I Dared to Call Him Father

No Greater Love

Living Under the Volcano

This omnibus edition first published 2001

ISBN 0 85476 833 5

Published by
KINGSWAY PUBLICATIONS
Lottbridge Drove, Eastbourne, BN23 6NT, England.
Email: books@kingsway.co.uk

Designed and produced for the publishers by
Bookprint Creative Services, P. O. Box 827, BN21 3YJ, England.
Printed in Great Britain.

Reproduced from the original typesetting
of the single-volume editions.

I Dared to Call Him Father

BILQUIS SHEIKH
WITH RICHARD SCHNEIDER

KINGSWAY PUBLICATIONS
EASTBOURNE

To my grandson Mahmud, my little prayer partner,
who has been a source of joy and comfort
to me through many lonely hours

1.

A Frightening Presence

The strange prickly feeling grew inside me as I walked slowly along the graveled paths of my garden. It was deep twilight. The scent of late narcissus hung heavy in the air. What was it, I wondered, that made me so uneasy?

I stopped my walk and looked around. Inside my home some distance across the broad lawn the servants were beginning to flick on lights in the dining area. Outside all seemed peaceful and quiet. I reached out to snip off some of the pungent white blossoms for my bedroom. As I leaned over to grasp the tall green stems, something brushed past my head.

I straightened in alarm. What was it? A mist-like cloud—a cold, damp unholy presence—had floated by. The garden suddenly seemed darker. A chilling breeze sprang up through the weeping willows and I shivered.

Get hold of yourself, Bilquis! I scolded. My imagination was playing tricks on me. Nevertheless, I gathered my flowers and headed quickly toward the house where windows glowed in warm reassurance. Its sturdy white stone walls and oaken doors offered protection. As I hurried along the crunchy gravel path I found myself glancing over my shoulder. I had always laughed at talk of the supernatural. Of course there wasn't anything out there. Was there?

As if in answer, I felt a firm, very real and uncanny tap on my right hand.

I screamed. I rushed into the house and slammed the door behind me. My servants ran to me, afraid to make any comment at all, for I must have looked like a ghost myself. It wasn't until bedtime that I finally found the courage to speak to my two handmaids about the cold presence. "Do you believe in spiritual things?" I asked, on concluding my story. Both Nur-jan and Raisham, one a Muslim, the other a Christian, avoided answering my question but Nur-jan, her hands fluttering nervously, asked me if she could call the village *mullah*, a priest from the mosque, who would bring some holy water to cleanse the garden. But my common sense had returned and I rebelled at submitting to the superstition of the ignorant. Besides, I didn't want any word of this to spread in the village. I tried to smile at her concern, and told her, a little too abruptly I'm afraid, that I didn't want any holy man on my grounds pretending to remove evil spirits. Nevertheless, after the maids left the room, I found myself picking up my copy of the Koran. But after struggling through a few pages of the Muslim Holy Book, I wearied of it, slipped it back within its blue silken case, and fell asleep.

I slowly awakened the next morning like a swimmer struggling to the surface, a thin high chant piercing my consciousness:

> *"Laa ilaaha illa Ilaah,*
> *Muhammed resolu'llal"*

The sing-song words drifted through the filigree of my bedroom window:

> *"There is no God but Allah:*
> *And Muhammed is his Prophet."*

It was a comforting sound, this Muslim call to prayer because it seemed so utterly normal after the previous night.

It was a call I had heard almost without exception every morning of my 46 years. I envisioned the source of the rolling chant.

Some moments before in the little nearby Pakistani village of Wah, our old muezzin had hurried through the door at the base of an ancient minaret. Inside its cool interior he had trudged up curving stone steps worn smooth by the sandals of generations of Muslim holy men. At the top of the prayer tower, I could imagine him hesitating at the carved teak door leading to the parapet to catch his breath. Then, stepping outside to the railing, he threw back his bearded head and in syllables fourteen hundred years old called the faithful to prayer.

> *"Come to prayer, come to salvation,*
> *Prayer is better than sleep."*

The haunting cry floated through the morning mist across cobblestone lanes in Wah still cold from the October night, drifted across my garden to curl along the house's old stone walls now ruddy in the light of the rising sun.

As the last wisps of the ancient chant hung above me, I remembered the eerie experience in the garden the night before, and quickly turned to morning routines that would be comforting just because they were so ordinary. I sat up and reached for the golden bell on my marble bedside table. At its musical tinkle, my maid Nur-jan hurried in out of breath as usual. Both of my handmaids slept in a room adjoining mine and I knew that they had already been up for an hour, waiting for my call. Morning tea in my bed was a *must*. Nur-jan began laying out my silver brushes and combs. She was a willing teen-aged girl, plump and giggly, but a bit clumsy. When she dropped a brush, I scolded her sharply.

Raisham, my other handmaid, older and quieter, a tall graceful woman, slid into the room bearing a large covered tea tray. She placed it on my bed table, drew back the

white linen to expose the sterling service and poured me
a cup of steaming tea.

Sipping the scalding ambrosia, I sighed in satisfaction; tea
was better than prayer. My mother would have been
shocked at my thought. How many times had I watched
her place her prayer rug on the tiled bedroom floor, then,
facing the holy city of Mecca, kneel and press her forehead
to the rug in prayer. Thinking of my mother I looked over
to the dressing case on my table. Fashioned centuries ago
of sandalwood and covered with engraved sterling silver, it
had belonged to Mother and her mother before her. Now it
was my heirloom to treasure. After finishing two cups of
tea I leaned forward, a sign for Raisham to begin brushing
my graying waist-length hair while Nur-jan carefully worked
on my nails.

As the two worked, they gossiped in easy familiarity about
news from the village, Nur-jan chattering and Raisham
making quiet thoughtful comments. They talked about a
boy who was leaving home for the city and a girl soon to
be married. And then they discussed the murder that happened in a nearby town where Raisham's aunt lived. I could
sense Raisham shudder as the news came up. For the victim
had been a Christian. She was a young girl who had been
staying in a Christian missionary's home. Someone had
stumbled across her body in one of the narrow lanes criss-
crossing her village. There was supposed to have been an
investigation by the constabulary.

"Any news about the girl?" I casually asked.

"No, Begum Sahib," said Raisham quietly, as she carefully began to work a braid in my hair. I could understand
why Raisham, a Christian herself, didn't want to talk about
the murder. She knew as well as I did who had killed that
girl. After all, the girl had forsaken her Muslim faith to be
baptized a Christian. So the brother, infuriated by the
shame this sin had brought upon his family, had obeyed
the ancient law of the faithful that those who fall away from
their faith must be slain.

Even though Muslim edicts may be stern and harsh, their interpretations are sometimes tempered with mercy and compassion. But there are always the zealots who carry out the letter of the Koran law to the extreme.

Everyone knew who had killed the girl. But nothing would be done. It had always been this way. A year ago, the Christian servant of one of the missionaries ended up in a ditch, his throat cut, and nothing had been done there either. I put the sad little story out of my mind and made ready to get up. My maids hurried to the closet and returned with several silken saris for my selection. I pointed to a jewel-embroidered one and after they helped drape it about me, they quietly bowed themselves out of my chamber.

Sunlight now flooded my bedroom, giving its white walls and ivory-colored furnishings a saffron glow. The sunlight glinted from a gold-framed photograph on my dressing table and I stepped over and picked it up, angry, because I had put the picture face down the day before; one of the servants must have set it up again! The engraved frame enclosed a photograph of a sophisticated-looking couple smiling at me from a corner table in a luxurious London restaurant.

In spite of myself I looked at the picture again, as one does when he keeps pressing a hurting tooth. The dashing man with dark mustache and burning eyes had been my husband, General Khalid Sheikh. Why did I keep this picture! Hate surged within me as I looked at the man I once felt I could not live without. When the photo had been taken six years before, Khalid had been Pakistan's Minister of Interior.

The glamorous-looking woman next to him had been me. As daughter of a conservative Muslim family which for seven hundred years had been landed gentry in this cool-climated Northwest Frontier Province of what had once been northern India, I had been hostess to diplomats and industrialists from all over the world. I had been accustomed to sojourns in Paris and London where I spent my time shopping on the Rue de la Paix or in Harrods. The lithsome woman who smiled from the photo no longer existed, I thought as I looked in the mirror. The soft pale skin had bronzed, the lustrous black hair was now streaked with gray, and disillusionment had etched deep lines in her face.

The world of the photograph had crumbled into fragments five years before when Khalid left me. Suffering the shame of rejection, I had fled the sophisticated life of London, Paris and Rawalpindi to seek refuge here in the quiet peace of my family's ancestral estate nestled at the foot of the Himalayan Mountains. The estate comprised the little hill country village of Wah where I had spent so many happy days as a child. Wah was surrounded by gardens and orchards which many generations of my family had planted. And the big stone palatial home with its towers, terraces and huge echoing chambers seemed as old as the snow-crowned Safed Koh mountains which loomed in the west. However, my aunt also lived in this house and desiring further seclusion, I moved to a smaller house the family had built on the outskirts of Wah. Inset like a jewel in twelve acres of gardens, this house, with bedrooms upstairs and living, dining and drawing rooms downstairs, promised the solace I needed.

It gave me more. For when I arrived, much of the extensive gardens had become overgrown. This was a blessing, for I buried much of my sorrow in the lush soil as I plunged into the restoration of the grounds. I made some of the twelve acres into formal gardens with walls and flower beds and left some of the area natural. Slowly the gardens, with their countless musical springs, became my world until by then, in the year 1966, I had the reputation of a recluse who secluded herself outside of town nestled amongst her flowers.

I looked away from the gold-framed photo in my hand, placed it face down again on the table and turned to my bedroom window looking toward the village. Wah . . . the very name of the village was an exclamation of joy. Cen-

turies before, when this was but a hamlet, the legendary
Moghul emperor Akbar traveled through here and his
caravan stopped to rest by a spring in what was now my
surroundings. He gratefully sank down under a willow, and
exclaimed in joy, "Wah!" thus naming the area forever.

But the memory of this scene gave me no release from
the unsettled feeling which had been hovering over me
ever since the strange experience of the evening before.

However, I tried to dispel it as I stood at my window. It
was morning again, I told myself, the next day, a safe time
with familiar routines and warm sunlight. The previous
night's episode seemed as real, but as remote, as a bad
dream. I drew the white drapes aside and breathed in
deeply of the fresh morning air, listening to the hissing of
the sweeper's broom on the patio. A fragrance of wood
smoke from early morning cooking fires drifted up to me
and the rhythmic thumping of water-mill wheels sounded
in the distance. I sighed in satisfaction. This was Wah, this
was my home, this was, after all, safety. This was where
Nawab Muhammad Hayat Kahn, a prince and feudal landowner, had lived seven hundred years ago. We were his
direct descendants and my family was known throughout
India as the Hayats of Wah. Centuries ago the caravans of
emperors would turn off the Grand Trunk Road to visit my
ancestors. Even in my earlier days notables from all over
Europe and Asia would take the same road, once an ancient
caravan route across India, to see my family. But now,
usually only members of my family would follow it to my
gate. Of course this meant that I didn't see many people
who were not part of my immediate household. I did not
much care. My fourteen house servants were enough company. They and their ancestors had served my family for
generations. Most important, I had Mahmud.

Mahmud was my four-year-old grandson. His mother,
Tooni, was the youngest of my three children. A slim at-
tractive woman, Tooni was a medical doctor at Holy Family
Hospital in nearby Rawalpindi. Her former husband was a

prominent landlord. However, they had an unhappy marriage and their relationship deteriorated a little each year. During their long bitter disagreements, Tooni would send Mahmud to visit me until she and her husband reached another uneasy truce. One day, Tooni and her husband came to see me. Could I keep one-year-old Mahmud for a while until they settled their differences?

"No," I said. "I do not want him to become a tennis ball. But I will be willing to adopt him and raise him as my own son." Sadly, Tooni and her husband never could settle their differences and they finally divorced. However, they did approve my adopting Mahmud, and it was working out quite well. Tooni came to see Mahmud often and the three of us were very close, particularly since my two other children lived far away.

Later that morning Mahmud pedaled his tricycle across the brick terrace shaded by almond trees. He had been with me for over three years and this lively cherubic child with deep brown eyes and button nose was the only joy of my life. His pealing laughter seemed to lift the spirit of this secluded old house. Even so I worried about how he would be affected by living with such a downcast person as me. I tried to compensate by making sure his every need was anticipated, and this included his own staff of three servants, in addition to my own eleven, to dress him, bring out his toys and pick them up when he was through playing with them.

But I was troubled about Mahmud. For several days he had refused to eat. This was particularly strange, for the boy was always visiting the bake kitchen to cajole my cooks into giving him sugar biscuits and snacks. Earlier that morning I had gone downstairs, walked through the terrazzo entranceway out to the terrace. After exchanging a warm hug with Mahmud, I asked his servant if the child had eaten.

"No, Begum Sahib, he refuses," the maid said in a near

whisper. When I pressed Mahmud to take some food, he just answered that he was not hungry.

I was really disturbed when Nur-jan came to me alone and suggested timorously that Mahmud was being attacked by evil spirits. Startled, I looked at her sharply, remembering the disquieting experience of the night before. What did all this mean? Once again I asked Mahmud to eat, but to no avail. He wouldn't even touch his favorite Swiss chocolates which I had imported especially for him. His limpid eyes looked up to me when I offered him the package. "I'd love to eat them, Mum," he said, "but when I try to swallow it hurts." A cold chill ran through me as I looked at my little grandson, once so lively and now so listless.

I immediately summoned Manzur, my chauffeur, also a Christian, and ordered him to get the car out. Within an hour we were in Rawalpindi to visit Mahmud's doctor. The pediatrician examined Mahmud carefully and he reported that he could find nothing wrong.

Fear chilled me as we rode back to the estate. Looking at my little grandson sitting quietly beside me, I wondered. Could Nur-jan *possibly* be right? Was this something that went beyond the physical? Was it . . . something in the spirit world attacking him? I reached over and put my arm around the child, smiling at myself for entertaining such ideas. Once, I remembered, my father had told me about a legendary Muslim holy man who could perform miracles. I laughed aloud at the idea. My father was displeased, but that was the way I felt about any such claims. Still, today, holding Mahmud close as the car turned off the Grand Trunk Road onto our lane, I found myself toying with an unwelcome thought: Could Mahmud's problem be related to the mist in the garden?

When I shared my fears with Nur-jan, her henna-tipped fingers flew to her throat and she begged me to call the village *mullah* and ask him to pray for Mahmud and sprinkle holy water over the garden.

I debated her request. Even though I believed in basic

Muslim teachings, for several years I had drifted away from
the many rituals, the praying five times a day, the fasting,
the complicated ceremonial washings. But my concern for
Mahmud overcame my doubts and I told Nur-jan that she
could call the holy man from the village mosque.

The next morning Mahmud and I sat at my window impatiently awaiting the *mullah.* When I finally saw him
making his way up the steps of the veranda, his thin ragged
coat flapping about him in the chilling fall wind, I was both
sorry I had asked him and angry that he wasn't walking
faster.

Nur-jan brought the bony old man to my quarters, then
withdrew. Mahmud watched the man curiously as he
opened his Koran. The *mullah,* whose skin matched the
ancient leather of his holy book, looked at me through
crinkled eyes, laid a gnarled brown hand on Mahmud's head
and in a quavering voice began reciting the Kul. This is the
prayer every Muslim recites when he is about to begin
any important act, whether to pray for the sick or to enter a
business agreement.

The *mullah* then started to read from the Koran in Arabic
—the Koran is always read in Arabic since it would be
wrong to translate the very words that God's angel had
given the prophet Muhammad. I became impatient. I must
have started to tap my foot.

"Begum Sahib?" the *mullah* said, holding the Koran out
to me. "You, too, should read these verses." He referred to
the Sura Falak and Sura Naz, verses to be repeated when
one is troubled. "Why don't you repeat these verses as
well?"

"No," I said, "I will not. God has forgotten about me and
I have forgotten about God!" But at the hurt look on the
old man's face I softened. After all, he had come here at
my request and with Mahmud's welfare in mind. "All right,"
I said, taking the worn volume. I let it fall open, then read
the first verse my eyes fell on:

*Muhammad is the Messenger of God, and those who
are with him are hard against the unbelievers. . . .*

I thought of the Christian girl who had been murdered,
and about the mist that appeared in my garden shortly
after she was killed, and above all about Mahmud's mysterious ailment. Could they be related? Surely any angry
spiritual power would never link me and Mahmud with a
Christian. I shuddered.

But the holy man seemed satisfied. Despite my reserva-
tions he returned for three days in a row to recite verses
over Mahmud.

And, just to complete the series of mysterious, unsettling
events, Mahmud did get better.

How was I supposed to think about all these happenings?

I was soon to find out. For without knowing it, events
had been set in motion which would shatter the world I'd
known all my life.

2.

The Strange Book

After these experiences I found myself drawn to the Koran.
Perhaps it would help explain the events and at the same
time fill the emptiness within me. Certainly its curved
Arabic script held answers which had often sustained my
family.

I had read the Koran before of course. I remembered
exactly how old I was when I first started learning Arabic
so that I could read our holy book: I was four years, four
months and four days old. This was the day every Muslim
child began to unravel the Arabic script. The moment was
marked by a great family banquet, to which all my relatives
came. It was then, in a special ceremony, that the wife of
our village *mullah* began teaching me the alphabet.

I especially remember my Uncle Fateh (we children
called him Grand Uncle Fateh; he wasn't really my uncle—
all older kinsmen are called Uncle or Aunt in Pakistan).
Grand Uncle Fateh was the relative closest to our family,
and I remember clearly how he watched me at the ceremony, his sensitive aquiline face glowing with pleasure as I
heard again the story of how the angel Gabriel began
giving Muhammad the words of the Koran on that fateful
"Night of Power" in the year 610 A.D. It took me seven years
to read the holy book through for the first time but when I

16

finally finished, there was cause for yet another family celebration.

Always before, I had read the Koran as an obligation. This time, I felt I should really search its pages. I took my copy, which had belonged to my mother, relaxed on the white eiderdown coverlet of my bed, and began to read. I started with the initial verse, the first message given to the young prophet Muhammad as he sat by himself in a cave on Mount Hira:

> *Recite: In the name of thy Lord who created,*
> *Created Man of a blood clot.*
> *Recite: And thy Lord is the Most Generous,*
> *Who taught by the Pen,*
> *Taught man that he knew not.*

At first I was lost in the beauty of the words. But later on in the book there were words that did not comfort me at all:

> *When ye have divorced women, and they have reached*
> *their term, then retain them in kindness or release them*
> *in kindness.*

My husband's eyes had been like black steel when he told me that he didn't love me any more. I shriveled inside as he spoke. What had happened to all our years together! Could they be dismissed just like that? Had I, as the Koran said, "reached my term"?

The next morning I picked up the Koran again, hoping to find in the curling script the assurance I needed so desperately. But the assurance never came. I found only directives for how to live and warnings against other beliefs. There were verses about the prophet Jesus whose message, the Koran said, was falsified by early Christians. Though Jesus was born of a virgin, he was not God's son. *So say not "Three,"* warned the Koran against the Christian concept of the Trinity. *Refrain; better is it for you. God is only One God.*

After several days of applying myself to the holy book, I put it down one afternoon with a sigh, got up and walked down to my garden where I hoped to find some peace in nature and in old memories. Even at this time of the year, the lush greenness persisted, brightened here and there by colorful alyssum which still blossomed. It was a warm day for fall and Mahmud skipped along the paths where I had walked as a child with my father. I could picture Father now, walking beside me here, wearing his white turban, impeccably dressed in his conservative British suit from Savile Row as befitted a government minister. Often he would call me by my full name, Bilquis Sultana, knowing how much I enjoyed hearing it. For Bilquis was the first name of the Queen of Sheba and everyone knew Sultana signified royalty.

We had many good conversations. And in later years we enjoyed talking about our new country, Pakistan. He was so proud of it. "The Islamic Republic of Pakistan was created especially as a homeland for South Asian Muslims," he said. "We're one of the largest countries under Islamic law in the world," he added, pointing out that 96% of our country's population was Muslim, with the rest made up mostly of scattered groups of Buddhists, Christians, and Hindus.

I sighed and looked up beyond my garden trees to the lavender hills in the distance. I could always find solace with my father. In his later years I had become a companion to him, often discussing our country's rapidly changing political situation with him and explaining my views. He was so gentle, so understanding. But now he was gone. I remembered standing by his open grave in the Muslim cemetery of Brookwood outside of London. He had travelled to London for surgery and had never recovered. Muslim custom requires that a body be buried within 24 hours of death and by the time I reached the cemetery his coffin was ready to be lowered into the grave. I couldn't believe I'd never see my father again. They unfastened the coffin lid so I could have one last look at him. But the cold gray clay in that box was not him; where had he gone? I stood there numbly wondering about it all as they refastened the coffin, each shrill squeal of the screws biting into the damp wood sending pain through me.

Mother, with whom I was also very close, died seven years later, leaving me completely alone.

There in my garden, shadows had lengthened and again I stood in twilight. No, the comfort I had sought in memories proved only to bring achings. Softly in the distance I could hear the muezzin's sunset prayer call; its haunting strains only deepened the loneliness within me.

"Where? Oh Allah," I whispered to the prayer rhythms, *"where* is the comfort You promise?"

Back in my bedroom that evening I again picked up my mother's copy of the Koran. And as I read I was again impressed by its many references to Jewish and Christian writings which preceded it. Perhaps, I wondered, I should continue my search among those earlier books?

But that would mean reading the Bible. How could the Bible help since, of course, as everyone knew, the early Christians had falsified so much of it. But the idea of reading the Bible became more and more insistent. What was the Bible's concept of God? What *did* it say about the prophet Jesus? Perhaps after all I should read it.

But then came the next problem: where would I get a Bible? No shops in our area would carry one.

Perhaps Raisham would have a copy. But I dismissed the thought. Even if she did, my request would frighten her. Pakistanis have been murdered for even appearing to persuade Muslims to turn traitor-Christian. I thought of my other Christian servants. My family warned that I should not employ Christian servants because of their notorious lack of loyalty and untrustworthiness. But I didn't let that bother me; as long as they could fulfill their duties, I was satisfied. Doubtless they weren't very sincere anyhow. After all, when the Christian missionaries came to India, they found it easy to make converts among the lower classes. Most of these were the sweepers, people so low in the social order that their work was limited to cleaning the streets, walks and gutters. We Muslims called these servile ones "rice Christians." Wasn't that the reason they accepted a false religion, mainly to get the food, clothes and schooling which the missionaries doled out?

We looked upon the missionaries themselves with amusement; they busied themselves so eagerly over these poor creatures. In fact, only a few months before, my chauffeur Manzur, a Christian, asked if he could show my garden to some local missionaries who had admired it through the fence.

"Of course," I said gratuitously, thinking of poor Manzur who evidently wanted so much to impress these people. A few days later from my drawing room window I watched the young American couple stroll through the garden. Manzur had referred to them as the Reverend and Mrs. David Mitchell. Both had pale brown hair, pale eyes and wore drab western clothes. What colorless creatures, I thought. Even so, I did pass word on to the gardener to give these missionaries some seeds if they wished them.

But thinking of them gave me my answer to getting a Bible. Manzur would get one for me. Tomorrow I would give him the assignment.

So I summoned him to my apartment the next morning. He stood at attention before me in his white pantaloons, the nervous twitch in his face making me uneasy, as it always did.

"Manzur, I want you to get me a Bible."

"A Bible?" his eyes widened.

"Of course!" I said, trying to be patient. Since Manzur didn't know how to read, I was sure he didn't own a Bible. But I felt he could get one for me. When he mumbled something I could not understand I repeated, simply but firmly, "Manzur, get me a Bible."

He nodded, bowed and left. I knew why he was resisting

my request. Manzur was made of no firmer stuff than Raisham. They were both remembering that murdered girl. Giving a Bible to a sweeper was one thing; bringing a Bible to a person of the upper classes was quite something else. Word of this could get him into deep trouble indeed.

Two days later Manzur was driving me to Rawalpindi to see Tooni.

"Manzur, I do not have the Bible as yet."

I could see his knuckles whiten on the steering·wheel.

"Begum, I will get you one."

Three days later I summoned him to the house.

"Manzur, I have asked you to bring me a Bible three times, and you have not." The twitch in his face became more noticeable. "I'll give you one more day. If I do not have one by tomorrow you will be fired."

His face turned ashen. He knew I meant it. He wheeled and left, his chauffeur boots clicking on the terrazzo floor.

The next day just before a visit from Tooni, a little Bible mysteriously appeared on my downstairs drawing room table. I picked it up, and examined it closely. Cheaply bound in a gray cloth cover, it was printed in Urdu, a local Indian dialect. It had been translated by an Englishman 180 years before and I found the old-fashioned phraseology difficult to follow. Manzur had evidently got it from a friend; it was almost new. I leafed through its thin pages, set it down and forgot about it.

A few minutes later Tooni arrived. Mahmud ran in just behind her, squealing, because he knew his mother would have brought him a toy. In a minute Mahmud raced through the French doors to the terrace with his new airplane, and Tooni and I settled down to our tea.

It was then that Tooni noticed the Bible resting on the table near me. "Oh, a Bible!" she said. "Do open it and see what it has to say." Our family views any religious book as significant. It was a common pastime to allow a holy book to fall open, point blindly at a passage to see what it said, almost like having it give a prophecy.

Lightheartedly, I opened the little Bible and looked down at the pages.

Then, a mysterious thing happened. It was as if my attention were being drawn to a verse on the lower right hand corner of the right page. I bent close to read it:

> *I will call that my people, which was not my people; and her beloved, which was not beloved. And it shall be, that in the place where it was said unto them, Ye are not my people, there shall they be called sons of the living God.*

Romans 9:25–26 *

I caught my breath and a tremor passed through me. Why was this verse affecting me so! *I will call that my people, which was not my people. . . . In the place where it was said unto them, Ye are not my people, there shall they be called sons of the living God.*

A silence hung over the room. I looked up to see Tooni poised expectantly, ready to hear what I had found. But I could not read the words out loud. Something in them was too profound for me to read as amusement.

"Well, what was it Mother?" asked Tooni, her alive eyes questioning me.

I closed the book, murmured something about this not being a game anymore, and turned the conversation to another subject:

But the words burned in my heart like glowing embers. And they turned out to be preparation for the most unusual dreams I have ever had.

* Modernized to Phillips' Translation

3.

The Dreams

It wasn't until the next day that I again picked up the little gray Bible. Neither Tooni nor I referred to the Bible again after I had switched the conversation to another subject. But throughout the long afternoon the words in that passage simmered just below the surface of my consciousness.

Early in the evening of the next day, I retired to my bedchamber where I planned to rest and meditate. I took the Bible with me and settled among the soft white cushions of my divan. Once again I leafed through its pages and read another puzzling passage:

> But Israel, following the Law of righteousness, failed
> to reach the goal of righteousness.
>
> Romans 9:31 *

Ah, I thought. Just as the Koran said; the Jews *had* missed the mark. The writer of these passages might have been a Muslim, I thought, for he continued to speak of the people of Israel as not knowing God's righteousness.

But the next passage made me catch my breath.

---

* Modernized to Phillips' Translation

23

> *For Christ means the end of the struggle for righteous-*
> *ness-by-the-Law for everyone who believes in him.*
>
> Romans 10:4 *

I lowered the book down for a moment. Christ? *He* was
the end of the struggle? I continued on.

> *For the secret is very near you, in your own heart, in*
> *your own mouth. . . . If you openly admit by your*
> *own mouth that Jesus Christ is the Lord, and if you*
> *believe in your own heart that God raised him from the*
> *dead, you will be saved.*
>
> Romans 10:8–9 *

I put the book down again, shaking my head. This directly
contradicted the Koran. Muslims knew the prophet Jesus
was just human, that the man did not die on the cross but
was whisked up to heaven by God and a look-alike put on
the cross instead. Now sojourning in an inferior heaven, this
Jesus will someday return to earth to reign for forty years,
marry, have children, and then die. In fact, I heard that
there is a special grave plot kept vacant for the man's remains in Medina, the city where Muhammad is also buried.
At the Resurrection Day, Jesus will rise and stand with
other men to be judged before God Almighty. But this
Bible said Christ was raised from the dead. It was either
blasphemy or. . . .

My mind whirled. I knew that whoever called upon the
name of Allah would be saved. But to believe that Jesus
Christ *is* Allah? Even Muhammad, the final and greatest of
the messengers of God, the *Seal of the Prophets*, was only
a mortal.

I lay back on my bed, my hand over my eyes. If the
Bible and Koran represent the same God, why is there so
much confusion and contradiction? How could it be the
same God if the God of the Koran is one of vengeance
and punishment and the God of the Christian Bible is one
of mercy and forgiveness? I don't know when I fell asleep.

* Modernized to Phillips' Translation

Normally I never dream, but this night I did. The dream was so lifelike, the events in it so real, that I found it difficult the next morning to believe they were only fantasy. Here is what I saw.

> *I found myself having supper with a man I knew to be Jesus. He had come to visit me in my home and stayed for two days. He sat across the table from me and in peace and joy we ate dinner together. Suddenly, the dream changed. Now I was on a mountain top with another man. He was clothed in a robe and shod with sandals. How was it that I mysteriously knew his name, too? John the Baptist. What a strange name. I found myself telling this John the Baptist about my recent visit with Jesus. "The Lord came and was my guest for two days," I said. "But now He is gone. Where is He? I must find Him! Perhaps you, John the Baptist, will lead me to Him?"*

That was the dream. When I woke up I was loudly calling the name, "John the Baptist! John the Baptist!" Nur-jan and Raisham rushed into my room. They seemed embarrassed at my shouting and began fussily to prepare my toilette. I tried to tell them about my dream as they worked.

"Oh, how nice," giggled Nur-jan as she presented my tray of perfumes. "Yes, it was a blessed dream," murmured Raisham as she brushed my hair. I was surprised that as a Christian, Raisham wouldn't be more excited. I started to ask her about John the Baptist but checked myself; after all, Raisham was just a simple village woman. But who *was* this John the Baptist? I had not come across the name in what I had read so far in the Bible.

For the next three days I continued reading both the Bible and the Koran side by side, turning from one to the other. I found myself picking up the Koran out of a sense of duty, and then eagerly turning to the Christian book, dipping into it here and there to look into this confusing new world I had discovered. Each time I opened the Bible a sense of guilt filled me. Perhaps this stemmed from my strict unbringing. Even after I had become a young woman, Father would have to approve any book I read. Once my brother and I smuggled a book into our room. Even though it was completely innocent, we were quite frightened, reading it.

Now as I opened the Bible, I found myself reacting in the same manner. One story riveted my attention. It told of the Jewish leaders bringing a woman caught in adultery to the prophet Jesus. I shivered, knowing what fate lay in store for this woman. The moral codes of the ancient east were not very different from ours in Pakistan. The men of the community are bound by tradition to punish the adulterous woman. As I read of the woman in the Bible standing before her accusers, I knew that her own brothers, uncles and cousins stood in the forefront, ready to stone her.

Then the Prophet said: *Let him who is without sin cast the first stone* (John 8:7).

I reeled as in my mind's eye I watched the men slink away. Instead of supervising her lawful death, Jesus had forced her accusers to recognize their own guilt. The book fell into my lap as I lay there deep in thought. There was something so logical, so right about this prophet's challenge. The man spoke truth.

Then three days later I had a second strange dream:

> *I was in the bedchamber when a maid announced that a perfume salesman was waiting to see me. I arose from my divan elated, for at this time there was a shortage of imported perfumes in Pakistan. I greatly feared running low on my favorite luxury. And so in my dream I happily asked my maid to show the perfume salesman in.*
>
> *He was dressed in the manner of perfume salesmen in my mother's day when these merchants travelled from house to house selling their wares. He wore a black frock coat and carried his stock in a valise. Opening the valise, he took out a golden jar. Removing the cap, he handed it to me. As I looked at it I caught my breath; the perfume glimmered like liquid crystal. I was about to touch my finger to it when he held up his hand.*

"No," he said. Taking the golden jar he walked over and placed it on my bedside table. "This will spread throughout the world," he said.

As I awakened in the morning, the dream was still vivid in my mind. The sun was streaming through the window, and I could still smell that beautiful perfume; its delightful fragrance filled the room. I raised up and looked at my bedside table, half expecting to see the golden jar there.

Instead, where the jar had been, now rested the Bible!

A tingle passed through me. I sat on the edge of the bed pondering my two dreams. What did they mean? Where I had not dreamed in years, now I had two vivid dreams in a row. Were they related to each other? And were they related to my recent brush with the realities of the supernatural world?

That afternoon I went for my usual stroll in the garden. I was still bemused by my dreams. But now something else was added. It was as if I felt a strange delight and joy, a peace beyond anything I had ever known before. It was as if I were close to the Presence of God. Suddenly, as I stepped out of a grove into a sun-flooded open area, the air around me seemed to be alive with another lovely fragrance. It wasn't the fragrance of flowers—it was too late for any of the garden to be in bloom—but a very real fragrance nonetheless.

In some agitation I returned to the house. Where did that fragrance come from? What was happening to me? Who could I talk to about what was happening to me? It would have to be someone with a knowledge of the Bible. I had already swept aside the thought of asking my Christian servants. In the first place it was unthinkable to ask information of them. They probably had never even read the Bible and wouldn't know what I was talking about. No, I had to talk to someone who was educated and who knew this book.

As I considered this question a shocking idea came to

mind. I fought the thought. That would be the last place I should go for help.

But a name kept returning to me so compellingly that I finally rang for Manzur.

"I want you to get the car out for me." And then as an afterthought I added: "I'll be driving myself."

Manzur's eyes widened. "Yourself?"

"Yes, myself, if you please." He left, reluctantly. Rarely had I taken my car out that late in the evening. I had been an officer in the Royal Indian Army women's division in World War II and had driven ambulances and staff cars thousands of miles over all kinds of terrain. But wartime was one thing and even then I was in the company of someone. The daughter of Nawab nobility was not expected to drive her own car in normal life, especially not at night.

But I knew I couldn't risk Manzur knowing what I was about to do and resultant servants' gossip. I was convinced there was only one source where I could find the answer to my questions: Who was John the Baptist? What was this fragrance all about?

So it was with extreme reluctance that evening that I headed for the home of a couple I barely knew, the Reverend and Mrs. David Mitchell who had visited my garden that summer. As Christian missionaries, they were the last people with whom I'd want to be seen.

4.

The Encounter

My black Mercedes idled in the driveway. Manzur stood at the driver's door which he kept closed until the last moment protecting the car's warmth against the chill of that autumn evening. His dark eyes were still questioning my decision, but without comment. I got into the warm car, settled behind the wheel and drove off into the twilight, the Bible on the seat beside me.

Everyone knew where everyone else lived in this village of Wah. The Mitchells' home stood near the entrance of the Wah cement works from which my family derived part of its income. It served as the center of a strange little community about five miles outside of town. The homes had been built as temporary quarters for British troops during World War II. I recalled from the few times I had ventured into the area that the drab, uniform houses had lost most of their whitewash; their tin roofs showed signs of much patchwork. A strange mixture of expectancy and fear filled me as I drove along. I had never been in a Christian missionary home before. I was hopeful of learning the identity of my mystery man, John the Baptist, and yet I feared a certain—what should I call it, "influence?"—from those who might answer my question.

What would my forebears think of this visit to a Christian

missionary? I thought, for instance, of my great-grandfather who had accompanied the famed British General Nicholson through the Khyber Pass in one of the Afghanistan wars. What shame this visit would bring on my family. We had always associated the missionaries with the poor and social outcasts. I imagined a conversation with an uncle or aunt in which I defended myself by telling them of my strange dreams. "After all," I said in the scene I was playing out in my mind, "anyone would want to find out the meaning of such vivid dreams."

As I approached the Mitchells' area in the dim light of early evening, it was just as I remembered it, except that the look-alike bungalows seemed, if possible, even more drab. After searching up and down narrow lanes, I found the Mitchells' house near the cement works, just where I thought it would be, a small whitewashed bungalow, sitting in a grove of mulberry trees. As a precaution I started to park some distance away until I caught myself. I was being far too afraid of what my family thought. So I parked squarely in front of the Mitchells', picked up the Bible and moved quickly toward the house. The yard, I noticed, was neat and the screened veranda well maintained. At least these missionaries kept their place in good repair,

Suddenly, the house door opened and a group of chattering village women filed out, dressed in the typical *shalwar qamiz*, a loose pajama-like cotton outfit, with a *dupatta* (scarf). I stiffened. They would know me of course; nearly everyone in Wah recognized me. Now the story would be gossiped all over the area that Begum Sheikh had visited a Christian missionary!

And sure enough as soon as the women saw me in the light that came from the Mitchells' open front door, their chatter ceased abruptly. They hurried past me to the street, each touching hand to forehead in the traditional salute. There was nothing I could do but continue toward the door where Mrs. Mitchell stood staring out into the dusk. Up close she looked just as I remembered her, from

seeing her at a distance about town, young, pale, almost
fragile. Only now she was wearing a *shalwar qamiz* like
the village women. As soon as she saw me her mouth fell
open. "Why . . . why, Begum Sheikh!" she exclaimed,
"What? . . . But. . . . Come in," she said. "Come in."

I was glad enough to step inside the house, away from
the village women's eyes which I knew would be fixed on
my back. We went into the living room, small and simply
furnished. Mrs. Mitchell drew up what appeared to be the
most comfortable chair for me near the open fire. She herself did not sit down, but stood folding and unfolding her
hands. I glanced at a circle of chairs in the middle of the
room. Mrs. Mitchell explained that she had just completed
a Bible study with some local women. She gave a nervous
cough. "Uh, will you have some tea?" she said, brushing
back her hair.

"No thank you," I replied. "I have come to ask a question." I looked about. "Is the Reverend Mr. Mitchell here?"

"No. He is on a trip to Afghanistan."

I was sorry. The woman standing before me was so
young! Would she be able to answer my questions?

"Mrs. Mitchell," I ventured, "do you know anything about
God?"

She sank down into one of the wooden chairs and looked
at me strangely; the only noise in the room was the low
hiss from the flames in the fireplace. Then she said quietly,
"I'm afraid I don't know too much *about* God, but I do
know Him."

What an extraordinary statement! How could a person
presume to know God! Just the same, the woman's odd confidence gave me confidence too. Before I quite knew what
was happening, I found myself telling her about my dream
of the prophet Jesus and the man named John the Baptist.
Strangely, I had difficulty controlling my voice as I related
the experience. Even as I told her, I felt the same excitement I felt on that mountain top. Then, after describing
the dream, I leaned forward.

"Mrs. Mitchell, I've heard about Jesus, but *who* is John the Baptist?"

Mrs. Mitchell blinked at me and frowned. I felt she wanted to ask if I had really never heard of John the Baptist, but instead she settled back again in her chair. "Well, Begum Sheikh, John the Baptist was a prophet, a forerunner of Jesus Christ, who preached repentance and was sent to prepare the way for Him. He was the one who pointed to Jesus and said: 'Look, the Lamb of God who takes away the sins of the world.' He was the one who baptized Jesus."

Why did my heart skip at the word "baptized?" I knew little about these Christians, but all Muslims had heard of their strange ceremony of baptism. My mind flitted to the many people who were murdered after their baptisms. And this also happened under British rule when supposedly there was freedom of religion. Even as a child I had put the two facts together: a Muslim was baptized, a Muslim died.

"Begum Sheikh?"

I looked up. How long had we been sitting there silently? "Mrs. Mitchell," I said, my throat tight, "forget I am a Muslim. Just tell me: what did you mean when you said you know God?"

"I know Jesus," Mrs. Mitchell said and I knew she thought she was answering my question.

Then she told me what God had done for her and for the world by breaking the dreadful deadlock between sinful man and Himself by personally visiting this earth in the flesh, as Jesus, and dying for all of us on the cross.

The room was quiet again. I could hear trucks passing on the nearby highway. Mrs. Mitchell seemed in no hurry to speak. Finally, hardly believing my own ears, I took a breath and heard myself saying quite distinctly, "Mrs. Mitchell, some peculiar things have been happening at our house lately. Events of the spirit. Good and bad, both. I feel as if I were in the midst of an immense tug of war, and I need all the positive help I can get. Could you pray for me?"

The woman appeared startled at my request, then, collecting herself, she asked if I wanted to stand up, kneel or sit down as we prayed. I shrugged, suddenly horrified. All were equally unthinkable. But there was this slender, youthful woman kneeling on the floor of her bungalow. And I followed her!

"Oh Spirit of God," said Mrs. Mitchell in a soft voice, "I know that nothing I can say will convince Begum Sheikh who Jesus is. But I thank You that You take the veil off our eyes and reveal Jesus to our hearts. Oh, Holy Spirit, do this for Begum Sheikh. Amen."

We stayed on our knees for what seemed like forever. I was glad for the silence, for my heart was strangely warmed.

At last Mrs. Mitchell and I arose. "Is that a Bible, Madame Sheikh?" she asked, nodding toward the little gray volume which I clutched to my breast in one hand. I showed her the book. "How do you find it?" she asked. "Easy to understand?"

"Not really," I said. "It is an old translation and I'm not at home in it."

She stepped into an adjacent room and returned with another book.

"Here is a New Testament written in modern English," she said. "It's called the Phillips translation. I find it much easier to understand than others. Would you like it?"

"Yes," I said, not hesitating.

"Start with the Gospel of John," Mrs. Mitchell advised, opening the book and placing a bit of paper in it as a bookmark. "That's another John, but he makes the role of John the Baptist very clear."

"Thank you," I said, touched. "And now I think I've taken too much of your time."

As I prepared to leave, Mrs. Mitchell said: "You know, it's so interesting that a dream brought you here. God often speaks to His children in dreams and visions."

As she helped me on with my coat, I wondered if I should share something about my other dream with her. The one about the perfume salesman. It seemed so . . . bizarre. But as had happened several times already in this strange evening, I found myself filled with a boldness that seemed almost to come from outside of me. "Mrs. Mitchell, can you tell me if there is a connection between perfume and Jesus?"

She thought for a moment, her hand on the door. "No," she said, "I can't think of any. However, let me pray about it."

As I drove home, I experienced for the second time that same fragrant Presence I had sensed in my garden earlier that day!

When I got home that night I read a little out of the portion of the Bible called "The Gospel of John," where the writer talked about John the Baptist, this strange man clad in camel skin who came out of the wilderness, calling people to prepare for the coming of the Lord. And then, there in the safety of my own bedroom, seated on my divan, surrounded by memories and traditions that were seven centuries old, a thought slipped sideways into my mind, unbidden, unwanted, quickly rejected. If John the Baptist was a sign from God, a sign pointing toward Jesus, was this same man pointing *me* toward Jesus, too?

Of course the thought was untenable. I put it out of mind and went to sleep.

That night I did sleep soundly.

As the muezzin called me to prayer the next morning, I was relieved to find myself seeing things clearly again. What a bizarre series of thoughts I had toyed with in the night! But now as the muezzin reminded me where truth lay, I felt secure again, away from these disturbing Christian influences.

Raisham came in just then, not with tea but with a note which she said had just been delivered to the house.

It was from Mrs. Mitchell. All it said was: "Read Second Corinthians, Chapter 2, Verse 14."

I reached for the Bible she had given me and searched until I found the chapter and verse. Then, as I read, I caught my breath:

> *Thanks be to God who leads us, wherever we are, on Christ's triumphant way, and makes our knowledge of Him spread throughout the world like a lovely perfume!*

I sat there in bed, and re-read the passage, my composure of a minute ago shattered. The knowledge of Jesus spreads like a lovely perfume! In my dream, the salesman had put the golden dish of scent on my bedside table and said that the perfume "would spread throughout the world." The next morning I had found my Bible in the same spot where the perfume had been laid! It was all too clear. I didn't want to think about it any more. Ring for tea, that's what I must do. Ring for my tea and bring life back into its proper focus quickly before something else went awry.

Even though Mrs. Mitchell had invited me back, I felt it best not to return. It seemed a prudent logical decision that I must now investigate this Bible on my own. I did not want to be pushed by any outside influence. However, one afternoon Nur-jan rushed into my room with an odd look in her eyes. "The Reverend and Mrs. Mitchell are here to see you," she gasped.

My hand flew to my throat. Why would they come *here?* I wondered. However, quickly composing myself, I asked the maid to bring them into the drawing room.

Sandy-haired David Mitchell, a lanky man with crinkly eyes, radiated the same friendly warmth as his wife. The two seemed so happy to see me that I forgot my discomfort over them coming to my house.

Mrs. Mitchell started to shake hands, then at the last minute threw her arms around me instead. I was stunned. No one outside the family, not even our closest friends, had

ever embraced me in this way before. I stiffened but Mrs.
Mitchell appeared to take no notice of my reaction. I found
—in retrospect, I have to admit—that this display pleased
me. There could have been no sham in her greeting.

"I'm so happy to meet 'the Flower Lady'," David exclaimed in a jovial American accent.

I glanced at Mrs. Mitchell and she laughed. "I should
explain. When you came to our house, I wanted to let David
know right away by telegram for we had often talked about
you since we visited your garden last spring. However, I
didn't want to use your real name, to protect you. As I was
wondering how to refer to you in the wire, I glanced out my
window and saw the flowers that had grown from the seeds
your gardener gave us. The name came to me: 'Flower
Lady,' and that became our code name for you."

I laughed. "Well, from now on, you can call me Bilquis."

"And please," she said, "call me Synnove."

It was a strange visit. I suppose I was half expecting
pressure from the Mitchells to accept their religion, but
nothing of the sort occurred. We drank a cup of tea and
chatted. I did question Jesus being called the "son of God,"
for to Muslims there is no greater sin than to make this claim.
The Koran states again and again that God has no children.
"And this 'trinity'?" I asked. "God is three?"

In answer, David compared God to the sun which mani-
fests itself in the three creative energies of heat, light and
radiation, a trinity relationship which together makes the
sun, yet singly is not the sun. And then shortly they left.

Again for several days I found myself alone with two
books—the Koran and the Bible. I continued to read them
both, studying the Koran because of the loyalty of a lifetime, delving into the Bible because of a strange inner
hunger.

Yet, sometimes I'd draw back from picking up the Bible.
God couldn't be in both books, I knew, because their mes-
sages were so different. But when my hand hesitated at
picking up the book Mrs. Mitchell gave me, I felt a strange

letdown. For the past week I had been living in a world of beauty, not a visible garden created by me from seeds and water, but an inner garden created from a new spiritual awareness. I first entered this world of beauty by way of my two dreams; then I became aware of this world a second time on the night I met the indefinably glorious Presence in my garden; and I had known it once again when I obeyed the nudging that prompted me to visit the Mitchells.

Slowly, clearly, over the next few days I began to know that there was a way to return to my world of beauty. And reading this Christian book seemed, for reasons that I could not grasp, the key to my re-entering that world.

And then one day little Mahmud came up to me holding the side of his head and trying not to whimper. "My ear, Mum," he cried in a pain-filled voice. "It hurts."

I bent down and examined him carefully. His usual ruddy brown complexion had paled, and although Mahmud was not a child to complain, I could see the tear stains on his little round tan cheeks.

I put him right to bed and crooned softly to him, his black hair too stark against the pillow. And then, after his eyes closed, I went to the telephone and rang the Holy Family Hospital in Rawalpindi. Within a minute Tooni was on the phone. She agreed that we should check Mahmud into the hospital the next afternoon for a complete examination the following day. I would be able to stay in an adjoining room and a maid would be given a smaller room adjacent to that.

It was toward evening when we checked into the comfortable arrangement. Tooni had the evening free to spend with us. Soon, Mahmud and his mother were giggling over some pictures Mahmud was coloring in a book she had brought him. I was propped up in bed reading my Bible. I had also brought the Koran with me, but by now I read the Koran out of a sense of duty, more than interest.

Suddenly, the room lights flickered, and then went out. The room was dark.

"Another power failure," I said, exasperated. "Did you see any candles?"

In a moment the door opened and a nun stepped inside with a flashlight. "I hope you don't mind the dark," she said cheerily. "We'll get some candles shortly." I recognized her as Dr. Pia Santiago, a slightly built, bespectacled Filipino who was in charge of the whole hospital. We had met briefly on a previous visit. Almost at once another nun came in with candles and in a moment warm light flooded the room. Mahmud and Tooni resumed their visit and I was left to make conversation with Dr. Santiago. I couldn't help notice her staring at my Bible.

"Do you mind if I sit with you for a while?" Dr. Santiago asked.

"It would be a pleasure," I said, assuming it was just a courtesy visit. She moved to a chair near my bed and with a rustling of her white habit sat down.

"Oh," she said, taking off her glasses and wiping her brow with a handkerchief, "has this ever been a busy night."

My heart warmed to her. Muslims always had respect for these holy women who give up the world to serve their God; their faith may be misplaced, but their sincerity was real. We chatted but as the conversation continued, I could tell that this woman had something on her mind. It was the Bible. I could see her glancing at it with mounting curiosity. Finally she leaned forward and in a confidential tone asked, "Madame Sheikh, what are you doing with a Bible?"

"I am earnestly in search of God," I answered. And then, while the candles burned lower, I told her, very cautiously at first, then with mounting boldness, about my dreams, my visit with Mrs. Mitchell, and my comparing the Bible and the Koran. "Whatever happens," I emphasized, "I must find God, but I'm confused about your faith," I said finally, realizing that even as I spoke I was putting my finger on something important. "You seem to make God so . . . I don't know . . . *personal!*"

The little nun's eyes filled with compassion and she leaned forward. "Madame Sheikh," she said, her voice full of emotion, "there is only one way to find out why we feel this way. And that is to find out for yourself, strange as that may seem. Why don't you pray *to* the God you are searching for? Ask Him to show you His way. Talk to Him as if He were your friend."

I smiled. She might as well suggest that I talk to the Taj Mahal. But then Dr. Santiago said something that shot through my being like electricity. She leaned closer and took my hand in hers, tears streaming down her cheeks. "Talk to Him," she said very quietly, "as if He were your father."

I sat back quickly. A dead silence filled the room. Even Mahmud and Tooni's conversation hung between thoughts. I stared at the nun with the candlelight glinting off her glasses.

Talk to God as if He were my father! The thought shook my soul in the peculiar way truth has of being at once startling and comforting.

Then as if on cue everyone started talking at once. Tooni and Mahmud laughed and decided that the parasol should be colored purple. Dr. Santiago smiled, rose, wished us all well, gathered her habit about her and left the room.

Nothing else was said about prayer or Christianity. Yet I moved through the rest of that night, and the next morning, stunned. What made the experience especially mysterious was that the doctors could find nothing wrong with Mahmud and Mahmud kept saying that his ear did not hurt him one bit. At first, I was irritated at all the time and trouble this had taken. Then the thought occurred to me that perhaps, just perhaps, in some mystic way God had taken advantage of this situation to bring me into contact with Dr. Santiago.

Later that morning Manzur drove us all back to Wah. As we turned off the Grand Trunk onto our lane, I could see the gray roof of my home through the trees. Usually, I looked forward to home as a retreat from the world. But today there seemed to be a difference about my house, as if something special would happen to me there.

We drove up the long driveway, Manzur sounding the horn. The servants ran out and surrounded the car. "Is the little one well?" they all asked at once.

Yes, I assured them, Mahmud was fine. But my mind was not on homecoming festivities. It was on this new way to find God. I went up to my bedroom to consider all that had been happening. No Muslim, I felt certain, ever thought of Allah as his father. Since childhood, I had been told that the surest way to know about Allah was to pray five times a day and study and think on the Koran. Yet Dr. Santiago's words came to me again. "Talk *to* God. Talk to Him as if He were your Father."

Alone in my room I got on my knees and tried to call Him "Father." But it was a useless effort and I straightened in dismay. It was ridiculous. Wouldn't it be sinful to try to bring the Great One down to our own level? I fell asleep that night more confused than ever.

Hours later I awoke. It was after midnight, my birthday, December 12th. I was 47 years old. I felt a momentary excitement, a carry-over from childhood when birthdays were festivals with string bands on the lawns, games, and relatives coming to the house all day. Now, there would be no celebration, perhaps a few phone calls, nothing more.

Oh, how I had missed those childhood days. I thought of my parents as I liked to remember them best. Mother, so loving, so regal and beautiful. And Father. I had been so proud of him, with his high posts in the Indian government. I could still see him, impeccably dressed, adjusting his turban at the mirror before leaving for his office. The friendly eyes under bushy brows, the gentle smile, the chiseled features and aquiline nose.

One of my cherished memories was seeing him at work in the study. Even in a society where sons were more highly regarded than daughters, Father prized his children equally. Often, as a little girl, I would have a question to ask him and I would peek at him from around the door of his office, hesitant to interrupt. Then his eye would catch mine. Putting down his pen, he would lean back in his chair and call out, "Keecha?" Slowly, I would walk into the study, my head down. He would smile and pat the chair next to his. "Come, my darling, sit here." Then, placing his arm around me, he would draw me to him. "Now, my little Keecha," he would ask gently, "What can I do for you?"

It was always the same with Father. He didn't mind if I bothered him. Whenever I had a question or problem, no matter how busy he was, he would put aside his work to devote his full attention just to me.

It was well past midnight as I lay in bed savoring this wonderful memory. "Oh thank you . . ." I murmured to God. Was I really talking *to* Him?

Suddenly, a breakthrough of hope flooded me. Suppose, just suppose God were like a father. If my earthly father would put aside everything to listen to me, wouldn't my heavenly Father . . . ?

Shaking with excitement, I got out of bed, sank to my knees on the rug, looked up to heaven and in rich new understanding called God "My Father."

I was not prepared for what happened.

5.

The Crossroads

"Oh Father, my Father . . . Father God."

Hesitantly, I spoke His name aloud. I tried different ways of speaking to Him. And then, as if something broke through for me I found myself trusting that He was indeed hearing me, just as my earthly father had always done.

"Father, oh my Father God," I cried, with growing confidence. My voice seemed unusually loud in the large bedroom as I knelt on the rug beside my bed. But suddenly that room wasn't empty any more. *He* was there! I could sense His Presence. I could feel His hand laid gently on my head. It was as if I could *see* His eyes, filled with love and compassion. He was so close that I found myself laying my head on His knees like a little girl sitting at her father's feet. For a long time I knelt there, sobbing quietly, floating in His love. I found myself talking with Him, apologizing for not having known Him before. And again, came His loving compassion, like a warm blanket settling around me.

Now I recognized this as the same loving Presence I had met that fragrance-filled afternoon in my garden. The same Presence I had sensed often as I read the Bible.

"I am confused, Father . . ." I said. "I have to get one thing straight right away." I reached over to the bedside table where I kept the Bible and the Koran side by side.

I picked up both books and lifted them, one in each hand. "Which, Father?" I said. "Which one is Your book?"

Then a remarkable thing happened. Nothing like it had ever occurred in my life in quite this way. For I heard a voice inside my being, a voice that spoke to me as clearly as if I were repeating words in my inner mind. They were fresh, full of kindness, yet at the same time full of authority.

"In which book do you meet Me as your Father?"

I found myself answering: "In the Bible." That's all it took. Now there was no question in my mind which one was His book. I looked at my watch and was astonished to discover that three hours had passed. Yet I was not tired. I wanted to go on praying, I wanted to read the Bible, for I knew now that my Father would speak through it. I went to bed only when I knew I must for the sake of my health. But the very next morning I told my maids to see that I was not disturbed, took my Bible again and reclined on my divan. Starting with Matthew, I began reading the New Testament word by word.

I was impressed that God spoke to His people in dreams, five times in the first part of Matthew, in fact! He spoke to Joseph on behalf of Mary. He warned the Wise Men about Herod, and three more times He addressed Joseph concerning the protection of the baby Jesus.

I couldn't find enough time for the Bible. Everything I read, it seemed, was directing me to take some kind of closer walk with God.

I found myself standing at a great crossroads. So far I had met, personally, the Father God. In my heart I knew I had to give myself totally to His Son Jesus or else to turn my back on Him completely.

And I knew for certain that everyone I loved would advise me to turn my back on Jesus. Into my mind crowded the memory of a special, precious day years before when my father took me to our family mosque, just the two of us. We stepped into the soaring vaulted chamber. Taking my hand, Father told me with great pride and with strong identification that twenty generations of our family had worshipped there. "What a privilege you have, my little Keecha, to be part of this ancient truth."

And I thought of Tooni. Surely this young woman had enough worries already. And there were my other children; although they lived far away, they too would be hurt if I "became a Christian." And then there was my Uncle Fateh, who had watched so proudly the day I was four years, four months, four days old and began learning to read the Koran. And there was beloved Aunt Amina and all my other relatives, some hundred "uncles," "aunts" and "cousins." In the east, the family becomes *biraderi*, one community, with each member responsible to the other. I could hurt the family in many ways, even interfere with the opportunities of my nieces getting married, as they would have to live in the shadow of my decision if I chose to join the "sweepers."

But most of all I worried about my little grandson, Mahmud; what would happen to him! My heart caught at the thought of Mahmud's father. He was a very volatile man, who might easily try to take the boy from me if I became a Christian, therefore clearly demonstrating that I was unstable.

That day as I sat reading and thinking in my quiet room, these thoughts seared my heart. Suddenly, the realization of the pain I might inflict on others became too much for me and I stood up, crying. I threw a wrap around me and walked into the cold, winter garden, my refuge where, it seemed, I could think best.

"Oh Lord," I cried, as I paced the graveled path, "could You really want me to leave my family? Can a God of love want me to inflict pain on others?" And in the darkness of my despair, all I could hear were His words, the words which I had just read in Matthew:

> *Anyone who puts his love for father or mother above his love for me does not deserve to be mine, and he*

*who loves son or daughter more than me is not worthy
of me. . . .*

Matthew 10:37-38

This Jesus did not compromise. He did not want any
competition. His were hard, uncomfortable words, words I
did not want to hear.

Enough! I couldn't take the pressure of the decision any
longer. On impulse I ran back to the house, summoned
Manzur and announced to the somewhat startled housekeeper that I was going to Rawalpindi. I would be gone
for a few days. She could reach me at my daughter's if there
were need. Manzur drove me into Rawalpindi where I did
spend several days feverishly shopping, buying toys for
Mahmud, perfumes and saris for myself. Not surprisingly,
as I continued my spree, I found myself drifting away from
the warmth of His Presence. Once when a shopkeeper
spread out a piece of cloth and showed me the gems em-
broidered in a rich design, I suddenly saw the shape of the
cross in the pattern. I snapped at the shopkeeper and fled.
The next morning I went back to Wah neither determined
to remain a Muslim nor determined to become a Christian.

Then one evening as I relaxed before the fire, I found
myself picking up the Bible again. Mahmud was in bed.
It was quiet in the living room. A wind in the garden rattled
the windows, the fire snapped and hissed.

I had read straight through all the Gospels and the Book
of Acts, and that night I had reached the last book in the
Bible. I was fascinated by Revelation, even though I understood very little of it. I read as if directed, strangely confident. And then abruptly I came to a sentence that made
the room spin. It was the 20th verse of the third chapter of
Revelation:

*See, I stand knocking at the door. If anyone listens to
my voice and opens the door, I will go into his house
and dine with him, and he with me.*

And dine with Him, and He with me!

I gasped, letting the book fall in my lap.

This was my dream, the dream where Jesus was having dinner with me! At the time I had had no knowledge of a book called Revelation. I closed my eyes and once again I could see Jesus sitting across the table from me. I could feel His warm smile, His acceptance. Why, the glory was there too! Just as it had been with the Father. It was the glory that belonged to His Presence!

Now I knew that my dream had come from God. The way was clear. I could accept Him, or reject Him. I could open the door, ask Him to come in permanently, or I could close the door. I would have to make my full decision *now*, one way or the other.

I made up my mind and knelt in front of the fire.

"Oh God, don't wait a moment. Please come into my life. Every bit of me is open to You." I did not have to struggle, or worry about what would happen. I had said Yes. Christ was in my life now, and I knew it.

How unbearably beautiful. Within a few days I had met God the Father and God the Son. I got up and started to prepare for bed, my mind whirling. Did I dare take one more step? I remembered that in the book of Acts, at Pentecost, Jesus had baptized His followers with the Holy Spirit. Was I supposed to follow this same pattern? "Lord," I said, as I laid my head back on my pillow, "I have no one to guide me except You Yourself. If You intend for me to receive this Baptism in the Holy Spirit then of course I want what You want. I am ready." Knowing I had placed myself completely in His hands, I drifted off to sleep.

It was still dark when I was awakened in a state of vibrant expectancy that morning of December 24, 1966. I looked at my luminescent clock and the hands pointed to 3:00 A.M. The room was bitterly cold but I was burning with excitement.

I crawled out of bed and sank to my knees on the cold rug. As I looked up, I seemed to be looking into a great light. Hot tears flowed down my face as I raised my hands to Him and cried out: "Oh Father God, baptize me with Your Holy Spirit!"

I took my Bible and opened it to where the Lord said:

> John used to baptize with water, but before many days
> are passed you will be baptized with the Holy Spirit.
> Acts 1:5

"Lord," I cried, "if these words of Yours are true, then give this baptism to me now." I crumpled face down on the chilled floor where I lay crying. "Lord," I sobbed, "I'll never want to get up from this place until You give me this baptism." Suddenly, I was filled with wonder and awe. For in that silent pre-dawn room I saw His face. Something surged through me, wave after wave of purifying ocean breakers, flooding me to the tips of my fingers and toes, washing my soul.

Then the powerful surges subsided, the heavenly ocean quieted. I was completely cleansed. Joy exploded within me and I cried out praising Him, thanking Him.

Hours later, I felt the Lord lift me to my feet. He wanted me to get up now. I looked out the filigreed windows and saw that it was nearly dawn.

"Oh, Lord," I said, as I lay back in my bed. "Could the heaven you speak of be any better than this? To know You is joy, to worship You is happiness, to be near You is peace. *This* is heaven!"

I doubt if I slept two hours that early dawn. In no time at all my maidservants came in to help me dress. For the first morning that I could remember, I did not say one cross word to them. Instead there was an air of calm and peace in the sun-flooded room. Raisham actually hummed a song as she brushed my hair, something she had never done before.

All that day I roamed through my house, silently praising God, hardly able to contain the joy within myself. At lunch,

Mahmud looked up from his pancakes and said: "Mum, you look so smiley; what has happened to you?"

I reached over and tousled his shiny black hair. "Give him some *halwa*," I told the cook. This dish made from wheat, butter and sugar was his favorite sweet. I told Mahmud that we would be celebrating Christmas at the Mitchells' home.

"Christmas?" said Mahmud.

"It's a holiday," I said, "a little like Ramazan." That, Mahmud did understand. Ramazan was the month of the Muslim year when Muhammad received his first revelation. So for this month, each year, Muslims fast from sunrise to sunset each day until at last the drums thunder in the mosques and we load ourselves with delicacies, sweet and sour fruit, spinach leaves dipped in batter and fried, delicately cooked eggplant, succulent kabobs. Christmas I supposed would indeed be a little like Ramazan. And I was right. When David met us at the door of the Mitchells' house, the scent of delicious cooked foods floated around him, and laughter sounded from within the room.

"Come in! Come in!" he exclaimed, drawing us into the living room filled with a holiday spirit. A Christmas tree glowed in the corner and the laughter of the two Mitchell children, just a little older than Mahmud, rang out from another room. Mahmud happily joined them at their play.

I could not contain my joy any longer. "David!" I cried, using his first name without thinking, "I am a Christian now! I have been baptized in the Holy Spirit!"

He stared at me for a moment, then drew me into the house. "Who told you about the Holy Spirit Baptism?" he asked, his gray eyes wide. He began laughing joyously and praising God. Hearing his "Hallelujah!" Synnove rushed into the room from the kitchen and David again asked: "Who told you?"

"Jesus told me," I laughed. "I read it in the Bible's Book of Acts; I asked God for it and received it."

Both David and Synnove looked bewildered. But then

suddenly they rushed to me. Synnove put her arms around me and broke into tears. David joined her. Then the three of us stood there, arms around each other, praising God for what He had done.

That night I began a diary into which I put all the wonderful things the Lord had been doing for me. If I should die—and I had no idea what might happen to me once word got out that I had become a Christian—at least I wanted this record of my experience to remain. As I sat at my desk writing my experiences, I did not realize that He was making preparations to begin my education.

6.

Learning to Find His Presence

Several surprises were waiting for me over the next several days, following my threefold encounters.

For one thing, I found I was experiencing dreams or visions, but quite unlike the two dreams that had started this whole incredible adventure. In fact my first experience left me shaken. I was resting in bed one afternoon thinking of my Lord when suddenly I felt as if I were floating right out my window. I felt sure I was not asleep and found myself passing right through the window filigree, and I caught a glimpse of the earth below. I became so frightened that I cried out in fear, and suddenly I found myself back in bed. I lay there slightly dazed, breathing shallowly, feeling a tingling in my legs as if they had been asleep, and then the blood was rushing back.

"What was it, Lord?" I asked. And then I realized that He had given me a special experience. "I'm so sorry, Lord," I apologized, "but You have picked up a coward."

Late that night it happened again. Only this time I talked to God through the experience and told Him I wasn't afraid. As I slipped back through my window I could only think I had been "floating" in a spiritual way. "But what is Your reason, my Lord?" I asked.

Turning to the Bible I searched His Word for something

of this, for I began to fear that it might be something not of the Lord.

I sighed in relief when I read in the Acts of the Apostles (8:39) where the Spirit of the Lord suddenly whisked Philip away to the distant city of Azotus after he had baptized the Ethiopian eunuch.

Then I was given further confirmation when I read Paul's second letter to the Christians at Corinth. In chapter 12, in speaking of visions and revelations from the Lord, he wrote of being "caught up into the third heaven." He felt that only God knew whether or not it was an actual physical experience, and I felt the same about mine. As Paul added: "This man heard words that cannot . . . be translated into human speech."

I heard words, too, that I cannot translate but I shall never forget the scenes. During one such experience I saw a steeple soaring into heaven; suddenly before me were hundreds of churches, new ones, old ones, churches with different architectural styles, and then a beautiful gold church. Again the scene shifted and I saw downtown areas of cities rolling before me, modern centers and old-fashioned village squares. It was all so clear; I could discern the skyscrapers, clock towers, and quaint ornate buildings.

Then my heart shook as I saw a man riding a red horse, his right hand wielding a sword; he galloped about the earth under cloud masses. Sometimes he rose until his head touched the clouds, and sometimes his steed's flashing hooves scraped the earth.

I couldn't get over the feeling that these must have been given to me for a particular, still unknown, reason.

I also found as I read the Scriptures that it was an experience completely unlike any other time I had spent with the Bible. Something happened to me as I went through the book; instead of reading the Bible, I found myself living it. It was as if I stepped through its pages into that ancient world of Palestine when Jesus Christ walked the stony roads of Galilee. I watched as He preached and taught, as He lived out His message in everyday situations, and as He displayed the power of the Spirit, and finally as He went to the cross and passed victoriously through the experience of death.

I also discovered to my surprise that the effect of Bible reading was beginning to be felt by others. This was brought home to me one morning when my maids were preparing my toilette. Nur-jan was arranging the silver combs and brushes on a tray when she accidently spilled the whole thing. There was a great clatter. She stiffened, her eyes wide; I knew she was expecting my usual onslaught. And indeed I was about to scold her when I caught myself. Instead, I found myself saying, "Don't worry, Nur-jan. They didn't break."

Then there was a peculiar boldness that began to take shape in my life. Up until then I had been afraid to let anyone know of my interest in Christ. For one thing, I dreaded the thought of people making jokes about the "sweeper Begum." Of more concern, I was afraid my family would ostracize me; Mahmud's father might even try to take him away. I was even fearful lest some fanatic take to heart the injunction: *he who falls away from his faith must die.*

So I was really not anxious to be seen at the Mitchells. The group of women who came out of David's and Synnove's house that first night still gave me concern. My own servants certainly knew that something unusual was happening to me. When I put all this together I was living in a state of constant uneasiness, not knowing when the pressure against me would begin.

But after my three encounters with God, I found myself making a surprising admission to myself one day. As far as I was concerned, my decision to become a Christian was now public information. As the Bible says, I was "confessing Jesus with my lips." "Well," I said to myself as I stood at my bedroom window one day, "we'll just let the results fall where they may."

I didn't expect results quite so quickly. Soon after Christmas, 1966, the downstairs maid came to me with her eyebrows arched, "Mrs. Mitchell is here to see you, Begum," she said.

"Oh?" I said, trying to sound casual, "show her in." My heart pounded as I walked to the door to meet my guest. "I am so honored to have you visit," I said, making sure that the maid, hovering in the background, heard me.

Synnove came to invite me to dinner. "There will be a few others there, people we are sure you would like to meet," she said.

Others? I felt the old wall rise within me. Synnove must have caught the hesitant look in my eyes for she sought to reassure me. "Most of them are Christians," she said. "Some are English, some Americans. Would you come?" her eyes pleaded hopefully.

And of course—with more enthusiasm than I felt—I said that I would be delighted.

I wondered why many Christians were so often shy! I had been in contact with Christians before, usually at state dinner parties I had hosted as wife of a government official. The dinners were formal events, served by uniformed servants, amidst Belgian lace, with centerpieces of fresh flowers; lengthy affairs, with numerous courses each served separately on its own Spode china. There were many Christians of different nationalities among the guests, but not one of them ever mentioned his faith, even when it would have been a natural part of the conversation. The people I'd meet at the Mitchell's, I felt, would not be so backward.

The next day I drove the now becoming familiar route to the Mitchells' house. David and Synnove greeted me warmly and introduced me to their friends. I wonder how I would have felt if I'd known at the time how large a role some of these people were going to play in my life.

The first couple were Ken and Marie Old. Ken was an Englishman whose blue eyes twinkled humorously behind thick glasses. He was a civil engineer who wore an air of informality as easily as he wore his rumpled clothes. His wife Marie was an American nurse with a practical air offset by a beautiful smile. The others were warm and friendly people, too.

And then to my horror I found myself the center of attention. Everyone was eager to hear about my experiences. What I expected to be a quiet dinner turned out to be a question and answer period. The dining room was still— even the several children sat quietly—as I told about my dreams, and about my separate meetings with the three personalities of God. At the end of the dinner David complimented his wife on the meal but said he felt that the spiritual nourishment of my story was even richer.

"I agree," said Ken Old. "I've seen you before, you know. I used to live in Wah. I would pass your garden in the early morning and admire your flowers. Sometimes you were in the garden but I must say you don't look like the same woman." I felt sure I knew what he meant. The Bilquis Sheikh of a few months ago had been an unsmiling person. "You are like a child," Ken went on to say, "who has suddenly been given a gift. In your face I see an incredible wonder at that gift. You treasure it more than anything you have ever possessed."

I was going to like this man.

I had enjoyable conversations with the others, and I realized that I had been right. These Christians were very different from Christians I had met at other dinner parties. Before the evening was over, each person had told a little about what the Lord was doing in his life. David was right. The meal was excellent, but the true feeding came from the Presence in that little house. I had never known anything similar, and I found myself wishing I could get this same feeding regularly.

Which is why, as I was about to leave, the comment from Ken struck me with such impact. Ken and Marie came up and took my hand. "You'll need some regular Christian fellowship now, Bilquis," said Ken. "Will you come to our house on Sunday evenings."

"Could you?" asked Marie hopefully.

And that is how I began regular meetings with other Christians. Sunday evenings we met at the Olds' house, a brick dwelling whose living room could barely hold the dozen people who crowded in. Only two were Pakistanis, the rest were Americans and Englishmen. I met new people, too, such as Dr. and Mrs. Christy. This thin energetic-looking American doctor was an eye specialist and his wife a nurse. Both were on the local mission hospital staff. At the meetings we sang, read the Bible, and prayed for each other's needs. It quickly became the high point of my week.

Then one Sunday I didn't particularly feel like going. So I rang up the Olds and gave some excuse. It seemed a little thing, but almost instantly I began to feel uneasy. What was it! I walked through the house restlessly checking on the servants' work. Everything was in order, yet everything seemed out of order.

Then I went to my own room and knelt down to pray. After a while Mahmud crept in, so quietly that I didn't know he was there until I felt his little soft hand in mine. "Mum, are you all right?" he asked. "You look funny." I smiled and assured him that, yes, I was all right. "Well you keep walking around *looking*. As if you'd lost something."

Then he was gone, skipping out the door and down the hall. I looked as if I had lost something?! Mahmud was right. And I knew right then what it was I had lost. I'd lost the sense of God's glory. It was gone! Why? Did it have something to do with my not going to that meeting at the Olds'? With my not having fellowship when I needed it?

With a sense of urgency I phoned Ken and said that I'd be there after all.

What a difference. Immediately I felt, actually felt, the return of warmth to my soul. I did go to the meeting, as I promised. Nothing unusual took place there, yet again I knew I was walking in His glory. Ken had apparently been right. I *needed* fellowship. I had learned my lesson. I determined from then on to attend regularly unless Jesus Himself told me not to go.

As I drew a little closer to God, here a step, there a step, I found myself hungering even more for His word through the Bible. Everyday, as soon as I arose, I would begin reading it with a never-failing sense of *nowness*. The Bible became alive to me, illuminating my day, shedding its light on every step I would take. It was, in fact, my lovely perfume. But here too I found a strange thing. One day Mahmud and I were to go to see his mother for the day. I was late getting to bed the night before and really didn't feel like getting up at dawn to have an hour with the Bible, so I told Raisham to wake me with my tea just before we were supposed to set off.

I didn't sleep at all well that night. I tossed and twisted and had bad dreams. When Raisham came in, I was exhausted. And I noticed that the entire day didn't go right.

Strange! What was the Lord saying to me? That He expected me to read the Bible *every* day?

That was the second time when I seemed to be stepping out of the glory of the Lord's Presence.

But the experience, nonetheless, left me with a strange sense of excitement. For I had the feeling that I was sitting on an important truth without realizing it. There were times when I was in the Presence and experienced that deep sense of joy and peace, and there were times when I lost the sense of His Presence.

What was the key? What could I do to stay close to Him?

I thought back over the times when He had seemed unusually close, way back to my two dreams and to the afternoon when I sensed the exquisite fragrance in my winter garden. I thought about the first time when I had gone to the Mitchells' and about the later times when I had read my Bible regularly, and gone to the Sunday meetings at the Olds'. Almost always these were times when I knew the Lord was with me.

And I thought about opposite times too, moments when I knew that I had lost this sense of His nearness. How did the Bible put it? *And grieve not the Holy Spirit of God* (Ephesians 4:30, KJV). Is that what happened when I scolded the servants? Or when I failed to nourish my spirit with regular Bible reading? Or when I just didn't go to the Olds'?

Part of the key to staying in His company was obedience. When I obeyed, then I was allowed to remain in His Presence.

I got out my Bible and searched in John until I found the verse where Jesus says:

> *When a man loves me, he follows my teaching. Then my Father will love him, and we will come to that man and make our home within him.*
>
> John 14:23

That was the Bible's way of expressing what I was trying to say. To stay in the glory. *That* was what I was trying to do!

And the key was obedience. "Oh Father," I prayed, "I want to be Your servant, just as it says in the Bible. I *will* obey You. I've always thought it a sacrifice to give up my own will. But it's no sacrifice because it keeps me close to You. How could Your Presence be a sacrifice!"

I had never got used to those times when the Lord seemed to speak so directly to my mind, as I am convinced He did right then. Who else but the Lord would have asked me to forgive my husband! *Love your former husband, Bilquis. Forgive him.*

For a moment I sat in shock. Feeling His love for people in general was one thing, but to love this man who had hurt me so much?

"Father, I just can't do it. I don't want to bless Khalid or forgive him." I recalled how once I had childishly even asked the Lord not ever to convert my husband because then he would have the same joy that I had. And now God was asking me to *love* this same man? I could feel anger rising within me as I thought of Khalid, and quickly put him out of my mind. "Maybe I could just forget him, Lord. Wouldn't that be enough?"

Was it my imagination or did the glow of the Lord's Presence seem to cool? "I can't forgive my husband, Lord. I have no capacity to do so."

My yoke is easy and my burden is light (Matthew 11:30).

"Lord, I can't forgive him!" I cried. Then I listed all the terrible things he had done to me. As I did, other wounds surfaced, hurts that I had pushed into the back of my mind as too humiliating to think about. Hate welled within me and now I felt totally separated from God. Frightened, I cried out like a lost child.

And quickly, miraculously, He was there, with me in my room. Flinging myself at His feet, I confessed my hate and my inability to forgive.

My yoke is easy and my burden is light.

Slowly, deliberately, I swung my terrible burden over to Him. I let go of my resentment, my hurt, and the festering outrage, placing it all in His hands. Suddenly I sensed a light rising within me, like the glow of dawn. Breathing freely, I hurried to my dresser and took out the gold-framed picture and looked down at Khalid's face. I prayed: "Oh Father, take away my resentment and fill me with Your love for Khalid in the name of my Lord and Savior, Jesus Christ."

I stood there for a long time, looking at the picture. Slowly the negative feeling within me began to fade. In its place came an unexpected love, a sense of caring for the man in the photo. I couldn't believe it. I was actually wishing my former husband well.

"Oh bless him, Lord, give him joy, let him be happy in his new life."

As I willed this, a dark cloud lifted from me. A weight was removed from my soul. I felt peaceful, relaxed.

Once again I found myself living in His glory.

And once again I found myself wanting never to leave His company. As a reminder to myself of this desire, I went downstairs, late as it was, and found some henna dye. With it I drew a large cross on the back of both hands to remind me always.

Never, if I had anything to say about it, would I again deliberately step away from His company.

It would take me a long time, I was sure, to learn the skill of living in the glow of His Presence, but it was a training time I welcomed with immense excitement.

And then one night I had a terrifying experience. I did not know I would be hearing from another side.

7.

The Baptism of Fire and Water

I had been sound asleep that night in January 1967 when I was startled awake by my bed shaking violently.

An earthquake? My heart was gripped by a nameless terror. And then I sensed a horrible malevolent presence in my room; one that was definitely evil.

Suddenly I was thrown out of my bed; whether I was in my physical body or spirit I do not know. But I was pushed and thrown about like a straw in a hurricane. The face of Mahmud flashed before me and my heart cried out for his protection.

This must be death coming for me, I thought, my soul quaking. The awful presence engulfed me like a black billowing cloud and instinctively I screamed out to the One Who now meant everything to me. "Oh Lord Jesus!" At this I was shaken mightily, as a dog ravages his prey.

"Am I wrong to call on Jesus?" I cried to God in my spirit. At this a great strength surged through me and I called out: "I *will* call on Him! Jesus! Jesus! Jesus!"

At this the powerful ravaging subsided. I lay there worshipping and praising the Lord. However, sometime around 3:00 in the morning, my eyelids became too heavy and I slipped to sleep.

I was awakened in the morning by Raisham bringing me

my morning tea. I lay there for a moment feeling such a sense of relief. As I closed my eyes in prayer, I saw the Lord Jesus Christ standing before me. He wore a white robe and a purple cape. He gently smiled at me and said, "Don't worry; it won't happen again."

I felt then that my harrowing experience was Satanic, a test Jesus permitted for my own good. I recalled the cry that came from deep within my soul: "I *will* call on His Name, I *will* say Jesus Christ."

My Lord was still standing before me. *It is time for you to be baptized in water, Bilquis,* He said.

Water baptism! I had heard the words distinctly, and I didn't like what I heard.

As soon as I could I dressed and asked Nur-jan and Raisham to see that I wasn't disturbed until lunchtime. I stood at the window thinking. The morning air was cool; and pale steam drifted up from the garden springs. I knew that the significance of baptism is not lost on the Muslim world. A person can read the Bible without arousing too much hostility. But the sacrament of baptism is a different matter. To the Muslim this is the one unmistakable sign that a convert has renounced his Islamic faith to become a Christian. To the Muslim, baptism is apostasy.

So, here was a difficult testing point. The issue was clearly drawn. Would I yield to the fear of being treated as an outcast, or worse, as a traitor, or would I obey Jesus?

First of all I had to be certain that I was really obeying the Lord, and not some illusion. For I was far too new at being a Christian to trust "voices." How could I test my impression better than through the Bible. So I went back to my Bible and read how Jesus Himself had been baptized in the Jordan. And I looked again at Paul's letter to the Romans where he talked about the rite in terms of death and resurrection. The "old man" dies, and a new creature arises, leaving all his sins behind.

Well, that was that. If Jesus was baptized, and if the Bible called for baptism, then of course I would obey.

That very moment I rang for Raisham.

"Please ask Manzur to get the car ready," I said. "I'm going to visit the Olds after lunch."

Shortly I was once again seated in Marie and Ken's small living room when I burst forth in my usual way. "Ken," I said, facing him squarely, "I'm sure that the Lord has told me to be baptized."

He looked at me for a long moment, his brow furrowing, perhaps trying to fathom the depth of my intention. Then Ken leaned forward and said, very, very seriously: "Bilquis, are you prepared for what may happen?"

"Yes, but . . ." I started to answer. Ken interrupted, his voice low.

"Bilquis, a Pakistani I met the other day asked if I were a sweeper in my own country." He looked at me levelly. "Do you realize that from now on you would not be *the* Begum Sheikh, the respected landowner with generations of prestige? From now on you will be associated with the sweeper Christians here?"

"Yes," I answered. "I do know that."

His words became still firmer and I steeled myself to look directly at him.

"And do you know," he continued, "that Mahmud's father can easily take him away from you? He could label you an unfit guardian."

My heart was stung. I had worried about this, but hearing Ken say it aloud made the prospect sound all the more possible.

"Yes, I know, Ken," I said weakly. "I realize many people will think I am committing a crime. But I want to be baptized, I must obey God."

Our conversation was interrupted by the unexpected arrival of the Mitchells. Ken immediately told them we had something important to discuss. "Bilquis," he said, "wants to be baptized."

Silence. Synnove coughed.

"But we don't have a tank for it," said David.

"How about the church in Peshawar?" asked Marie. "Don't they have a tank?"

My heart sank. Peshawar is the capital of the North-West Frontier Province. In every sense of the word it is frontier territory, a provincial town populated by conservative Muslims noted for their quickness to take action. Well, I thought, there goes any secrecy I might want to keep. The whole town would know within an hour.

It was left that Ken would make arrangements for us to go to Peshawar. We should hear from the pastor there in a day or two.

That evening my phone rang. It was my Grand Uncle Fateh. I loved this elderly gentleman dearly. He was always so interested in my religious instruction.

"Bilquis?" My uncle's authoritative voice sounded upset. "Yes, Uncle?"

"Is it true that you are reading a Bible?"

"Yes." I wondered how he knew. What else had he heard?

Uncle Fateh cleared his throat. "Bilquis, don't *ever* talk about the Bible with any of these Christians. You know how argumentative they are. Their arguments always lead to confusion."

I started to interrupt him but he rode over my words. "Don't invite anyone . . . ," he emphasized ". . . *anyone* to your house without consulting me! If you do, you know that your family will not stand by you."

Uncle Fateh was quiet for a moment as he paused to catch his breath. I took advantage of the opening.

"Uncle, listen to me." There was a strained silence on the other end of the wire. I plunged ahead. "Uncle, as you'll remember, no one has ever entered my home without an invitation." My uncle would remember, all right; I was well known for ruthlessly refusing to see callers who had not arranged their visits beforehand.

"You know," I concluded, "that I will meet whomever I like. Goodbye, Uncle."

I hung up the phone. Was this an omen of things to

come as far as the rest of my family was concerned? If Uncle Fateh reacted so strongly just hearing that I read the Bible, what would happen when he and the rest of my family learned about my baptism? I didn't like to think.

Which only added fuel to my drive to be baptized right away. I wasn't sure I *could* resist pressure from scores of people I loved.

No word came from Ken.

The next morning as I was reading the Bible, I again ran across the story of the Ethiopian eunuch to whom Philip had brought the message of God. The first thing the eunuch did, as soon as he saw water, was to jump down out of the carriage to be baptized. It was as if the Lord was telling me all over again, "Get your baptism and get it now!" I felt sure He meant that if I waited much longer, something or someone might prevent it.

I leaped from my bed, realizing with fresh power that huge forces were marshalling to block me from what the Lord wanted me to do. I put down the Bible, summoned my maids who quickly dressed me and shortly I was speeding to the Mitchells'.

"David," I said, while we were still standing in the doorway, "is there any answer from Peshawar?"

"No, not as yet."

My voice rose. "Can't you baptize me here? Today? Now?"

David frowned. He ushered me in out of the cold morning air. "Now, Bilquis, we can't be in too much of a hurry about such a big step."

"I must obey my Lord. He keeps telling me to press on." I told him about my morning Bible reading, and about the new insistence from the Lord that He wanted me baptized before anything happened to me.

David held out his hands in helplessness. "I must take Synnove up to Abbottabad this afternoon and there isn't anything I can do now, Bilquis."

He put his hand on my arm. "Be patient, Bilquis. I'm sure we'll hear from Peshawar tomorrow."

I drove over to the Olds'.

"Please," I cried as Ken and Marie greeted me, "is there any way for me to be baptized immediately?"

"We asked our pastor," Ken said, taking me by the arm and leading me into the living room. "He says the whole matter has to go through the Session."

"Session?" I echoed. "What is that?"

He explained that his pastor wanted to baptize me but he had to get approval from his church's governing board. "This could take up to several days," he added, "and meanwhile anything could happen."

"Yes," I sighed, "word *would* get out." My mind raced desperately over all the possible circumstances.

Then Ken told me an amazing thing. In the middle of the night he had heard a man's voice directing him to *"Turn to page 654 in your Bible."* What a strange way, he thought, of giving a Bible reference. It was Job 13 and 14, and the verses shone out from the page. He read the verses that had so blessed him and which seemed meant for me. They started: *Wherefore do I take my flesh in my teeth, and put my life in mine hand? Though he slay me, yet will I trust in him.*

Was I ready for even *this*, I wondered? Was my trust *that* strong? I stood up and took Ken's arm. "Give me my water baptism now. And then, though He kill me, I am ready. I'll be better off in Heaven with my Lord."

I slumped down into a chair and looked up at Ken, apologizing. "I'm sorry, Ken. I'm getting upset. But one thing I know: the Lord said I should be baptized now. I shall put it to you bluntly. Are you going to help me or not?"

Ken sat back in his chair, ran his hand through his sandy brown hair. "Of course," he said, looking at Marie. "Why don't we go to the Mitchells' and see if there isn't something we can do?"

We drove back across the winding streets of Wah. For a while we sat quietly with the Mitchells in their living room in prayer. Then Ken sighed deeply, leaned forward and spoke to all of us. "I'm sure we all agree God has been guiding Bilquis in a most unusual way up until now. And if she insists her urgency to be baptized is from God, then let us not be a hindrance to her." He turned to David. "You're going to Abbottabad. Why don't Marie and I take Bilquis up there today, meet you and Synnove, and arrange for Bilquis' baptism there this afternoon? We'll forget about Peshawar."

Suddenly, it seemed the right thing to do and we all started making preparations. I hurried home, had Raisham pack an extra set of clothes which the Olds said I would need. "Something water won't hurt," Ken said.

Yet in the midst of all this I still felt uneasy. I even sensed the waning of my closeness to the Lord. Hadn't He in so many ways given me a specific urgent instruction? Hadn't He directed me to have my water baptism *now?*

A thought flicked through my mind. I dispelled the idea. It was unthinkable.

But when the thought persisted I asked my Lord in prayer: "Would it be all right, Father God?"

And thus on January 24, 1967, began a most unusual baptism.

Raisham stood before me, in answer to my call.

"Yes, Raisham," I said again. "Please fill the tub."

She turned to her duty, a puzzled expression on her face; never had I taken a bath at this hour of the day.

Raisham announced that my tub was ready; I dismissed her. What I proceeded to do may have some theological problems. But I wasn't thinking in theological terms. I was simply trying to be obedient to a strong urge which was backed up by Scripture. I was supposed to be baptized *now*, and with the impediments that I felt marshalling themselves, I had doubts about waiting even until the afternoon.

So, because I wanted more than anything else in the world to stay in the Lord's Presence, and the way to do that was through obedience, I walked into the bathroom and stepped into the deep tub. As I sat down, water rose almost to my shoulder. I placed my hand on my own head and said loudly: "Bilquis, I baptize you in the name of the Father and of the Son and of the Holy Ghost." I pressed my head down into the water so that my whole body was totally immersed.

I arose from the water rejoicing, calling out, and praising God. "Oh Father, thank You. I'm so fortunate." I *knew* that my sins had been washed away and that I was acceptable in the sight of the Lord.

I did not try to explain to Raisham what I had done and in her usual reserved manner she pointedly did not ask. Within a few minutes I was dressed, waiting for the Olds to take me to my baptism in Abbottabad. Again I didn't know what the theology of the situation was. I did know my motives. These Christian friends had taken such care of me, helping me. They had gone through a lot for me and I didn't want to confuse matters further. I would go ahead with the baptism, although some untrained instinct told me I had already done what the Lord wanted of me. I tried to read the Bible but my Spirit rejoiced so that I was unable to concentrate. I was back in the Glory again, just as I always was when I obeyed Him explicitly, with the Bible as my only check.

"Begum Sahib, Begum Sahib?"

I looked up. It was Raisham. The Olds were downstairs, waiting.

I told Mahmud I would be away for the rest of the day. I felt it better if he were not too involved in an event that might have unpleasant consequences. Then I went down to join Ken and Marie.

It was a two-hour drive to Abbottabad, along a road that was lined with firs and pines. I didn't mention my tub baptism. Instead I told about the many times I had travelled this same road on family outings, followed by several autos piled high with luggage. Silently I wondered if I should feel disloyal to this old heritage.

We arrived at the mission to find the Mitchells waiting with a Canadian medical doctor and his wife, Bob and Madeline Blanchard, who were our hosts. Along with them stood a Pakistani man. "This gentleman," said Synnove, "is Padri Bahadur, the minister who will baptize you."

I looked around at the others, including an Anglican doctor and another Pakistani minister.

"Perhaps this is prophetic, Bilquis," said Synnove. "Perhaps through you many Christians will be drawn closer, for this may be the first time in Pakistan that Baptists and Presbyterians and Anglicans have all gotten together in a common baptism."

There was an air of excitement about the room. Doors were closed, shades were drawn and I imagined what it was like back in the first century when Christians had their baptisms in the catacombs under Rome.

As we prepared for the ceremony, I looked around and asked, "But where is the tank?"

It developed there was none. Ken said that I would have to be sprinkled.

"But Jesus was immersed in the Jordan," I said.

We had crossed a river just before arriving at the mission station. "Why not take me back to the river?" I asked; but then I remembered that it was bitterly cold and others would have to get into that water too and I didn't press the point. Especially since I was certain that I had already received the sacrament.

And so I was baptized again, this time by sprinkling. While I was being sprinkled, I thought how the Lord must be chuckling. After the ceremony, I looked up to see tears streaming down the faces of others in the room. "Well," I laughed, "all this crying certainly doesn't encourage me!"

"Oh Bilquis," sniffed Synnove, coming up to throw her arms around me. She couldn't go on.

"Congratulations," said each of the others. Synnove sang a hymn, Ken read from the Bible, and then it was time to head for home again.

It was a quiet drive. There was no anxiety amongst us; it felt good just to be with Christians. We all said goodbye again amid tears, and I went into my house.

The comfortable mood was shattered as soon as I stepped through the door. The housekeeper rushed up to me, eyes wide, anxiety in her voice.

"Oh Begum Sahib, your family has been here asking about you! They say they know that you are mixing with Christians and. . . ."

I put up my hand. "Now stop!" I commanded, silencing the chatter. "Tell me who came."

As the housekeeper recited the names of those who had come to my house that day, a new apprehension filled me. These were the senior members of my family, uncles, elderly cousins, aunts, people who would come to my house in this manner only on a vitally important concern.

My heart sank. That night I ate with Mahmud, trying not to show my own fears, but just as soon as he went to bed I retired to my own room. I looked out the filigreed window; the snow had stopped falling and under the winter moon I could make out the outlines of the garden I loved. All around me I sensed the comfort of the old house I loved so much, my sanctuary, my retreat.

And now? Would I even be able to keep my home? It was a strange thought, for I had always had the security of family, money and prestige. Yet I felt without doubt that it was also a prophetic thought. The forces which I knew to be marshalling against me had already begun to express themselves through my family. Much of my "power," much of my "security" lay in the family. What would happen if suddenly they all began, at once, to oppose me?

Surely this was the very reason the Lord insisted that I have my baptism quickly, immediately. He knew me. He knew where I was most vulnerable.

I stood there looking out the window. Shadows from swaying trees played through the filigree.

"Oh Lord," I prayed, "please don't let them descend on me all at once. Please let them come one at a time."

No sooner had I breathed these words when there was a knock at the door. The downstairs maid came in to hand me a package. "This was just delivered for you," she said. Impatiently I tore off the wrapping to find a Bible. Inscribed on the fly leaf was: *To our dear sister on her birthday—* It was signed: "Ken and Marie Old."

I held it to my breast, thanking God for such good friends. Then I opened it and my eye was attracted to a page on which these words seemed to stand out: *I will scatter them abroad. . . .*

At the moment the meaning of these words was a mystery to me.

8.

Was There Protection?

I awakened the next morning full of apprehension. Today the family would come again, either en masse or one at a time. Either way I dreaded the awful confrontation. I dreaded the accusations, the angry warnings, the lures and threats which I knew were coming. Above all, I hated hurting them.

Not quite believing that God would answer my request, I had Raisham bring out my finest saris, chose the most attractive, issued word to the gate servant that I would be happy to see all visitors today, and then went to the drawing room. There I sat on one of the white silk chairs and read while Mahmud played with his toy cars, weaving them in and out of the paisley design of the large Persian rug on the floor.

The giant carved clock in the hall struck ten o'clock, eleven, and finally noon. Well, I thought, it looks as if they plan an afternoon visit.

Lunch was served and then while Mahmud napped I continued waiting. At last at three o'clock I heard the sound of a car stopping outside. I was steeling myself for battle when the car drove away! What was happening? I asked the maid and she said it was just someone making a delivery.

Evening darkened the tall windows of the drawing room.

71

and shadows gathered high on the ceiling. Then there was a phone call for me. I glanced at the clock; it was seven. Were they phoning instead of coming in person?

I picked up the phone to hear a soft voice I recognized very well—Marie Old. She sounded quite worried. Word of my conversion was certainly out already, as yesterday's invasion of relatives showed. So why the concern?

"Are you all right?" Marie said. "I've been anxious about you."

I assured her that I was fine. As soon as I hung up the phone, I called for my wraps and asked that the car be sent around. At this time of the year, my family did not normally visit after eight o'clock so I felt it was safe to leave. Odd, how not one relative had called or visited.

I wanted reassurance from one of my Christian family. The Olds? Why had Marie called so mysteriously? I drove to the Olds' house and was surprised to find it completely dark.

And then, quite unexpectedly, quite abruptly, I was alarmed. As I stood at the gate leading into their yard I could feel fear settle over me, touching me with clammy cold horror. Dark thoughts came at me from dark corners of the yard. Surely I had been foolish to come out alone at night! What was that back in the shadows? My heart raced.

I turned. I was about to run for the car.

And then I stopped. No! This was no way to be acting. If I were a part of the Kingdom, I had a right to the King's protection. Standing there in the awesome darkness, still very much afraid, I deliberately willed myself back into the King's hands. "Jesus. Jesus. Jesus." I said over and over again. Incredibly the fear lifted. As soon as it had come, it was gone. I was free!

Almost smiling now, I turned toward the Olds' house. After a few paces, I saw a crack of light coming between two drawn curtains in the living room. I knocked.

The door slowly opened. It was Marie. When she saw

me she gave a sigh of relief and quickly drew me into the house and hugged me.

"Ken! Ken!" she called.

He was there in a moment. "Oh thank God!" he exclaimed. "We were quite worried about you." Ken told me that the Pakistani Padri at my baptism had become quite concerned for my safety and had told them that they had made a mistake in leaving me alone.

"So, that's why you were so concerned on the phone, Marie!" I suppressed a nervous laugh. "Well, I expect the whole country will soon know about my conversion, but thank you anyhow. So far, nothing has happened. Even my family didn't show up and you can't know how grateful I am for that answer to prayer."

"Let's thank the Lord," Ken said, and the three of us knelt together in their living room as Ken thanked God for my protection and asked Him to continue to watch over me.

So, I returned home, the richer for having called on God's help in the face of fear by taking advantage of the Name of Jesus. My servants said there had not been a phone call all that evening. Well, I thought as I prepared for bed, watch out for tomorrow.

Again, I waited in the drawing room all day, praying, thinking, studying the white mosaic floor tiles and the paisley print of the Persian rugs. There was not a word from anyone.

What was going on? Was this some kind of a cat and mouse game?

And then I thought to check with the servants. In Pakistan if you want to know anything, ask a household servant. Through an uncanny grapevine, they know everything about everybody.

Finally, I pinned down my handmaid Nur-jan: "Tell me, what happened to my family?"

"Oh Begum Sahib," she answered, suppressing a nervous giggle, "the strangest thing happened. It was as if everybody was busy at once. Your brother had to go to the annual Winter Cricket Tournament." I smiled; to my brother, cricket was more important than a sister who was on her way to hell. "Your Uncle Fateh had to go out of the province on a court case; your Aunt Amina needed to go to Lahore; two of your cousins were called out of town on business, and . . ."

I stopped her; she need not go on any further. The Lord had said He would scatter them and scatter them He did. I could almost hear my Lord chuckle. It wasn't, I felt sure, that the concerned members of my family would leave me alone, but now they would come one by one.

And so it was. The first emissary was my Aunt Amina, a regal woman in her seventies whose eastern beauty somehow always looked out of place in my drawing room with its modern western furniture. For years we had a close relationship of love and trust. Now as she walked in, her magnolia complexion was paler than usual and her gray eyes were rimmed with sadness.

We chatted a bit. Finally I could tell she was coming to the real reason for her visit. Clearing her throat, she sat back and, trying to sound casual, asked: "Er . . . Bilquis . . . uh . . . I have heard . . . that you have become a Christian. Is it true?"

I only smiled at her.

She shifted uneasily in her chair and continued. "I thought people were spreading false rumors about you." She hesitated, her soft eyes imploring me to say that it wasn't true.

"It is no lie, Aunt Amina," I said. "I have made a complete commitment to Christ. I have been baptized. I am now a Christian."

She slapped her hands over her cheeks. "Oh, what a great mistake!" she cried. She sat very still for a moment, unable to add anything. Then, slowly gathering her shawl around her, she stood and with frozen dignity walked out of my house.

I was crushed, but I asked the Lord to protect her from

the devastating hurt she was feeling. I knew I had to discover His own prayer for my family. Otherwise, I would
leave a swath of damaged loved ones behind me. "Lord,"
I said, "the ideal thing of course would be to have every
one of these people come to know You. But I know that if
they aren't converted, I know You still love them, and right
now I ask that You touch each of these dear ones of mine
with Your special blessing, starting, if You will, with my
Aunt Amina. Thank You, Lord!"

Next day I had to say the same prayer. This time it was
for Aslam, a dear elderly male cousin who came to see me.
A lawyer, he lived about 45 miles from Wah. As the son of
my father's brother, he had inherited many of my father's
characteristics, the same warm smile, the gentle sense of
humor. I was fond of Aslam. From his attitude, I was sure
that he had not heard the full particulars of my problem.
We exchanged a few pleasantries, and then Aslam said:

"When is the family meeting? I'll pick you up and we'll
go together."

I chuckled. "I don't know when the family meeting will
be, Aslam, but I do know that I'll not be invited because
the meeting is about me."

He looked so confused I knew that I had to explain everything. "But please go to the meeting, Aslam," I said, when I
had finished. "Maybe you can put in a good word for me."

I watched him sadly make his way out of the house; it
was obvious, I thought, that a climax was approaching. I
had better get to Rawalpindi and Lahore as soon as possible. I didn't want Tooni and my son Khalid to hear
garbled stories about me. There was nothing I could do in
person about my daughter Khalida, for she lived in Africa.
But I could face Khalid and Tooni. The very next day I
set off for Lahore. Khalid had done quite well in business,
and his home reflected it. A lovely town bungalow, it was
surrounded by wide verandas and an immaculately groomed
lawn.

We drove through his gate, parked by the entrance and

walked up onto the broad veranda. Khalid well alerted by family and by a long phone call from me, hurried out to greet me. "Mother! How glad I am to see you," he said, though I sensed he welcomed me with a little embarrassment. We talked all that afternoon about what I had done, but in the end I knew Khalid did not understand at all.

Next I had to see Tooni. I drove to Rawalpindi and went straight to the hospital. I asked that Tooni be paged, and as I waited I wondered how I should go about telling her. Doubtless she had been hearing stories already. She certainly was aware firsthand that I had been reading the Bible. She may even have overheard fragments of my conversation with the Catholic nun, Dr. Santiago, in this same hospital when Mahmud had been admitted. One thing she surely did *not* know: how life-changing that visit with Dr. Santiago had been, for it was this little nun who encouraged me to pray to God as my Father.

"Mother!" I looked up to see Tooni hurrying toward me, her chestnut hair in stark contrast to her white starched uniform, her face beaming, her arms outstretched.

I rose, my heart pounding. How was I going to break the news to her! I tried to think of gentle ways, but the fear of pressure from Tooni was too much. Without daring to be circumspect, I blurted it out. "Tooni," I said, "be prepared for a shock, dear. Two days ago I was . . . I was *baptized*."

Tooni froze, her hand half extended, her sensitive eyes filling with tears. She slumped on the couch next to me. "I thought it would be coming to this," she said in a voice I could hardly hear.

I tried to comfort her, with no success. "There's no point in pretending to work," Tooni said. So she got permission to leave early and together we drove over to her apartment. Tooni's phone was ringing as she unlocked the door; she rushed in, picked the receiver up, and turned to me. "It's Nina." This was a niece who also lived in Rawalpindi. "She wants to know if it's true." She turned back to the phone as

Nina had evidently started talking again; even from where I stood I could hear Nina's voice rising. Then Tooni said softly: "Yes, it's true Nina. She's done it." Nina must have slammed down the phone, because Tooni took the receiver from her ear, looked at it, shrugged, and slowly replaced it on its cradle. It would be best to give her time to collect her thoughts. So I collected my things.

"Come see me, darling," I said, "when you feel you can. We'll talk." Tooni made no objections at all, so within minutes I was on the Grand Trunk Road headed home. The minute I arrived home my servants clustered around me. Nur-jan was wringing her plump hands and even Raisham's face was paler than usual. The phone had been ringing all day, relatives had been at the gate since early morning asking for me. Even as the servants chattered, the phone rang again. It was my sister's husband, Jamil, who worked with a British oil firm. I had always thought of Jamil as a man of the world, but now his voice didn't sound very self-assured.

"Bilquis, I have heard the strangest thing and cannot believe it," he said bluntly. "A business friend told me that he heard you had become a Christian. Of course, I laughed at him and assured him that could never happen."

Word really was spreading rapidly. I said nothing.

"Bilquis!" Jamil's voice was insistent. "Did you *hear* me?"

"Yes."

"That story isn't true is it?"

"Yes."

There was another silence. Then: "Well, that's nice," Jamil snapped. "You've just lost more than you can know. And for what? For just another religious viewpoint. That's what." He hung up.

In ten minutes Tooni was on the phone sobbing. "Mama, Uncle Nawaz just called to say that now Mahmud's father will be able to get him back. Nawaz says no court will allow you to keep him!"

I tried to comfort her but she hung up sobbing.

Late that evening while Mahmud and I were dining in my bedroom, Tooni and two of my nieces came to the house. I was startled by their ashen faces.

"Please sit down and join me," I said. "I'll have the servants bring your meal up."

Tooni and my nieces just picked at their food. I was happy to see the two young girls, but it was clear they weren't happy to see me. The conversation was trite and all three women kept glancing at Mahmud and making oblique suggestions that he go away to play. It was only after he finally did leave that one of the nieces leaned forward anxiously.

"Auntie, do you realize what this means for *other* people?" She broke into tears. "Have you thought of anybody else?" Her question was echoed in the brown eyes of my other niece who sat silently across from me.

I reached across the table and took the girl's slim hand. "My dear," I said sorrowfully. "There is nothing I can do but to be obedient."

Tooni now looked at me through tearful eyes and, as if she had not heard a word I said, begged me. "Mother, pack up and leave. Leave while there's something . . . or some-*one* . . . to leave with."

Her voice rose. "Do you know what people are saying? You'll be attacked. Your own brother may be compelled to take action against you!" And then she broke down sobbing. "My friends say you'll be murdered, Mommy!"

"I'm sorry, Tooni, but I'm not going to run away," I answered gently. "If I leave now I'll be running for the rest of my life." Determination rose within me as I spoke. "If He wishes, God can easily take care of me in my own house. And no one, *no one*," I said, "is going to push me out." I sat up in my chair, suddenly feeling very dramatic. "Let them come and attack!"

And then, as I sat there feeling so fiercely sure of myself, something happened. The warm personal Presence of God was gone. I sat, almost in panic, oblivious to the voices rising around me. But just as suddenly I realized what had happened. The old me, full of pride and stubbornness, had taken over. *I* was deciding what would happen, that no one would push me out of my home.

I sank back in my chair, barely aware that Tooni was speaking to me.

". . . all right, then, Mommy," Tooni cried. "So you've become a Christian. Must you become a Christian martyr also?" She knelt by my chair and laid her head on my shoulder. "Don't you realize that we love you?"

"Of course, dear, of course," I murmured, stroking her hair. Silently I asked His forgiveness for being so head-strong. Wherever He wanted me to go was fine, even if it meant leaving my house. As I said this in my heart I once again felt the Presence of the Father. The whole exchange had taken but a few minutes, but even as the three women sitting in front of me continued talking, I was aware that life was going on at another level too. The Lord was right then, at that moment, working with me, teaching me. He was in the very process of showing me how to stay in His Presence.

". . . so we will, then? All right?" It was Tooni's voice and I had no idea what she was asking me to agree to. Fortunately she went on. "If Mahmud's father comes after him, you can let me take him. I haven't become a Christian," she added pointedly.

Eventually the three girls quieted down. I asked them if they wouldn't like to spend the night and they agreed. As I bid Tooni and my nieces goodnight, I thought how our roles had changed. Once I was so protective and wor-ried over them; now we were equally worried for each other. That night I prayed: "Lord, it's so difficult to talk to a person who doesn't have faith in You. Please help my family. I'm so worried for the welfare of my loved ones."

As I drifted off to sleep, I again seemed to have left my body as if floating. I found myself standing on a grassy slope surrounded by pine trees. A spring bubbled near me.

All about me were angels, so many that they seemed to form a hazy mist. I kept hearing one name, "Saint Michaell". The angels gave me courage. And then I was back in bed. I got up and, still sensing this spiritual strength, went to Mahmud's room. I pointed to him in his bed and then went to my daughter's and nieces' rooms and did the same. I went back to my bedroom and got down on my knees. "Lord," I prayed, "You have shown me so many answers, now show me, I pray, what You are going to do with Mahmud. I would like to give Tooni some assurance."

I felt urged to open my Bible and this passage leaped up from the page: Genesis 22:12—"Lay not thine hand upon the lad, neither do thou anything unto him. . . ."

"Oh, thank You Father," I sighed.

At breakfast I was able to assure Tooni. "Darling, nothing is going to happen to your son; you never need worry." I showed her the Scripture given to me. Whether my faith was contagious or Tooni was touched by the Holy Spirit, I don't know. But her face did relax and she smiled for the first time in two days.

My daughter and nieces left my house on a somewhat less somber note that day. But the flow of other relatives and friends continued.

A few days later Raisham announced that there were *seven* people, all very dear concerned friends downstairs wanting to see me. I didn't want to face them without Mahmud. The boy should know everything that was going on. So I found him and together we went downstairs to the drawing room. There they sat in straight-backed formality far forward on their chairs. After the tea and cakes and small talk, one of those present cleared his throat. I steeled myself for what I knew was coming.

"Bilquis," said a friend I'd known since childhood, "we love you and we have been thinking over this thing you have done and we have a suggestion which we think will be of help to you."

"Yes?"

He leaned forward and smiled.

"Don't declare your Christianity publicly."

"You mean keep my faith a secret?"

"Well . . ."

"I can't," I said. "I can't play games with God. If I must die, I die."

All seven of them seemed to edge closer to me. An old friend of my father glared at me. I was about to glare back but caught myself. They thought they had my welfare at heart.

"I'm sorry," I said, "I just can't do what you ask." I explained that my faith had quickly, in little more than a month, become the most important thing in my life. "I cannot keep quiet about it," I said. I quoted them the Scripture where the Lord says: "Every man who publicly acknowledges me I shall acknowledge in the presence of my Father in Heaven, but the man who disowns me before men I shall disown before my Father in Heaven" (Matthew 10:32, 33).

"But," said another elderly gentleman, "you are in a very peculiar situation. I'm sure your God wouldn't mind if you kept quiet. He knows you believe in Him. That's enough." He quoted the Koran law on apostasy. "We're afraid," he said, "that someone will kill you."

I smiled but no one else was smiling. It was a pointless discussion, as they saw. When they rose to go I was given my ultimatum.

"Remember, Bilquis, if you get into trouble, none of your friends or family can stand by you. The ones who care the most will have to turn their backs on you."

I nodded. I well understood their words. I wished now that I had sent Mahmud out to play in the garden so that he would have heard none of this. When I looked at him, though, sitting on his little chair beside me, he just smiled. "It's all right," he seemed to be saying.

There were near tears as the group prepared to leave. A close friend of my mother kissed me. "Goodbye," she said.

She repeated the word with a strange emphasis. Then she broke into tears, pulled herself away and hurried out the door.

The house seemed like a tomb after they left. Even Mahmud's usual noisy play was subdued.

Three weeks passed when the only sound in my house was the hushed voices of servants. If it weren't for the Mitchells and the Olds and for our regular Sunday evening meetings, I wonder if the freeze-out might not have worked.

Each day the family battle line was seen more clearly. I saw it in the anger on the face of a cousin I met in the bazaar. I felt it in the scornful glance of a nephew I passed on the street in Rawalpindi. It was there in the cold voice of an aunt who called to say that she wouldn't keep a luncheon appointment. The boycott had begun. My phone remained silent, and no one pulled the bell cord at my gate. Not one member of the family came to call, even to scold. I could not help but recall a verse from the Koran (Sura 74–20): *If you renounced the faith, you would surely do evil in the land and violate the ties of blood. Such are those on whom Allah has laid His curse leaving them bereft of sight and hearing.*

In a very real way this was happening. I had violated the ties of blood and I undoubtedly would not see or hear from my family anymore.

The normal chatter and laughter of the servants had quieted as they slipped in and out of my rooms. I could hardly get them to talk to me beyond the usual, "Yes, Begum Sahib."

And then one morning the boycott took a strange turn. There was a soft click of my door and I turned to see Nur-jan quietly enter to minister my toilette. It was so unlike her usual exuberance. Raisham stepped in even more solemn than usual. As they proceeded to their tasks, they did not speak and I was bothered by the haunted look on both of their faces.

I waited for some word but Nur-jan continued her tasks

silently, without the usual gossip or chatter. Raisham's face was graven. Finally, with a little of the old fire in my voice, I said:

"All right, I can tell something is wrong. Tell me about it."

The brushing halted as I heard the news. Except for Raisham, standing before me now, all of my Christian servants, including Manzur, had fled my house in the middle of the night.

9.

The Boycott

What did it mean, this defection? Four servants quitting!
In a town like Wah where any job was hard to come by,
their decisions were hard to understand.

It was fear of course. Manzur was afraid because I
asked him to get me a Bible and had him drive me to the
home of missionaries. The other three Christian servants
must have picked up his concern. They must have heard
the rumblings of a volcano which would soon erupt and
didn't want to be caught in the overflow.

But what about Raisham, this Christian servant who now
began to brush my hair again? I could feel her graceful
hands tremble as she started her work.

"And you?" I asked.

She bit her lip as she continued her brushing. "I probably
shouldn't stay," she said softly. "It's going to be . . ."

"Very lonely," I concluded her statement.

"Yes," she said, swallowing, "and . . ."

"And you're afraid. Well, if you left, Raisham, I wouldn't
blame you. You have to make up your own mind, just as I
did. If you do stay though, remember that Jesus *told* us we
would be persecuted for His sake."

Raisham nodded, her dark eyes moist. She took a hairpin
out of her mouth and proceeded to do up my hair. "I know,"
she said sadly.

Raisham was quiet the rest of the day. Her concern affected Nur-jan who was approaching quiet hysteria. The next morning when I awakened I could hardly bring myself to ring the little bell. Who would be with me now? My bedroom door opened slowly and Nur-jan came in. Then, in the near darkness of winter's early hours another form followed. It was Raisham!

Later, I told her how much I appreciated her staying. She blushed. "Begum Sahib Gi," she answered softly, adding the affectionate third salutation which means, May you have long life, "as you serve the Lord, so I will serve you."

With the rest of my Christian servants gone, my house became even quieter, partly because I did not replace them all. My needs were simpler now that no family came by. I decided not to rehire Christians for a while. I found a new chauffeur, a Muslim named Fazad and a new Muslim cook's assistant, but I hired no one else. I was especially glad for Mahmud who continued to play happily in the house or garden. I encouraged him to invite friends over from the village, which suggestion Mahmud accepted quickly. Most of the children were slightly older, five or six, while Mahmud was still only five. But Mahmud nevertheless was their natural leader; I didn't think it was simply that he was their host, rather that seven hundred years of leadership was in the child's genes and could no more be denied than could his limpid brown eyes.

How much of this heritage was I putting in jeopardy? How much of the boy's rightful family ties was I threatening? Just yesterday he had asked again when his cousin Karim was going to take him fishing. Karim had promised to teach Mahmud the mysteries of catching the trout that slipped among the mossy rocks of our garden stream which joined the Tahmra River.

"Mum!" Mahmud had asked. "When is Karim going to come?"

I looked down at the boy whose eyes were shining, and I just didn't have the heart to tell him that his fishing party would never take place. Mahmud could not have been very drawn to Christianity so far. I read him Bible stories which he loved so much that I moved his bedtime from 8:00 to 7:30 so we could have plenty of time for them. But what were a few stories compared with a fishing trip. And friends. For bit by bit Mahmud's friends began to stop coming over. Mahmud couldn't understand this, and when I tried to explain it to him he looked at me in puzzlement.

"Mum," he said, "who do you love better, me or Jesus?"

What should I say! Especially right now when he was lonely. "God has to come first, Mahmud," I said, paraphrasing the Lord's warning that unless we put family after Him, we are not truly His own. "We have to put God first," I said, "even before the people we love most in the world."

Mahmud *seemed* to accept this. He *seemed* to be listening when I read him the Bible. Once, after I had read to him, "Come unto me all ye who are heavy laden and I will give you rest," I heard his nap-time pleas: "Jesus, I love You and I will come unto You, but . . . please don't give me rest. I don't like resting." He would even fold his hands and pray, but I knew that it was hard on him being alone and seeing me alone. Not one relative, friend or acquaintance turned off of the Grand Trunk Road any more toward my house; never did the phone ring.

Then at 3:00 one morning my white bedside phone did clamor. I reached toward the instrument, my heart pounding. No one would call at this hour unless there had been a death in the family. I picked up the phone and at first heard only heavy breathing. Then three words were thrown at me like stones:

"Infidel. Infidel. Infidel."

The phone went dead. I lay back on my bed. Who was it? One of the fanatics my uncles constantly warned me about? What might they do?

"Oh Lord, You know that I don't mind dying. But I'm an awful coward. I cannot stand pain. You know how I faint when the doctor gives me a needle. Oh, I pray that I will be able to bear pain if it comes." Tears filled my eyes. "I guess I'm not made of the stuff of martyrs, Lord. I'm sorry. Just let me walk with You through whatever comes next."

What did come next was a threatening, anonymous letter. "Let's be clear. There is only one word to describe you. Traitor." Then there was another letter and shortly still another. They all contained warnings. I was a turncoat and I would be treated as such.

Late one afternoon in the early summer of 1967, about six months after my conversion, I stood in my garden with the crumpled remains of one such letter in my fist. It was particularly vitriolic, calling me worse than an infidel, a seducer of the faithful. True believers, the letter said, had to burn me out like gangrene was burned out of a healthy limb.

Burn me out? Was this more than just a figure? I walked further into the garden, around which glowed beds of tulips, hyacinth and alyssum. Spring had blossomed into summer. Quinces flourished in the garden, and the last of the white petals were falling from the pear trees. I turned and looked back at my house. "They wouldn't touch my house!" I exclaimed inwardly. They wouldn't burn out a Begum! But, as if to confirm that I could no longer count on the protection of position and wealth, a caller came to pay me a visit. He was announced by a servant.

"General Amar is waiting to see you, Begum," she said.

My heart jumped. I looked through the garden gate and sure enough, there stood a familiar olive drab command car. General Amar was a dear old friend from my Army days. During World War II, I had been associated with him and now he was a top general in the Pakistani Army. We had kept in touch with each other through the years, particularly when my husband was Minister of the Interior and worked closely with him. Was he, too, coming to condemn me?

Soon I could hear his footsteps crunching on the pathway of the garden as he strode to meet me, all spit and polish in a natty khaki uniform, jodhpurs and leather boots. He took my hand, leaned over and kissed it. My apprehension lessened; evidently he was not on a mission of battle.

He looked at me, his dark eyes glinting humorously. As always the General came right to the point. "Is it true what people are saying?"

"Yes," I said.

"What made you do this?" he exclaimed. "You've put yourself in a very dangerous situation! I've heard rumors that some people want to kill you!"

I looked at him silently.

"All right," he added as he sat down on a garden bench, his leather belt creaking. "You know I'm like a brother to you?"

"I hope so."

"And, as a brother, I feel fondly protective toward you?"

"I hope so."

"Then, remember that my home is always open to you."

I smiled. This was the first kind thing anyone had said to me.

"*But*," the general went on to say, "there is something you should know. That offer is a personal one." He reached over to a blossom, pulled it to him and sniffed it, then turned back to me, adding, "Officially, there wouldn't be much I could do, Bilquis."

"I know." I took the General's hand, we got up together, strolled onto the terrace and inside the house. As we walked I told him things had not been easy.

"And they won't get easier, my dear," my friend said in his matter of fact way. Later, after I had ordered tea in the drawing room, he asked with a quizzical smile: "Tell me, Bilquis, why did you do it?"

I explained what had happened and found that General Amar was listening carefully. How extraordinary! Here I was, without realizing it, doing what the missionaries called *witnessing*. I was speaking about Christ to a Muslim, and a high official at that. And he was listening! I doubt that I really reached General Amar that afternoon but he was in a reflective mood half an hour later when he bid me goodbye in the summer twilight, again pressing his lips to my hand.

"Remember, Bilquis," he said huskily, "anytime you need my help . . . anything I can do as a friend . . ."

"Thank you, Amar," I said.

He turned, his boot heels clicked down the hallway tiles and out into the early evening darkness to his waiting command car. And our solitary, strangely sad, visit was over. "I wonder if I'll ever see him again," I thought.

For the first time during this boycott, during the anonymous letters and phone calls, during the warnings of old friends, I was learning what it was to live from hour to hour. It was the opposite of worrying. It was waiting to see *what He was going to allow.* For I was convinced that nothing occurred without His permission. I knew, for instance, that pressure against me must become more intense. If that did happen, then He would have allowed it and I must learn to search for His Presence in the midst of seeming disaster. I would just live hour to hour, staying near Him. Yes, that was my key. Learn to keep His company, so that whatever happened, whenever it happened, I would still be in His glory.

With the increasing family pressure, I thought I knew how King David felt when, fleeing from his son, Absalom, he picked up his lyre and sang: *"But thou, O Lord, art a shield for me; my glory . . ."* (Psalms 3:3). The glory which, I understand, he considered the unspeakable blessedness, joy, and felicity of the saints in heaven.

For the moment the pressure from my family was, still, the boycott. Not one member of the family came to call, even to scold. With rare exceptions none of my old friends called either. The sneers in the marketplace continued. So did the calculated exclusion from great moments in the family: births, deaths, weddings. Whenever I allowed myself to dwell on the loneliness this caused, I'd feel the glory begin to fade, and immediately I'd turn my thoughts by a sheer act of will to the times Jesus too had felt lonely.

It helped. But I found, a little to my surprise, that I desperately needed simple companionship. I who had been so aloof was now in need of closeness. Not even the Olds and the Mitchells came to the house anymore. For their own protection I advised them not to visit me.

One gray afternoon I retreated to my bedroom to read the Bible. It was unusually cold for early summer. A sharp wind rattled my windows. As I started to read, I felt a warmth on my hand and looked down to see a patch of sunlight resting on my arm. I glanced out of the window just in time to see the sun disappear again behind the clouds. For just one minute, it seemed He had reached down and touched my hand for comfort.

I looked up, "Oh my Lord," I said. "I am so lonely; even my cheeks feel dried up from lack of talking. Please send someone to talk to today."

Feeling somewhat foolish for asking for such a childlike thing, I returned to my Bible. After all, I had His company and that should be enough. But in a little while I was startled to hear an odd sound in the house, odd since it had been absent so long. There were voices downstairs.

I threw on my robe and flew out into the hall to meet Nur-jan running toward my room out of breath. "Oh, Begum Sahib," she squealed, "the Olds are here."

"Praise God," I exclaimed and hurried to meet them. Of course I saw Ken and Marie at our Sunday services in their house, but this was different, a midweek call. Marie rushed to me, taking my hand. "We just had to see you, Bilquis," she said, her blue eyes sparkling. "For no reason at all except we love being with you."

What a visit that was. I realized as we talked that I had been making a mistake not asking people over to visit me. Pride had kept me from admitting the need. Suddenly I had an inspiration. Why not invite people to my house on Sunday for the meetings? But wouldn't this be heaping gunpowder on the flames? I tried to quench the thought but it would not go away. Just as my friends were about to leave I said, quickly:

"Would you like to come here this Sunday night?"

The Olds looked at me a bit shocked.

"I mean it," I said, extending my hands sideways. "This old house needs some life."

And so it was decided.

That evening as I prepared to retire, I thought how wonderfully the Lord provides for us. When my family and friends were taken from me, He replaced them with His own family and friends. I slept peacefully and awakened to the feel of a warm sun streaming through my window. I got up and opened the window, reveling in the soft breeze that drifted in. In its earthy garden aroma I could smell the warm breath of the full summer now upon us.

I couldn't wait for Sunday evening to come. By Saturday afternoon that old house was filled with flowers; every floor, every window was scrubbed until it shone. I hinted to Raisham that she might like to join us but she became a bit flustered; she was not ready for such a bold step yet and I didn't press.

Sunday crept by while I kept Mahmud out of the drawing room, straightened the Persian carpet, constantly rearranged the flowers, and found a speck of dust here and there to wipe away. But at last I heard the gate open and cars crunch up the drive.

The evening was everything I had hoped for, with song and prayer and telling each other what the Lord was doing. Just twelve of us, plus Mahmud, sitting around comfortably in the drawing room, but I'd have sworn there were a thousand other guests too, unseen, welcome.

The evening had another peculiar purpose too, one I had not foreseen. It turned out that my Christian friends were still quite worried for me.

"Are you being extra careful?" It was Marie talking.

"Well," I laughed, "there is not much I can do. If someone wants to harm me, I'm sure he'll find a way."

Ken looked around the drawing room and out the large glass doors into the garden. "You really *don't* have much protection here," he said. "I hadn't quite realized how vulnerable you are."

"How about your bedroom?" asked Synnove. Everyone

felt it wise to look over my room, so we all trooped up. Ken was particularly concerned by the windows, looking out on the garden; they were protected only by a glass pane and filigree screen.

He shook his head. "It really isn't safe, you know. You should do something about it, Bilquis; have some kind of heavy metal grill installed. Anyone could get through this."

I said I would see to it the next day.

Was it my imagination or did His glory fade just a little as I made the promise?

Eventually we said goodbye and I retired happier than I had been in a long time. The next day, however, as I was about to send for the ironworker in the village, I was once again aware of the quickly receding glory of the Lord. Why? Was it because I was about to take an action that was based on fear? It certainly did seem that every time I started to call the ironworker my action was stopped.

And then I realized why. When word got around the village that I was having my window barred, everyone would realize that I was fearful. I could just hear the gossip. "Ha! What kind of religion is Christianity, anyway. When you become a Christian you become fearful?" No. I decided, I would not have the window barred.

That night I went to bed confident that I had made the right decision. I fell asleep at once but suddenly I was awakened by a sound. I sat up, startled, but without fear. Before me appeared a breathtaking sight.

Through the walls of my room, in a supernatural way, I could see my whole garden. It was flooded with a heavenly white light. I could see every rose petal, every tree leaf, every blade of grass, every thorn. And over the garden hung a calm serenity. In my heart I heard my Father saying, "You did the right thing, Bilquis. I am with you."

Slowly the light faded and the room was dark again. I switched on my bedside lamp, lifted my arms and praised God. "Oh Father, how can I thank You enough? You have so much concern for each of us."

The next morning I called all of my servants together and told them that they could sleep in their own homes from now on if they chose to do so. Only Mahmud and I would sleep in the big house. The servants exchanged glances, some in surprise, some in joy, one or two in alarm. But I knew one thing at least had been accomplished. The decision put an end to any thought of protecting myself. And with the decision the glory came back and stayed for a longer time than usual. Perhaps this was necessary for the next turn of events.

One morning when Raisham was brushing my hair she remarked casually: "I hear that your Aunt's son, Karim, has died."

I shot out of my chair and looked at her incredulously. "No," I gasped. Not Karim, who was supposed to take Mahmud fishing! He was one of my favorites! What had happened? Why did I have to find out about even Karim's death through the servants! With steely willpower I got control of myself and forced my body back down into the chair so that Raisham could go on with her work. But my mind raced on. This could be just a rumor, I thought. Raisham could have mistaken the name. My heart rose a little. Later, I asked an elderly member of the staff to find out for me what had really happened. She went into the village and in an hour returned, downcast.

"I am sorry, Begum Sahib," she said. "But it is true. He died last night from a heart attack and the funeral is to-day."

Then, this servant who had a facility for learning everything, gave me news that hurt even more. My aunt, the servant told me, knowing how much I loved her son, had specifically asked my family to "be sure and tell Bilquis that my boy has died." No one followed her wishes.

Later I sat at my window pondering it all. I had been excluded from family events for six months, but never had the boycott hurt as it did now.

As I sat rocking softly I began to pray for His help and, as always, the help came. This time it was as if a warm cloak were placed gently on my shoulders. And with that sensation came an unusual plan of action. The very idea shocked me. It was so bold I knew it must be of the Lord.

10.
Learning to Live in the Glory

As I sat at the window overlooking my garden, where Karim and I had played as children, a strong monsoon wind blowing up from India bent the tops of the trees. In it I seemed to be catching an extraordinary message which I could not believe I was correctly hearing.

"You can't really be telling me that Lord," I said smiling. "I'm just hearing voices! You don't want me to go to *Karim's funeral.* It would be unseemly. It would be in poor taste. I would end up offending people who are in mourning."

Even as I objected, I recognized once again the sense of His Presence beginning to fade. Immediately, with this sign, I began to wonder if perhaps I really were being told to do this extraordinary thing, to go straight into the face of the hostilities of the boycott.

Finally, breathing a deep sigh, I got up from my place at the window, shrugged and said aloud, "I'm beginning to learn, Lord. My sense of the right thing to do is nothing compared with Yours! I'll go, since You are telling me to go."

And, of course, the sense of His Presence returned.

What an extraordinary series of experiences I was having with this coming and going of His glory. Still, I had the feeling that I was just on the verge of understanding what this was all about. How would I be able to learn to stay in His Presence for an ever increasing percentage of time? I did not realize that over the next two months I was to have a series of experiences which would take me a step further in this learning process.

I stood in the cobblestone lane in front of Karim's house, hesitating. In spite of my promise to obey, I felt as if I were a lonesome dove being thrown to a thousand cobras. Taking a deep breath I headed toward the stone house which stood among others like it. I walked into the court-yard and stepped onto the veranda, subject to the stares of the village people who were sitting around quietly. I went inside the old-fashioned house with its carved ceilings and white plastered walls where Karim and I had so often laughed, played and romped together.

There was no laughter now. On top of the gloom of the family in mourning was added the chill of a score of con-temptuous glances directed my way. I looked toward a cousin with whom I had been very close. Our eyes met for a minute; my cousin quickly turned her head and began talking with a neighbor.

Now squaring my shoulders I stepped into the living room of Karim's house, then sat down on one of the thick cotton mattresses which had been placed on the floor sur-. rounded by bolsters and cushions to lean on. I smoothed the sari around my legs. Suddenly people seemed to wake up, realizing who I was. The quiet soothing conversation that had filled the room suddenly halted. Even the women say-ing their beads, each bead signifying a prayer to Allah, ceased and looked up. The room, which had been hot with the early summer heat and with the scores of bodies packed shoulder to shoulder, suddenly seemed chilled.

I said nothing, made no attempt to be sociable, simply lowered my own eyes and said my own prayers. "Lord

Jesus," I whispered to my heart, "do be with me as I represent You to this group of dear friends and relatives who are so saddened by Karim's death."

After fifteen minutes the quiet flow of conversation began again. It was time to pay my respects to Karim's wife. Holding my head high, I arose from the mattress and stepped into the adjoining room where Karim's body lay in its tall, deep coffin, structured according to the Muslim belief that a dead person must be able to sit up when the angels came to question him before he enters heaven. I gave my condolences to Karim's wife, then looked at the quiet face of my dear cousin shrouded in the new white cotton burial cloth and whispered to myself a prayer to Jesus for this man's spirit. Oh, how I wished I had been able to talk to him before he died.

A low humming filled the room as close family members prayed for Karim. The ladies stood and read verses from the Koran. It was all part of the life and death rhythm which I knew so well. I was turning my back on it all. Before sunset today, there would be a procession to the cemetery with all of the family following the bier. At the grave side the pallbearers would place the coffin on the ground and the priest would call out, *God is most great. Lord, this is Thy servant, the son of Thy servant. He used to testify that there is no God but Thee, and that Muhammad is Thy servant and Thy messenger.* . . .

As I stood listening to the soft moaning in the room, I saw Karim's mother kneeling at the bier. She looked so forlorn, I suddenly felt an overwhelming urge to go to her side. Did I dare? Would it be an affront? Should I say anything to her about Jesus? Probably not. Just my being there as a Christian was bringing Jesus to her side in a caring way.

So I stepped over to Karim's mother and put my arms around her, telling her in a soft crooning voice how sorry I was. "Karim and I were so close. May God bless you and comfort you." Karim's mother turned her face to me. Her dark tear-filled eyes thanked me and I knew that Jesus was even then comforting her sorrow-filled heart.

But Karim's mother was the only one in the room who seemed to accept what I was doing. As I left her and returned to sit down among the mourners, one male cousin —a close one too—made quite a show of rising to his feet and shuffling out of the room. Another cousin followed. And then another.

I sat there struggling with the emotions of my own sorrow for Karim and his family on the one hand and with this deep embarrassment on the other. My heart pounded. The hostility was reaching through my protection. It was all I could do to keep seated for the appropriate amount of time until I could stand, make my goodbyes and walk out of the room. Finally when I did leave I felt every eye in the household staring at me.

In my car I sat for a moment at the wheel, trying to collect myself. I had obeyed, but the cost was high. Certainly I would prefer to have remained at home rather than walk right straight into the maw of this open anger.

If I thought I would have to walk through this valley only once I was wrong. A few weeks later, just as midsummer's heat was beginning to settle over our district, another cousin died. Again, I heard of his death through my household. Again, obeying the Lord's direction, I found myself reluctantly walking into a room full of mourners, to the chilly discord of hate. As an act of will I focused my concern away from myself and toward the one person there who was really bereaved, my cousin's widow. She had a child just going on five, the same age as Mahmud. She looked so forlorn standing by herself at the coffin that I wept for her and for her husband.

And then just as I had done at Karim's funeral, I found myself being propelled toward this desperate woman. As I approached our eyes met, and I saw hesitation cross her tear-stained face. Then, with a look of sudden determination, knowingly going against the will of her family, she extended her hand to me. As I held her brown and shaking hand in my own I wept in silence. We exchanged only one or two words, but my heart was praying fervently that the Holy Spirit would reach into her bereavement and keep His promise, even to this Muslim dear one, "Blessed are they who mourn."

"Thank you, Bilquis, thank you," the widow said in a whisper as at last she released my hand. I embraced her and walked out of the room.

Oddly, there were two more funerals in quick succession. This was quite unusual even for a family of our size. But in each case I was told very clearly, very distinctly, by the Lord to get out of my safe little house and go into the place where I was needed. I was not to do too much talking. I was to let my caring presence be its own witness.

And all the while the Lord was working with me. He had so much to teach me, and He was using these funerals as His classroom.

It was during one of these visits to a family funeral that I discovered the next great secret of staying in His Presence.

At a Muslim funeral no one cooks or eats until the body is buried. This usually amounts to a day's fasting and is really not an ordeal. However, that day, as I sat isolated in the crowded room, I suddenly found that I wanted my usual afternoon tea. It was something, I said to myself, which I simply could not do without.

Finally, unable to control my desire, I stood and mumbled an excuse. I had to wash my hands, I said. I slipped out of the house and down the street to a small cafe. There I had my precious tea and returned to the mourners.

Immediately I felt a strange aloneness, as if a friend had left my side. Of course I knew what it was. The comforting Presence of His Spirit had left me.

"Lord," I said to myself, "what have I done?"

And then I knew. I had told a lie when I was excusing myself.

"But it was only a white lie, Lord," I said. I sensed no comforting from the Spirit. Just a deadness.

"But Lord," I pressed, "I don't have to follow those Muslim mourning practices any more. And besides, I just can't do without my tea. You know that."

No sense of His Spirit.

"But Father," I pressed on, "I couldn't tell them that I went out for tea and cake. That would have hurt them."

No Spirit.

"All right, Father," I said. "I understand. It was wrong for me to lie. I realize that I was seeking the approval of men and that I must live only for Your approval. I am truly sorry, Lord. I hurt You. With Your help I will not do that again."

And with those words His comforting Presence flooded me again, like rain falling on a parched lake bed. I was relaxed. I knew that He was with me.

And that was how I learned to move back into His Presence quickly. Whenever I did not feel His nearness, I knew that I had grieved Him. I would search backwards until I spotted the time *when I last knew His Presence*. Then I would review every act, every word or thought until I discovered where I had gone astray. At that point I would confess my sin and ask His forgiveness.

I learned to do this with increasing boldness. Through these exercises in obedience I learned the beautiful secret of repentance. Repentance, I discoverd, was not tearful remorse so much as admitting where I had gone wrong and avowing with His help never to make that mistake in the future. As I realized my own weakness, I could call upon His strength.

It was during this time that I discovered there was no such thing as an innocent white lie. A lie is a lie and is always of Satan, the father of lies. He uses "harmless" white lies to get us started in this insidious habit. Lies pave the way for greater temptations to come. Satan whispers that a white lie is "consideration" for other people. We bend ourselves to the world instead of to Jesus who is the Truth.

Though I learned this lesson at the funeral of a relative, it was the beginning of a new kind of life for me, one where I attempted to weed out all lying. From that day on I would try and catch myself every time I was about to commit a white lie. Once a missionary friend invited me to a gathering which I did not want to attend. I was all set to make the excuse that I had another engagement. A warning signal sounded within me and I stopped myself just in time. Instead, I found that I could be truthful and still not hurt anyone's feeling by simply saying, "I'm very sorry, but I won't be able to be there."

Or, there was the day when I sat down to write a letter to a friend in London and almost automatically began writing that I had been out of town for some time and had not been able to answer his last letter. I stopped, pen poised in midair.

Out of town? I had been here all the time. I crumpled the paper, dropped it into the wastebasket and started again. "Dear Friend: Please forgive me for not answering your wonderful letter sooner. . . ."

Little things, certainly. But I was learning that to be careful in small things made it much easier to handle the larger temptations as they came. Besides, life was so much easier when I didn't have to spend a lot of time contriving.

Slowly, surely, it began to dawn on me that I was trying to live with Christ as my constant companion! Of course, it just wasn't possible to do this. So often I caught myself falling into my old ways! But I kept trying.

And in the process I discovered the practical side of the promise, "But seek ye first the kingdom of God, and his righteousness; and all these things shall be added unto you" (Matthew 6:33, KJV). For, as I made the attempt to put God first, some of my other heartfelt needs were given back to me.

One afternoon Raisham came to my room with a startled expression on her face.

"There's a lady in the drawing room waiting to see you," she said.

"Who is it?" I asked.

"Well, Begum Sahib, if I'm not mistaken it's the mother of Karim."

Surely she must be mistaken! Karim's mother would not be coming here!

I walked downstairs wondering who then it could be. But, as I turned the corner into the drawing room, sure enough there stood the mother of my dead cousin. Hearing my steps she looked up, came over and threw her arms around me.

"Bilquis," Karim's mother said, tears forming in her eyes, "I just had to come personally to tell you something. At first, at the funeral, I didn't see you among all the people. But I need to tell you how much comfort you were. It's . . . I don't know . . . something new. Something warm and special."

And at last I saw why I had not been allowed to speak of Jesus directly to Karim's mother during the time of her crushing bereavement. For that would have been to take advantage of her. Now however the situation was quite different. Gently and softly there in my drawing room I spoke to her about how much Jesus meant to me and how He was slowly and inexorably changing so many of my old imperious ways, replacing them with His warm human personality.

"It's true," Karim's mother said. "You did care. You really wanted to share my sorrow."

It was a short visit but a wonderful one. Encouraging in two directions: First, that another human being had actually noticed a change in me; and second, I hoped that this was the beginning of a break in the family boycott.

It didn't happen quickly though. Every time the phone rang it was one of my missionary friends. So one morning just before Mahmud's sixth birthday, when the phone rang I expected to hear Marie. Instead I heard the friendly voice of the mother of the second cousin who had died.

"Bilquis?"

"Yes."

"Bilquis, I just wanted to say how much I appreciate the help you gave my son's wife. She told me you really spoke to her heart."

How interesting. For I had said little. It was Christ who had done the consoling.

We exchanged a few pleasant words and then hung up.

Once again I could not help but be amazed at how Jesus had done the work through me when I said little or nothing about Him directly. It was my being there, representing His Spirit in this time of need that had been the helper.

Over the weeks a few other family members came for short visits. They'd drop by to see Mahmud on his birthday, bringing him sweets and toys. Ostensibly the reason for their visit was to see the boy. Actually, I knew, it was just a good excuse. They really had come to soften some of the hurt of the boycott. The visits were always strained and short. But they were bright, welcome chinks in the terrible wall that had been raised around me.

Almost a year had passed since I had made the decision to accept Christ's call. How the time was flying! Soon my birthday would be here again. One year since I had given myself to the Lord. And now I was looking forward to my first real celebration of Christmas. I had of course seen Christmas celebrations when I was in Europe. But never had I known what Christmas was like viewed from the heart. I borrowed a creche from the Mitchells. When they came to the house with the little manger scene they also brought a small fir tree, and we all sang, "O Christmas Tree . . . O Christmas Tree . . . ," while Mahmud squealed with delight. The servants put the tree in the drawing room and we all decorated it with paper ribbons.

There was something wrong, however.

Much as I enjoyed these festivities, there wasn't much real meaning in them. I began to wonder if I could celebrate Christmas in a way that expressed the change that had come into my life.

And then an idea came to mind. Why not throw a party for everyone—missionaries, and people from the village, even the sweepers. Immediately I heard the warning voice of my family cautioning me not to make a display of my faith; and I also heard the General's voice warning me that he could no longer give me official protection if I got in trouble. I knew the idea of such a Christmas party would be a threat to many. Yet, after much prayer it seemed to me my Presence was strongest when I began to make plans for the unusual gathering.

So I went ahead on Christmas Day and threw the party which caused such a stir in Wah. The village people arrived early and congregated around the tree in the drawing room. Then the missionaries came. Synnove led everyone in song. And then to my astonishment one of the servants announced that an aunt and some cousins from Rawalpindi had arrived on a drop-in visit!

My heart leaped. How would they react! I need not have worried—they reacted in typical upper class-fashion, I'm afraid. First their jaws dropped, then they quietly retired to another room where they sat alone in strained silence.

I did not want to ignore either group so I spent my time going from room to room. It was like running back and forth from a hot shower to a cold shower.

Finally, perhaps because of my own persistence, a few members of my family began to relax. Some even went into the drawing room and joined the festivities around the tree. By the end of the party they were passing small talk with the Olds and the Mitchells, if not with the sweepers.

The party heralded, I hoped, the start of a different kind of year. Not an easier one, just a different one. Because immediately in front of me lay many confusing crossroads which could lead me into trouble if I took a wrong turn. For along with the smattering of relatives and friends who were now returning, came a different kind of visitor. They were people who were determined to convert me back to the Muslim faith. I had a feeling that there were interested onlookers, anxious to see how I would react to these voices beckoning me back home. Should I keep a discreet silence, or should I really speak my mind?

The answer came to me, again, in terms of my Presence. For whenever I tried to be devious I felt uncomfortable and alone. But whenever I answered the loaded questions forthrightly and in love, then I felt that the Lord Himself was right with me.

One afternoon, for instance, there was a soft knock on my door. I was surprised, for it was two o'clock in the afternoon.

"Yes?" The door opened. It was Raisham. "Begum Sahib, you have a visitor."

There was a hesitancy in her soft voice. I had told Raisham that I preferred not to be bothered between noon and three in the afternoon. It was not an order however. A year ago I would have ordered Raisham sharply not to bother me for any reason between noon and three. Now I explained to her that I no longer considered time as something I owned; it belonged to the Lord. If something came up which she herself thought I should see to, then of course she was to come to my room no matter what the hour.

"Begum Sahib, the man is an Englishman." There was a glint of amusement in her brown eyes. "He says he wants to talk about God."

"All right," I said, wondering. "I'll be right down."

Waiting for me in the drawing room was a pale, sandy-haired Englishman. I was interested in noting that he wore typical Pakistani clothes, a white shirt and baggy trousers. With his pale face and white clothes he almost blended into the white walls of my drawing room. After apologizing for dropping in without an appointment, he came to the point.

He said that he had travelled all the way from Karachi to see me; since he had converted from Christianity to Islam, members of my family thought we had interests in common. "Ah," I said to myself, "now I understand. Knowing how much I like the British, they think I will be impressed by an Englishman who has left his Christianity for Islam."

My visitor hemmed and hawed and launched into the purpose of his visit.

"Begum," the man said, "one thing really disturbs me about Muslims who convert to Christianity. It is the Bible. We all know that the Christian New Testament has been changed from what God gave."

He was expressing Islam's main charge against the Bible, that it had been so altered that today's version is untrustworthy. The original, Muslims claim, had agreed with the Koran.

"I hope you won't think I'm being facetious," I said. "I really do want to know something. I've heard often that the Bible was changed but I've never been able to learn who changed it. When were the changes made and what passages were corrupted?"

My visitor leaned back and looked up to the carved ceiling beams, his fingers drumming the arm of his chair. He did not answer. It was unfair of me I guess. As far as I knew there were no answers to these questions.

"You see," I went on, drawing on research I had made, "in the British Museum there are ancient versions of the Bible which were published nearly three hundred years before Muhammad was born. On every issue between Christianity and Islam these old manuscripts are identical with today's Bible. The experts say that in every basic essential today's Bible has not been changed from the original. This is important for me personally. For, to me the Bible has become an alive Word. It speaks to my soul and feeds me. It helps guide me. . . ."

My visitor got to his feet in the middle of my sentence.

". . . and so," I went on, "I find it quite important to

know if there really are places where I'm fooling myself. Can you tell me?"

"You talk about the 'Word' almost as if it were living," my visitor said.

"I believe that Christ is living, if that's what you mean," I said. "The Koran itself says that Christ was the Word of God. I would love to talk with you about it sometime."

"I must be going."

And that was that. I saw my visitor to the door and invited him back. He never did return but others came, some well primed for battle and with such misconceptions! I'll never forget the man who accused Christians of worshipping three separate Gods.

"Your so-called Trinity consists of God, Mary, and Jesus!" he said. "You Christians say that God took a wife who was Mary and from their union Jesus was born. Allah can't have a wife!" he laughed.

I prayed quickly. And a clear line of thought came to mind.

"Do you read the Koran?" I asked.

"Of course."

"Well then, do you remember how the Koran says that Christ was given the Spirit of God?" I had often wondered how the Koran could have such marvelous truths as this. "You perhaps have heard of Sadhu Sundar Singh, the devout Sikh to whom Jesus appeared in a vision. This is how Jesus explained the Trinity to him: 'Just as in the sun there are both heat and light, but the light is not heat and the heat is not light, but both are one, though in their manifestation they have different forms, so I and the Holy Spirit, proceeding from the Father, bring light and heat to the world. . . . Yet We are not three but One, just as the sun is but one.'"

It was quiet in the room when I finished. My guest was deep in thought. Finally he arose, thanked me for giving him time and silently left the house.

As I watched his forlorn figure walk down the graveled driveway it occurred to me to wonder whether my little

visits with people like the Englishman and this zealot were
really being used by the Lord. I had no way of knowing,
for I never heard from either of them again. It didn't matter.
I perhaps should not even wonder about results. The only
thing that did matter to me was obedience. If the Lord
asked me to talk to these people, then that is what I should
do.

As the winter rolled into spring, the Lord seemed to give
me other ways of speaking too. I went to Lahore and—
after a good but strangely uncommunicating visit with my
son Khalid—I purchased a hundred copies of the Bible to
give away to anyone who was interested. I also bought a
quantity of Christian tracts. I gave them away at every opportunity, even leaving them in public restrooms. I'm not at
all sure this did any good. Once, when I went back to the
restroom, I found my little stack had dwindled but then I
looked in the wastebasket. There, crumpled up, were the
copies of my tracts.

"It seems so pointless, Lord," I said. "Am I doing what
You want? Why is it, Lord," I said raising my hands to my
waist in supplication, "that not one single time have I been
able to see the results of talking about You?" There was the
English convert to Islam, and the General, and all the
servants who had fled, and the hundreds of times I had
talked with members of my family and with friends—not
one of these times bore visible fruit. "It's so puzzling, Lord!
I just don't understand why You aren't using me."

As I prayed the sensation of Christ's Presence grew ever
stronger in that room. He seemed to fill the atmosphere
with strength and comfort. I heard in my heart the distinct
suggestion, "Bilquis, I have only one question to ask you.
Think back over those times when you have talked with
your friends, and with your family. Think back over the
times you have accepted people who have come to argue.
Have you felt My Presence during those visits?"

"Yes Lord. Yes indeed I have."

"My glory was there?"

"Yes Lord."

"Then that's all you need. It is so often this way with friends. And family. The results are not your problem. All you have to worry about is obedience. Seek My Presence, not results."

So I continued on my course. The odd thing is that it became an increasingly stimulating and invigorating time. Once the Lord had taken my eyes off the "results" and turned them to His Presence, I could enjoy meeting friend after friend, relative after relative without the slightest feeling of frustration. I learned to take advantage of opportunities. Whether the conversation was on politics or clothes, I would ask God to prompt a question which would give me an opening. For example, once when I was talking to a niece, the conversation drifted to my former husband, who was now Pakistan's ambassador to Japan.

"What if Khalid came to your house?" she smiled, lifting an eyebrow.

I looked at her directly. "I would welcome him. I would serve him tea." My niece looked at me incredulously. "I have forgiven him," I continued. "And I hope that he has forgiven *me* for all that I did which hurt him."

"How can you forgive that way!" My niece knew that the breakup had been most difficult.

I explained that I certainly could not forgive in my own strength. I had asked Jesus to help me. "You know," I said, "Jesus invited us all to come to Him with our burdens. Jesus took my burden of hate from me."

My niece sat quietly for a while. "Well," she said, "that is a Christianity I have not heard about. If you're going to talk like that I'll be one of the first to come and learn about your Jesus."

Even here I was disappointed. I had high hopes. I believed that indeed my niece might return to the subject but she never did.

I did have times when the glory left me during this period. It always occurred in the same fashion. I would slip into Satan's trap of convincing me that I sounded pretty good! My arguments were really quite profound!

One day for instance a friend asked me, "Why do you have to be so exclusive? You'll have to admit that we all worship the same God, whether Christian, Muslim, Hindu, Buddhist or Jew. We may call Him by different names and approach Him from different directions, but in the end it's the same God."

"You mean He is like a mountain top to which different paths lead?"

He settled back balancing his cup of tea and nodded. And then I flew to the attack.

"Well," I said, "He may be a mountain top but there is only one path to Him, through Jesus Christ. The Lord said: 'I am the way, the truth and the life.' Not just *a* way," I added sharply, "but *the* way."

My friend put down his cup of tea, grimaced and shook his head. "Bilquis," he said, "did anyone ever tell you that you still come across as haughty?"

And instantly I knew that the man sitting in front of me was speaking for God. My arguments were right. They were Biblical and sound. But the Spirit had left. *Bilquis* was right. *Bilquis* was stating truth. Quickly I said a prayer of repentance and asked the Lord to take over.

"I'm sorry," I laughed. "If I come across as smug because I'm a Christian, then I'm not acting as Christ would want. The more I learn about Christ the more I need correcting. The Lord has so much to teach me and I know He is speaking right now through you."

My visitor left, perhaps closer to the Lord, perhaps not. I doubt that I shall ever know. But I do know that I was, step by painful step, learning to listen and to obey.

And then one night I had another one of those frightening experiences which came only after I had become a Christian. I was in my room preparing for bed when I suddenly felt a powerful presence of evil at my bedroom window. Instantly my mind turned to my Protector and I was warned from going near the window. I dropped to the floor in prayer, asking my Lord to cover me as a mother hen covers her chicks and I felt the strong cloak of His protection. When I arose, the presence at the window was gone.

The next morning, I drove over to the Mitchells. The sun shone brightly on their street but I was still shaking inside. Yet, as I walked up to their door, I felt hesitant about mentioning what happened to me for fear they wouldn't understand.

At the door, Synnove hugged me, then stepped back, her blue eyes questioning me.

"What's wrong, Bilquis?" she asked.

"Well," I ventured, "why do frightening things keep happening after one becomes a Christian?"

She ushered me into the living room where we sat down.

"I don't really know what you mean," she said puzzled. "Has someone threatened you?"

"Not someone," I answered, *"something."*

"Oh?" she said, and arose and got her Bible. "Here," she said, sitting down and flipping through its pages, "in Ephesians 6 it speaks about that kind of thing." She read: *"We are up against the unseen power that controls this dark world, and spiritual agents from the very headquarters of evil."*

She looked up at me.

"That must be it," I said telling her something about what happened that night.

She listened thoughtfully, and then said, "Why don't you talk to the Olds about it?"

"Well," I said, giving a nervous laugh, "I don't know if I want to even *talk* about it any more."

And that's how I felt at the beginning of our get-together with the Olds that evening. I decided not to bring it up. I'd simply make a fool of myself, I thought. It was probably just my imagination.

However, as I sat talking with Marie Old on a sofa before the fire, I couldn't help mentioning it. I tried to sound light-hearted.

"The strangest thing happened to me last night, Marie," I said. "I had the most frightening experience and I can't explain it."

Her husband, Ken, in his usual relaxed manner, had been sitting in a window seat behind us reading a book. Hearing me, he laid his book down, looked up and sensing my reluctance to talk about it, he, in his own quiet way, gently drew me into explaining the whole episode.

When I finished, I tried to laugh. "And then again," I said lightly, "I may have had too much curry at dinner last evening!"

"Don't minimize the things the Lord will bring you through," he said quietly. "Supernatural things *do* happen." He walked around the sofa and sat in a chair facing us. His face was serious.

He explained the supernatural presence of evil and how God can allow it to come upon a person as a test. As an example, Ken pointed out in the Old Testament how God permitted Satan to attack Job and how He allowed the Evil One to tempt Christ in the wilderness. Both of these, Ken pointed out, were tests. And in each case, he added, Satan's intended victim emerged victorious because of his outspoken faith in God. I couldn't help remembering the attack I suffered the second night before my baptism.

Slowly, the learning continued. But what I did not know as I gratefully considered Ken's comforting teaching, was that the Lord had already started a process which was to leave me more and more alone, yet not lonely; more and more cut off from my family, yet part of a great, supportive family; more and more cut off from the roots which meant so much to me in Wah, yet with deepening roots in a new City.

It was because of these upcoming tests of endurance that He had been placing me, time after time, in situations where I had to depend solely on Him.

11.

Winds of Change

The weaning process began one Sunday a few weeks later, during our regular prayer meeting. I thought that both the Olds and the Mitchells seemed unusually somber that evening.

"What's wrong?" I asked as we walked into the Olds' drawing room. Ken leaned his head back and stared at the ceiling.

"Marie and I are leaving on a year's furlough," he said abruptly.

My first reaction was panic at the thought of abandonment. What would I ever do without the Olds! Of course I would still have the Mitchells, but I depended on both families, together, to be my support. The Mitchells had brought me into my first contact with the church; the Olds had walked closely with me. Was this just a beginning? How long before I lost both families?

Marie must have read my heart. For she stepped over and took my hand. Tears filled her eyes as she spoke.

"My dear," Marie said, "you must realize that it will always be this way. Those we love will always be leaving. Only Jesus stays with you forever."

Ken now joined his wife at my side.

"There's another thing, Bilquis," Ken said. "You can be sure the Lord never leads you out of a safe situation unless He has a purpose. Because of that, you can start rejoicing now, even in the midst of the hurt."

We had only a few weeks more together, the Olds, the Mitchells and I. The departure date grew closer, carrying with it a sense of doom. We all tried to be faith-filled about the vacuum that would be created by Ken's and Marie's leaving but it was play-acting, not at all real.

It was a sad day when the Mitchells and I and others in our small Christian group went to the Olds' house for a goodbye send-off. We did our best even at this last moment to make it a celebration, but our hearts were heavy. We tried to see the moment as a chance not to "let them go" but to "send them out."

It was a brave show. But in our hearts, as we saw the Olds' heavily-loaded automobile lumber off toward the Grand Trunk Road, it seemed to us all that life could never again be as rich.

As I drove back to my own home that day I had a strange sensation of being on my own, now, alone in a hostile community. How ridiculous. The Mitchells were still in Wah, after all!

The weaning process took a new and unexpected turn late one morning, some months after the Olds left, when Dr. Daniel Baksh phoned me. He said he and Dr. Stanley Mooneyham, representing a group called World Vision, headquartered in California, U.S.A., would like to visit me. I had never heard of his organization but my doors were open to anyone, even people who were curious to see what a Muslim-turned-Christian looked like.

Both arrived a few days later. When we finished dinner, Dr. Mooneyham began to speak and it was clear that he was no curiosity-seeker. He was interested in my conversion, all right, but I sensed that he would have been equally interested in the conversion of my gardener. As we sipped tea, he came to the point.

"Will you come to Singapore, Madame Sheikh," Dr. Mooneyham asked, "to testify for the Lord?"

"Singapore?"

"Billy Graham is arranging a large conference there called *Christ Seeks Asia.* It will be for Asiatic Christians of all kinds—Indonesians, Japanese, Indians, Koreans, Chinese, Pakistanis. Your testimony will be an inspiration to us."

It didn't sound right. I had enough to do right there in Wah without taking off for other parts of the world.

"Well," I said, "I'll pray about it."

"Please do!" Dr. Mooneyham said and then shortly he bid me goodbye.

Long after Dr. Mooneyham left, I sat on the veranda thinking and praying, as I had promised, about the invitation. One side of me said that I should take advantage of the opportunity. Another side of me said I should not even think of it.

And then an idea occurred to me.

My passport. Of course. It was just about to expire. It would have to be renewed if I were to go to Singapore. At that time in Pakistan there was much red tape involving passports. The situation was *impossible.* Some people sent their passports in for renewal and *never* got them back.

Why not let this situation act as a voice for the Lord? If He wanted me to go, He would take care of this passport detail.

That very afternoon I filled out the necessary information and posted the passport to the proper officials. As I slipped it in the mail box I had very little doubt that this would be my "No" to the Singapore trip.

A week later an official-looking government envelope came in the mail.

"Hmm," I smiled, "this will be the first step in getting my renewal, some more forms to fill out. And so it will go on for months."

I opened the envelope.

There, all renewed and officially stamped, was my passport.

So it was, a few months later, that I said goodbye to six-year-old Mahmud and drove down to Lahore. There I had a short visit with my son, Khalid, before going on to Karachi where I would board the jet for Singapore. Although it was now 1968 and a year and a half had passed since the Lord met me, Khalid was much like the rest of my family, now showing little interest in my discovery. I suspected that he considered me, at 48, embarked on a strange kind of trip. But I was to be respected as his mother, and we had an enjoyable visit.

Later as I boarded the jet in Karachi and considered the project I was just now undertaking, I had the impression that Khalid was right. What in the world was I doing on this airplane headed for Singapore! There were a lot of Christians aboard and I wasn't too sure I liked what I saw. I shrank from their exuberance. They were singing Gospel songs, shouting back and forth to each other across the aisles, sometimes raising their hands and crying, "Praise the Lord!" I was embarrassed. There was an artificial quality about the joy, not unlike the forced gaiety I had occasionally seen among conventioneers on the streets of London. I found myself muttering that if this was what it meant to travel in Christian circles, I wasn't interested.

What made the moment worse was that, for reasons which I could not define, I felt this trip held a personal significance beyond my safari to Singapore. It was as if the trip were prophetic, foretelling the type of life I would be called upon to lead.

"Oh no, Lord," I said to myself. "You must be playing with me!" Prophetic in what sense? That I was going to have to spend a lot of time among extroverts, traveling in jet airplanes? Back in Wah I was just getting comfortable in my role as a Christian, but that was in a provincial village. There I was in control, at least. Christianity to me was a very private joy, to be shared on my own terms. I definitely did not like the idea of parading myself before hundreds, perhaps thousands of strangers.

As the plane took off I stared out of the window, watching Pakistan fall away below me into the mist. Even though I knew that I would be coming back within just a few days, something warned me that in a very real sense this was a beginning. Although I would return to my home in the physical sense, in another sense I would never come back. This—this group of Christians on an airplane—was my home now.

What could I possibly mean by that! The idea appalled me.

From the Singapore airport we went straight to the conference hall where the meetings were already in progress.

And suddenly, quite to my surprise, I found that I was having a very different reaction to this group of assembled Christians.

There were thousands of men and women in the conference hall, the largest number of people I had ever seen gathered in one place. As I walked into the hall, everyone was singing "How Great Thou Art." I felt the familiar Presence of God's Spirit and had never known it to be so palpitating. Almost instantly I wanted to cry, not out of sadness but out of joy. Never before had I seen such a large crowd of people praising the Lord. I could hardly grasp it. So many people, from so many countries! Different races, different dress! Galleries of praising Christians seeming to rise forever.

Now this was different! Not at all like the group of people on the airplane. I then realized what I had been experiencing on the plane. Everything was suddenly very clear. Those people on the jetliner had been shy, nervous, perhaps even afraid. Afraid of the newness, afraid of flying. They were bluffing and posturing, not in the Spirit in spite of the language. They were no more moving in the Spirit than I was when I scolded one of the servants or reacted violently to an uncle when he tried to pressure me back into Islam. The problem had been their language. Christian talk fooled

me. I should have recognized their Christianese as such,
covering up a hurting.

But here in this conference center it was different. So-
cializing was over, worship had begun. If the prophecy I
had felt meant being with groups like this, *that* I could appreciate and accept.

One thing still bothered me. Was I really supposed to
stand up in front of these thousands of people to talk? It
was one thing to speak about my experiences to people I
knew personally in Wah. But here? With all these strange-
looking people from so many different continents? I did not
feel at all safe.

I hurried over to my hotel where I tried to settle down. I
looked out the window at teeming Singapore. How different
Singapore was from London and Paris. People jostled each
other on the streets, hawkers sang their wares and auto-
mobiles threaded through the melee, constantly sounding
horns. The very press of people seemed to menace me here
just as it did in the conference hall. I shuddered, thrust
the curtain closed and retreated to the other end of the
room where I sat down and tried to calm myself.

"Oh Lord," I cried, "where is Your comforting Spirit?"

And suddenly I recalled a childhood experience of walking with my father through the marketplace in Wah. Father
cautioned me to stay by his side but, always active, I wanted
to run off. One day I did. A flower display caught my attention and I ran over to it. Suddenly I realized that my
father was not at my side. Panic filled me and I burst into
tears. "Oh Father," I said, "come find me and I won't ever
run away from you again!" Even as I spoke, there he was,
his tall slender figure coming quickly toward me through
the crowd. I was with him again! All I wanted now was to
stay by his side.

As I sat in the hotel room, I realized that in fact I had
left my heavenly Father again. By allowing myself to become anxious, I had run off from His comforting Presence.
When would I learn that I cannot worry and trust God at

the same time! I relaxed in my chair and felt at peace again.

"Oh thank You, Father," I said weeping in relief. "Please forgive me for stepping away from You. You are here, You are in that hall. I'll be safe."

A few minutes later in the hotel lobby, I felt a hand on my arm and heard a familiar voice. I looked around to see Dr. Mooneyham.

"Madame Sheikh, so good to have you here!" Dr. Mooneyham seemed happy enough to see me. "Are you still willing to speak?" It was as if he had been reading my mind.

"Don't worry about me," I said, smiling. "I'll be fine. The Lord is here."

Dr. Mooneyham just stood there, studying my face, as if making a decision about how to interpret my words. After all, I had been using Christianese too, and he wasn't going to take it at face value, possibly let it fool him as it had fooled me on the airplane. Dr. Mooneyham's eyes were reading my very soul. Then suddenly he seemed satisfied.

"Good," he said abruptly. "You're slated for tomorrow morning." He looked at his watch. "You'll have lots of prayer support."

Dr. Mooneyham had understood me correctly. The sense of security lasted through the next morning too, when indeed I did get up in front of those thousands of people gathered in the auditorium to speak of the way the Lord had found me in such a strange way. It was not at all difficult speaking. He was with me as I stumbled and fumbled my way through the talk, embracing me and encouraging me, assuring me that *He* was doing the communicating and not I. And as people surrounded me in loving fellowship after my talk, it was as if I had taken the first step in a new kind of work for the Lord.

The Lord also arranged my meeting a man who would become very important in my life, though I didn't realize it at the time. I was introduced to Dr. Christy Wilson, a kind gentleman who was pastor of a church in Kabul, Afghanistan, which ministered to foreign nationals. We found a rapport in the Lord's Spirit as we discussed his work.

Then, the meetings were over and I was on my way back to Wah. Once again I sensed that the whole trip had a strangely foretelling character, as if God had asked me to come with Him to Singapore so that I could learn more about a type of work He wanted me to do.

Well, I said to myself, at least I'll be headquartered in Wah. Perhaps I wouldn't mind *too* much, going out on an occasional trip from my comfortable and secure ancestral home.

But as the car turned off the Grand Trunk Road toward our house in the trees, I had no way of knowing that the weaning process was going to shatter more of that security.

12.

A Time for Sowing

The next separation step came in the sad news that the Mitchells were leaving on furlough. It would be some time before they would return to Pakistan.

It was more than a year after Singapore. I was sitting in the Mitchells' living room with our small band of Christian professional men and women from the area. It was a sad occasion, the final get-together before David and Synnove left. I could not help thinking of the first time I had come to this same low-verandaed house as a hesitant seeker. So much had happened since then. I looked at the faces of these two who had been so close to me in my introduction to Christ: tall David, his hair graying, and earnest Synnove who had prayed for me so consistently.

"I'm going to miss you terribly, you know that," I said as we all stood on the small lawn in front of the Mitchells' house. "How will I ever get along without your fellowship!"

"Maybe the Lord is teaching you to get along without it," said Synnove. "He's always stretching us, you know, Bilquis, until we don't have a safe handhold left except Him."

It sounded good, but I still didn't like being stretched and told Synnove as much. She just laughed. "Of course you don't, dear Bilquis. Who ever wants to leave the safety of a womb. But adventure lies ahead!"

Synnove got into their old car and closed the door. One more embrace through the window and suddenly the Mitchells' car was rolling dustily away, away from the forlorn whitewashed buildings that had been officers' quarters during the war. Their car disappeared around the corner. Adventure, indeed! Here I was a lonesome Christian in a Muslim town. Would I be able to make it alone?

Several weeks passed, during which time, frankly, it was hard for me to sense the adventure Synnove promised, or the direction and purpose that Ken Old had foretold when he and Marie left what semed such a long time ago. The Sunday evening meeting of Christians continued, first in one home then in another of the five of us who were left, but without the leadership of the Olds and Mitchells the meetings seemed to flounder.

Then one night after a listless meeting an idea struck me. Were we making a mistake trying to do things exactly as the Mitchells and the Olds had done? Our little group was surely going to atrophy if we didn't get some new blood in our midst. What would happen—and I felt my pulse quicken just at the thought—what would happen if we asked people to join the fellowship who were not professionals—not doctors and engineers and missionaries? Suppose we asked Christians and non-Christians alike, the sweepers, the lower classes, to join in fellowship. Perhaps in my own home since it was large and convenient. When I suggested the idea to our fellowship there was some initial resistance, then skeptical agreement. We decided to go ahead. Through direct invitations and through the grapevine also, I passed word along that a Christian evening would be held at my house Sunday night.

I was surprised at how many people turned up. Most were from Rawalpindi where word had travelled. And, just as I hoped, not all were Christians either. Many were simply hungry to find out more about the Christian God.

With those of us from the original group as leaders, we sang and prayed and tried to do what we could to minister to the individual needs of the maids and day laborers and school teachers and business people who also came to the house.

Soon there was a fresh feeling to the Sunday fellowship. The responsibility was awesome. I and the others who were leaders in this small group spent hours on our knees, hours close to the Lord and the Word, trying to be sure that in no smallest way did we diverge from the direction He wished us to take. All of a sudden the "resultless" period I had been experiencing was reversed. I was able to see actual conversions. The first to come to the Lord was a young widow. She cried her hurt and lonesomeness out and then asked the Lord in. It was extraordinary to see the transformation in her personality, from a gloomy, defenseless creature to a hope-filled child of God. Shortly a mechanic from a nearby garage came into the Lord's Kingdom, then a file clerk, then a sweeper.

And all in my own home. I felt honored indeed, although I kept wondering when I would start to hear from the family about this smudge on our reputation. But no one complained. Not yet, anyhow. It was as if the family didn't want to admit what was happening. One day I tripped on a tile in my terrace, fell and suffered a slight bone fracture. My family didn't come; they telephoned instead. But at least they were telephoning!

If opposition to my slowly evolving Christian life was lessening from my family, it was still coming from within me at times. I was yet a very private person, possessive, counting my land and garden my own.

Across the lawn from my house is a road leading to the servants' quarters. Growing next to this road is a tree called the ber, which has a red fruit similar to the cherry. That summer after the Mitchells left, children from the village (perhaps encouraged by reports of a change in my personality) began coming right onto my property to climb the ber and help themselves to its fruit. The intrusion was bad enough, but when their shouts and squeals interrupted my rest time, I leaned out of my window and ordered the gardener to chase the children away. That very day I had the gardener cut the tree down. That would solve the problem permanently!

As soon as the tree was destroyed I realized what I had done. With the tree gone, so was the joy and peace of the Lord's Presence. For a long time I stood in my window staring at the empty place where it had been. How I wished now that the tree were still there so that I could hear the joyful shouts of the children. I realized what the true Bilquis Sheikh was like. All over again I knew that in my own natural self I would never be different. It was only through the Lord, through His grace, that any change could ever take place.

"Oh Lord," I said, "let me come back into Your Presence again please!" There was only one thing to do. Scattered throughout my garden were large trees heavy with summer fruit. The very next day I issued an open invitation to the village children to come and enjoy! And they did too. Even though I'm sure they tried to be careful, branches were broken, flowers trod upon.

"I think I see what You're doing, Lord," I said one afternoon after the children had gone home, and I was surveying the damage. "You found the garden itself to be a place that stood between us. You are weaning me even from the garden! You've taken it away to give to others. But look how they were enjoying it! It's Your garden. I give it up to them with great pleasure. Thank You for using this to bring me back into Your comforting Self."

He did return too. Until, that is, I once again needed a pruning. This time it wasn't the garden, it was my precious rest.

One cold November afternoon I was resting when Mahmud slipped into my room. He was becoming a youth now and his good-humored features foretold a handsome young-man-to-be. But now his face was concerned.

"Mum, there's a woman outside who wants to see you. She's got a baby in her arms."

I lifted my head. "Mahmud," I said, forgetting my own instructions to Nur-jan and Raisham, "You're eight years old now! You *know* that I don't want to see anyone at this time of day."

Mahmud had hardly left the room before the thought struck me: what would the Lord have done? And, of course, I knew what He would have done. He would have gone to the woman immediately, even if it were the middle of the night.

I called to Mahmud, who had not gone far enough down the hall to miss hearing me. Once again he stuck his brown face through the door.

"Mahmud," I said, "what does the woman want?"

"I think her baby is sick," Mahmud said, coming now into the room. I could see the concern in his eyes.

"Well bring her to the reception room then," I directed as I prepared to go downstairs.

In a moment I joined Mahmud, the woman and her child. The woman was dressed in the coarse, baggy clothes of a peasant. She might have been the baby's grandmother. She had a wizened face, shrunken shoulders and her pantaloons bagged around a thin frame. Only when she lifted her face and stared at me with deep brown eyes could I see that she herself was little more than a child.

"What can I do for you?" I asked, my heart melting.

"I heard about you in my village, and I walked here."

The place she mentioned was twelve miles away. No wonder the poor thing looked so tired. I sent servants for tea and sandwiches. I wondered if she were still nursing the baby; in some villages mothers nurse their children up to three years of age. The baby's eyes stared listlessly at the crystal chandelier, its tiny mouth still. I laid hands on the child's forehead to pray for him; it was hot and dry. As I laid hands on the mother's head, I could feel generations of my family wincing. In the old days, I would have been horrified if even this peasant's shadow had fallen on me.

My heart went out to these little ones, the mother and the child, as I asked God for healing in the name of Jesus. When the maid came I told her also to bring some vitamins for the mother. We visited for half an hour, the mother telling me of her life with a husband who had been crippled in an accident, the new baby, not enough food. And indeed she was nursing the baby—it was the cheapest way to feed him. When the mother finally rose to go, I restrained her with a gesture.

"No," I whispered. "Not yet. We must find some way to see to it that you and the baby are taken care of." Immediately as I said this, the old Bilquis Sheikh began to grow nervous. What if word got out to other needy people in Wah that the Begum Sahib in the big garden provided a soft touch? Wouldn't we be swamped with lines of other skinny, emaciated, sickly, desperate people?

But even as my heart whispered this question, I knew that I had no choice. Either I had meant it or I had not meant it when I gave myself *and all that I possessed* to the Lord.

". . . and, of course, your husband needs attention too. Let's get you all to the hospital. And let's get some decent food into your bodies. Then, if your husband still can't find work, let me know."

That's all there was to the visit. I made arrangements for the hospital to bill me and waited. But the woman never returned. I was a little surprised. When I asked the servants if they knew what had happened to her, they—as usual—had the answer. She and the baby and her husband had indeed gone to the hospital, and now they were all better. The husband had work. My ego bridled at first at the ungratefulness of this woman for not returning to give thanks, but the Lord checked me. "Is that why you helped her? So that you could be thanked? I thought thanksgiving was supposed to go to Me!"

And of course He was right. I went back in my mind to the place where I first felt that *I* had taken care of this woman. Then I asked the Lord to forgive me, and never to allow me to fall into that trap again. "Lord," I sighed, "Your arm must be tired from picking me up so often."

It seemed through those days that I would have little moments of success in the job of living close to the Lord, only to be brought back to earth quickly with resounding failure. I wondered if this were the pattern usually followed in the Christian life. Since I had no one to talk to then, I had to carry these questions secretly.

One morning while Nur-jan was administering my toilette a redbird fluttered to the window sill.

"Oh!" I exclaimed, "look at what the Lord has sent us this morning!"

There was silence as Nur-jan quietly went on brushing my hair. I was a bit surprised; Nur-jan was normally so talkative. Then she observed shyly, "Begum Sheikh, do you know that when you start talking of the Lord your whole appearance changes?"

That afternoon I placed an order for several more Bibles at the mission shop in Islamabad. They were a special kind of Bible, designed for children. I had discovered the usefulness of these Bibles with Mahmud. I discovered also that the servants around the house were picking up the brightly illustrated little book. When the Bibles arrived, I made a special point of giving one to Nur-jan. Imagine my joy when one day she came to speak to me privately.

"Begum Sahib," Nur-jan said, her plump face full of emotion, "I have something to tell you. Do you remember how you have so often told us that if we want to know this Jesus, all we have to do is ask Him to come into our heart?" At this she broke into tears. "Well I did, Begum Sahib.

And He did come in. I have never felt such love, ever; in my whole life!"

I couldn't believe my ears. I threw my arms about the girl and embraced her. We danced a little crying waltz around the bedroom.

"What an incredible piece of news, Nur-jan. Now we are three Christians—you and Raisham and I. We must celebrate!"

So Raisham and Nur-jan and I all had tea together. It wasn't the first time I had drunk tea with people of the serving class. But it still gave me a slight shock. As the three of us Christians daintily sipped our drinks and nibbled at our cake together, chatting like old friends, I found my mind wandering. What had happened to the woman who had retreated to this same estate, to hide from wealthy society? Here she was, sitting with the maids. How my family and friends would be scandalized. How my old friends and family would wonder! I thought back to the way I used to vent my frustrations in sharp orders and outbursts of temper. If I noticed dust on a chair rung, if the servants chatted too loudly in the kitchen, if my lunch were delayed a moment, the whole household could depend on an outburst. The Lord had really been working with me, and I felt His company with great satisfaction.

It was not that I wanted to become a saint. But I was beginning to learn that my responsibility of being a representative of Jesus Christ would not allow me to do anything that would dishonor His Name. And He was also teaching me that one's actions spoke louder than words when it came to witnessing for Christ.

But then I noticed a strange thing at our evening meetings. Nur-jan was not among the dozen villagers who were now joining us in my drawing room. How odd! One day after she had done my hair I asked her to stay behind for a moment. Wouldn't she like, I said, to join us this Sunday?

"But Begum," Nur-jan said, startled, her face whitening, "I just cannot talk about what happened to me, or go to a meeting. My husband is a devout Muslim. We have four children. If I say that I have become a Christian he will just turn me out."

"But you *have* to declare your faith," I insisted. "There is no other way."

Nur-jan stared at me unhappily, then left the room, shaking her head and mumbling. I could just barely make out the words, "But it can't be done."

A few days later I was visiting the Reverend Mother Ruth whom I had also come to know at the Holy Family Hospital. I always enjoyed talking to her. The Reverend Mother mentioned how many people in Pakistan are secret believers.

"Secret believers!" I exclaimed. "I do not see how that is possible. If you are a Christian why aren't you shouting the news!"

"Well," said Mother Ruth, "look at Nicodemus."

"Nicodemus?"

"He was a secret believer. Check chapter three of the Gospel of John."

I opened my Bible then and there and began to read how this Pharisee came to Jesus late one night to find out more about His kingdom. I had often read this stirring chapter but not until then did I realize that of course Nicodemus was a secret believer.

"Perhaps at a later date Nicodemus expressed his belief openly," the Sister said. "But as far as the Scriptures show, he was careful not to let his fellow Pharisees know."

The next day I called Nur-jan into my room and read the verses about Nicodemus to her. "I'm sorry I made you uncomfortable," I said. "In time the Lord may show you how to declare your faith. In the meanwhile, just listen carefully to His leading."

Her face brightened. Later I watched her humming happily at her work. "I hope I did the right thing, Lord," I said. "What I have to watch is that I not set myself up in judgment against anyone."

Just a few days later I discovered for myself, with new intensity, how difficult it was to become a Christian in this part of the world.

One afternoon the phone rang. It was one of my uncles, a relative who had been particularly sharp with me. Even as the family boycott began to thaw slightly, this uncle had never been in touch, never spoken. His voice on the phone was sharp.

"Bilquis?!"

"Yes."

"I hear that you are leading others astray. You are taking them from the true faith."

"Well, dear Uncle, that's a matter of opinion."

I could imagine the man's face getting flushed with the anger that showed in his voice. "It's one thing for you to make these decisions yourself. Quite another for others to follow. You must stop this, Bilquis."

"Uncle, I appreciate your concern but I must remind you that you are to run your life and I will run my own."

The very next day when my new chauffeur was driving me home from a visit with Tooni, a man stood in the road and tried to stop the car. My chauffeur knew that I often stopped for hitchhikers. But he did not want to stop this time.

"Please don't ask me to stop, Begum," he said in a determined voice. He swerved around the man, his tires squealing on the edge of the highway.

"What do you mean?" I leaned forward in the seat. "You don't think that man was trying to . . . ?"

"Begum . . ."

"Yes?"

"Begum, it's just that . . ." the man lapsed into silence and all my questioning could not drag any further information out of him.

But it was just a week later that another one of my

servants slipped into my room minutes after I had retired for my afternoon rest.

She closed the door behind her.

"I hope you will not mind," she said in a low whisper. "But I simply must warn you. My brother was in the mosque in Rawalpindi yesterday. A group of young men began talking about the damage you are doing. They kept saying something would have to be done. Soon. To shut you up."

The girl's voice was shaking.

"Oh Begum Sahib," she said, "must you be so open? We are afraid for you and for the boy."

My heart skipped. Now it was my turn to wonder whether it had not been best to remain a secret believer in this land, and yes, even in this family where Jesus was anathema.

13.

Storm Warnings

Two months passed after the report of threats against me. Nothing occurred more threatening than hostile glances from a few young men, and I began to wonder if the alarms were groundless.

Now it was Christmastime again, a few years after I had found the Babe of Bethlehem. Even though some family members had been visiting me, the warning phone call from my uncle reminded me that relationships within my family were still strained and I felt it would be a good idea to have a dinner party for my relatives and friends, to see if now we could do something further to heal the breach.

So I spent considerable time making up a guest list. Then one evening, before going to bed, I slipped that list into my Bible for safekeeping, intending to have the invitations sent out the next morning.

But that was never to take place.

For when I opened the Bible the next morning to take out the list my eyes fell on a passage. Incredibly, it read:

> *When you give a luncheon or a dinner party, don't invite your friends or your brothers or relations or wealthy neighbors, for the chances are they will invite you back, and you will be fully repaid. No, when you give a party, invite the poor, the lame, the crippled and the blind.*

132

> *That way lies real happiness for you. They have no*
> *means of repaying you, but you will be repaid when*
> *good men are rewarded—at the resurrection.*
>
> Luke 14:12

"Lord, is that Your word for me?" I wondered, holding
the Bible in one hand and the guest list in the other. Sure
enough, most of my relatives and neighbors and friends
were well-to-do. I had told myself this was an opportunity
to get Muslim and Christian together, but actually I saw
that pride had been showing through. I wanted to demonstrate to my family that I still had friends among the
wealthy class.

I crumpled up the list.

Instead, I did exactly what the Bible said. I made up a
list of widows, orphans, unemployed and poor people of
the village and then invited all of them to attend Christmas
dinner. This included everyone, even all the beggars. I
made some of the invitations myself, others I passed along
through my own staff. News like this travels fast and soon
my servants were bringing back word that the whole village
was planning to come. For a moment I had misgivings. All
those *people*. I thought of the pair of silk handmade Persian
rugs I had recently ordered for the living room. Oh well, I
thought, I could put the good things up out of the way during that time.

So we started preparations. Mahmud's eight-year-old enthusiasm was infectious as he helped me gather presents
for the people who would come. We found woolen shirts
for the boys, brightly colored garments for the young girls,
rolls of red, pink and purple cloth for the women, warm
pantaloons for the men, wraps and shoes for the children.
The servants and I spent hours wrapping the gifts, tying
the packages with silver ribbons.

One day there was a knock on the door. A group of
womenfolk from Wah were standing outside. They wanted
to help. "Not for pay, Begum," their spokesman explained.
"We just want to help you put on the dinner."

Suddenly the whole celebration had become a community affair. For decoration, I asked a family of potters in the village to make lamps, the small oil pottery lamps still commonly used in that part of Pakistan. I ordered 500 of them. I had the village women come to the house, where we made wicks by twisting cotton into strands. As we worked, natural opportunities arose to talk about Christ. As we placed the lamps around the house, for instance, I told the story about the wise and foolish virgins.

The food was another exciting project. Again the village women helped me prepare typical Pakistani sweets and sliced almonds and the delicious legus nuts. They pounded silver paper into strips so thin we could stick them on the sweetmeats as a colorful foil.

The village people began to arrive at the house on December the 24th and continued coming for what turned out to be a week's festival. How beautiful all the lamps were decorating every cranny, sitting cheerily along rails and sills. Mahmud had a wonderful time playing with the village children. I had never seen these children's eyes sparkle so, nor, for that matter, Mahmud's. Squealing and laughing filled the house. From time to time Mahmud would come to me with requests.

"Mum," he would say, "there are five more boys standing outside; can they come in?"

"Of course," I laughed, patting him on the back and feeling sure that there were more children in our house right now than lived in all of Wah. When I talked with the villagers about how Christ had instructed us to treat each other in this way their response was, "Did He *really* walk with people like us?"

"Yes," I said, "and today what we do for others, we do for Him."

Finally, after the festivities were over and I was able to slump down in a chair without worrying about sitting on a sleeping child, I sighed in contentment to God. "Is this what You wanted me to do?" And I seemed to hear the soft response: "Yes." And then I noticed: I had forgotten to put up the new Persian rugs. Yet they seemed none the worse for wear.

Many of the poor never forgot that party. About a month later, I heard through one of the servants about a funeral in Wah. The wife of the local *mullah* complained loudly that I had made a mistake losing my faith. Someone else, however, replied: "Have you seen the Begum Sahib lately? Have you done any of the things she has done since she became a Christian? If you want to learn anything about God, why don't you go see her?"

But there was another side to this experience too. For I learned that there were forces in Wah which did not take kindly to the party.

"Begum Sahib," an old retainer who worked in our garden stopped me one day. He touched his forehead. "A minute please?"

"Of course."

"Begum Sahib Gi, there is talk in the town that you should know about. One speaks about how the Begum has become a problem. There are those in the village who say they will have to do something about you."

"*About* me?" I said. "I don't understand."

"Neither do I, Begum Sahib. But I just feel you should know. . . ."

Warnings like this, sometimes coming close together, sometimes spread months apart, began to occur with increasing regularity over the next year. It was almost as if the Father were trying to prepare me for a difficult time to come.

One day, for instance, three small boys came to our house from the village. Later I wondered if they were God's messengers, arriving in these little forms. For Mahmud came to me with news from the boys. He was shivering and his eyes were wide with fear.

"Mum, do you know what my friends said? They said

that in the village people were planning to kill you. They will do it after Friday prayers." He began sobbing. "If you die, I will kill myself!"

What was I to do! I gathered Mahmud's eight-year-old form in my arms, stroked his tousled black hair and tried to comfort him. "My dear child," I said, "let me tell you a story." And I recounted to him the tale of Jesus' first sermon in Nazareth, when the crowd became so angry and determined to stone Him. "Mahmud," I said, "Jesus passed through the midst of them. There wasn't a thing anyone could do to Jesus until and unless the Father allowed it to happen. The same is true with you and me. We have His perfect protection. Do you believe that?"

"Do you mean we will never be hurt or harmed?"

"No, I don't mean that. Jesus was hurt. But only when His time had come to suffer. We do not need to live a life of constant fear that something terrible will happen to us. For it cannot happen to us until our moment has come. And maybe that will never happen. We will simply have to wait and see. But in the meantime we can live in great confidence. Do you understand?"

Mahmud looked at me and his brown eyes softened. Suddenly he smiled, wheeled on the spot and ran off to play, shouting happily. It was the best answer to my question he could possibly have given.

I wish I could say that I myself felt as confident. Not that I disbelieved what I had said to Mahmud. It was that my faith was not yet childlike. I rose and carried my Bible out into the garden. My heart was not exactly light. How dare they try to force me from my land!

The fall weather was crisp and dry; as I slowly walked along the graveled path, I could hear a fish splash in my little stream and the far-off call of a bird. Chrysanthemums and other summer leftovers cheered the path. I breathed the pleasant sparkling air. This was my land, and my people. This was my country. My family had served it well for seven hundred years. This was my home, and I could not, *would not* leave it!

Yet events were taking place which were totally out of my control, and which did not bode well for my stubborn determination to stay in my home.

In December of 1970, four years after my conversion, Pakistan had its first national one-man-one-vote election. It looked as if the People's Party would carry the day. And that was not exactly good news for me. For none of my highly placed friends were also friends of this party. "Islam our Faith, Democracy our Policy, Socialism our Economy" was the new party's slogan. It was a slogan designed to appeal to the man on the street. I know that the common ordinary Pakistani felt a new sense of power. Was this good for me? Probably it was good for the new Bilquis, but there was an inherent danger too. For nothing fires the zeal of a fanatic more than the belief that his government will back him in his exploits. My old reputation was certainly not that of a democrat; socialism did not fit the age-old traditions of our family; and Islam?—well, now I was a traitor.

I followed the events somewhat from a distance. One day, however, an old government friend of my father's from Sardar arrived. Despite his despair over my new faith, he had tried to stay close to me. From time to time he would call or visit just to make sure that everything was all right.

Now he sat with me on the white silk-covered divan in our drawing room, sipping tea.

"Bilquis," he said, his voice low, "are you aware of what is happening and how it can affect you?"

"Do you mean with the Pakistan People's Party?"

"They won the election of course. How much do you know about Zulfikar Ali Bhutto."

"I knew him well," I said.

"Don't you read the paper? Listen to the radio?"

"No, you know I don't take time for that."

"Well, I advise that you do take time. The government situation has changed. I doubt if you can count on him as you did on previous presidents," he added. "You have, my dear, lost what influence you may have had in high circles. That era is over."

Half an hour later as I waved my old friend out of the driveway and returned to call the maid to clean up, I realized that a strange thing had happened with my old friend's visit. It was as if he had spoken for the Lord, preparing me for the fact that my protective, influential friends were gone, bringing me one more step toward total dependence on the Lord.

It wasn't too long before I began sensing a growing hostility. I saw it in the eyes of men as I walked in Wah. I'll never forget the change in the attitude of a minor official with whom I discussed taxes on my property. In the past he had been a servile man, bowing and touching his forehead. Now the little fellow was openly hostile. It was evident in his clipped remarks and the contemptuous way he slapped the forms down in front of me.

And later as I was strolling along the road outside my house, I glimpsed a man who usually went out of his way to speak to me. Now I noticed something quite different. He caught sight of me, quickly turned his head and began to study the horizon as I passed. Inwardly, I chuckled. "Lord, don't we all behave like children!"

Interestingly, the new government seemed to have little effect upon my household staff. Except for Nur-jan, who was still quietly enjoying her new walk with Jesus, and Raisham, my other Christian servant, my entire staff were faithful followers of Muhammad. Yet a real affection existed between us. More than once my Muslim servants slipped into the bedroom to plead with me. "Please, Begum Sahib Gi," they said in low voices, "if you should have to leave . . . or if you should decide to leave . . . don't worry about us. We'll find work."

What a different relationship I had with my staff now than a short four years before.

Dreams, too, played a remarkable role during that time. Dreams had always been a part of my Christian experience, ever since the day I first met Jesus, who came in a dream to feast at the table with me. Now these strange and mystic experiences, such as Paul said he experienced, became even more active.

One night I found myself taken out in spirit and crossing the ocean at a terrific momentum. Like the speed of light I came to what I felt was New England, though I had never been to America. I came before a house, or was it a nursing home? I floated into a room with twin beds. In one lay a middle-aged woman with a round face, clear blue eyes and a mixture of gray and white short hair. A white embossed cotton spread in a triangular pattern covered the bed. She was obviously very ill; I sensed she had cancer. A nurse sat in a chair reading. And then I saw my Lord in the corner of the room. I kneeled down before Him and asked what I should do.

"Pray for her," He said. So I went to the woman's bed and prayed fervently for her healing.

In the morning I sat at my window still awed by what had happened in that room across the sea. Why did Jesus ask me to pray for the woman? He was right there. Yet He had asked me to pray for her. I was beginning to get a glimmer of a tremendous revelation. Our prayers are vital to our Lord. He works through them. I was led to the fifth chapter of James: *Believing prayer will save the sick man; the Lord will restore him and any sins that he has committed will be forgiven. . . . Tremendous power is made available through a good man's earnest prayer. . . .*

Thus our prayer releases this power into the person for whom we plead.

Another time I envisioned walking up a gangplank as if boarding a ship. The gangplank led into a room. Christ was standing in the room. He seemed to be giving me instructions. Then I walked back down the gangplank. At the end of it a lady was waiting, dressed in western clothes, a skirt and jacket. She appeared to have been waiting for me. She came up to me, linked her arm in mine and started to take me away.

"Where are we going, Lord?" I asked over my shoulder. But He would not tell me.

The dream seemed to be saying that I would be going on another trip. Although this time I would be going to an unknown destination, Jesus would be watching over the journey. The dream left me in a state of preparedness so that I was not startled by the news an old friend brought me.

In March 1971, just a few months after Bhutto had taken office, I had a vist from Yaqub, an old government friend. He had been close to our family for years. In fact, when my husband was Minister, there was a time when Pakistan was in an economic decline with a serious trade imbalance. Yaqub and I had helped inaugurate a self-help program which came to be called the *Simple Living Plan*. The basic idea was to encourage Pakistan industries to produce our own goods, lessening the need for imports.

We had followed each other around the country helping small factories and cottage industries get started. We had encouraged local people to weave fabric and then start production of clothing. We, ourselves, had voluntarily entered an austerity program, wearing homespun garments. It was all to the good, for the *Simple Living Plan* was a success. As local factories began to thrive, the economic condition of Pakistan improved. Through the years since, Yaqub would occasionally visit me to discuss politics and world affairs. He knew a good deal about our family holdings, for he had visited the many estates we had throughout Pakistan, and he knew that most of our funds were tied up in real estate.

"Bilquis," he said, in a tone that was apologetic, "some friends and I have been talking and . . . er, the subject of your financial health has come up. Have you considered selling some of your land? I'm not sure how safe it is for you to have all of your funds tied up in real estate, with Bhutto promising land reform."

What a thoughtful thing for Yaqub to do. And not without risk either. With the growing hostility toward the ruling class of yesterday, his government staff car outside my house could easily serve to bring criticism on his own shoulders.

"Thank you, Yaqub," I said, trying to control my voice. "But as things stand now I am determined. Nothing—nothing at all will force me to move out!"

It was an infantile thing to say of course. The old Bilquis with her imperious, stubborn way was showing through. Nonetheless it was an attitude which did not surprise my friend at all. "That's the answer I expected, Bilquis," Yaqub said, stroking his moustache and laughing. "Just the same, the time may come when you may want to leave Pakistan. If you need help . . ."

"If the time does, my good friend, I will be sure to remember your offer."

Another dream: this time from Raisham, usually so reserved.

"Oh Begum Sheikh," my maid cried, kneeling her tall slender form by the divan on which I sat in my bedroom that cold night I met the Lord. "I've had a horrible dream. Can I tell you about it?"

"Of course."

I listened closely. Raisham told me that in her dream some evil men had come into the house and were holding me prisoner. "I fought with them," she cried. "I called out 'Begum, run!' And in the dream I saw you running out of the house and escaping."

The maid's dark brown eyes were moist with tears. It was I who had to comfort her. But for me this was not difficult. In the words which I spoke, I found myself listening to advice which I should take to heart. "My dear," I said, "I have been hearing much from the Lord lately about the possibility of having to flee. And this may occur. I at first refused to believe. But now I am beginning to wonder."

"It is possible," I said, lifting her pale chin upwards and smiling, "that I may have to go. But if I do, it will be in the Lord's timing. I am learning to accept that. Can you believe me?"

The little maid was silent. Then at last she spoke, "What a wonderful way to live, Begum Sahib."

"It is indeed. It is the only way. Nothing, any longer, is in my own control."

And although I did believe everything I said, as the young maid disappeared from my bedroom, I found myself not quite as in charge of my emotions as I may have sounded. Fleeing? Running away? Me?

The series of message "experiences" began to come more rapidly in the autumn of 1971. One day Nur-jan came to me breathless and taut with emotion.

"What is it, Nur-jan?" I said as she started to brush my hair, her hands trembling.

"Oh, Begum Sahib," Nur-jan sobbed, "I don't want you to be hurt."

"Hurt by what?"

Nur-jan dried her eyes. She told me that her brother, her own brother, had been to the mosque the previous day, and that a group of men had said that at last the time had come to take action against me.

"Do you have any idea of what they meant?"

"No, Begum Sahib," Nur-jan said. "But I am afraid. Not only for you but for the boy, too."

"A nine-year-old child? They wouldn't . . ."

"Begum Sahib, this is not the country it was even five years ago," said Nur-jan seriously, so unlike her usually bubbly self. "Please be careful."

And indeed, it wasn't but a few weeks later that it happened.

It had been such a lovely day. Autumn was in the air. The monsoon season was over and the weather was crisp and dry. Nothing untoward had happened for days on end and I found myself saying that after all we were living in a modern age. It was 1971, not 1571. Holy wars were a thing of the past.

I went up to my room for my prayer hour.

But suddenly, without knowing why, I had the strongest urge to get Mahmud and to rush outside to the lawn!

What a foolish thing to do. But the urge was so definite that I dashed down the hall, woke Mahmud up from his siesta, and without explanation hurried the groggy and protesting child down the hall.

Still feeling foolish, I dashed down the stairs, threw open the French doors and ran outside.

The moment I stepped onto the terrace, I smelled acrid smoke. Someone was burning pine boughs. We had a long-standing rule that no one was allowed to burn trash on my land. I went in search of the gardener and when I rounded the side of the house was instantly filled with horror.

There, heaped against the house, was a mound of dried pine boughs, ablaze. The crackling flames, hot and fast, raced up the side of the building, leaping high.

I screamed. The servants came running. Soon some were rushing back and forth to the streams with buckets filled with water. Others had unreeled the garden hose and were spraying the flames but our water pressure was low. For a moment it looked as if the fire was going to catch the timbers which stuck out from the end of the building under the roof. They began to smoke and smoulder. There was no way to throw water that high. The only way we could keep the house from burning down was to quench the flames themselves.

On we raced, against time. The ten servants which were on the staff formed a line to the stream passing buckets of water from one person to another, sloshing it over in their hurry.

On everyone worked for half an hour, until finally the leaping flames began to be brought under control. We stood, about a dozen of us, in a circle around the fire. All of us were perspiring, all of us shaking. In another few minutes the house would have been ablaze, impossible to quench.

I caught Nur-jan's eye. She shrugged ever so slightly and nodded her head.

I knew exactly what she was thinking. The threat had been carried out. I looked at the wooden roof beams, their ends charred black, and the soot stains on the white walls of my house. I thanked the Lord that nothing else had happened and shuddered to think of what could have happened if I had not been directed outside at that very moment.

An hour later, after the police had come to investigate, make their notes, question me and the staff, I was once again seated in my room. I picked up the Bible to see if the Lord had anything special to say to me.

One phrase leaped off the page.

"Haste thee, escape thither; for I cannot do anything till thou be come thither" (Genesis 19:22).

I put the book down and looked up. "All You have to do now is show me the *way* You want me to leave. Will it be easy, or will it be hard?

"And above all, Lord," I said, this time with tears suddenly filling my eyes, "what about the boy? Can he come too? You have been stripping me of everything. Does that include the child as well?"

One day six months later, in May of 1972, the Lord spoke to me still again through another dream. Raisham came to me with worry written in her eyes.

"Begum Sahib," Raisham said, "is the cash box safe?"

She was referring to the portable strong box in which I kept the household cash.

"Of course it's safe," I answered. "Why?"

"Well," Raisham explained, obviously trying to control

her voice, "I had a dream last night in which you were motoring on a long trip. You had the cash box with you."

"Yes?" I said. This wasn't too unusual, since I often carried the cash box with me on trips.

"But the dream was so *real*," Raisham insisted. "And the sad part is that as you were traveling, people stopped you and stole the cash box."

She trembled and once again I had to comfort her with assurance that the loss of my money would lead me into a still closer dependence on God. After she went back to her work I thought about that dream. Could it be prophetic? Could it be telling me that my finances would be taken from me? Would I soon be completely on my own, hurtling into the unknown with no means of support?

These were astonishing days. For just two months later, on a hot July day in 1972, a servant came to announce the arrival of my son Khalid.

"Khalid?" My son still lived in Lahore. Why a special trip, especially in this intense heat? What was so important that it could not be handled on the telephone?

Khalid was waiting for me in the drawing room. "Son!" I exclaimed as I walked in. "How great to see you! But why didn't you phone?"

Khalid came over and kissed me. He closed the drawing room door and, without preamble, he plunged into the purpose for his visit. "Mother, I've heard a frightening rumor." He stopped. I tried to smile. Khalid lowered his voice and went on, "Mother, the government is going to expropriate much private property."

My mind went back to the visit from my government friend who had said the same thing, more than a year earlier, back in March, 1971. Was his prophetic visit coming to pass now? Khalid told me that Bhutto was starting his land reforms and that it was very likely that my properties would be among the first to be nationalized.

"What do you think I should do?" I asked. "Will they take it all or just part?"

Khalid got up from his chair and walked over to the garden window, deep in thought. Turning back to me he said:

"Well, Mother, nobody knows. Perhaps it would be best to sell *some* of your properties in small lots. That way the new owner will be protected from a total government take-over."

The more I thought about it, the more I felt Khalid's suggestion made sense. We drove over to discuss the issue with Tooni, all of us agreeing that this was the right way to proceed. It was decided then. Khalid would go back to Lahore. We would join him there to arrange the paperwork. Tooni, Mahmud and I would follow shortly.

So it was that one hot morning in July of 1972, the three of us found ourselves nearly ready for the drive to Lahore to see real estate agents about my properties. As I stepped out of the house I was struck by the beauty of my garden. Summer blossoms were at their height and even the springs seemed to tinkle louder than usual.

"We'll be back in a few weeks," I said to the assembled staff on the front steps of the house. Everyone seemed to accept the idea. Everyone that is but Nur-jan and Raisham. Nur-jan suddenly burst in tears and rushed away.

Sadly I went up to my bedroom to pick up an item I forgot. When I turned again into the hall to go back downstairs, Raisham was standing in front of me. She took my hand, her eyes wet with tears.

"God go with you, Begum Sahib Gi," she said softly.

"And He with you," I answered.

Raisham and I stood in the hall silently together, saying nothing but understanding everything. Somehow I sensed that I would never see this tall slender person again—she with whom I had become so close. I squeezed her hand and whispered, "There is no one who can do my hair like you."

Raisham put her hands to her face and rushed away from me. I was about to close the bedroom door when something stopped me. I walked back into the room and stood there.

A hush settled over the white-furnished room. The morning sun flooded in from the garden window. This is where I had come to know the Lord.

I turned my back on the room and on my precious garden, where I had so often known the Lord's Presence, and headed outside to the car.

There were people I would be extremely glad to see in Lahore. First, of course, Khalid, his wife and their teenaged daughter. Then there was the possibility of seeing the Olds. I had written that I would be coming to Lahore. Their new mission was in a village some distance from the town, but I hoped that I could see these old friends.

Lahore, as usual in July, was broiling, its ancient streets steamed with rain from the last monsoon. As we threaded our way through the crowded downtown streets, a loudspeaker on a minaret above us crackled, then broke into the metallic voice of a muezzin's noontime prayer. Traffic suddenly lightened as cars and trucks pulled to the curb. Drivers climbed down to the sidewalk, laid out their prayer mats and began prostrating themselves.

Tooni could only stay with us for a very short time because of prior obligations. After we got the necessary paperwork done and had a short visit, Khalid took us to the railroad station so that Tooni could catch her train. It was a poignant moment at the station, more poignant than I could understand. According to plan, Mahmud would be seeing his mother again in just a few days. Yet we all sensed something unusual about the leave-taking. Mahmud, lanky for nearly ten, tried to hold back the tears as he kissed his mother. Tooni cried openly as she embraced the boy. Suddenly I found myself crying too and we all three hugged each other there on the station platform.

Finally, Tooni threw her dark chestnut hair back and laughed: "Oh come on, we're not having a funeral."

I smiled, kissed her again, and Mahmud and I watched her climb aboard the coach. As the engine tooted and the

cars slowly began to leave the station, a pang caught my
heart. I searched for Tooni's face in the coach window. We
located her and both Mahmud and I blew kisses.

Hungrily, I fastened Tooni's face in my mind, etching it
in my memory.

The next day I spent time with realty men who advised
me that my property sale would take several weeks. Khalid
assured us that we would be welcome as long as we wanted
to stay.

The one thing that disturbed me was that I would not
have spiritual fellowship. I knew now why disciples went
out two by two. Christians *need* each other for sustenance
and counsel.

I called the Olds. How great it was to hear Marie's voice!
We laughed together and cried together and prayed together on the phone. Though their schedule prevented
them from coming to Lahore, they could of course put me
in touch with Christians in town. Marie mentioned especially a college professor's wife, Peggy Schlorholtz.

Strange! Why did my heart beat faster at the name?

Within minutes, Peggy and I were on the phone with
each other. Within hours, she was in Khalid's drawing room.
When she saw me her face broke into a smile.

"Tell me, Begum Sheikh," she said, "is it true that you
met Jesus for the first time in a dream? How *did* you come
to know the Lord?"

So there in the drawing room I told Peggy the whole
story, just as it had begun six years before. Peggy listened
intently. When I finished she took my hand and said the
most amazing thing.

"I wish you would come to America with me!"

I looked at her, dumbfounded. But again my heart was
racing.

"I mean it," said Peggy. "I'm leaving soon to put my son
in school. I'll be in the States for four months. You could
travel with me and speak to our churches there!"

She was so enthusiastic that I did not want to dampen

her spirits. "Well," I said smiling, "I do appreciate your invitation. But let me pray about it."

The next morning a maid brought a note to me. I read it and laughed. It was from Peggy. "Have you prayed yet?" I smiled, crumpled the note and did nothing. It was just too preposterous to think about.

Unless. . . . Suddenly the events of the past two years crowded into my mind in a momentous sweep. The dreams. The warnings. The fire. My determination to do whatever the Lord wanted—even if it meant leaving my homeland.

No, I had not really committed Peggy's question to the Lord. But I did now. I placed the trip in His hands. It was difficult because I knew with a part of me which I could not understand, that if I left it would not be just for four months. It would be forever.

"Lord, I will say it once again. You know how much I want to stay in my land. After all, I'm 52 years old, and that's not time to start all over again.

"But," I sighed. "But . . . that is not the most important thing is it? All that really matters is staying in Your Presence. Please help me, Lord, never to make a decision that would take me away from Your glory."

14.

Flight

Odd, how after the Lord changed my mind about leaving Pakistan, sudden roadblocks emerged.

One, for instance, that seemed insurmountable was a regulation that citizens of Pakistan are only allowed to take five hundred dollars out of the country. As my dependent, Mahmud could take 250 dollars. How could Mahmud and I possibly live for four months on 750 dollars? This by itself seemed enough to keep us from considering Peggy's suggestion further.

Then a few days later, Peggy invited me to her home for a visit. As we chatted, Dr. Christy Wilson's name came up in the conversation. She knew him too. I was quite concerned about him since I had heard he had been ejected from Afghanistan by the Muslim government which then had destroyed the church he had built in Kabul for foreign nationals.

"Do you have any idea where he is?" I asked.

"Not really," Peggy said.

Just at that moment the phone rang. Peggy went to answer it. When she returned, her eyes were wide, "Do you know who that was?" she said. "It was *Christy Wilson!*"

After we got over our startled, laughing surprise, we began to ask ourselves if this were more than "coincidence."

Dr. Wilson, Peggy said, was just passing through Lahore. He wanted to come out for a visit. Of course I was glad, for it would be good to catch up on news, but I had an intuitive sense that more than casual visiting was going to occur.

We had a marvelous reunion at Peggy's house the next day. I brought Dr. Wilson up-to-date on events in Wah and in my own life. Then Peggy told him about trying to persuade me to come to the United States. He became quite enthusiastic about the idea.

"There are several problems though," Peggy said. "The first is the regulation that Bilquis can take only five hundred dollars out of the country."

"I wonder . . . ," Dr. Wilson said stroking his chin. "I have some friends who might. . . . Perhaps I could send a wire. . . . I know a man in California. . . ."

After a few days Peggy phoned, all excited. "Bilquis," she shouted. "It's all arranged! Dr. Bob Pierce of Samaritan's Purse will sponsor you! Do you think you could be ready to leave in seven days?"

Seven days! Suddenly the enormity of the idea of leaving my homeland swept over me. For I still felt convinced that if I did in fact leave, it would be forever. I understood what Rudyard Kipling meant in his lines:

> God gave all men all earth to love,
> But, since our hearts are small,
> Ordained for each one spot should prove
> Beloved over all . . .

Wah . . . my garden . . . my home . . . my family. . . . Could I seriously contemplate leaving them?

Yes, I could. I could consider nothing else if I were truly convinced that this were God's will. For I knew what would happen if I deliberately disobeyed. His Presence would disappear.

Over the next twenty-four hours another confirmation appeared to come through. Khalid told me at supper that there was only one minor detail left to cover, then all of the real estate problems would be over. "I think you can say quite safely, Mother," Khalid said, "that as of today you have divested yourself of the properties you wanted to sell."

Then suddenly doors slammed. Not by God, so it seemed, but by my country. For still a regulation came in, to the effect that no Pakistani can leave the country unless all of his income taxes have been paid. Mine had been paid, but I needed a statement to that effect. I had to get an Income Tax Clearance Certificate. Only with this could I buy tickets for the United States.

Four of my seven days before departure were gone; only three were left now as my son Khalid and I walked into the government office to get the Clearance Certificate. Khalid and I thought there would be no problems at all, since my papers were in order.

The office was on a busy street in downtown Lahore. However, when I stepped into that building, something struck me as strange. It was far too quiet for the usual bureaucratic office where clerks ran hither and yon and someone always seemed to be arguing with a staff member.

Khalid and I were the only ones in the office except for a bald-headed clerk who sat at the far end of the counter reading a magazine. Stepping up to him, I told him what I wanted.

He looked up only partially and shook his head. "Sorry lady," he said putting his head back down into the magazine again, "there's a strike on."

"A strike?"

"Yes, Madame," he said. "Indefinitely. No one is on duty. There's nothing anyone can do for you."

I stood staring at the man. Then I withdrew a few feet. "Oh Lord," I prayed aloud, but in such a way that only my son could hear me, "have You closed the door? But why did you encourage me so far?"

Then a thought struck me. Had He really closed the door? "All right, Father," I prayed. "If it is Your will that Mahmud and I go to America, You'll have to be the one to arrange for my clearance." A strong sense of confidence filled me and I found myself addressing the clerk.

"Well, *you* seem to be on duty," I said. "Why can't *you* give me my clearance?"

The man glanced up from his magazine with a dour expression. He seemed the type who was always happy to say no.

"I told you, lady, there's a strike on," he grunted.

"Well, then, let me see the officer in charge." One thing I had learned in my government work was that when I wanted something done, I should always go to the highest authority.

The clerk sighed, slapped down his magazine and escorted me to an office nearby. "Wait here," he grunted again, then disappeared into the office. From it I could hear a low murmur of voices, then the man emerged and motioned me in.

Khalid and I found ourselves facing a handsome middle-aged man sitting behind a scarred desk. I explained my need. He leaned back in his chair, twirling a pencil. "I'm sorry Madame . . . Madame . . . what did you say your name was?"

"Bilquis Sheikh."

"Well, I'm very sorry. There's absolutely nothing we can do during this strike. . . ." But suddenly a light of recognition flooded his eyes.

"You aren't the Begum Sheikh who organized the *Simple Living Plan?*"

"I am."

He slammed his fist on the table, then shot up. "Well!" he said. He drew a chair over and asked me to sit down. "I think that was the most wonderful program our country ever had."

I smiled.

Then the officer leaned across his desk in a confidential manner. "Now let's see what we can do for you."

He got me to explain precisely what the problem was and I told him that I was supposed to be in Karachi to catch a plane for the United States in three days. The man's face took on a resolute look. Standing up, he called out to the clerk on the counter. "Tell that new assistant to come in here."

"I have," he said to me in a very low voice, "a temporary stenographer. He is not part of the regular work staff and isn't on strike. He can type up the Certificate. I *myself* will put on the seal. I'm glad to help."

A few minutes later I had the precious Certificate in my hand, fully executed. As I left, I confess, I waved the paper at the surprised little clerk who looked up from his magazine just long enough to see my smile and hear my "God bless you."

As we left the government office building a few minutes later, an astonished Khalid mentioned to me that it had taken only twenty minutes to complete the entire business. "That was less than it would have taken if everyone had been on duty!" he said.

My heart singing, I tried to explain to Khalid that the Lord wants our *companionship*. When we pray, He wants to work *with* us. It was the Moses' Rod Principle. If I had just put the problem in the Lord's hands without stepping out in faith myself, I might never have gotten the Clearance. I had to step out by doing everything I could. I had to ask to see the man in charge. Just as God required Moses to strike the rock with a rod, He asks us, too, to *participate* in the working of miracles.

Khalid seemed a bit taken aback by my enthusiasm but recovered and added with a smile: "Well, I'll say one thing, Mother. I notice that instead of 'thank you' you always say 'God bless you.' And when you say that, it's the most beautiful thing I've ever heard."

Now that all my papers were in order I wondered if I could take a quick trip back to Wah to say goodbye, for by then I was convinced that this trip would be for more than four months. However, when I brought up the subject, Khalid said:

"Didn't you hear about the flood?"

Heavy rains had struck the portion of Pakistan between Lahore and Wah. Many square miles of land were flooded. All traffic was snarled. The government had taken over transportation.

My heart sank. I would not even be allowed to say good-bye. The Lord was asking me to make a clean break, like Lot being told not to look back.

I had planned to leave Lahore on Friday morning, two days off. I would fly to Karachi, the jumping-off place for the United States. Peggy and her son would begin their trip in New Delhi. Their Pan American New York-bound plane would stop at Karachi and Mahmud and I would join them on the plane there. On Thursday morning, however, an unusually strong urge swept over me not to wait. My anxiety centered around Mahmud. Surely grapevine efficiency had taken the news back to Wah that we were not on a simple visit to Lahore but were on our way out of the country. Wasn't it probable that relatives might try to take Mahmud away from my "corrupting" influence? Would I be stopped on some pretext or other? A strong sense of danger spurred me.

No, I wouldn't wait. I would leave that very day. I would go to Karachi, stay with friends, and lie low.

So that afternoon, after a flurry of packing, Mahmud and I said quick farewells to Khalid and his family and hurried to the airport. We flew out of Lahore with a definite sense of relief. We were on our way!

Karachi was, as I remembered it, a rambling desert and seashore town nestled against the Indian Ocean. It was a hodgepodge of the old and new, of gangling camels brushing against Rolls Royces, of buzzing fly-filled bazaars next to smart shops offering the latest Parisian fashions. Perfect. The town was so large we would just be swallowed up in it.

We were staying with friends and I was shopping downtown, preparing for our departure for America the next day. Suddenly a strange oppression came over me. I closed my eyes as I leaned against a wall for support and prayed for my Lord's protection. I was given the strong leading that Mahmud and I were to move to a hotel that night. I tried to shake it off. "This is silly!" I told myself. Then I remembered the story of the Wise Men being warned in a dream to leave early by another route.

Shortly, we were checked into the Air France Hotel at the Karachi Airport. I took Mahmud to the room as quickly as possible, ordered our meals sent up, and together we simply waited. Mahmud seemed restless. "Why do we have to be so secretive, Mum?" he asked.

"I just think we ought to be quiet for a little while, that's all."

That night before the flight, I lay awake in bed wondering. Why was I so apprehensive? There was no real reason for it. Was I letting my nerves take over? Was I overreacting to the threats of the past? The fire? I slept fitfully and only for a few hours. By two o'clock in the morning I was up and dressed, again prodded by a strong sense of urgency. Again I felt ridiculous. It was unlike me. The only way I could explain it was that the hour had come for me to *leave* the hotel and I was being *propelled* by the Lord. I hustled a groggy Mahmud into his clothes, then gathered our bags, placing them by the door for the bellman to pick up.

It was three o'clock in the morning. The flight was at five. Mahmud, still sleepy-eyed, stood with me in front of the hotel waiting for a taxi to take us to the terminal. I looked at the waning moon and wondered, would this be the last time I would see this moon in my own country? An early morning breeze wafted a scent of narcissus, probably from a flower box, and my heart cried out, for I sensed that I would never see my garden again.

Finally the doorman flagged a cab. Mahmud and I climbed in. I prayed as we wove our way through traffic. Even at this early hour the airport avenues were busy. As cars pulled alongside at stoplights I nervously sank back a little deeper into the seat. "We're just being quiet for a little while," I quoted myself, trying to sound as reassuring to my own ears as I had to Mahmud. No, that wasn't the way. What I really needed to do was to pray. "Lord, do take away this nervousness. Nervousness is not founded in You. I cannot trust You and worry at the same time! And yet if this urgency is of You, Lord, there must be a reason and I will obey."

We pulled into the terminal and got out onto a bustling sidewalk where the rumbling thunder of jet engines and the cacophony of hundreds of voices blended in an atmosphere of urgency. My heart caught as I looked up and saw my country's flag, the star and crescent on its green background, snapping in the breeze. I would always respect that flag, my people, and their Muslim faith. A porter hurried our luggage over to the check-in counter where I was grateful to see it disappear into seeming safety.

Just 40 pounds of luggage each. I smiled as I thought of our family trips on other days to the interior when thousands of pounds of luggage were taken for just a few week's stay and my sisters still cried for the clothes that we couldn't take along.

We had an hour to wait before plane time. Keeping Mahmud close to me, I felt it best for us to mix in with the crowd in the terminal so we wouldn't be noticed. But I couldn't shake the sense of impending danger. Again I scolded myself for needless worry. The Lord is in charge, I told myself. He is guiding me out of this situation, and all I need to do is obey.

Then Mahmud asked to go to the restroom. We walked down the hall to the men's room. I waited in the corridor.

Suddenly the loudspeaker called out our flight.

"Pan Am flight for New York City now ready for boarding."

My heart jumped. Where was Mahmud! We must be going!

Finally the men's room door opened. No, it was a turbanned Sikh who stepped out.

I found myself edging to the door. What was I doing! Certainly no woman in a Muslim country would be caught going into a men's room even to look for a nine-year-old missing youngster.

Now they were calling our flight again. "Pan Am flight for New York City is now ready for departure. All passengers should be aboard."

Oh no!·My heart cried. I had to do something. I pushed the men's room door back and shouted, "Mahmud!"

A little voice answered, "I'm coming Mum. . . ."

I breathed a deep sigh and fell back limply against the wall. Soon Mahmud came out. "Where were you? What kept you!" I cried.

No matter. I didn't wait for an answer but grabbed the boy's hand and ran. Now we rushed down the long hall to the boarding gate. We found ourselves among the last passengers getting aboard.

"Wow, Mum!" cried Mahmud. "What a ship!"

What a ship indeed. The 747 airliner was huge. We were both excited. I had never seen such a big plane before.

As I was about to step aboard I hesitated for a moment, at this last touch of Pakistan's soil.

But we had to keep moving. Inside the plane, which seemed like an auditorium to me, a stewardess directed us toward our seats. Where was Peggy? What would I do in the States without her?

And then, there she was! Working her way up the aisle toward us. Peggy threw her arms about me.

"Oh precious lady!" she cried. "I was so worried. I· couldn't see you in the crowd at the boarding gate!" I explained what had happened and Peggy seemed relieved. She introduced us to her son who was with her. "Too bad we can't sit together," she said. "We just had to take the seats they gave us."

Frankly, it was just as well. My thoughts were not social

at that time. They were on the realization that I was leaving my homeland. I felt sad, certainly, but at the same time *complete*. I couldn't understand it.

Soon Mahmud was being Mahmud. He made friends with a stewardess who took him into the cockpit for a visit. Mahmud came back enthralled. I was pleased. The stewardess asked us to put on our seat belts. I looked out the window to see the first rays of dawn spearing the eastern sky. The engines rumbled and a surge of excitement filled me. Our ship began to lumber down the runway. I looked behind me but could not see Peggy.

But Mahmud's face was there, next to me. And it shone with excitement as the jet engines exploded into thunder at takeoff. I took Mahmud's hand and began to pray.

"What now, Lord? Again I have such a feeling of *completion!* You have brought me out of my homeland, like Abram. Not knowing what comes next, yet complete. Satisfied, because I am with You."

Even embarrassment over my fears and nervousness didn't bother me now. All I knew was that I had obeyed the Lord in every way. And I had to admit that I would never really know what might have happened if I had not followed His every command and moved as I did.

Tiny lights whisked by the windows and suddenly the rumbling of wheels beneath us ceased. We were airborne! In the light of early dawn, I could see the shoreline of Pakistan on the Indian Ocean receding below us.

I held out my hand to Him. He was my only security. My only joy was staying in His Presence. As long as I could stay there I knew that I would be living in the glory.

"Thank You, God," I breathed. "Thank You for letting me travel with You."

Postscript

Bilquis Sheikh went on to live in the USA, a woman with no country to call her own, but with more of a heart for every nation. Having had to leave behind her garden on the other side of the world, she created another one on the hillside behind the little house in California which she shared with her grandson Mahmud. She died in 1997.

NO GREATER LOVE

No Greater Love

JOY BATH
with SHIRLEY COLLINS

KINGSWAY PUBLICATIONS
EASTBOURNE

Foreword

It is never easy to give an answer to the age-old question, 'How does a loving God allow suffering?' It is sometimes even harder to understand why, when someone serves God all their life, suffering follows. *No Greater Love* confesses that it does not try to give slick answers to either of these questions, but it does continually show that despite the hardships and testings of Joy Bath, plus many other characters mentioned in her memoirs, God is always to be trusted. A peace that passes all understanding fills our hearts when we put ourselves into the hands of the Almighty, no matter what happens to us.

Roy Castle
Spring 1994

Introduction

How can one person judge the life of another? It was a privilege to ghost-write this book for Joy. I make no pretence of being the same kind of selfless person she was. She gave her time sacrificially, and I have undoubtedly spent more of my time on earth enjoying myself. We could work together because we were both travelling the same road: we shared the same Christian faith.

In my walk with God I have been impressed by the work of the Reverend Malcolm Herbert. Two decades ago he and I attended the same youth group. Now he is a vicar, currently in Woking. He has spoken these words of wisdom which are relevant to society, and to how it may regard people such as Joy; people the world may consider insignificant: 'We live in a society which majors on success and despises failure. But the world is groaning like a woman in labour. And us with it. We are simultaneously part of the problem and the answer. We are not called to succeed, but to follow Jesus.'

Joy was not a natural writer. Her diaries contained mundane things like, 'Washed my hair. Did the washing up before lights out.' Mixed in with these comments were simple statements such as, 'Helped with a Caesarean section.' She did not boast of her achievements; would not mention how the lives of thousands of patients had been saved through the medical knowledge of herself and her colleagues. To discover the stories behind her daily jottings it was necessary to sit alongside Joy and talk at length. Drawing out the facts from such a retiring and phlegmatic individual was not easy. In the process I discovered a modern-day saint with a terrific sense of humour.

I also spoke to a number of friends, colleagues and members of the Bath family, who provided additional insights into Joy's life. The Bishop of Salisbury told me: 'In the end, when you meet death face to face, there is nothing else in which to put your trust except God.'

Joy Bath trusted God—in life and in death.

Shirley Collins

I

'It won't work! This jack—it doesn't fit our wheels, Joy.'

I watched, helpless, as Debbie Brown, my nursing Sister, tried to lift the pick-up to change a punctured tyre. Too ill to be of much practical help, I felt anxious about our predicament on a dirt road in the middle of nowhere.

The sun rose higher, along with my temperature and Debbie's temper. We were both red in the face when I suggested she ought to stop for a cool drink. In her best Irish brogue she told me to push off—to go and sit under the shade of the nearest bush. I watched my colleague from a distance. Of medium height, slim build and with a fair complexion, we are very much alike: both lacking in muscle power and unsuited to an African heatwave.

It was Sunday 8th March 1992. The weather had been extremely hot almost since the year began, when the rains failed to come. Zimbabwe's worst drought in living memory marked the start of a different kind of aridity in my own life. We were on our way to Harare, setting off early to avoid the intolerable heat of the day. The Elim Mission Hospital truck was due for a service, and I was hoping to find a cure for a prolonged fever, nasty cough, sore throat and various aches and pains which refused to respond to antibiotics. Poorly on and off for about a year, the symptoms had escalated over the previous month until my chest hurt just in breathing.

Debbie persevered for well over an hour. When people

9

get angry, they somehow gain extra strength. In her frustration she found a way to make the jack stay on the wheel. Slowly, inch by inch, one corner of the truck was raised off the ground. The job was three-quarters done when I spotted an approaching bus. It stopped and all the passengers piled out, eager to help.

'You know, I'm actually annoyed those guys arrived after I'd done the hardest part,' Debbie frowned, as the journey recommenced.

'You should demand a discount from the garage. Part of the service has been done already!' Realising the humour of the situation we laughed, relieved to be *en route* once more.

Arriving in Harare around midday, exhausted, grubby and dishevelled, all I could manage was to shower and collapse into bed. Thankfully we were at the home of senior Elim mission workers Peter and Brenda Griffiths; old friends who were not expecting me to provide scintillating conversation over lunch.

Next morning I was well enough to visit the local doctor's surgery for a thorough examination, and go for blood and urine tests. More antibiotics were prescribed— this time for pus on the tonsils. Though I had no idea I could be a risk to anyone, I remember commenting that the young lady who took the blood sample should have been wearing rubber gloves.

Three days passed with Peter and Brenda. The cough and chest pain became much worse so the local doctor advised admission to hospital. An empty bed was found in St Anne's, Harare. While Peter rummaged through Brenda's shelves for a suitable nightdress and dressing gown for me to borrow, I rang my parents in England. About to leave for a holiday in Spain, they sounded really concerned and considered cancelling. Thinking they were overreacting, I persuaded them to go ahead as planned.

Back at the Mission prayers were said for me. Dr Roger

Drew, who gave treatment in the early stages, kept in touch with Peter by telephone. Tuberculosis or typhoid might account for my problems. When pneumonia was diagnosed, Roger became alarmed. He needed to visit Harare to buy some electrical equipment so he decided to check on me at the same time.

One morning, as a nurse helped me to bathe, I commented on my sudden weight loss. Two-thirds of the patients I cared for as Matron of the seventy-bed Mission hospital had AIDS. I had begun to look like one of them. The nurse made no reply, but must have said something to the consultant as he came to me requesting an AIDS test.

'It really isn't necessary,' I replied. 'During a visit home in 1990 I had a test, which was negative.'

'You could have become infected since then.'

'We've been careful to wear rubber gloves at work, sterilising them with bleach before re-using. There's been no unprotected exposure.' I thought of my young niece back in England, who organised a glove collection as a safeguard against AIDS infection.

'I'm afraid I must insist you take another test now,' he said firmly.

I had faith in Dr Wiles, and submitted. At least I would be able to prove him wrong.

My rough breathing disturbed some of the other patients. Moved to a side ward, I waited with Roger on Saturday 21st March for the results of the blood test for AIDS. For me there was no stomach sickening anxiety, as I was confident the result would be negative, even though the evidence was ominous. Roger had looked at my latest chest X-ray. It was very abnormal, and an accompanying report raised the possibility of sarcoidosis—a fleshy tumour. But why should someone like me, a non-smoker, develop such a thing?

Whatever the cause, my condition would soon begin to

improve, I told myself, and before long I would return to the demanding job I enjoyed so much. It was not to be. I was unaware that Roger already knew the worst. Informed the day before, he had been trying to prepare me to face the truth. Now Consultant Dr Wiles was coming towards us, the gravity of his expression warning that something was wrong. He looked down at the floor for an instant, hesitated, then looked me straight in the eye. 'You've tested HIV-positive.'

'I can't be,' I protested and demanded a retest, adding, 'I don't remember any needle-stick injuries. It must be a mistake.'

'I'm sorry,' he said, leaving me to come to terms with the shock and feelings of disbelief.

Peter Griffiths entered at that moment. It was quite early in the morning, but he had been waiting in the foyer at Roger's request. The three of us sat and wept together for ages. When Dr Wiles returned he said something of great significance, although it gave little comfort at the time.

'For you, Joy, the fact that you are HIV-positive is not a matter for shame, but for pride.'

'Yes,' said Peter. 'You have the virus only because of your calling and dedication to service.'

'You must realise you are seriously ill, and it's best that you return to England as soon as possible,' continued Dr Wiles.

'I'll make the necessary arrangements,' volunteered Roger.

'And I'll go back to Katerere with Roger and tell everyone at the Mission,' said Peter, ever the calm organiser, though he looked shaken.

Roger had a real battle to get me on a plane to Heathrow. Very politely he was told to delay travel until his patient was feeling better. Only when he spoke to the British Airways doctor in London, fully explaining the situation, did things begin to move. In the meantime I really appreciated the visit of a contingent from the Mission around my bedside. Emotions were running riot as we said our goodbyes. No one knew what to say; no words seemed adequate. Pastor Munembe was there, Mai Simango—who had worked closely with me in the Sunday school—all the national nurses, and Debbie.

After the others had gone Debbie stayed behind. Now she was telling me of her long-standing fears that I might have AIDS. Though I knew I would never work in Africa again, the full implications of my physical state had not yet struck home. As far as I was concerned I had contracted the HIV virus and developed pneumonia as a result. The fact that Debbie was talking about AIDS didn't register in my mind. That was one more hurdle yet to be faced.

Three days later, strapped to a stretcher and with an oxygen mask over my face, I made the ambulance ride from St Anne's to Harare Airport. Peter and Debbie were also in attendance, together with Roger, who was travelling with me. It must have looked a fearful scene to other passengers—like something from a television soap—but this was real-life drama. Some doubted I would survive the long journey. They were praying hard that life would still be present by touchdown and beyond, to Southampton General Hospital.

I slept most of the way while Roger watched the in-flight movie, *Terminator 2: Judgement Day*. Charity and mission workers normally take the cheapest seats. Due to my state of health we travelled First Class. Roger joked that he would be returning as baggage. Thanks to his diplomacy, no one on the plane or at Elim Headquarters was aware of the full story of my condition. I wanted my parents to be the next to know, and I wanted to be the person to tell them. When we were able to talk together their reaction

13

was strange, as if my words were fulfilling some kind of prophecy.

'We feel the Lord has prepared us for this. We're not at all surprised,' said Mum. At that moment all I wanted was for them to put their arms around me and hold me tight. I found out later that that was what they wanted too, but at the time it was difficult—I had tubes everywhere, and they didn't want me to break down and cry in case it restricted my breathing even further.

I arrived in England at the time of the Elim Pentecostal Church's annual conference, which was being held at Butlin's, Bognor Regis. Many members were following my career with interest. When those at the conference heard the latest news, which Roger had drafted into an official statement, 4,000 people rose from their seats, joined hands and prayed for me. I believe those prayers had an effect. After responding to treatment for pneumocystis pneumonia (PCP) I was well enough, a few days later, to address the conference via a live telephone link. The nurses were left wondering whether their patient was a new celebrity.

I began to feel more comfortable. Then, about three weeks after the initial diagnosis, the reality of my illness began to sink in. I had attended AIDS courses and nursed AIDS patients for four years. Only now did it dawn on me that PCP plus HIV-positive equals full-blown AIDS; a death sentence. Coming from a pentecostal background I automatically began asking God for healing, and questioned how I could have contracted the disease.

I still have no idea how it happened. There are theories about bleach weakening the protection of surgical gloves, and stories of medics becoming infected through body fluids splashing in the eyes. Or it could have been via my feet—in such sultry weather we were inclined to wear open sandals or flip-flops. There may have been an abrasion or cut on a toe . . . only God knows. In the end, no matter how much of a turmoil my mind and emotions might be in, I had to learn to leave the incident with the Lord, along with the subject of my healing. Otherwise I could forfeit my inner peace.

With the PCP sufficiently under control I became an outpatient at the end of April, under care of the Royal South Hants Hospital. Arriving home at my parents' house, a celebratory photograph was taken to one side of the car. I had gained some weight, but my appearance was changed. While in Southampton my hair started falling out, sometimes in large handfuls. Consultants advised that the HIV virus can cause this, but it also frequently happens to those who have had a serious illness.

One evening I was trying to wash my hair over the sink, but the hair loss was really bad. Heartbroken, I wondered if I would end up completely bald. My youngest brother Keith heard me crying. He came into the bathroom and gave me a lovely hug. I realised how fortunate I was to be within a supportive and loving family, when so many AIDS victims are abandoned by relatives and friends.

Roy, my eldest brother, and his wife Jacquie, made an appointment with a wig specialist in Swindon. I could have obtained a wig through the National Health Service, but someone wanted to make a gift, so I bought privately. The hairdresser was patient and professional, and the fitting was confidential, in a cubicle in one corner of the salon. Brushed into a style, the chosen wig looked wonderful. I walked out into the street feeling great, if a little self-conscious.

'Where is it then?' asked Roy, who had been waiting in the car park. 'Did you decide not to buy a wig in the end? Your hair do's very nice.' He was not just being kind, he really hadn't noticed. Several months later my own hair had grown back enough to leave the wig off. It was such a relief to go without it. Though no one ever knew my secret I felt vulnerable, especially when shopping on rainy days in Salisbury market. There was always the fear it might be hijacked by a passing umbrella!

My health continued to improve after being prescribed the drug AZT, though I was kept on the lowest dose to avoid becoming anaemic. A pentamidine nebuliser helped the PCP, providing a fine spray for inhalation. Apart from dry, mottled skin and periods of tiredness, few signs of a fatal virus were apparent.

'Why you, Joy? Your life's been spent serving God and helping others. Why should you suffer in this way?' When they learned I had AIDS, questions like this started coming from many people. I had no pat answers then, or now, but rest in the confidence that God never makes mistakes. He called me and promised to be with me.

2

For as long as I can remember I have wanted to be a nurse. Coupled with this ambition has been a keen desire to travel, inspired by tales of far away lands brought to my parents' home in Wiltshire by visiting missionaries. Pentecostal Christians do not exactly believe in predestination, but a pre-school photograph taken in the 1950s shows a budding medic in best uniform holding my favourite toy Topsy, a black doll.

As I grew up the longing to be a nurse remained, though there was no confidence I would be able to gain the necessary qualifications. The thought of entering my father's business instead, the greengrocery trade, did not seem anywhere near as exciting. On reaching the fourth year at secondary school I sat an English Language RSA examination and, to my astonishment, passed. This encouraged me to stay on a further twelve months. Then came a two-year pre-nursing course at Salisbury Technical College. I managed to get the necessary credentials and began training to be a nurse at Poole General Hospital in 1968.

Three years later, soon after passing finals and qualifying as a State Registered Nurse, I attended an Elim Pentecostal Church conference in Blackpool. Among those speaking at a missions rally were a number of workers from Rhodesia. My memory fails to recall the names and faces of all the speakers, but I remember that a lively young teacher called

Mary Fisher was among them. She sang two hymns as solos and had a fine voice and I thought she looked youthful for a missionary—about the same age as I was. I had no idea then that we would one day be together in the same compound, or that she would lose her life in a terrible massacre.

Someone was appealing for doctors to volunteer for service in Katerere, as a married couple who began Elim's work there were reaching retirement age. I thought, 'I could never be a doctor, but maybe they can use a nurse,' and made my way to the front. A number of young people were gathering near the stage to dedicate their various careers to God. When it became obvious that no one was signing up nurses I joined this group, saying a simple prayer.

At the end of the week I went home and began pestering the Almighty about future prospects in a more fervent way. No definite answers seemed to come from above, but Dad offered some divine inspiration: 'It wouldn't do any harm to qualify in midwifery. Surely they'll need those skills in any developing country.' I joined a class in Bristol.

About a year later, when the course had just ended, I received an unexpected visit from the local pastor. A member of the Elim Missionary Council, he had recently returned from a meeting where the Mission hospital in Rhodesia was on the agenda. Matron Joyce Pickering was now the only expatriate there, and desperately overworked. In a letter she had written, 'If you can't find a doctor, please send a nurse with midwifery training.'

When I heard of this plea I had a tremendous feeling of peace. Though only twenty-four and fairly inexperienced, I knew God was leading me out to Rhodesia. The minister went to great lengths to explain all the problems I could encounter. Others tried to discourage me, saying I should wait a few years. In my simple childlike faith I was sure that if this was my calling, God would not let me down.

Once I had said that I was willing to go, everything

happened very quickly, with departure fixed for the last week of July 1974. The weekend before there was a farewell service at the Elim church in Salisbury, where it was touching to see nursing friends as well as regular worshippers. As I had been a Sunday school and youth group leader as well as a church member, three official presentations were made. With each came a Scripture reading, prayerfully selected by different people. No one had discussed which verse to choose, but all were the same: 'Have not I commanded thee? Be strong and of a good courage; be not afraid, neither be thou dismayed: for the Lord thy God is with thee whithersoever thou goest' (Joshua 1:9, KJV).

A ripple of amazement went through the congregation. God was making it clear to me, and everyone else, that he was sending me in his strength. It was a wonderful confirmation.

Although it meant travelling on a weekday, the whole family hired a minibus to see me off at Heathrow. Several friends were also there. In those days overseas assignments could last for many years. No one knew for sure when they might see me again. It was a bitter-sweet occasion.

'I still don't understand why you want to spend your life tucked away in some foreign country,' sighed Pearl, my younger sister.

'It's the role I want, just as that is yours,' I said, patting her pregnant tummy. 'I'll want to hear all the news of my new niece or nephew.'

'We're all so proud of you,' cried Mum, hugging my neck one final time.

Less tearful, Dad was concerned for my safety. 'We always thought you'd make a good missionary. Do exactly as you're told by superiors and don't take any risks. There are rumours of discontent and guerrilla warfare.' Behind his words were many shadows. I told him not to worry.

From Salisbury, Wiltshire to Salisbury, Rhodesia.

Although the flight lasted sixteen hours, elation kept tiredness at bay. Descending the steps on landing, a surprisingly cold wind blew around my legs. I began looking around for Alan Renshaw, the mission worker who was to meet me. As I pushed my trolley along after passing through customs and immigration, a deep voice called out: 'Miss Joy Bath?'

I turned and saw a tall, thin man with wide shoulders.

'You look just like your photograph,' he grinned. 'We'll have some lunch first, before setting off for Katerere—it's nearly four hours away.'

Alan is a good talker and time went by quickly as we covered the journey of 140 miles, mostly on bumpy gravel roads. I was conscious of passing through acres of quiet, flat land with no one in sight, just tall grasses on either side and mountain peaks in the distance. Now and again there were a few round, brown thatched buildings grouped together.

'They're called *kraals* and are the homes of village people,' explained Alan.

'The large houses in the city looked very grand and European. These are more traditional, what Africa is really all about. But I don't see any animals.'

'Not at this time of day, it's too hot for them. You'd have to come out here at the crack of dawn, or last thing at night. Of course, there are plenty in the game reserves.'

We came upon the Elim Mission in a valley at the foot of a small hill. Around 5.30pm, just before nightfall, I met Joyce Pickering and deposited my luggage at her house, where I would live for the time being. A cheerful but no-nonsense Yorkshire woman, she gave the instant impression of being an extremely capable and practical person; reassuring qualities to find in a matron. Over a grand meal prepared by Alan's wife Anne at their home, in honour of my arrival, the four of us chatted about ourselves and my new surroundings.

'Our complex here is like a little bush town, sprawling over 100 acres,' said Alan. 'Apart from the hospital there's the main church, also serving smaller chapels in the area, and the secondary school, of which Peter Griffiths is the Principal. Most of the teachers are away this weekend at a Scripture Union camp.'

Anne cut in, 'There are limited shopping facilities for basic food and clothing, African style, and you can buy cooking utensils and the like round here. But nothing resembles Marks and Spencer.'

'Joy seems to have brought sufficient suitcases!' laughed Alan.

'Perhaps it's time we unpacked some of the contents,' suggested Joyce.

After helping to clear away the dishes, Joyce and I hurried back to her house to put some of my clothes on hangers. Electricity in the Mission compound came from a generator, which switched off towards the end of the evening. There was about half an hour of power left. As I went to bed that first night in Africa the air was full of unfamiliar noises, including the sound of drum beats in the distance. It was disconcerting to realise I could no longer reach for the light switch.

'What was all that going on in the middle of the night?' I asked Joyce the next morning.

'Nothing to worry about—just a religious sect a way off who hold all-night meetings.'

'It's Sunday tomorrow,' I ventured. 'There's church for us, I expect, with or without the teachers?'

'There certainly is, and you're the special guest! By afternoon the teachers will be back. Today I'll give you a tour of your workplace and show you the house that will be your own after decorating.'

Most of the buildings in the compound were framed at ground level by neat gardens edged with white stones.

Exotic fruit trees—lemon, grapefruit, passion, pawpaw and banana—stretched their branches above tin or thatched rooftops. The hospital seemed very different and strange at first. There were far more staff than I had imagined. Trained nurses wore white uniforms and starched caps, while unqualified ones had blue dresses with white collars and cuffs. They all looked clean and smart, and greeted me with a polite, 'Hello, Sister Bath.' I shook that many hands and heard so many names I thought I'd never remember everyone. It was several weeks before I knew each face and name, and could match both together.

The following day, as I walked down to the Mission church, I imagined my parents attending their morning service. I was asked to say a few words and saw before me a sea of black faces, all friendly and smiling. It was enough to dispel any homesickness. I noticed that men and boys sat apart from the women and girls. The right-hand side of the congregation was sparse, as most of the men were away working, only coming home for holidays. The girls had fascinating hairstyles. Many had braids starting at the roots, twisted into different designs with black thread.

Other early impressions still remain with me. Nursing mothers carry their babies with ease on their backs in a special cloth called an *inbereko*. A crying baby receives breast milk immediately, whether Mum is on her own or in company. Families have new babies on average every two years. Older children help in looking after infants, and it is common to see three-year-olds with tiny babies on their backs, jigging them up and down to stop them crying.

That inaugural Sunday afternoon marked the first of many weekly visits for tea with Peter and Brenda Griffiths. They had worked with the founders, Cecil and Mary Brien, so I asked about the early days.

'The story begins in South Wales, in general practice in a

22

small Rhondda Valley town,' started Peter. Knowing this was a long yarn, Brenda reached for the teapot to refill our cups.

'The Briens were considering their future careers, and Cecil drove to Swansea one weekend, to take advice from Rhys Howells, founder of the Bible College of Wales. He was told: "Return home, and do what the senior partner at the practice tells you." Before surgery opened next morning, the boss rebuked him: "This preaching of yours in the streets of the town on your afternoons off is unbecoming to a medical man. You should go to Africa as a missionary." So he did as the doctor ordered!'

'Just like that, eh! But how did the Briens know where to start?'

'They didn't at first. They began by getting some experience at an established mission on the Mvura Dhona range of mountains, overlooking the Zambezi escarpment in the northern border region of Rhodesia. There they both worked as medics, learned the Shona language, and saw many people become Christians. After a time Mary Brien felt God was speaking to her through the Bible. A few verses just seemed to hit her in the eye, as if they were highlighted.' There was a pause as Peter reached for his Bible and thumbed through pages of the Old Testament to read: '"And the Lord spake unto me, saying, Ye have compassed this mountain long enough: turn you northward . . . unto a land that I will shew thee. . . . And they departed from the mount of the Lord three days' journey" (Deuteronomy 2:2–3; Genesis 12:1; Numbers 10:33, KJV).

'Cecil and Mary prayed together, asking for God's guidance. They also wrote to a friend back home, the Reverend Leslie Green. He replied almost immediately, saying they must leave their present posts and join forces with an Elim minister and his wife at a church in Umtali.

Around then, a white Rhodesian in the congregation there had a strange dream, which he told to that same minister, the Reverend Jesse Williams. It concerned a group of Africans from Chief Katerere's kingdom, carrying empty pots, looking for water.

'The Briens obeyed their message, even though it meant going south rather than north, and on a journey of two days, not three. Travelling in their truck, they slept the first night in Salisbury's Coronation Park, then drove on towards the Mozambique border and Umtali. Jesse Williams told them about the dream, and how it related to a region north of Umtali, in Inyanga North, where no missionaries had ever settled. Cecil and Mary were convinced that this was the place for them. However, they had to wait a while for agreement from the authorities before setting off to work.

'In August 1951 they eventually journeyed a third day and reached the Gairezi Valley in Katerere, where the road literally ended. Driving between trees and rocks, they came to rest on the banks of the Manjanja River. Now this stretch of water was reputed to be evil, the name meaning "stream of the lion spirit". Pitching their two tents they set up home, later adding a mud hut which became the dining room.

'Immediately they began preaching the gospel to inquisitive tribesmen in the Shona language, referring to Satan as the evil spirit, who took the place of God in people's hearts. "Jesus, his Son, will give you living water," they cried. The message had instant appeal. A young lad, Rhinos Mukwewa, became the first convert in the area. He is now a teacher and a leader in one of the local fellowships.'

'An inspiring story!' I commented. 'But what of their progress in medical terms?'

'It began slowly, as the local people were suspicious of

foreigners when it came to healing, preferring traditional methods. The Briens stretched a tarpaulin from the end of their truck over a framework of poles, and started a dispensary. Then there were clinics, where the Bible was opened, the gospel read and patients prayed over before treatment was given. They described to me their first operation, a herniotomy, performed on a table by the light of a hurricane lamp held aloft by an African assistant. Mary, the anaesthetist, put the patient under by dripping ether onto a mask. A valuable microscope was kept steady on top of Mary's ironing board. And things which needed to be cool were placed inside an old safe and submerged in the river until required.'

'The water comes down from the mountains, and the supply has never dried up, even in times of drought,' added Brenda. This was testimony in itself to the fruitfulness of the site. Still, I was thankful that working conditions had improved considerably since then.

'The Mission as it now stands is the result of Cecil and Mary Brien's faith and hard work. Nowadays there could be up to 1,000 people in the compound at times, wouldn't you say?' Peter rounded off the intriguing tale with a look towards his wife, which was also a signal to fetch more tea.

Established almost a quarter of a century before my arrival, the Elim Mission at Katerere had become well-known for miles around as a centre for health and education. In spite of this, I soon realised that the local witch-doctors remained a problem for the hospital. Highly respected members of the community, they had a real hold on people.

It was still common for sick people to go to the traditional healer first. Only if there was no improvement would an approach be made to us, and by that time the patient could be at death's door. Roots and leaves of various plants do have medicinal properties. The problem is that in

Africa's long, dry heat these become concentrated, poisoning instead of healing; the equivalent of taking an overdose. We tried explaining this to relatives of patients, but they still had more confidence in their own ways than ours. Many people died as a result, especially children. Their small bodies are more vulnerable to toxins.

There were no strict visiting hours in the hospital. Relatives of patients stayed at the bedside all day, and often slept underneath at night, if home was a long way off. If a person was seriously ill, and there seemed to be no immediate improvement taking place, relatives would assume the worst, asking that the patient be allowed to go home. There they could die in their own surroundings, with traditional rites being performed. We would argue against this—particularly as a longer course of treatment could often save the life—but it was not unusual for patient and family to flee the compound.

In spite of such disappearances, the wards and out-patients' clinic always seemed to be full of people. We dealt with virtually everything from infectious diseases to broken limbs and accident cases. And there was never a shortage of expectant or new mothers with tiny babies requiring attention. Efficient and businesslike, Joyce was panicked by nothing and no one. At work she was firm to the point of appearing stern at times, especially with the staff. In leisure hours she was just the opposite, and full of fun.

It was a relief to discover that all the Elim workers there were ordinary people. In my mind I had the misconception that they might be super-spiritual beings, giants of faith. I came to the conclusion that perhaps the great Christian pioneers—the first disciples, Francis of Assisi, William Tyndale, the Wesley brothers, Billy Graham, and maybe even Cecil and Mary Brien—were somehow different from myself and my new friends. The former were brave innovators; we just carried on with the work.

I was frequently tired, but always happy. With any new job come the staging posts of initial unfamiliarity, the feeling that one cannot absorb any more facts, and the gradual regaining of confidence as tasks are achieved and skills mastered. Through all of these I remained in a positive mood, feeling my role was the realisation of so many hopes and dreams.

3

The year 1976 saw a number of comings and goings at the Mission, beginning with the arrival of the Evans family in the spring. Philip was a teacher and the new deputy head, and Susanne had secretarial experience, which was needed for Peter's office. With them came their three young children, Timothy, Rachel and Rebecca (although the eldest two were later to be schooled elsewhere). The newcomers arrived twice: the first time they were refused entry on landing, and directed back to England. It seems Phil annoyed the authorities by declaring he would be a conscientious objector in the event of a civil war. Peter Griffiths managed to smooth things over.

Brenda Griffiths was suffering from insomnia. When the school closed for the Easter holidays, Peter decided to combine a check-up at the doctor's in Salisbury with his speaking engagement at a Scripture Union event near Bulawayo. He was confident that Phil could manage things in their absence, but wavered in this opinion after a worrying conversation with a member of the security forces. The latter operated a camp a couple of miles away and it was normal to see army vehicles driving through the compound. This time they stopped, seeking out Peter to bring news that two bands of guerrillas had come over the border from Mozambique. Perhaps he should think again about the trip. There might be trouble brewing.

'Political activists, some said to be Communists and

based outside Rhodesia, are stirring the native people up,' Peter told Phil. 'There's been no activity around here so far, but last year the school was visited by two terror-ists—in civvies—as part of a general reconnaissance. They were members of the Zimbabwe African National Union.'

'But these boys may be from another faction. Whoever they represent, there's no guarantee they'll pay us a visit. And SU are expecting you—best not disappoint them,' Phil replied. So somewhat reluctantly Peter and Brenda put their things in the car and left.

The Renshaws and others were away on vacation. A single lady, Joan Caudell, was the only other expatriate teacher on site between terms. She was spoken to by a friendly contact in the security forces.

'The Avila Catholic Mission, not far from here, was entered by a group of terrorists,' she said gravely to Phil and Sue, relating the message. 'They were armed, and threatened people.'

'Was anyone hurt?' asked Phil.

'No.'

Peter and Phil had not told all of the remaining Eur-opeans about their misgivings, only Joyce, and Roy Lynn, our caretaker. Now Sue was party to the information, she had disturbing tidings of her own to add.

'I heard some of the African women talking this week. There are freedom fighters in the district. I didn't think anything of the conversation at the time. Could they be a danger to us? I'm scared.'

Oblivious to all this, I was very much enjoying the company of my parents, who turned out to be intrepid travellers. This was their first visit to Africa, and together we climbed the hill behind the Mission for a clear view of the valley. It stretches as far as the eye can see, with the mountains of Mozambique in the distance. While up there we found some primitive bushman paintings, which fascinated my parents. Then Mum's mood changed.

'There's a man behind us,' she whispered as we began our descent. 'I think he's carrying a rifle.'

I turned slightly. 'It looks more like a walking stick. But even if it is a gun, he's probably out hunting.' The man kept his distance and did not bother us, but Mum remained uneasy. When we got back I had a shift to work in the labour ward and forgot the incident.

Meanwhile, Joan had moved in with the Evans family so she would not be alone at night. Ian Smith, the Rhodesian Prime Minister, was giving an important speech on the radio. They listened intently as he declared that the country was in a state of war, a fight for independence. His words added to their fears and all three of them prayed for God's protection before going to bed. The children were already asleep. Not long after the generator went off, the household was roused by a group of men shouting revolutionary slogans.

I was now living in my own place. I had given my parents my bed and was in a small guest room. Exhausted after a long and happy day, I had fallen into a deep sleep. Dogs are a useful addition to any missionary household, and Sandy, my alsatian–labrador cross, was a good security guard, disposer of unwanted reptiles and alarm clock. He could be quite fierce, and his loud barking woke me up.

'Who's there?' I shouted through the window. Sometimes the nurses would come and ask me to go to the hospital in the middle of the night. I could see no torchlight, and there was no reply to my call. Disgruntled, I scolded the animal and went back to bed.

Meanwhile, although he had only been in the country for two months, Phil Evans was doing remarkably well in talking his way out of a life-threatening situation. Refusing to open the door, he communicated with the callers by an open window.

'We've had enough of domination by the whites! We are the freedom fighters!' they declared. 'The whites passed laws which don't apply to them, saying we can't have guns, and must carry identity cards. We refuse to have cards, but we will carry guns!' Their weapons were raised in the air.

'This is a Christian Mission and we don't want to get involved in any fighting,' reasoned Phil. Then, in a flash of inspiration, he told them the story of how he was turned back at the airport for being a conscientious objector. This seemed to please the visitors. They calmed down a little, and listened until he had finished speaking. Phil could see white teeth in the darkness outside as they nodded their approval.

One man was not smiling. '"Love your enemies", "turn the other cheek", I know these are the words of Jesus, who also threw people out of a temple—as we will drive out the whites from our country,' he said, with real venom. 'Now, give me your medicines so we can treat our wounded.'

Sue handed over a First Aid box and the guerrillas backed off.

'Be quiet, you noisy dog!' I called to Sandy who was still barking, and I rose from my bed a second time. Hearing voices I went outside, wearing only my night-dress, expecting to see a couple of nurses. From the garden path a group of people were visible, congregating under the large branches of what I called the flamboyant tree. One of the nurses was there, plus an African teacher. The rest were strangers, wearing camouflage battle dress and carrying machine guns.

The nurse was asked to go to Joyce's house, which was close to mine, and bring her out to join us. She arrived breathless, but not from hurrying. It was the only time I ever saw her unnerved. The spokesman of the military group introduced himself as a freedom fighter, before launching into a lengthy speech.

'Eighty years ago the whites came. African warriors fought brave battles, but could not win without guns. We have guns now. We will liberate Zimbabwe!'

'Down with identity cards! Down with Ian Smith!' they shouted in unison. 'Down with . . .'

'Yes, we understand,' I butted in impatiently. 'So if you've finished we'll go back to sleep. I've been delivering babies, I'm very tired, I have to be up early tomorrow, and it's cold standing out here.'

'We know you help our people, so you will not be harmed,' replied the spokesman. 'But I have many soldiers—more than these here—and they need medicines and bandages.'

I looked at Joyce. Did he mean the compound was surrounded?

'Can't you bring your wounded down to the hospital?' she suggested.

'No, we must not be seen by the security forces. Come.' He pointed the way with his gun.

'Please let me go indoors to put on a warm coat,' I requested.

'Very well,' he replied. The group waited while I fetched my dressing-gown.

Walking to the hospital, we were told the freedom fighters had already visited Phil and Sue's house.

'What about Roy?' whispered Joyce, but she was overheard. There was a murmur among the troops, then the African teacher spoke. 'They haven't bothered him, because they know he has a gun.'

Roy's house was a little way from the others. He was probably unaware of our predicament.

We gave them everything they asked for, with me all the

time grumbling that it was most unethical to supply medicines without seeing the patients. Just before they disappeared into the shadows I was asked if we had a two-way radio.

'No,' I answered truthfully. Neither did we possess a telephone.

'If you tell the security forces about us, we will come back and kill you,' they warned. Then they were gone.

Joyce was shaking like a leaf. I suggested a cup of strong, sweet tea at my house with Mum and Dad. My parents! In the commotion I had forgotten they were there. Hearing the dog bark, they assumed I had been called to attend to a medical emergency. Dad needed rest and was asleep when we arrived back. At the start of their stay he had been disturbed at night when rain leaked through the thatched roof onto his side of the bed. Mum was wide eyed and worrying. A kind of sixth sense mothers seem to have told her something was wrong. As soon as I started relating it all to them, Mum remembered the man on the hill with a gun. Was there any connection? I didn't know.

When I was face to face with the freedom fighters I was not afraid at all. In fact I was indignant that they had come at night and woken me up. It wasn't until I started explaining what had happened to Mum and Dad that I began shaking all over. It was as if something clicked within me, and I realised Joyce and I had been in a very dangerous situation. If the terrorists had been drunk, or if they had taken offence at our words, they could have become angry. Who knows what they might have done to us?

I needed to read something from the Bible to calm my nerves and Dad's copy was handy. It was a Gideon publication, so he looked in the front index, where readings are listed for life's situations. Under the heading 'Where to find help when in danger' was Psalm 91. I took the book to read aloud, but became too emotional to continue. Dad carried on at verse 5: ' "Thou shalt not be afraid for the terror by night; nor for the arrow that flieth by day." ' The whole psalm was so appropriate. After a time of prayer together we all retired to our beds again. Mum, Dad and Joyce lay awake for the rest of the night. I slept like a log until morning, comforted by those words.

The next day we expatriates left Katerere for Salisbury, in several vehicles and at different times, so as not to arouse suspicions. Roy Lynn returned to keep an eye on things after escorting Joyce to safety. With hindsight I can see that it was unwise of us to up and go, but we were all inexperienced and nervous about the consequences of the nocturnal visit. Had we known our African co-workers better at that time, we would have realised they could be trusted. If we had confided in two leading pastors, Pious Munembe or Ephraim Satuku, they would have led us to make the right decision. The nationals could not understand why the missionaries had left so suddenly. This caused a slight distancing of relationships. I feel we failed them badly.

The guerrillas who had come to the Mission were cornered by the security forces a few days later. A number were killed, and the rest arrested and taken to Salisbury to stand trial. We all met for a conference to decide the future, and voted to return. The single ladies would be allowed to be in their own homes during the daytime, but would stay with the families at night. When Joyce or myself had to be on duty at night, one of the men would accompany us to the hospital and stay there until the work was done. This was tough on them as we could be up for hours, especially if there was a complicated birth happening. Also, the mosquitoes had a good feed as our protectors read by flickering lamplight to keep themselves awake.

The security situation began to deteriorate. Not many days would pass without us hearing of landmine explosions or encounters between terrorists and the authorities. However, all through the war no violence occurred within the Mission compound. It was as if all our prayers for peace in the midst of the hostilities were answered. Perhaps the surrounding circle of freedom fighters had been replaced by invisible angels.

One Sunday I returned from church and was cooking lunch when through the kitchen window I saw army vehicles arrive at the hospital. A civilian lorry had been blown up by a landmine and there were casualties needing immediate attention. The soldiers explained that there were no army medics in the area, so they had come to us for help. Peter took me to the scene with an African nurse. We travelled in convoy in his Peugeot 404. It was all right to be seen sandwiched between their trucks, but to sit with the security forces would lead people to believe we were taking sides.

By a little bridge near Kajozo an ancient five-ton truck was smashed and lying on its side. The driver was breathing his last. Nearby was a young man, moaning loudly. We parked some distance away in case the weight of the vehicles set off more mines, and walked back to the horrific scene. Behind us, the soldiers were watching the bush, guns at the ready, expecting attack at any time.

I ascertained that the man who was moaning had cracked ribs, and moved on. A young mother lay dead on the ground, with her tiny baby still at the breast. It was unhurt, though in need of nourishment. The slogan 'breast is best' is so true in developing countries. Feeding bottles are a death sentence if sterilising fluid cannot be bought, or incorrect proportions of milk and water are mixed. The water must be clean too. I wondered how this little ebony cherub was going to survive without a mother.

Another woman, still alive but unconscious, needed help first. Both legs were broken and bent the wrong way up

35

from the shins, like a rag doll. Ants had already started to burrow into wounds around her heels. Scooping them out, we patched her up as best we could, putting on splints and setting up a drip. A man with a deep leg wound also required a drip. He had lost a great deal of blood. We gave injections of morphine to those who were in pain.

The casualties were taken away by helicopter, which made two trips and could not stay long in the area for fear of attracting the attention of guerrillas. I handed the infant to a rather juvenile co-pilot. He didn't seem to know how to hold a baby, so it was a new experience for both of them. As the chopper took off for the last time the pilot shouted, 'The doctor sends his compliments to the sister for a first-class job!'

The whole thing was a dreadful experience, especially for Peter, who was unused to seeing mangled bodies and had nightmares for months afterwards. We received feedback that everyone except the young man was doing fine. I was wrong about him and he died. He had a ruptured spleen, not cracked ribs. But at the time I examined him, his condition did not seem critical. Generally the person who is able to cry out is usually the least injured.

God works in mysterious ways. It might have been Phil Evans lying there. An hour earlier that Sunday morning he was driving the Mission's two-ton truck along the same road, with a group of churchgoers as passengers. Before reaching the bridge he mysteriously lost control of the wheel and slid off the road. No one was hurt.

On Tuesdays it was my habit to drive to a village called Kambudzi to hold a clinic. When Pastor Munembe told Peter that the place had become unsafe, he came to discuss the matter with me.

'I want you to make the final decision, but I advise you to

36

discontinue working there for the time being,' he frowned. As he stood before me I thought hard.

'Peter, those are poor and deprived people, in desperate need of medicines. I'll carry on running the clinic if you'll come with me.' He agreed, and became quite a useful form-filler in the process, while I carried on with the nursing.

During the first journey we anxiously scanned the road ahead for any signs of landmines, not realising we had already driven over one. We only became aware of it when an army truck behind us exploded. Thankfully the vehicle, unlike ours, was heavily reinforced. The only injury was to a trooper who was blown clear. He had landed on his rear end, damaging his coccyx.

At least one highway, to the district administrative centre at Inyanga, began to look like the lunar surface, with deep holes everywhere. Every so often this fifty-five-mile route was littered with debris, marking the sites where military vehicles had been blown apart. It was time to take certain precautions with our travel. The school lorry carried sand bags on the back and the tyres were filled with water. The Mission truck was fitted with metal plating. For the hospital, a hardy Rhino was purchased; a Land Rover ambulance offering more protection beneath our feet than most standard models. It was open at the top, until a tarpaulin was added, and looked like a white bath tub on wheels, with a red cross painted on each side.

We were instructed only to journey outside the compound by these specially adapted modes of transport, and not to venture out after dark. When going to particularly sensitive areas I had to wear a crash helmet and put cotton wool in my ears. Seat belts had to be worn on every trip. As the war intensified we had to contend with ambushes as well as the possibility of being blown up.

Peter was having a time of prayer and meditation one day when he felt compelled to read the biblical account of Ezra.

Part of the story concerns a journey to Jerusalem, past enemy lines. Ezra was too ashamed to ask the king for bodyguards, having previously declared, 'The hand of our God is upon all them for good that seek him' (Ezra 8:22, KJV). So he set off without a military escort, but arrived safely, reporting, 'The hand of our God was upon us, and he delivered us from the hand of the enemy, and of such as lay in wait by the way' (v 31).

Later on, I burst into Peter's office somewhat distraught, with a plea for help. 'I've a patient in labour who may need a Caesarean and can't be treated here. This is her tenth child, and the previous pregnancies have weakened her, so the uterus isn't contracting as it should. It may rupture. With a younger mother I could try fixing up a drip containing a drug to encourage the contractions. But I daren't risk it with this one.'

'Are you saying she has to be taken to Inyanga now?'

'That's right.' I was amazed by Peter's unusually calm manner. Night was falling. He knew the risks.

He said, 'Don't mind me sounding a little righteous, but God gave me prior warning of this. We have his permission to break the curfew.'

We went in the two-ton truck, with the patient and a relative lying down in the back. None of us dared speak for several miles and the silence was eerie. Coming onto the brow of a hill, my heart jumped. Fires were spreading across the valley below.

'It's nothing to worry about,' reassured Peter. 'They're just burning off the stubble in the fields—farmers do it every year about this time.'

Of course! I should have known that, coming from the West Country.

The journey was completed without incident and the woman taken to a government doctor.

Peter was required to report to the police station,

saying where we had come from, and giving the name of a hotel where we would spend the rest of the night.

'You were lucky to get through,' remarked the duty officer. The Principal of Elim Secondary School rose to his full, bantam height, determined to give credit where it was due.

'No, the hand of our God was upon us,' smiled Peter rather sanctimoniously.

4

'If any of us are killed in a landmine explosion, will we be classified as martyrs?' The question was hypothetical and said partly in jest, as a group of us met to talk about writing our wills and leaving instructions for funerals in the event of death in service. I felt I would rather be buried in Rhodesia to keep the costs down.

Suddenly, the blades of several helicopters whirred overhead. Choppers were landing in the compound. We rushed out to see what was happening.

'Civilian casualties, in shock, with minor injuries—nine young girls!' shouted a member of the security forces. 'We attacked a rebel camp, not realising they were entertaining their girlfriends.'

Joyce immediately sprang into action. 'Move the male patients into one ward to make room,' she ordered some junior nurses. Then she and I began giving the most badly shocked girls intravenous fluids. But we couldn't find any veins. Having worked in operating theatres in the past, Joyce had seen plenty of varicose vein surgery.

'I need to do something called an intravenous cut-down,' she explained. I marvelled as she made deep incisions around the ankles of two girls, in each case managing to find a vein.

Within a couple of days all the girls were feeling much better. They seemed popular, receiving visits from a number of smartly dressed young men. Later I heard that these were their boyfriends—rebels who had survived the attack. If the security forces had realised what was going on, we would have been in trouble for fraternising with their enemies.

Around this time road travel became so dangerous that Elim turned to the Mission Aviation Fellowship for help. Once a month a government doctor flew out from Umtali to an airstrip near Katerere. Leprosy sufferers received treatment close to the runway, before he made his way to the hospital to see any patients Joyce and I were worried about. Meanwhile the pilot was unoccupied.

On one occasion the doctor examined a physically small girl, who was due to give birth to her first baby. He confirmed our fears that a normal delivery would not be possible, adding, 'Sister Bath, Matron and I can manage without you for a time. Take this patient to Umtali in the plane. You'll be back before I've finished here.'

It was a windy day and the little Cessna was tossed about like a leaf. In addition, the pilot made swerving man-oeuvres to avoid being sighted by terrorists. Some of them now possessed ground-to-air and heat-seeking missiles. The expectant mother had never been in a plane before and was terrified. I tried to reassure her, and held her hand most of the way, but was feeling green with travel sickness myself. We deposited her safely at the hospital in Umtali and had an uneventful return trip. To quell my nausea I tried to concentrate on the view, picking out landmarks. The white stones bordering Katerere's brown plots and pathways looked like rows of white teeth around open mouths, beckoning hungrily from below. A dentist's nightmare! Still, it was good to reach *terra firma* again.

The curtailment of journeys by land was unhelpful to Joyce's personal life. She and Roy Lynn were in the early stages of courtship and needed to spend time alone together off site, so they could become better acquainted.

Joyce did well to maintain a professional coolness at work, but I detected a warm glow around her whenever the likeable little Irishman was around. Roy was slightly disabled and walked with a limp. By way of compensation he'd been blessed with good looks and the gift of the blarney. Through knowing him Joyce had mellowed, and there was a spin-off into our relationship.

Joyce and I began to pray together regularly for the African nurses. It was her idea. 'Perhaps it will lead them into deeper spiritual matters,' she said hopefully. Although many were Christians they seemed oppressed by the war waging all around us. Some had reverted to carrying pagan charms for good luck. There had even been tentative enquiries about the end of the world coming soon. We decided to invite them to an evening meeting about the power of the Holy Spirit. Attendance was not compulsory, and the staff dining hall provided a non-threatening venue.

Almost everyone not on duty turned up to hear what we had to say. Joyce was about to start speaking when someone appeared in the doorway. There was an emergency in the labour ward.

'I'll go,' I volunteered, rising from my seat. The message of Pentecost would have more clout delivered by the Matron. Joyce opened her mouth to protest, but I was out of the room before she could say anything.

A couple of hours later a transformation greeted my return. Worried expressions had become wide smiles on glowing faces. Eyes shone and voices were lifted in praise to God. Even the room's atmosphere had changed. Many were sitting in small groups and from their lips came the gentle murmuring of different languages. People were speaking in tongues for the first time!

'The Holy Spirit has come,' sighed one of the ladies contentedly.

'Yes, and I haven't led this kind of meeting before,' beamed Joyce, with tears of happiness in her eyes.

I owned up, 'I'm glad you did, because I wouldn't have known how!'

Peace and joy flowed from that meeting, permeating every corner of the hospital for months to come. Only after Joyce and Roy became engaged, and she left on furlough to prepare for the wedding, did things sour. But the events were unconnected. I thought it was my imagination at first—paranoia brought on by extra responsibilities. Or could it be that some of the nurses were standing around gossiping about my marital status? Perhaps, like me, they were wondering whether a husband was going to appear on the scene. Eventually they came to see me *en masse*.

'We want more money,' said a spokeswoman.

I explained that they were all due for a rise in salary at the end of the following month.

'*I marii*—how much?' she asked. No one was impressed by my reply.

'That is too little,' said a second girl, while another threatened, 'We want more, or we will not stay here.'

'I'm seeing *mufundisi* Griffiths later. I'll mention the matter to him.' Sensing the group was becoming hostile I edged away, while agreeing to take the matter higher.

I was actually going to Peter and Brenda's for supper. When I arrived there they could see I was upset and were very supportive.

'The management committee, which takes advice from Africans, has overall responsibility for salaries. If the staff are not happy they must make a formal complaint,' said Peter.

'I think someone from outside's been causing trouble deliberately,' suggested Brenda. 'You know how Peter McCann is constantly losing things? Well, the other day

43

the boy who works around the house went to fetch fire-wood, and hasn't been seen since!'

This raised a chuckle. Bearded and bespectacled, Peter McCann looked every inch the absent-minded professor. As a science teacher, he could not be faulted. In everyday living he was a complete scatterbrain, testing the patience of his wife Sandra to the absolute limit.

Brenda went on, 'It would seem the lad's been press-ganged into joining the freedom fighters. There've been a number of similar disappearances.'

'War is always hardest on civilians,' mumbled Peter Griffiths, momentarily becoming eight years old again and reliving German bombing raids on Swansea.

'There are staff problems at the school too,' said Brenda. 'The Renshaws are returning to Britain when their current contract ends. They have a number of family commitments to sort out.'

'But Catherine Picken is coming back here to teach English and sport,' replied Peter, returning to the present. 'She's been away looking after her elderly mother since before you arrived, Joy. And you'll not have to manage senior hospital duties alone for much longer. Wendy White will soon be here.'

After the meal I walked away from their house with mixed thoughts and feelings. The Renshaws were leaving. I would miss their cheery faces and helping hands. I pictured Anne Renshaw fitting Staff Nurse Evelyn's ample curves into a stylish wedding gown. An altered seam here, a pressed hem there, and a lovely head-dress of fabric flowers. The effect was topped off to perfection by a dainty parasol. Anne is like a fairy godmother to African brides. Over the years she has persuaded more than a score of Elim women in Europe to turn out from storage their precious white dresses, lying unused, and donate them to mission stations. Evelyn was marrying Pious Munembe and, as

44

with most converts, wanted a white wedding 'like the English Christian girls'. Her chief bridesmaid looked lovely in a long dress loaned by myself.

That was my first experience of an African wedding and it was a day to remember. After a moving service, the reception was held outside the church. There was much singing and dancing in the hot sunshine. The guests sat at long tables and enjoyed a cooked meal of chicken served in a tasty gravy with the staple grain *sadza*—a versatile maize, on this occasion made into a kind of porridge. I was amazed that there was enough food to go round as it is not customary to send out official invitations for such events; the cooks just have to guess at how many to cater for. Every guest gave a present and the master of ceremonies shouted out what it was. This was followed in each case by applause and cheering, with traditional '*Rrululul!*' shrieking sounds, made by rolling the tongue. The whole process took several hours. Finally a family Bible was presented by Mai Satuku, in a flourish of low bowing movements.

Immediately after her wedding Evelyn became Mai Munembe. *Mai* is a respectful title for older women, who are generally always either married or widowed. The nearest word in English is 'Mrs'. Spinsters like myself, who are old enough to be married but aren't, pose a problem. There is no word in Shona to describe us. By default I have been addressed as *Mai* on many occasions.

I began to think about the new nurse coming out from England, Wendy White. Older than me, she would probably be called *Mai* as well, though she was single. I was looking forward to having an extra member of staff. But Wendy was newly qualified, a university graduate and social worker who had decided to switch careers in midlife. There would be a lot for her to learn about coping with limited resources and facilities. Would she be capable,

45

and willing, to take orders from me, a younger woman? I dearly hoped so.

A crowd of memories and expectations raced through my mind during the short walk to Phil and Sue's place. I was resident there at nights with Joan Caudell. It was surprising to see Sue outside the house with a bundle of something in her arms. I quickened my pace as it had started to rain. Sue was carrying a load of firewood, and I helped her inside with it. She explained how, like the McCanns', her hired help had also gone missing.

'I do hope those two haven't got themselves into any trouble,' she fretted. I watched as she shook her long brown hair loose from a pony tail. It was quite wet from the rain. Then she busied herself around the kitchen, sorting a pile of Becky's clothes for mending.

'You look really at home here, Sue,' I said, remembering how she had suffered from culture shock after arriving in Katerere.

'Oh, I am. Phil has always fitted in, but it took me a few months to carve out my own little niche. Now we're both sure this is the right place to be. We'll sit tight and ride out the storm, however rough it gets.' She referred simultaneously to the war and the downpour happening outside. The seasonal rains had come.

Three disturbing incidents shook morale at the Mission over the next few weeks. Everyone's faith and staying power were tested. In the south of Rhodesia an armed African in military uniform robbed a Catholic bishop and nun before shooting them dead. A second nun, who was able to hide, escaped detection and gave the authorities a description of the roadside attack and the attacker. In another part of the country a Catholic priest left his house to lead a service, but never arrived at the church. A search revealed no body or clues as to his whereabouts. Then, at a place called Musami, in the direction of Salisbury, seven Catholic mission workers were murdered.

It was with great trepidation that, a few days after this last event, Peter and Brenda Griffiths met Wendy White at Salisbury Airport. They felt duty bound to brief her on the latest developments in the war, giving her the option to back out at the last minute.

'The situation has become much more dangerous,' cautioned Peter. 'For the first time expatriates have been killed. We'll understand if you want to change your mind and return to England.'

The slim, elegant woman listened to what he had to say. Smiling graciously, head tilted to one side, she replied, 'It would take more than that to keep me from the Lord's work.'

Members of the Mission team were not prone to gossiping about one another, but everyone agreed that having Wendy around was like working with royalty. She was an exceptionally devout Christian, while at the same time being a lady from the upper classes: well-bred, well-spoken and schooled in social etiquette (an unusual and rather intimidating combination). She came with excellent references and was a good nurse, but had the annoying habit of always being right.

Shortly after Wendy's arrival I took her off compound to a baby clinic. Heavy rains had reduced the bush roads to rutted tracks of squelching mud, several inches deep. It was hard to drive the Rhino in such conditions. Even on dry roads strength and skill were needed for this vehicle, as the metal reinforcements had raised the height of the steering wheel. One almost had to stand upright to reach it. Consequently, I asked a male handyman—one of Roy Lynn's African assistants—to drive us to Chiwarira that day.

On the way back it began to rain heavily. When we reached a river bed that was normally dry, it had become a mighty rushing torrent. The driver stopped before attempting to go further. Should we wait for the flood to subside, or try to drive through it? Not wanting to be the one to make the decision, I left it to him. 'We'll go on,' he said, biting his bottom lip and looking rather worried.

Halfway through, the engine spluttered and stalled. We were stranded in the middle, and could feel the force of the brown flow buffeting the Rhino. The armour plating was watertight, but we began to move downstream.

'Help us, God!' I cried.

'We should praise the Lord,' declared Wendy.

I thought, *That sounds very good and spiritual, but what can we be happy about at a time like this?*

As if reading my mind, she said, 'Believe he is going to save us, and thank him in advance. Remember, "Faith is the substance of things hoped for, the evidence of things not seen"' (Hebrews 11:1, KJV).

We praised the Lord in English and in tongues for what seemed like a very long time. Mostly I didn't know what I was saying, but my heart was telling God that I didn't want to die yet. Nor did I appreciate his sense of humour in sticking me in a makeshift boat with Mary Poppins.

The water level appeared to be dropping. Trapped by mud, the Rhino halted. The driver rolled up his trouser legs, climbed out and waded to the bank. He reached it safely and waved to us before running off to fetch help. We were quite close to the Mission, so it wasn't long before he came back in a truck with Roy. They towed us out of the river and home to Katerere. Still the Rhino refused to start. Roy had to strip the engine right down in his workshop, to clear out the debris, before it could be used again. He was not amused.

I regularly wrote letters to my parents containing news of my experiences. They read the dramatic details of this account to my paternal grandparents and the facts were changed down the line. The next thing I heard was, 'Joy was sailing down the river and came face to face with an angry four-legged Rhino!'

In the meantime Peter Griffiths was in hot water with the security forces. Despite the numerous military skirmishes around the Mission, we believed we could continue our work through a policy of neutrality. The previous year we had had no choice but to hand over medicines when the freedom fighters visited. Since then, Peter had been contacted by guerrillas and had not informed the authorities. As a result he was arrested and found himself in court. His defence was as follows:

'News went along the grapevine that we were using vehicles which were reinforced against landmines. One of our ministers received a message, saying some guerrillas wanted to talk with me, and that I should preach at Kambudzi Church the following Sunday and await further instructions there. I was also told to take a collection among the teachers and bring the proceeds with me, to show good faith towards the rebels' cause. I took the service and afterwards shook hands with people at the door, as is our custom. Nothing unusual happened. I was just about to leave when Pious Munembe—the pastor, and headmaster of the local primary school—said there was a teenager waiting for me in the vestry. The young man had a note from "the comrades", telling me that he would guide me to them. When Pious heard this, he offered to go too.

'The three of us travelled in the cab of my truck for a couple of kilometres, until the lad said it was time to stop. We went on foot into the hills. Arriving at a clearing at the top of a slope we saw two sentries with automatic weapons. Then we came across a platoon of about a dozen armed combatants. I shook hands with them, greeted them in Shona, and went to sit down on the ground. Their leader told me to sit on a blanket, which I saw as an encouraging gesture.

49

'We were questioned for about an hour, mainly about why we had reinforced our vehicles. They saw this as a sign that we did not trust them to warn us if and when they planted landmines. I said that without a doctor it was sometimes necessary to rush patients off to Inyanga in the middle of the night, when there was no time to wait for warnings. They accepted this explanation.

'I suggested that if we stayed there much longer the security forces might spot my truck at the side of the road, and investigate. The platoon commander asked if I had brought the money from my teachers. I said that if I had asked for money, they would have become upset and might leave the school. Then it would have to close. However, I had brought $100, which came from the school funds. But this left me with a problem. How would I account for the missing money? As a Christian I could not lie, and neither could I enter into my financial statement, '"Gift to the comrades."

'Pious seemed to get a little nervous at this point, exclaiming, "Give them $50!" One of the combatants, who had been sitting on a tripod-mounted machine gun, came to the rescue by saying, "If he can't fiddle the books for $100, he can't do it for $50 either!" The commander seemed to understand, and we were allowed to leave without making a contribution.'

Pious backed up Peter's account, but the prosecution still wanted to know why the meeting had not been reported. Peter admitted he was guilty in this respect, but replied, 'Because I feared retribution on myself, Pious and the teachers. If that happened the school would be finished.' The court was lenient and Peter was freed. This time.

No one wanted to close the school or hospital. Both were providing vital services to the community. Yet we worried about what the authorities would do if the guerrillas made contact again. Then came a devastating blow which caused an urgent reappraisal of our whole position. The five-ton lorry, which was a lifeline for Mission supplies, hit a landmine on the way to Salisbury. Although heavily reinforced it was a complete write-off. The driver injured his back, and the man next to him—who was not wearing a seat belt—plunged through the windscreen and was killed. Another passenger lost a leg. Suddenly the reality of living in a war zone came too close for comfort. The vehicle was needed daily for bringing 1,000 meals to the school. The hospital sometimes used it for transporting large quantities of medicines and equipment. A replacement would be costly, and what if that were blown up too, with further loss of life?

Peter Griffiths was head of the Mission team, but the most senior Elim official in the country was Ronald Chapman, at Umtali. He attended a conference in Katerere with all of us, to discuss the future. Most were totally unprepared for what he had to say.

'Eagle Preparatory School is on the market for rental. It's in an area where there's been virtually no terrorist activity—the Vumba district—only a twenty-minute journey from Umtali. As Field Director for this part of Africa, I propose the secondary school moves there from next term.'

'That's a radical suggestion,' voiced Catherine Picken. 'What about the rest of the pupils?'

'The primary school mainly consists of day children and local teachers. It can remain where it is—there's no sense in uprooting people unnecessarily.'

'Brenda and I have been here about fourteen years, and are soon to go on furlough,' said Peter. 'I think this is the time for Phil to take over as Principal of the secondary school.' Phil looked at once pleased, unworthy and embarrassed. He began fiddling nervously with his spectacles.

'And the hospital?' I shrieked, the high tone of my voice reflecting the anxiety I now felt.

'It can become more of a clinic, run by less experienced nurses who live around Katerere. I understand Evelyn Munembe has sufficient qualifications to take overall responsibility?' Mr Chapman's eyes were staring into mine, demanding an answer. When I didn't give one, he continued, 'It may be the time, and God's will, for expatriates to step back and relinquish some of the work to capable, indigenous leadership. Not only at the hospital, but in the churches too.' He looked around at the collection of glum faces.

I found my voice. 'Yes, Evelyn would be an excellent choice. Wendy and I could . . . ?'

'No definite decisions can be made today. Approval will have to be given by Elim Headquarters at Cheltenham. However, the secondary school will need a nurse cum matron.'

'And a caretaker.' Roy Lynn entered the conversation. 'Joyce and I will be married by then. She could look after any sick pupils.'

Joan Caudell was also going on furlough. For her the choice was simple: she wouldn't be returning in the autumn. It was mooted that Wendy should fill the gap. She seemed very distressed at this idea, saying that while her degree qualified her to teach, God had called her to medical service. 'I'll have to think and pray about all this,' she scowled.

'And what about me?' I asked, almost in tears. Again Mr Chapman looked me full in the face. It felt as if everyone was staring at me, waiting for him to speak.

'You've been here almost exactly three years. Perhaps it's time to look for another position.'

5

Over the following weeks Wendy and I had a lot of heart-searching to do. The unexpected blow we had both received formed a common bond between us. Secretly we prayed that the proposed changes would be blocked by Elim Head-quarters, and for a while it seemed as if the favour would be granted. Before his wedding to Joyce in Yorkshire, Roy Lynn represented Katerere Mission at an Elim Council Meeting. The members were unwilling to sanction the splitting off of the school from the hospital. However, it was agreed that their representative, John Smyth, would travel to Rhodesia to assess the situation.

By the time he arrived Wendy had made her peace with God. 'If the decision is made to move to the Vumba, I will take it as the Lord's will for me to go there. After all, I am qualified to teach English and History,' she told me.

'At least you've had some choice as regards your future,' I replied bitterly. Wendy shot me a reproving glance. Still feeling hurt and angry, I could reach no such plateau of acceptance that my first overseas assignment was coming to an end.

When John Smyth saw how things were, he began to realise it was in Elim's best interests for the school to be sited elsewhere. Individually we were all given a chance to say what we felt, before coming together to hear the verdict. The earlier recommendations were confirmed. I had no option but to obey orders and start packing for home. I was heartbroken.

Before the August holidays a second-hand lorry was obtained to ferry load after load of furniture and non-essential goods to Eagle School. On about the sixth trip it hit a landmine. Thankfully, no one was hurt. The engine was destroyed and the cab windows were blown out, but the rest of the vehicle and its contents remained intact. A breakdown truck arrived, complete with military escort, to tow the lorry to Umtali. Unfortunately the driver was none too careful on the dirt roads. Probably driving too quickly in order to get out of the danger zone, he rolled our lorry and did what the landmine had failed to do, completely destroying it and the load.

At the end of term, three buses came to take the boarders to Umtali. From there they would travel back to their homes. About fifty miles down the road the first bus hit a landmine. Two students, Leonard and Daniel, were killed. A third boy, Jotham, lost a leg. Terrified, the remaining youngsters clambered onto the other buses. The second one arrived safely, but the third bus hit another mine and caught fire. Everyone was able to escape through the windows, which had blown out in the explosion. The driver was the only fatality. For the final clearance of essential equipment and personnel the services of a furniture removal firm were hired, protected by a heavy military escort.

A few days later Mary Fisher and I started a memorable holiday in Durban, South Africa. We seldom saw the sea as Rhodesia was land-locked, and we really appreciated a fortnight spent largely on the beach. While we were relaxing in the sun, our peace was shattered by the tragic news of a huge bomb exploding in Woolworths in Salisbury. Eleven people were killed. How long could this carnage go on, we wondered?

Mary was apprehensive and nervous about teaching in the new location. Her large eyes opened even wider in anticipation, as she described the whereabouts of Eagle School.

'It's very close to the Mozambique border. A beautiful setting, high up in the mountains, where the climate is cool and damp—*Vumba* means misty. The tourist guide books liken the area to England's Lake District.'

'Better take your wellies, then,' I advised. Having Mary around was good therapy. Her incessant chatter helped me to come to terms with the fact that I was leaving. And she was such an innocent it was impossible to hate her for having a job I couldn't do for lack of the right qualifications.

To have another string to my bow would prevent me from being in this kind of difficult situation again, I considered. After completing my midwifery course I had toyed with the idea of going to Elim Bible College. Now the opportunity presented itself again. I took this as the way forward and, back at the Mission, enrolled by post for two years of theological study.

Then it was time to say *chisarai zvakanaka*—goodbye— to Rhodesia. I arrived home on 25th August 1977, to be met by a crowd of family and friends. Three years had passed since I'd seen most of them, and everyone was talking at once, trying to tell me something different. A niece had been born to me via Pearl, and here she was, Charlotte, already walking and attempting to join in the conversation. Travelling back to Wiltshire in the church minibus, I did my best to catch the excitement of the moment, but I had a throbbing pain in my head, and ached all over.

Mum had prepared a huge spread for the whole family. I just wanted to have something to quench my thirst, and then go to sleep. The following day I felt worse and had a high temperature. The doctor was called, and he prescribed

55

antibiotics. It was thought I might have flu. Somehow I managed to get to the hairdresser's, and then went on to a big homecoming celebration at church. Attendance was mandatory as the Mayor and Mayoress of Salisbury were guests of honour. Afterwards I collapsed into bed and stayed there. Four days later jaundice started to make itself evident. The doctor came again and hepatitis A was diagnosed. It took a number of weeks to recover, which made me late starting at Elim Bible College.

The two years spent in residence there in rural Surrey were of tremendous benefit in many ways. My relationship with God took on a new dimension. At that time the college was housed in an old mansion at Capel, set within large grounds. There were plenty of places and opportunities for private reading and contemplation. Good thing too, as I had to share a room with three and sometimes four other students.

Settling down to full-time studies was not easy. I found it difficult to concentrate, and the long hours spent poring over books resulted in eye strain. In addition, there were practical jobs for students to do. At first I was on the cleaning rota, which meant one work period before breakfast and a longer session each afternoon, vacuuming long corridors. I hadn't regained my strength from the hepatitis and by the end of each day was completely exhausted. Later I was given lighter duties serving in the dining room, for which I was grateful.

Fellow students didn't quite know how to treat a real live missionary. Some tried to put me on a pedestal, or treat me like a china doll. Determined to show I was normal, I went out of my way to be involved in as many pranks as possible. Water fights and dunking people in baths of cold water soon showed them my true colours.

I was surprised to find little zeal for overseas mission among the theological students. A conversation with one young man left me particularly disturbed. His main objection was that in the middle of the jungle there would be nowhere for him to go for dental treatment if he developed toothache. This seemed a worrying lack of faith and common sense in someone training to be a pastor!

There were a number of foreign students at Elim Bible College then, including a white South African, and black Africans from Kenya and Guinea Bissau. During the holidays it was possible to take one or two to my home. It was fun for them to meet the family and learn Wiltshire English. When winter came they were fascinated by snow— something they had not seen before. One even went outside to roll in it.

As the temperature dropped and strong winds blew around Capel, I reluctantly put away my cotton dresses and brought out thick wollens which hadn't seen the light of day for four years. Still it seemed unbearably cold. Then someone had the bright idea of placing polythene sheets over the windows—a primitive form of double glazing which effectively cut out some of the draughts.

Peter and Brenda Griffiths returned to England shortly after me. It was to be a period of study leave, so that Peter could complete a post-graduate degree. The three of us met at Heathrow to see the Lynns off. Joyce's parents were also at the airport to say farewell. They were concerned for the well-being of their daughter and new son-in-law, even though Eagle School was thought to be in a quiet area, safe from Rhodesia's warring factions. Roy's expertise was badly needed for maintenance work. Joyce would conduct clinics locally when her medical knowledge was not required by staff and pupils.

A selfish little voice inside me was saying that I should be on the plane too. I tried to ignore it. The pair looked so happy and right together. Something Joyce said gave me a hint that she might be pregnant. It was odd that they went through the departure barrier without looking back for a final wave or glance. Peter noticed this too and remarked on it.

I didn't see him or Brenda again until Saturday 24th June 1978. A Midsummer Day etched in my memory for all time. But I was aware that Peter had been sent back to Rhodesia in the spring for a few days, as there were fears of unrest in the Vumba district. On his return, he told me by letter that everyone was happy and wanted to stay at the new site, where they were at least safe from the threat of landmines.

He wrote: 'We came to the firm conclusion that as the school and the young lives in it were important for the future of the country, the work must continue.' Roy—who had experience of living in the strife-torn areas of Northern Ireland—was adamant that 'mission workers just can't keep running away'.

However, the murder of two Salvation Army teachers working in the country, plus a series of anonymous threatening notes sent to our personnel, persuaded Headquarters at Cheltenham to instigate further changes. Elim International Missions Director Leslie Wigglesworth instructed Ronald Chapman to ensure that non-African staff left the school after lessons each day. Accommodation was to be found within the urban safety of Umtali.

The last Saturday in June was Elim Bible College Open Day and Graduation Day for final year students. Peter was to give the address, and planned to speak on the true story of a group of missionaries in Ecuador who were murdered by Auca Indians. Late morning I was busy with last-minute cleaning jobs. A voice came over the tannoy, 'Will Joy Bath please report to the Principal's office.'

I had no idea why I was being summoned, but hurried along there. When I entered, the room seemed full of members of staff and foreign students. The atmosphere was tense and people were looking around nervously. One or two were crying. Wesley Gilpin, the Principal, welcomed me with a nod of his head. Then he began to speak.

'I have to tell you all that a dreadful massacre took place last night in Rhodesia, in a remote region near the Mozambique border. I don't have all the details yet, but it is suspected that the victims were our mission workers.'

My initial reaction was one of peace. It couldn't possibly be my former colleagues, because they had gone to live in Umtali, only commuting to Eagle School during the day. But over the next few hours, as information filtered in from Ronald Chapman and various news networks, it became clear that it was our people. Their belongings had been packed into cases, and the workers were scheduled to move into new homes the following morning. Instead, as dawn broke, their dead bodies were being discovered on a grassy bank near the sports field. The attack was so violent that some were almost unrecognisable.

By the cricket scoreboard lay a mature woman with dishevelled clothing, including a yellow cardigan. In one hand was clutched a matching scarf, which she had intended to put over her greying hair to conceal the fact that she was wearing curlers. A long-handled axe was embedded in the back of her head. Catherine Agnes Picken: an overseas veteran with eighteen years of fine service to her credit. She first worked in the Belgian Congo in the 1950s, but left there because of ethnic troubles.

A young man wearing a trendy purple sweater and trousers was found with his hands tied behind his back. His face had been split open. Philip George Edward Evans: BSc, Phd. Two weeks earlier a premonition had prompted him to send an album of precious family photos to his mother for safekeeping.

The face of another man had been bludgeoned by a piece

of wood. But his beard was still visible. Peter McCann: BSc and former student of Elim Bible College.

Spread-eagled on the ground was a woman in a blue top and slippers, her left arm stretched out towards a tiny baby. Eileen Joyce Lynn: SRN, midwife and newly delivered of her own child, Pamela Grace. How often I had watched and learned from our resourceful Matron, a cheeky lock of dark curls poking around the side of her cap as she worked. Her hair was now matted with blood, and beside her the daughter born just three weeks ago had been bayoneted to death.

A few yards away a man in a checked shirt was found, horribly mutilated. Robert (Roy) John Lynn: an Elim Bible College graduate. His eyes had apparently been gouged out, and his body was riddled with knife marks. The man who had refused to run away from trouble had been stabbed in the back at least fifteen times.

Then there was a group of two women and three small children: Susanne Eugena Mary Evans with Rebecca, who was four-and-a-half years of age; and Sandra McCann with her son Philip, aged five, and daughter Sharon Joy, four years old. All had been beaten about the head viciously. One of the youngsters had the imprint of a boot on her face. The mothers also had bayonet wounds around the neck, and were naked from the waist down.

Under a tree in a nearby copse a young woman in a denim dress, with long dark hair, was huddled in a foetal position. Elisabeth Wendy Hamilton White: SRN, BA, Dip Soc Stud; daughter of a supermarket magnate and granddaughter of the man who pioneered the Mersey Tunnel. Her murder was possibly the most gruesome. She was severely beaten, and bayoneted in the head, neck, chest and groin. That would probably be because she angered her captors by telling them about Jesus. Eloquent Wendy would not have gone down without a verbal fight.

There was one piece of good news. Mary Fisher: triple graduate of Swansea, Brunel and London Bible College, was still alive! A trail of blood led the security forces to a patch of long grass, where she had run to hide. Unconscious and hypothermic, she was rushed to hospital in the capital and placed in intensive care.

Twelve martyrs, and one brave soul fighting for her life. What kind of mindless beings could have sent my guileless friends into eternity so brutally? Whose politics could demand the savage crushing of young skulls, the raping of women and little girls? And why did no one come to their rescue? For some time I was too shocked to cry—my emotions were kept at bay by a questioning mind. I needed to know more.

It transpired that a large group of guerrillas had attacked the school after supper on the Friday night. Some gave the pupils a talking to in the dormitories, while others herded the British teachers out of their houses at gunpoint, to a quiet spot. The noise of the killings, away from the buildings, failed to reach the ears of a South African teacher, Ian McGarrick, who was in his room marking examination papers. It was he who made the grim discovery of the corpses early on that Saturday morning.

By early afternoon my mother arrived at Capel. Though deeply distressed, she kept saying, 'Thank God you weren't there! You're safe!' This finally brought out my grief. The two of us collapsed into a heap and cried for several hours.

The formalities of the day went ahead, but even now I wonder how Peter managed to stand up and speak. The main theme of his talk remained the same: believing in Christ is no insurance policy against death through missionary activities. Only the names of those who died were changed. Instead of mentioning Americans, his words were of our own dear folk.

Many memorial services were held over ensuing

weeks. And one verse from the Bible was repeated again and again: 'Except a corn of wheat fall into the ground and die, it abideth alone: but if it die it bringeth forth much fruit' (John 12:24, KJV).

Suddenly, the Elim Pentecostal Movement was at the centre of world events. British and foreign governments, Ian Smith, and leaders of other churches, were all discussing the massacre, adding to the already substantial amount of media coverage. The publicity resulted in many hundreds of volunteers coming forward for overseas service. If interest in missions was lax during my first year at Elim Bible College, the situation was totally reversed after the events of 23rd June 1978.

Tragically, Mary Fisher never regained consciousness and died in hospital. This brought the total number of martyrs to thirteen. People began to remark on how my life had been spared. Was it for some special purpose? I didn't think too much about it then. I never thought my lot would be to go through a different kind of martyrdom. My thoughts and heart were directed towards the families and relatives of those who died. In particular Timothy and Rachel Evans, who woke up one morning at boarding school to find they were orphans. I was only made redundant from my job. They had suffered a much greater loss.

6

What next? Towards the end of year two at Elim Bible College I was interviewed about my future plans. The Missions Board would not consider a return to Rhodesia. The situation was still dangerous. But there was an opening at a small clinic in India, with scope for gospel ministry. It was mine if I wanted it, but I wasn't sure. My feathers were still ruffled from the pain of being told to leave Katerere. And the loss of my friends weighed heavily on my heart. I thought and prayed about the offer for some weeks, before finally deciding to accept it.

On 11th July 1979 I found myself at Delhi Airport, being met by the small, motherly figure of Olive Jarvis. There were people everywhere, making a lot of noise as they went about their business. I could hardly hear what she was saying for the constant hubbub of excited voices—absolute bedlam. An overnight stop in a hotel provided some peace and quiet. Then it was back into the crowds again and on to the railway station for a 600-mile train journey to the state of Bihar.

Our compartment was full to overflowing, with bodies pressed together on all sides. Some alighted at each stop, but they were replaced by more people getting on the train. It was extremely humid. Such air as there was contained pungent smells. Though I had done my research and knew the population of India totalled over 700 million, the reality of being confronted with a large, jostling portion of humanity was claustrophobic.

It was impossible to avoid making comparisons. Africa is a continent of contrasts—luscious foliage or sun-bleached grasses; modern cities versus wide open spaces. Tribesfolk are distinguished by different physical characteristics and forms of dress. To my untrained eyes everything in India just seemed brown. From the houses to the burnt sienna dust of the roads and railway tracks. The people were mostly the same colour brown and as the majority were poor, so were their once bright clothes: browned with age and accumulated dirt.

Olive watched my reactions with a bemused expression on her face.

'This is the main train route to Calcutta, so it's particularly busy. Bihar is one of the most densely populated places in the world, and one of the poorest areas of India. I've been out here for twenty years and have grown used to the way of life.' There was a pause as the train halted. Vendors with grubby fingers pushed baskets and trays of refreshments through the open windows.

'Be careful what you eat and drink,' she advised. 'You could easily pick up a tummy bug. Even the bottles of water with screw tops probably aren't safe—they tend to fill them in the river.'

I wasn't tempted. Both food and liquid were brown too.

We were based at Dehri on Sone. A tiny, typically Indian town, without street lights or pavements. A high wall surrounded the only church and we went through large iron gates round the side to our single-storey house. It was divided into two: one part belonged to the Indian pastor, the remainder was shared by myself, Olive and a third worker, Sylvia Beardwell.

The house had few amenities. Electricity was fitful and often went off, or was too weak to be of any use. We

64

frequently resorted to candles or paraffin lamps. Running water was only available at certain times of the day, otherwise it meant a trip to a hand pump in the yard. Even when the water came on it was always cold—there was no hot.

We did have a nice walled garden, full of flowers. From it went a raised pathway through paddy fields to the dispensary, our place of work. This was also surrounded by a high wall. The place was primitive. Just one room divided into two was used for consulting and giving out medicines. Opposite was a shelter where women and children waited to be seen.

For cultural reasons it was not possible to see men. And we could only treat minor ailments as there was no doctor or equipment for anything else. Coughs, sores, impetigo, scabies, ringworm, diarrhoea and ear discharges were common. The patients were very poor, in various states of distress and illiterate. We had to find a way of keeping them in line or the last would push to the front and an uproar would result. A system was devised so the first ten who arrived were given blue cards, the next red and so on, to ensure they waited in order.

Usually the clinic was finished by midday. In the afternoons it was necessary to rest, due to the heat. But in the evenings we sometimes went out on visits, or else I would keep busy with language study. What a triumph it was to master the alphabet! Without it I couldn't even board a bus unless I asked someone for its destination—and most people didn't speak English. The first hymn I learned in Hindi was 'How great thou art'. It was very popular at that time, and sung at most meetings.

Sylvia was younger than Olive, but both ladies were quite a bit older than I was. In Rhodesia the expatriates formed a closely knit community and I enjoyed friendships with a variety of age groups. Here there were just the three of us foreigners, apart from a Scots lady who also resided in the town. Living so closely together, personality clashes and differences of opinion due to the generation gap would erupt now and then. I realised it was important to put things right as early as possible, before they were blown out of all proportion.

Olive was very kind and patient in helping me to adjust to my new environment. Diminutive but businesslike, Sylvia undertook to educate me in cultural matters. I believe this exercised her mind as well as my own.

'The reason we see so many ear patients is close breeding,' she told me one day. 'There is a social structure of castes. The main ones are *Brahmin*—the priests and their families, *Kshatriya*—warriors, and *Vaisya*—merchants. The three are not supposed to mix. Officially, discrimination is banned in this country, but it's part of Hinduism to stay within one's caste, and as most Indians follow that religion, marriages happen within family groups.'

'Aren't some people outside the castes, for example the Christians?'

'Yes. The tribal people tend to be Christian or Muslim. The *Harijan*—the untouchables—are technically the lowest caste, but many have become Buddhists. Sikhs have their own ways and customs, and would like to have their own independent state. They form a very small part of the whole population and are mainly found in the Punjab, to the north west, on the other side of Delhi.'

I found all the Indians intelligent and hard working; even those begging on the streets. But there was a gap in their mentality when it came to crossing social barriers. Not long after that lesson from Sylvia, I saw the dead body of a man lying in the middle of a Dehri on Sone street. It remained there for several days and was decaying by the time a member of the same caste came to take it away.

Some people might liken this situation to the story of the Good Samaritan. It reminded me of one of the opening scenes of a film, *The Magnificent Seven*. An outcast had died, and someone provided a coffin, but the undertaker and his men were too scared to take the body away for burial. They feared they would be shot by racially prejudiced townsfolk. Enter the Christlike hero Chris (played by Yul Brynner) and another brave soul called Vin (Steve McQueen). They drove the hearse, dodging bullets and shooting back at their attackers, until they reached the cemetery gates. A stirring moment in the history of moving pictures.

On another occasion I saw a man severely beaten by way of religious persecution. It stands out in my memory, happening in a land where all beliefs were supposed to be tolerated. However, at Christmas a subtle form of intolerance was shown towards Christians. Buying cards with a nice message was not easy, as most didn't mention the actual festival. Probably the makers were trying to avoid using the Lord's name. 'Season's Greetings' was the norm.

Carol-singing was popular with young church members. A group would set off after dark, cycling around the town and stopping at Christian homes. After singing they would be given food like sweet meats or *samosas*—triangular pastries filled with good things—before moving on. There was much merriment, and the visits went on late into the night. Christmas Day was a public holiday, but as most shopkeepers and market stall holders were Hindus or Muslims, it meant business as usual for them.

The climate was very unkind in Bihar. Summers were too hot and dry; the monsoon season was too hot and wet. With the rain came clouds of mosquitoes. My legs were always covered with bites. Winter was a welcome respite. The only complaint was that it didn't last long enough—only for about four months and then it was back to the burning heat again.

It was a relief to spend our holidays at a hill station.

There we had the company of other mission workers, and I spent a few hours each day at a nearby language school. The station was really a spartan cottage, with limited bathing and toilet facilities. We stayed there for about six weeks each summer to avoid the worst of the heat. In the hills the temperature stayed a little cooler, but not much.

To reach the station took a whole day. It involved a train journey, followed by a hair-raising ascent up a zigzag road in a taxi with bald tyres. I closed my eyes so as not to see the sheer drop either side of the steep track. Vehicles could only travel so far, and the last part of the climb had to be made on foot, carrying luggage and all. Once we arrived, it was necessary to fumigate the premises; rats having been the only occupants since our last visit.

Becoming more proficient in Hindi meant I could take on a Sunday school class at Dehri Christian Church. It was fun and when words failed me, actions and visual aids were used to get the message across. Compared to English children they were extremely well behaved.

I also began venturing out to see needy families on my own. A Muslim man was employed to look after the garden and drive our rickshaw—a three-wheeled bicycle with a seat at the back for passengers, and a hood to keep off the sun or rain. Once, on the way to a village, he turned off the main highway onto a side road, pedalling fast.

'Help!' I cried, as I fell out and landed on my head in a ditch. Hearing footsteps, I expected the rickshaw *wallah* to come and pull me out. But he just paced up and down the road until I hauled myself up. It was a long wait, as I suffered slight concussion and felt very dizzy.

'Why didn't you give me a hand?' I demanded angrily.

'It is not the custom for a man to touch a woman,' was the reply. Then he admitted sheepishly, 'But I have done another kind of wrong. I knew there was a problem with one of the wheels before leaving Dehri.'

When we arrived at our destination some villagers kindly made me a cup of tea as I was still giddy. And I was supposed to be ministering to them!

The visit of a delegation from Elim Headquarters caused a lot of excitement. John Smyth and David Butcher flew in from Delhi to a domestic airport. Olive and I went to meet them in a jeep with a hired driver. At some point on the way there the horn failed, so on the way back we stopped at a garage to get it fixed. While no one seemed to check on tyre conditions, it was illegal to drive without a horn. In India you need the horn all the time. We were certainly glad to have it working later on in the journey.

Ambling in the middle of the road was a herd of elephants. Not wild ones, but transport animals for wealthy people. The passengers were sitting on top. A keen amateur photographer, David Butcher gleefully reached for his camera to catch the unusual sight on film.

'We pose for you,' volunteered the elephant handler in Hindi. He seemed an obliging sort and the passengers were good natured, so John Smyth and I also took some snaps.

'You're very kind. Thank you. Enjoy the rest of the trip,' I said as we prepared to leave. At this, the handler began to get agitated. Arms waving in the air, he ordered the elephants to kneel down, completely blocking the road.

'I don't think they'll move unless you pay him!' laughed Olive.

She was right. We tried blaring the horn for some time. The noise attracted quite a crowd, but the elephants stayed put. We had to give in and pay up before we were allowed through.

The presence of the two visiting pastors meant evangelistic meetings could be held in Dehri on Sone. The Indian minister didn't do much in that line, and as the culture held no great respect for women, Olive, Sylvia and I were restricted in what we were allowed to do.

'We three are absolutely powerless!' moaned Sylvia during a private meeting with John Smyth and David Butcher.

'We're certainly not using the full range of medical and theological training we possess,' I chipped in.

'All we can do is pray,' said Olive.

The pastors agreed and we took time to bring the matter before the Lord in prayer.

Unbeknown to us, God was calling a man from South India—Augustine Jebakumar—to begin a major work in the North. The first we knew of it was when he arrived at Dehri on Sone with a small group of workers, including two young women. They said they were called the Gospel Echoing Missionary Society, GEMS for short, and began working within Dehri Christian Church.

Talented and enthusiastic, they were like a breath of fresh air through the district. Unfortunately, the staid members of Dehri Christian Church felt rather intimidated by their presence. In addition, jealousy developed over funding obtained from overseas for evangelistic campaigns.

God does not only use Christians in the furtherance of his work. A *Brahmin* lady was so impressed by the GEMS that she gave them five acres of land as a gift. It was in a country area, with plenty of room for expansion. The team moved out of town and set up on their own. One of their young women left to be married and I made a real and lasting friendship with the remaining girl, Jeya. We became like sisters. It was great to have someone of my own age to relate to.

After being unwell for some time, Sylvia was sadly diagnosed as having cancer of the bladder. She was flown home to England as treatment in India was difficult to obtain. I was working more and more with the GEMS team and feeling that was where the main thrust of my work should be. It made sense for Olive and me to close the dispensary and join the GEMS at their base. They had started an orphanage, and were about to open a school.

A number of business people had approached the GEMS requesting that a mission school be set up. Standards in government and private schools were poor and it was generally accepted that mission schools provided a high standard of education. Augustine asked if Olive and I would be willing to teach. As nurses we had no experience or qualifications to be school teachers, but no one seemed to mind. I became a teacher of English and Environmental Science, learning how to teach from books. The children were lovely and well disciplined. I felt fulfilled and really enjoyed the experience.

Two pieces of advice I still remember from those days are: real teaching is guidance—helping a pupil to find the answer themselves; and if a lesson hasn't gripped the teacher, it won't interest the child!

Once again, political events had a hand in changing the course of my life. In 1984 India's Prime Minister, Mrs Indira Gandhi, was assassinated by Sikh extremist members of her bodyguard. All foreigners without visas were ordered to leave. That included me. It was a hurried departure, but I believed that obtaining a visa was just a formality.

'I'll soon be back,' I told Jeya confidently.

'I'm not so sure, my friend,' she replied. 'Getting official papers sorted out can be a slow process at the best of times. Now the country is in mourning . . .'

Indians can be highly emotional people at times. I decided this was one of those times for Jeya, and chose to ignore her forebodings.

Once home I made an application to the High Commissioner of India in London, requesting a long-term visa. It was refused. I appealed against the decision, backing up my case with letters of recommendation from influential people in India. I never received a reply.

As time went on it became apparent that I was not going to be able to get back. I took a Teaching English as a Foreign Language course in London, and then a short course on tropical diseases in Liverpool. After this, as I'd been out of full-time nursing for ages, I joined a nursing agency in Salisbury, Wiltshire and for a year eased myself back into my favourite profession.

'I don't know where I'm heading, but I don't think I'll ever be returning to Africa,' I told a friend. The reply was, 'It's best to pencil in your plans for the future. Then you can always rub them out if God has other ideas.'

7

With the spring of 1987 came an unexpected summons to Elim Headquarters at Cheltenham. Brian Edwards had become Director of International Missions and was eager to meet with me. I had assumed he had in mind a general chat about my situation, but it wasn't long before the conversation with this tanned, rather suave man began to centre on Katerere.

'A lot has happened in nine years, Joy. Life in independent Zimbabwe, as the country's now called, is very different.' I nodded in agreement. He went on, 'Under a new government the health service has developed, and that is good. In practice it means more primary healthcare, ante-natal clinics and infant vaccinations. There's also an emphasis on family planning, and attempts are being made to curb the spread of AIDS.'

Leaning forward in an animated manner, he started tapping one end of a ball point pen on the desk. 'Staff at the Elim Hospital are run off their feet serving a population of about 60,000. Apart from the national workers there are currently three Brits there—a doctor and two nurses. A third nursing post has just been made available via the authorities. Can I put your name forward?'

Of course I said, 'Yes!' It was more than I could ever have hoped for.

After all the formalities were completed I flew out to South Africa in July, to be met by Peter and Brenda

Griffiths and their two sons. From there we travelled to Zimbabwe, with hardly a silent moment passing between us. I had a lot of catching up to do.

'Salisbury is now Harare, Umtali is Mutare, and Inyanga is Nyanga,' chanted the boys in unison.

'Katerere's stayed the same, in name anyway,' laughed Brenda.

The family had returned to Africa, so that Peter could resume his important work of helping to educate young minds.

'The last time we met was at a youth camp on the Isle of Wight,' I reminded him. 'Not long after the massacre.'

'Yes, let's fill in a few gaps. After coming out here to help prepare for the funerals, I spent some time arranging for the transfer of students to other schools. Although secondary school places were at a premium at the time, people were sympathetic. Places were found for all 300 children, albeit scattered throughout the length and breadth of the land. Splitting them up was providential. Many were able to start Christian groups in schools where none had existed before. But that's not all. Do you know of a lady called Janet Cunningham?'

'Vaguely. Didn't she start an organisation for women?'
'Yes, Homemakers. Well, she invited me to speak at a combined meeting of several groups of Homemakers on the subject of forgiveness. This had become a controversial issue since the media quoted various Christian relatives of our dead colleagues, speaking of forgiveness for those who murdered their sons and daughters. You see at the same time, the average white Rhodesian was crying out for revenge.'

Brenda took up the story. 'Peter was due to fly back to England the day before the meeting. He said he couldn't attend. Then Janet spoke to him again, and the next thing I knew, he'd delayed his departure by two days. She must be a persuasive woman!'

'Ah, but it was the right decision,' emphasised Peter. 'In my talk I pointed out that whatever we think about the idea of forgiveness for murderers, Jesus prayed that those who crucified him would be forgiven. Although we may not be murderers, we are all sinners, and all need the forgiveness of God found only through the cross, when we repent and call out to Jesus to save and forgive us. I made no sort of emotional appeal for people to commit their lives to Christ, but did point out that anyone interested in becoming a Christian could leave their name and address in a book after the meeting.'

'Did anyone?' I asked.

'Yes. Six ladies.'

There was some significance in the number six. Up in the Vumba mountains, God had allowed six grown women to be martyred and find entrance into his heavenly kingdom. Now I was hearing that after the very first external meeting since the massacre where Peter was able to speak of God's offer of forgiveness in Christ, six women had come forward. A shiver went down my spine.

As we came nearer to the Mission memories came flooding back and I went quiet, trying to control my emotions. A few obvious changes had been made, like new houses for staff, but no extra buildings had been added to the hospital. There were still some members of staff I remembered from before and I was amazed how the lilting Shona language all came back. Nurses who didn't know me had quite a surprise when they realised I could understand their conversations.

Dr Adrian Smyly was a primary healthcare specialist. He put a lot of effort into building up the preventive healthcare services to the community. More baby clinics were established and called ZEPIs (Zimbabwe Expanded Programme of Immunisation). They took place in fifteen different locations, including Nyamombe Refugee Camp, a two-hour drive from Katerere. Ante-natal and post-natal care were introduced at the ZEPIs, using the back of a Land Rover ambulance as an examination room.

It was marvellous to see the improvements in healthcare. In the 1970s we had treated sick children every day of the week, but other services were only available once a month. Now parents could bring their children from Monday to Friday for weighing, vaccinations, and treatment if they were sick.

A real bond of friendship and teamwork developed quickly between myself and the other two expatriate nurses Debbie Brown and Bobbie Marcus, the Matron. Evelyn Munembe had given up full-time work in order to have a family, but she was still active in the community whenever possible.

The days were busy and happy, like those during my first term of service before the civil war. If my thoughts strayed too much towards the massacre, there was always some job or other to be done around the hospital to occupy the mind. I wouldn't admit it, but I was putting a lid on deep emotional hurts.

Before returning to Zimbabwe I told a friend who is a journalist, 'God has forgiven the murderers, so I must too. I feel no bitterness towards them.' I meant what I said, but when the words came out in print and I read them, a great gaping sadness welled up inside me. Every now and again, during quiet moments, those words would come back, echoing around my head.

In June 1988 Mary Brien visited the Mission. Her husband had passed away, so she came as far as Nyanga with a nephew, before being collected by Bobbie Marcus and a group of ladies from the church. They travelled in an open pick-up and we heard their approach from some distance—

the ladies were singing a song of welcome with great gusto. People came running to the vehicle to greet her.

She was with us for five days, and from the time of her arrival until the time of her departure there was a constant flow of Zimbabweans waiting to see her, singing to her and bringing gifts. On the Sunday morning the church was packed with people wanting to hear her speak. She was an octogenarian, but had plenty of energy to stand and preach the gospel, and she gave an appeal at the end. It was a real thrill—for her and the expatriates—to see so many men respond. Some had made commitments years ago, but had grown indifferent. Others made a stand for Christ for the first time that morning. After the service a party took place outside the church. Representatives of various chapels and groups in the area sang songs and gave their appreciations to her.

I know it is wrong to put people into little boxes, but I marked Mary Brien down as being an old school type; a woman with a strong personality and full of determination. She was staying at Bobbie's house and had problems with the door keys. On finding herself locked in, she was seen climbing through a bedroom window one morning at 6am. Nothing was going to prevent her from joining the nurses for early morning prayers!

Any antagonism I felt towards Mary Brien was undoubtedly due to the fact that she had sussed me out. Somehow, she knew I needed healing from memories surrounding the massacre. We didn't talk much, but she urged me to pray in the manner of her late husband, 'Lord, help us to live in the light of eternity.'

Then it was the tenth anniversary of the massacre. Bobbie and Debbie were suggesting a trip to the Vumba. It was rare for all three of us to have days off together. Oh, how I tried to avoid going, and how glad I was afterwards that I went with them. Sometimes one has to be dragged out of the past in order to face the future.

Each of us had a profoundly moving experience as we stood by the graves of the martyrs. The plots are marked by simple white crosses and surrounded by specially planted jacaranda trees. An eerie stillness pervades the clearing, though it is a beautiful resting place.

Suddenly the silence was broken by the sound of violent sobbing. I realised it was me. At first it was as if someone else was crying and I was an onlooker. I sank to the ground. Cradled in the arms of my friends, there came a point of owning emotions I had suppressed for so long. A part of me had died and was buried with the victims. I needed to grieve.

When I was all cried out, the three of us stood and praised the Lord for bringing us together to work in Zimbabwe. In turn we rededicated ourselves, declaring our commitment to God, whatever it might mean. Then we sang two hymns: 'Here I am wholly available' and, remembering Mary Fisher's voice on flexidisc, 'For me to live is Christ, to die is gain'.

We turned to leave and Debbie remarked, 'They weren't so much heroes as those who simply believed they were called to do a work, and to carry on doing it until told otherwise.'

Bobbie was frowning, 'In my book that's exactly what heroes are.'

The scene from that old Western flashed through my mind's eye once again. 'They were our magnificent thirteen,' I mumbled.

Feeling fresh and clean, I fell silent on the way back to Katerere. I was thinking of some of the great paradoxes of the Christian life. Of Stephen, the first Christian martyr, who, although young, had an amazing ability as an evangelist, only to suffer death by stoning when he was being most effective for God. And James, who, as one of the inner circle of Jesus' disciples, received special revelation and training, only to be killed most brutally by Herod. Even more puzzling was the fact that after Herod arrested Peter, he was rescued by miraculous intervention, only to die for his faith later in Rome. I wondered why his life was spared on the first occasion.

I had been hearing rumours for some time that the man who led the rebel attack on Eagle School was now a Christian. There was formerly no desire within me to investigate the matter further, but the healing experience by the graves had stimulated my curiosity. At a convenient moment when visiting Peter Griffiths at home in Harare, I asked if he knew anything.

'Oh, plenty,' he said, with a mysterious smile on his face. 'I've been waiting for you to say something, but you weren't ready before.'

'Is it true?'

Peter nodded. 'The man, Gary Hove is his name, attended a Bible college here in the city. He wants to be a preacher.'

'You've met him?'

'We've had several chats. I'm sure his conversion was real.'

Peter went on to tell how, one Sunday morning just after Independence, Gary Hove was reading a newspaper in his room at an army camp in Bulawayo. His eye caught sight of an article in bold type, which commenced with the words 'Dear Comrades . . .' in bold letters. It was actually a paid advertisement inserted by a missionary called Margaret Lloyd, telling of the love of God towards everyone. Then it described the conversion to Christ of a Cuban Marxist called Raphael. At the end was a PO Box number.

'Gary read the piece aloud to some of his buddies. They

were all angry that a comrade, albeit a Cuban, should become a Christian. It was decided that Gary should write to Margaret, inviting her to meet all of them so she could answer questions about the Christian faith. This was a ploy on their part to lure her to the camp and kill her. The letter was written, and Gary put it into the thigh pocket of his fatigues.' Peter demonstrated the movement with his own hand.

'Walking to the mail box in the camp, his hand went to his pocket. The letter had disappeared! He couldn't remember exactly what he had said before, but he hurriedly wrote a second letter. By reply, Margaret sent some Christian literature and a Bible. He not only read what she sent him, but also began to visit churches.'

'Hungry for God,' I asserted.

'One night, back at the barracks, Gary and his friends shared a strange religious experience—a vision—in which they all saw a cross. Then Gary alone saw the hand of God coming down, as if in judgement, to smite him. He cried out to God for mercy, and asked to be saved from his sins!'

'Incredible!' I exclaimed. This was some story. 'It's just like Saul of Tarsus, who tried fervently to crush the early church, only to find Christ himself, and to become Saint Paul.'

'After the first time I met Gary, I arrived home to find an unexpected visitor—one of my ex-students—Colin Kuhuni.' Peter looked at me as if I should know this name. I didn't, and said as much.

'Colin is a bright young lawyer, trained to sift through evidence and look for facts. He happened to have been a student at the school when our friends were killed. Along with the other pupils, Colin was subjected to a propaganda talk from Gary and his platoon. I told Colin about my meeting with Gary and the story of his conversion. Immediately I had finished, Colin asked, "Tell me what he looks like." This wasn't difficult, as Gary is so tall and angular. When I gave the description Colin said, "He was the man who lectured us on that dreadful night." It seemed that God had brought Colin along that day to confirm I had met with the right man.'

'Phew! Did you question Gary about the massacre?'

'The second time we met. Apparently the whole thing was a revenge attack—there was nothing personal in it. Gary and twenty others carried out the murders in retaliation, after the security forces killed some of his people. I plucked up the courage to enquire how the missionaries reacted when they knew they were going to die, and what they might have said. His reply was that they prayed God would have mercy on their murderers and save them.'

Once again a shiver went down my spine. Almost as an afterthought, Peter said, 'One of the women—it had to be Wendy—shouted something like, "You can kill our bodies, but not our souls."'

Brenda came in at that point. I had taken up an entire afternoon of Peter's time, when he should have been looking at students' papers. After kissing them both fondly, I started off on the long drive back to the Mission.

The moon was up and full by the time I reached Rainbow Cottage, the little house which had been built for me. It was so called because the decorators had painted each room a different pastel colour, which was extended to the outside window frames. There was time for a toasted cheese sandwich before lights out. I chose to eat it by the blue window, enjoying the moon, and the stars which had come into view beside it. I pictured how those graves in that eerie Vumba clearing would look on a night like this.

'Yes, it would have been Wendy,' I said to myself, then went to bed.

Adrian Smyly's term of service came to an end. Everyone was grateful for the improvements he had brought to the Mission hospital's Maternal and Child Health Department. Over a period of eight years the numbers of children treated increased dramatically from 5,000 to over 18,000. In his place came Roger Drew, a young surgeon. He took one look at the operating theatre and declared, 'Some of this equipment is all right. I suppose the rest belonged to Cecil Brien. He probably bought it from Noah!'

The theatre was brought up to scratch, and we were able to do even more for the people of Katerere. Our inaugural major operation was a Caesarean section, performed in the middle of the night. It was the first of many, and we became quite expert. I gave the anaesthetic, Debbie would help with resuscitation of the baby, and a medical student assisted Roger. We had some failures. There are many risks to mother and baby during pregnancy and the birthing process.

One heavily pregnant patient came to the clinic with a vaginal discharge. I gave her something for it, but the infection refused to clear up. It was diagnosed as having been sexually transmitted. Although she had been delivered of several children already with no complications, this time the poor woman was growing larger every day, with no signs of going into labour. We let her go over ten months, hoping for a normal birth. But the baby grew too big for a vaginal delivery, and a Caesarean section was performed. This was risky because of the infection, but there was no other choice. The baby died, but the mother survived. She was tested and found to be HIV-positive.

We were continually aware in our work of the steady increase of AIDS. In 1990, 132 new patients were HIV tested at our hospital. Fifty-three of these were positive and five died during the year. In 1991, 199 were tested. Eighty were positive and fourteen died. Most of the infections were passed on through heterosexual relationships. Some patients were infants who had contracted the virus from their mothers.

I mentioned earlier that many of the men travelled to large towns and cities in order to find work. They came back for holidays and special occasions. In between times prostitutes satisfied their sexual desires. Many of the women already had AIDS from unprotected sex—often with customers such as truck drivers, who travelled to and from distant parts of Africa. When the men arrived home the virus passed to their wives, and any subsequent offspring. There is a cultural practice in Africa for widows to marry a member of their dead husband's family. As infected women were paired with previously uninfected partners, AIDS gained more victims. In some parts of the continent whole communities have been wiped out.

Eventually every patient at the Mission hospital was treated as potentially HIV-positive, whatever the diagnosis. To protect the staff, rubber gloves were available. We didn't have enough to use new ones with each patient. The gloves were washed, soaked in bleach and dried. Staff were also encouraged to wear rubber gloves when putting up drips and taking blood samples for the laboratory. Nurses were careful to wear heavy duty gloves when handling soiled laundry, and plastic aprons and gloves when changing bed linen.

Faced with the prospect of an early death, some people will try anything in the hope of finding a cure. A married couple from Harare came to Katerere, having heard of a tribesman using herbs on AIDS victims. The husband was very ill and this form of natural medicine made him worse. As a last resort, the wife brought him to us. Bedridden and seriously dehydrated due to continuous diarrhoea, there was little that could be done. The man died. If he had been admitted earlier, oral rehydration might have prolonged his life.

His widow was left with the awful problem of having to transport the corpse back to Harare. Tradition dictated that he must be buried in a family plot. She had no money, so I arranged for the body to be taken to a mortuary at Nyanga. There it could be kept in a refrigerator until she had the funds for the next stage of the journey. I thought that was the end of the distressing story, but after the wife had left with the body—weeping and wailing as is the Shona custom—in walked a daughter. She was unaware of her father's death. When I told her the sorry tale she became hysterical, violent, and had to be restrained.

In some places AIDS patients are treated as outcasts. In Katerere relatives are generally supportive. It is essential that families receive spiritual and medical help when patients leave hospital. An AIDS home visiting team was set up by the Mission hospital to enable the dying to be nursed in their own homes. The team is led by Mr Chitima, a church lay worker, assisted by Mai Sagwidza. She had previous experience in the Mission hospital's Rehabilitation Department. Qualified nurses administer medicines and whatever else is required.

This can involve the washing of open sores with soap and

water, or salty water, which acts like a disinfectant; giving fevered patients bed baths of cold water to help cool them; and rubbing aching muscles with soothing coconut oil. Paracetamol is often used as a painkiller. Other remedies utilise resources available locally. For example, the juice of a sliced onion mixed with sugar makes an effective expectorant for a dry cough. Packets of oral rehydration salts are used in the hospital for acute cases of diarrhoea, but for mild cases four teaspoons of sugar and half a teaspoon of salt, added to a litre of boiled water, will do just as well.

Family members learn simple but important skills, like how to turn a weak patient over to avoid bed sores. They can alleviate the discomfort of thrush in the mouth by providing salt water mouthwashes several times a day. The giving of moist meals containing tomato, banana and other kinds of juicy fruits and vegetables, provides vitamins, replaces body fluids, and at the same time helps to soothe sore mouths and throats.

I saw a number of youngsters orphaned through AIDS. The lives of others were touched by the deaths of brothers and sisters, aunts or uncles. One way I could reach out to these children was through Sunday school classes. Mai Simango, a Zimbabwean lady of about fifty years of age, was my partner in this venture. She was a boarding school mistress at Penhalonga, before obtaining a similar post at Elim Secondary School, which had now returned to Katerere.

For their own good, Mai Simango ruled the older children with a rod of iron. But she was very kind and loving to the little ones. They would flock around her buxom figure, seeking a cuddle, like chickens under the wings of a mother hen. When I went to her house to plan lessons we would always end up on our knees. Mai Simango was a woman of great prayer.

On a larger scale AIDS education became part of the

general school curriculum. To take effect, the best approach was to give advice at an age before the children became interested in the opposite sex. Older pupils, whose natural passions were already aroused, were less likely to listen to reasoned arguments. Adults, particularly leaders of communities, were targeted through talks and seminars.

For some time Bobbie Marcus' state of health had been a cause for concern. Little had been said in public, though members of Elim churches in Britain and Northern Ireland were aware she had been undergoing tests. She didn't have AIDS. The symptoms related to her mobility and nervous system. Multiple sclerosis was one possible explanation. She was flown home, where more tests revealed a less serious problem. Happily, she fell in love with Pastor David Tinnion and they were married. Bobbie never returned to work in Katerere.

Her departure led to an important event in my life. Saturday 18th February 1989 was highlighted in my diary as a day off. Nothing significant in that. However, the morning was disrupted by a visit from Brian Edwards and Peter Griffiths. The two had arrived at the compound the previous evening and we shared a meal together. It was a pleasant enough occasion, with no sinister overtones. Now they wanted to talk business. Why? In the kitchen I poured coffee for the three of us, and took it through to the lounge. Brian appeared tense as he took a cup.

'Joy, the hospital needs a new Matron,' he began. 'Evelyn Munembe is back, but with a family of her own to look after, she can't take on a full-time job. Debbie isn't quite ready yet, we feel, to take on overall responsibility. And none of the Zimbabwean nurses has enough qualifications for such a role. But someone else does.' As Brian paused to take a sip of black coffee I caught Peter's eye. He winked at me.

Brian continued, 'We—that's myself, the Missions Board

and Peter—would like you to have the post of Sister in Charge here at the Elim Mission Hospital.'

So that was it. An ordinary day had suddenly become rather special. My heart was beating faster as I replied, 'I'd like that very much. I hope I'll be worthy of your trust.'

I shook hands with Brian and received a fatherly hug from Peter. Then it was over to the hospital where Pastor Ephraim Satuku and Roger Drew confirmed the appointment. The rest of the day was spent writing letters home to tell members of my family the good news.

Official announcements were made at the hospital the next day, and prayers were said for me in church. I said my own private 'thank you' to the Lord—the one who put a yearning for nursing and Africa in my heart from childhood. I was on cloud nine and stayed there for several months, until the rains came.

It was mid-November. While driving to Harare one day to collect various supplies, my vision blurred as my head began to swim—with the heat, or so I thought. Concentration was difficult and I had to keep repeating to myself, 'Salaries from the bank, pick up lactogen, enquire about parcels.' A dark cloud followed me back to Katerere, but no rain fell.

A couple of days later I was having supper with Roger and his wife when a dramatic storm came on. We viewed it from the verandah. The lightning was quite beautiful to watch as it forked down the sky. The noise of the rain was almost deafening as it landed on adjoining tin rooftops.

'Good,' I sighed. 'This will clear the air, and hopefully my sickness.'

'I thought you'd been looking a bit pale,' said Roger. 'Is everything all right?'

'It's nothing really. Just a muzzy head and general malaise. Despite taking medication, the symptoms have persisted.'

The change of weather brought no relief. The following day I vomited and immediately felt better. About a month later, while on duty in the operating theatre, I started to feel ill again. If it wasn't the heat this time, perhaps the condition of the woman lying on the table was to blame. Attacked with an axe, she had suffered terrible head wounds. Was I experiencing a surge of emotions in a flashback to the injuries described at the Vumba massacre? No. Hours later, feeling hot and feverish, I popped a thermometer in my mouth to discover my temperature was up. I mentioned the matter to Roger, and was taken aback by his reply.

'You're off on holiday soon. Have a complete and thorough medical, including blood tests.'

'But I'm sure there's . . .'

'No need to worry? Maybe not. But whatever it is, it won't go away without proper treatment. Look, I don't want to scare you, but with all these AIDS patients coming in—you should have *that* test too.'

I was going home for my brother Tim's wedding. Shortly after I sailed through a check-up, and an HIV test showed me to be negative. I heaved a sigh of relief and returned to Zimbabwe. The sickness did not recur. From time to time most members of staff went through a period of anxiety about contracting AIDS. Roger had a particularly nasty scare.

A small boy was admitted, complaining of abdominal pain. A bowel obstruction seemed the obvious cause and Roger began an operation. No bowel contents were found, but the lymph nodes were swollen and bleeding. This could indicate typhoid, tuberculosis, lymphoma—or AIDS. Two nodes were removed for further investigation, and the boy was closed up.

Roger told me, 'The wound was sutured, the dressing neatly in place. I turned my attention to the instrument

88

trolley. All the needles were stuck to an adhesive pad in their container. They had been new, we'd just received them from England. I went to close the lid of the container to make it safe for the nurses who would soon be clearing up. One needle wasn't lying flat on the pad. As the lid came down the sharp end went through my glove and into my thumb. Taking the gloves off, I encouraged the wound to bleed, went quickly to the sink and washed it copiously with water. It looked such a trivial injury, yet I was only too well aware of the potential implications.'

The patient and his family were well-known to us. The father was a part-time shoemaker with a drink problem, two wives and a large number of children. He had tuberculosis, and the others were suffering from malnutrition. All had been tested for AIDS in the past with negative results, with the exception of one of the little girls. This didn't make sense. For a child of this age to be HIV-positive, the source had to be the mother, who had shown up negative. The mother and children were tested again. This time the results were positive. The boy died a few days later.

Now Roger had to be tested. The first blood sample, taken by Debbie, showed he was HIV-negative at the time of the injury. Then it was necessary to wait three months before taking a further test, to see if he had been infected through the needle. In the meantime every sniffle, ache or pain was a source of worry. Thankfully, the second test came back negative too. However, he admitted, 'The sense of relief was not as great as it should be. I'm negative now, but what about the next accident with a needle, or the one after that?'

Roger subsequently went through the dilemma that many other overseas workers have experienced in the face of danger. Fight or flight? He couldn't escape the problem, for all around were AIDS patients.

One morning, walking to the hospital, he saw a group of women sitting on the ground under the shade of a tree. Their tell-tale wailing meant only one thing: someone had died during the night. The notes of a patient were lying on the floor just inside his office door. They had been put there by one of the night nurses. Roger picked them up, sat at the desk and started to read them.

She was only a young woman. Single, but with a child a few months old. She had first come to the hospital complaining of a cough, weight loss and severe diarrhoea. She certainly looked as if she had lost weight, she was so emaciated. An X-ray showed that one side of her chest was full of fluid. Treatment was given, but her condition deteriorated. The previous day Roger had tried draining two litres of fluid off the chest. Obviously it had made no difference. A blood test confirmed she had AIDS. A few days later the child also died.

Another patient, who was pregnant, had such severe vaginal warts, caused through AIDS, that she couldn't deliver normally. She was given a Caesarean section. The baby survived and seemed fine. Though he was feeding, he did not grow at the normal rate, became sickly and ultimately died. Of AIDS.

'At times, I don't feel I can cope with the pressure,' said Roger. 'It must be similar to the predicament you were in during the war. But I think this is worse because this enemy is hidden, and therefore seems more sinister.'

But he did cope, eventually declaring, 'Though I wanted to leave and find a safer occupation, I realised two things: I can't just run away, and no job is without hazards. I could go home and who knows? An accident or unexpected illness could take me. Life is not something we can hold securely in our own hands. What did Jesus say? "For whosoever will save his life shall lose it: but whosoever will lose his life for my sake, the same shall save it" ' (Luke 9:24, KJV).

Meanwhile my own health was fine. However, my temperament was adjusting to some of the non-medical matters a Sister in Charge has to cope with. Like pilfering. Ten litres of diesel oil and two door frames were reported missing from the hospital storeroom. A close check was kept, and smaller items also started to disappear.

On Elim Secondary School's sports day, the people handling the refreshments ran out of sugar. Roger was around, and offered to go and fetch some from a small shop run by Mai Malvira. The sugar was kept in large containers, not pre-packed as in Western supermarkets. After weighing, his purchase was put into a plastic bag. Roger soon realised this was one of our sterilisation bags. Evidence!

Mai Malvira also had a job in the hospital. She was brought into my office for questioning, but denied theft. The explanation was that the bags were being thrown away. I was not satisfied, and suspended her pending further enquiries. The police had to be called in and an officer gave a talk to all the staff. It looked as if Mai Malvira was guilty, but I didn't want her sent to prison. We opted for a disciplinary warning, after which she was reinstated, but she failed to turn up for work. I believe this may have been due to embarrassment. Pastor Satuku mentioned the matter in church, to clear the air, so everyone knew the true story of what had been going on.

A happier occasion was the visit of President Mugabe to the hospital on 24th October 1990. He seemed impressed and stayed for several hours. It was very hot—another of those days when we were eagerly awaiting the rains. Due to the heat and old age, an elderly lady died while he was there. But we managed to steer him away and avoided the distress of letting him see the body being carried out. I believe she died of a heart attack. She only came in with an abscess on her face.

I was ill again in March and April of 1991, with fevers, aches and pains and then a rash—typical of the type common with typhoid fever. Roger started me on the treatment for typhoid and then I was driven in to Harare for further investigations. No conclusive diagnosis was made. If I had been tested for AIDS at that time, I wonder, would the result have been positive?

Next I had a strange rash on my thighs and abdomen in December. The doctor in Harare was most interested, but had no idea what it could be. He prescribed steroids, which seemed to help. As soon as the course was finished the rash came back with a vengeance—just for one day—before completely disappearing. I never had it again.

On 19th February 1992 I was helping in the operating theatre. A man had mangled his hand in a grinding machine and attempts were being made to tidy up his fingers. It was a long and delicate procedure. I started feeling hungry and then dizzy. The room was spinning round. I grabbed at one corner of the operating table in order to stay upright. No one seemed to notice me.

Suddenly, gripped by agonising abdominal pain, I cried out, 'Help! Go and fetch Debbie!' One of the African nurses ran out to fetch her. With my head on the table alongside the patient, I made sure he was kept asleep by shooting anaesthetic into a vein every time he moved. By the time Debbie arrived on the scene I was on the floor. But the patient was still asleep. I was escorted home, took some painkillers, and went to bed. When I woke up I felt fine, as if nothing had happened.

In the days that followed, the problems with my throat and chest developed. The next part of my story you know—the diagnosis of AIDS, my journey back to England and hospitalisation have already been told in

Chapter 1. But that is not the end. As a PWA (person with AIDS) I am not just sitting around waiting to die. The following pages show I am living a full life, as actively as possible. And God is leading me into a new understanding of himself and his ways.

9

After living abroad for so many years, I sometimes feel the world has passed me by. Whenever I have spent time at home in the past it has been hard to make many lasting friendships, because I would soon be off to another part of the world. In the same way, I have allowed myself to become distant from my family—to be less involved in their lives than if I had been in England throughout the last twenty years. Some members of the family have been mentioned in previous chapters. Now is the time for you to hear more, as I rediscover them.

My parents Victor and Violet have been happily married for over fifty years. They had six children. Unfortunately the first baby died. Some brothers and sisters are like peas in a pod. The five Baths have varying temperaments and have all done different things.

Roy is the eldest. He used to help in Dad's shop and now works for the Post Office. He lives with his family in Swindon. Jacquie, his wife, is a kind of extra daughter to Mum and Dad, and a sister to me. Originally from Jersey, she was adopted by another branch of the family and is technically my cousin. As a child she was always round at our house, playing with the rest of us. Roy and Jacquie have two grown-up children, Kevin and Mandi.

I came next, born on 17th April 1950. In some churches a child's first communion or confirmation service might be a cause for celebration. The Pentecostal way records when an individual makes their own decision to become a follower of Jesus. I became a Christian at the age of eight, which is quite young, but not that unusual. I received the baptism of the Holy Spirit at the age of sixteen.

Pearl was born after me. She has a husband called Trevor and daughters Charlotte and Geraldine. They all live in Salisbury. When Charlotte realised my second term of service in Zimbabwe was among AIDS patients, she organised a collection service for rubber gloves from local hospitals and clinics. She was just thirteen years of age at the time.

My brother Tim and his wife Yvonne live in Swindon with young Kristian and James. When Tim is not working as a chef, he and Yvonne can often be found in Russia. As part of Messianic Testimony to the Jews they deliver humanitarian aid to needy families in an orphanage, intensive care unit, and the Russian National Centre For Children With AIDS. Their work also involves sharing the gospel with Messianic believers. Russia is currently experiencing a dramatic spiritual awakening, and the Jewish community is no exception to this. Since the collapse of Communism, literally thousands of Jewish people have come to acknowledge Jesus as their Messiah.

Keith, my youngest brother, is married to Debbie. They are about to begin a family of their own. In the meantime he has several hundred four-legged babies to care for. Keith is a shepherd on Salisbury Plain. It's a rugged life, being out in all weathers.

Quite often Keith will come over for lunch. We have so much in common, sometimes our conversation horrifies Mum and Dad, especially if we are all enjoying a meal together. With Keith a shepherd and myself a midwife, the discussion frequently turns to the similarities between the birth of a baby and a lamb. It is natural for us to compare our different experiences, but either Mum or Dad will interject with, 'Please, you two! Not while we are eating.'

On one such occasion Keith was worried about an old ewe, who might have to be put down. She had developed a bad infection. Though Keith would ensure that any treatment was carried out humanely, he was upset at the thought of losing a member of the flock. I am surprised at the compassion and concern Keith shows for the sheep. If one of the lambs is sick or weakly, his wife is given the job of nursing it back to health in their kitchen.

I hate the idea of pain being experienced by any living thing. But for human beings it can come in many forms; physical, mental and emotional; persecution and rejection. It can act as a purifying process. It can be a benefit, remoulding a person and giving new strengths.

A student social worker called Emma has visited me on a regular basis. She is a tremendous girl who, as a sufferer of cerebral palsy, has already overcome many hurdles to reach her current role. I wonder whether she would have been so keen to succeed if she were not fighting a disability.

Some Christians, mostly those who do not understand how AIDS is spread, have made hurtful comments to me. They spit out accusations like, 'You must think we're naïve to say you caught it at work. From an affair, more like.' As a result I have started to feel a closeness to the Virgin Mary. Her pregnancy, while engaged to Joseph, must have prompted winks and nudges from the gossips. If she had told all and sundry that God was the father of her baby, she would either have been locked up for being insane, or stoned to death for blasphemy. Instead she not only bore all the taunts silently and with dignity, but was also able to utter a wonderful hymn of praise, which is nowadays known as the Magnificat. It has become something I recite often in my private times with God:

My soul glorifies the Lord and my spirit rejoices in God my Saviour, for he has been mindful of the humble state of his servant. From now on all generations will call me blessed, for the Mighty One has done great things for me—holy is his name. His mercy extends to those who fear him, from generation to generation. He has performed mighty deeds with his arm; he has scattered those who are proud in their inmost thoughts. He has brought down rulers from their thrones but has lifted up the humble. He has filled the hungry with good things but has sent the rich away empty. He has helped his servant Israel, remembering to be merciful to Abraham and his descendants for ever, even as he said to our fathers (Luke 1:46–55).

To keep things in perspective, I've encountered little negative reaction to my condition. However, I have been guilty of a few wrong attitudes myself towards other people. When visiting Southampton for hospital appointments, I have to report to the Genito-Urinary Clinic. This is more commonly known as the STD (Sexually Transmitted Diseases), VD or Special Clinic. It is embarrassing to sit in the waiting room there, never having had a sexual relationship. And it is not easy to have an unbiased attitude towards other patients. I have tried to reason the matter through, saying to myself that the other people are there because they are sick, and who am I to judge how they became ill?

I had an interesting discussion with Jacquie along these lines, which led to some radical conclusions:

1. I shouldn't ask or even think about how another person contracted AIDS, unless I am prepared to submit myself to their prejudices and suppositions about me.

2. As Jesus was the friend of sinners, he might have shown more sympathy and compassion than I have so far towards other AIDS sufferers. He might have shown more willingness to be identified with them.

3. How can I be more like him? When asked how I came to be infected, perhaps I should just say, 'Through my work in Africa,' and not go into long explanations about being an innocent victim.

I have had five or six boyfriends. The physical side of the relationships has never progressed as far as the sexual act. Even the naughtiest thing I ever did along these lines is really quite innocent. While training to be a nurse in Poole, a mutual attraction developed between myself and a patient. I used to draw the curtains around his bed so we could kiss and cuddle. That was as far as it went. The sheets always stayed between us. It was most unprofessional conduct and I was lucky not to be caught and thrown off the course. Nothing like that ever happened again.

Over the years it has been hard to see those close to me finding partners and getting married, while I am still single. Now I have AIDS there is even less possibility of ever having a family of my own. I often feel I would love to be married; to have someone to care for me and someone to care for. Then I look around and see so many marriages in shambles. Perhaps I am better off as I am.

Reaching out to make new friends at this stage in my life is such an effort. But I know I must do it, and have joined Salisbury AIDS Support Group. I made the first move, contacting the co-ordinator David Penney, and arranging to meet at his office. We chatted at length. He is a very understanding person, concerned for the downtrodden of our society. Among the many posters on the wall of his office, I noticed one which read something like, 'No one ever died of AIDS by caring.' I could accept what the poster was saying, but pointed out that's exactly the way I contracted AIDS. The poster has since been removed.

Occasionally I come across faces from the past. A girl who was one of my Sunday school pupils in the 1970s was recently baptised at Elim Salisbury Church. Although contact had been maintained with people there, she had faltered in her faith since childhood, until she heard me speak at a luncheon. Before being baptised, she walked to the microphone and said, 'Joy's done so much with her life. But over the last twenty years, what have I done with mine? Very little. This moment symbolises a new start for me.' It was touching to think that my testimony could have such an effect on someone else's life.

Since January 1993 I have undertaken a number of speaking engagements at churches and conferences. They have all been valuable in helping people to understand what it is like to have AIDS. I generally feel I should address the problem of why Christians suffer. This is a vast subject, but starting to explore it has helped me, and I trust it has helped others too.

I believe suffering is not a licence for self-pity, but a chance for the sufferer to teach and encourage others. Shakespeare said that all the world is a stage. The audience can see us playing our part well, or badly. If all is well, they receive something positive to take to their hearts and take home. If all they see is hatred and bitterness the message of the scriptwriter is lost; the time spent at the theatre wasted.

There are Christians who believe healing is waiting just around the corner for everyone who is sick. They see the absence of healing as proof of a lack of faith in the promises of God. Their reasoning is based on certain passages of Scripture, for example Matthew 7:7–11 and 21:18–22, which seem to indicate human beings can obtain anything they ask. Then there are the many instances of Jesus healing people miraculously. I do not doubt the abilities of the Almighty, but in becoming a Christian I became a follower of Jesus. He suffered an agonising death, and if that means I have to do the same for some reason, I must say, 'Thy will be done.'

Three passages of Scripture have been particularly helpful to me. Sometimes, as I read these aloud to congregations, I find it hard to control my emotions. The words seem so powerful and simple:

First, 2 Corinthians 1:3–11, especially:

> . . . the God of all comfort, who comforts us in all our troubles, so that we can comfort those in any trouble with the comfort we ourselves have received from God . . . Indeed . . . we felt the sentence of death. But this happened that we might not rely on ourselves but on God, who raises the dead (vv 3b–4, 9).

Second, 2 Corinthians 4, especially:

> We are hard pressed on every side, but not crushed; perplexed, but not in despair; persecuted, but not abandoned; struck down, but not destroyed. We always carry around in our body the death of Jesus, so that the life of Jesus may also be revealed in our body . . . Though outwardly we are wasting away, yet inwardly we are being renewed day by day. For our light and momentary troubles are achieving for us an eternal glory that far outweighs them all. So we fix our eyes not on what is seen, but on what is unseen. For what is seen is temporary, but what is unseen is eternal (vv 8–10, 16b–18).

Third, Philippians 1:20–21, especially:

> . . . Christ will be exalted in my body, whether by life or by death (v 20b).

These passages have also helped me to cope with a worsening state of health. Though I am certainly not living every day in the hope that it is my last, I am looking forward to an afterlife I am certain exists.

My parents' house benefits from the famous view of Salisbury Cathedral across green fields. One of my favourite pleasures on a fine day is to walk the rural lanes there, gazing at the water meadows from Britford Bridge. One Saturday I was out walking when I passed a house where a man was working on his car. Parts and tools were all over the pavement and I tripped on them. It wasn't that I was day dreaming. I just could not see them or the ground beneath my feet. For some months I had been experiencing bad headaches and blurred vision around the lower edges of my eyes. Now some of my peripheral sight had gone.

Dr Wilmot in Southampton said a virus named cytomegalo was responsible. If untreated, it could take my sight completely. He arranged for the fitting of a Hickman Line. This is a tube attached to a main vein near my heart, with the outer end about two inches long, sticking through my chest. With a bit of adjustment it remains hidden by my clothing. Five days a week an anti-viral solution called Ganciclovir is slowly injected through the Hickman Line. The process takes about two hours and I can administer the treatment myself. It seems to have helped stem the sight loss, but the headaches are still with me.

Normally supplies of Ganciclovir arrive at home by a special delivery service. But on one occasion a mix-up over the prescription meant I had to collect it from a hospital pharmacy in Southampton. Also waiting for drugs there was an African girl. She looked familiar, but I could not think whether we had met before. Then I remembered a conversation with a nurse which took place before I was allowed home to Salisbury.

'Joy, I don't know whether I should ask you this, but there's an African lady in the next isolation cubicle with the same problem as you, who doesn't know how she's going to cope. Would you have a chat with her?'

'Yes, I will. I'd like to meet someone else with my condition.'

'And you might be able to speak in her mother tongue?'

'Probably not. There are loads of different tribal languages. But I might be able to help in some way.'

I tried to keep my promise, but I was receiving a lot of visitors every day. Each time I was alone, she had someone at her bedside. By the time we were both free she was being discharged and her husband was taking her away. But here she was again, at the pharmacy. I seized the opportunity to introduce myself.

She was feeling much better, and had found a part-time job. We exchanged addresses and in due course she and her husband came to visit me. It was a great encouragement for both of us. And it was comforting for her to chat with another person who had lived in Africa.

I was also put in touch with another PWA, a young man in a more serious condition. I went to see him on several occasions. He was painfully thin, and had several infections, which eventually killed him.

Since coming back to England I have been able to attend two Elim conferences. At the most recent, intense headaches meant it was only possible to go to a few sessions. One of these was a children's meeting where I gave a talk. Afterwards they prayed for me, particularly a young coloured lad called Gideon. He showed real faith and it made me quite tearful. A younger child had a prophecy from the Lord: 'Jesus wants us to know he loves us all very much. And Joy, he's proud of you.' I was more blessed by the words of these little ones than by the carefully prepared lectures of seasoned preachers.

Work, church services, speaking engagements and conferences. You may be wondering whether I ever relax and have a good time. Members of some religions believe everything on earth has been put here for us to enjoy. To some extent Pentecostals agree with that, but in practice they try to avoid anything which might be termed worldly or extravagant. In doing so we have become separated from some of life's more innocuous pastimes. For most of us, going to church is the highlight of the week. We really enjoy it—possibly because the services are so lively and uplifting. The rest of the time we are too busy adhering to the Protestant work ethic to notice all the good things in the world around us. We have largely forgotten how to have a good time—at least I had until I was forced into early retirement.

Recently I have been on more outings and holidays, have had more fun, than ever before. I treasure memories of walking along a cliff path on Guernsey, followed by delicious crab sandwiches at Vazon beach; joining in a sing-song with others in the crowd during a carnival procession; sunlight sparkling on a calm sea, as I took a ferry to the Isle of Wight; just sitting at home watching the *Last Night of the Proms* on television with a box of chocolates on my knee.

I went to London's Oxford Street and travelled on an open-top bus to see the Christmas lights. What an experience! It was dark and freezing cold, but I was wrapped up warmly. There was a wonderful atmosphere, with the Salvation Army band playing carols and the beauty of the street lights and window displays. The trip was something I had wanted to do for years, but never managed it before. Then there was the joy of having the family together—all twenty-six of us—on Christmas Day.

I have found happiness in all kinds of everyday pursuits. The key is to relax, stop rushing from one task to the next worrying about the future, and enjoy what the present provides. Try it sometime. I only wish I had earlier.

During my enforced stay in England I have had a lot of time to reflect upon my life. I think it was while I was in India that I had a conversation with a fellow missionary about the right time to go home. My condition is fuddling my mind and I am unable to remember who the person was, but their words have remained with me. It was said that a missionary can get to the stage where Asia, Africa or some other continent is so much a part of them they cannot do without it. That's when it is time to return home. I now think that maybe I had reached that stage with Zimbabwe.

IO

Fairly recently, while reading part of the Sermon on the Mount (Matthew 6:31–34), I was struck by the words of Jesus, 'Do not worry about your life.' I am sure he did not mean we should not plan and prepare for the future as best we can. He did mean we should not be full of anxiety. He goes on to say, 'Therefore do not worry about tomorrow, for tomorrow will worry about itself. Each day has enough trouble of its own' (v 34).

What really impressed me about this teaching of Jesus was the air of authority with which it was delivered. He was not giving out advice, but commands. And how right he was to place emphasis on this matter. It is pointless to waste our lives sitting around fretting about things which may never happen. On the other hand, if we knew the trials we had to face in life beforehand, we would probably give up on every aspect before reaching adulthood.

Two letters posted from Nyanga just before Christmas 1992 shocked and saddened me. First Roger Drew wrote that Peter Griffiths was seriously ill. Then Peter himself told me that the outlook was bleak. Yet the start of his troubles seemed so small and insignificant.

At the beginning of November Peter was reading aloud, as a prelude to giving one of his regular Tuesday evening Bible studies to a large group of people. He could not pronounce some of the words properly. No one except Brenda seemed to notice, and he put the problem down to being overtired, plus the fact that the passage of Scripture—from Genesis—contained some tricky Hebrew names.

The next day Peter's speech was slurred from time to time. He wrote: 'I rang Debbie Murphree, the GP, and arranged an appointment. Foolishly ignoring her advice to get someone to drive me to her rooms, I drove myself. She found a slight weakness on the left side of the face, which could indicate I had suffered a minor stroke. After the examination she immediately arranged for me to see a consultant, Terry French, the following day.'

A CAT scan arranged through the consultant showed that a part of Peter's brain, about the size of a golf ball, appeared to have died. At least that was the first impression. When he saw the pictures Terry French commented, 'That's a pretty impressive infarct of the brain!'

An infarct is an area of dead tissue caused by interruption to the blood supply. This would probably fit in with the supposition that Peter had survived a stroke.

Peter had wisely asked his son Stephen to take him to this appointment. From Roger Drew's letter came the news, 'Stephen and his wife Anna had been due to fly to Mozambique that day, to begin work with the Leprosy Mission. Thank goodness they were delayed due to a shortage of aviation fuel. Peter had an epileptic fit in the car as they drove away, just outside the grounds of Terry French's office.'

The normally tranquil atmosphere of the consulting rooms was shattered by their return. Stephen, who is a doctor himself, helped to put up a drip and administered diazepam, a sedative, through a vein. An ambulance quickly arrived and Peter was taken to Parirenyatwa, a large hospital in Harare. Stephen was quite distraught by the sight of his stricken father. Of the fit, Peter said, 'Fully conscious throughout, I thought I was dying. I yielded myself to the Lord, thinking he was taking me home to heaven.'

Several more fits happened that day before Peter's condition calmed down. A neurosurgeon, Mr Auchterlonie, said surgical intervention would not be necessary. About a fortnight later, while Peter was still in hospital, he took a sudden turn for the worse, losing strength on his left side. A second CAT scan was done and this time the picture was enhanced by injecting dye. Terry French and Mr Auchterlonie realised that what appeared to be dead tissue was in fact a tumour.

Wrote Peter, 'I was transferred to the Avenues Clinic where Mr Auchterlonie operates from—literally! He did a biopsy of my brain. There was a two-day, agonisingly long wait for the results. They showed the tumour was malignant, and ought to be removed without delay. I signed the consent form for the operation.'

The apparent strokes were caused by the tumour bleeding into itself, swelling rapidly and putting pressure on certain areas of Peter's brain, resulting in paralysis down the left side of the body.

Roger saw him before surgery, and reported, 'Physically, he was worse. The left arm and leg were now also affected. Naturally, Peter was apprehensive about the operation. But he was doing his best to crack jokes—bad ones as usual—and responded well to a comment made by one of the nurses.'

She had come to wish him luck. Peter replied, 'I don't believe in luck. I believe in God. If this is my time to die, I'm ready.'

The operation went well, and the surgeon managed to remove all of the tumour. Peter recalled, 'The following days were just a blur. As a nurse, you'll realise how I must have looked, with tubes going into me and coming out of me in all sorts of places. And I was sedated up to the eyeballs. But in my confusion, God was revealing new depths of his love and graciousness. As I lay in that bed I marvelled at how God loves this world, and me as a part of it, and at how he deals with us in wonderful ways we do not deserve. I reflected with awe on the scene in Gethsemane, when Jesus saw the horror of his approaching death and said, "Father, if you are willing, take this cup from me; yet not my will, but yours be done" (Luke 22:42). Discharged from hospital, I am now at home. Mr Auchterlonie is setting up programmes of radiotherapy and chemotherapy at Parirenyatwa. The battle continues and I ask for your prayers.'

Strength, co-ordination and clear speech were returning to Peter. Progress was slow, but he was hopeful for the future. I was not so sure. It was no surprise when a third letter came through the letterbox a couple of months later, containing bad news. Peter wrote, 'I have been told there is no cure in medical science for my condition. The sort of tumour I had invariably returns. Radiotherapy simply controls the growth rate for a time, and may give me a little longer to live. So, you and I are in the same boat. Tell me how you cope.'

I knew Peter must be pretty low to send out such a plea, so I was on the telephone to him straight away. He didn't seem too bad, but admitted to struggling with despondency on waking each morning, due to thinking about the future.

He said, 'Depression fades somewhat as I become active and involved in the affairs of the day.'

We decided he was suffering from an over-fertile imagination. He was prone to thinking about what would happen if he became disabled to the point of being like a vegetable.

'Thoughts like that are not allowed!' I chided. 'Remember the Briens' prayer?'

'Lord, help us to live in the light of eternity. There are

times when I feel I'm beginning to learn to stand where God stands, and to take an overhead view of what's happening in this brief span of time. Then, in my disabled state, I stumble over some object, or falter in a simple everyday task like a clumsy child, and come back down to earth. It's very hard to accept. I've always been such an active person.'

For the next six months Peter and I supported each other with letters and telephone calls. In a way it was comforting to know that such an old and trusted friend was going through the same kinds of thoughts and feelings as myself. At one stage I had half a plan put together to fly over to Zimbabwe and visit Peter, Brenda and others. It was an impossible dream which never materialised. My health would not have stood up to such vigorous travelling.

The tumour began to grow again, and by late summer Peter's condition was deteriorating. Susie Sanguinetti, a friend who worked for the BBC World Service, began typing his letters to me. 'I am now walking around slowly and once more speaking with some slurring of my speech,' I read. The next paragraphs let me know in no uncertain terms that he would not be with us much longer.

I have given the family instructions for my funeral. I want to be buried, rather than stick to the European practice here of cremation. This is because my African friends find cremation a difficult idea. The preacher and leader of the service will be Dr Ken Jenkins, but Pious Munembe and Ephraim Satuku should also speak. They are so close to me and risked their lives for me during the war here.

I want two hymns which have special meaning for me. 'Amazing Grace', because I have become more amazed than ever that God should treat me, and the whole world, with grace we are not worthy to receive. And 'Ungatora Hako Pasi', which Brenda and I had at our wedding. The Shona roughly translates, 'You can take the world and all its joys. We for our part will take Jesus and all he offers. His grace is overwhelming and sufficient for all.'

Now I must go and take an aspirin gargle—a small thing you and I do in common! Your loving and very tired friend and colleague, Peter.

Those were the last words he ever wrote to me and I treasure them, like a person might hold on to an old pair of worn out shoes. Brian Edwards rang me on the morning of Tuesday 10th October to say that Peter had died at 9pm the previous evening. The funeral would be on the following Friday in Mutare, conducted according to Peter's wishes. A memorial service was held in Swansea on 6th November. I was able to attend, with Mum and Dad. A good number came and it was an incredibly moving occasion. Afterwards Peter's mother gave me a long and tearful hug.

We stayed overnight in Wales and travelled back the following day. I drove all the way there and most of the way home. As we left the M4 at Chippenham I moved over to let Dad take the wheel. Exhausted, I was also acutely aware of my failing eyesight. It was getting to the point where it was no longer safe for me to be in control of a car. Just as Peter's treatment had only delayed the growth in his brain, I feared the Ganciclovir was fighting a losing battle within my own body.

Over the next weeks my health began to deteriorate. I carried on with the treatment, but suffered dreadful migraines whenever I was up and about. So I stayed in bed, sleeping for most of the time. When I did manage to stagger about on my feet I experienced weird feelings of weightlessness, as if I were floating above the ground. These symptoms could have been due to stress and grief; reactions to Peter's death. They disappeared when I was presented with a wonderful surprise.

Early one morning the doorbell rang and my parents

instructed me to answer it. David Butcher and his wife were on the front step, both grinning from ear to ear.

'We picked up something special for you at Heathrow at the crack of dawn,' he said. 'Come and have a look in our car.'

I was intrigued as they led me through the door and a few paces up the drive. Someone was sitting on the back seat of the car. I couldn't see who until I looked inside.

'Jeya! I never thought it would be you out here.'

'I never thought to leave India—though I did visit Singapore last year—but you, my friend, are worth coming all this way to visit!'

We both wept happy tears and held each other for several minutes. Until David suggested the house would provide a more comfortable place to sit.

Jeya stayed about a week and was a real tonic. We are similar people, in spirit rather than looks, capable of holding deep conversations and discussions. I interviewed her as part of a Sunday service at Salisbury Elim Church and she shamed me by offering this lovely tribute to our friendship: 'God brings many people in our lives to be a blessing for us. God brought Joy into my life to give me joy.'

When it was time for Jeya to leave England I made the journey to Heathrow with her, escorted by Mike and Elisabeth Sherwood. He is an Elim pastor based in Essex, who formerly worked for Brian Edwards in Elim International Missions. Mike's face beamed as Jeya told how the GEMS has grown at an amazing rate in recent years. The work has expanded from Bihar to surrounding states and into the neighbouring country of Nepal.

Our parting was difficult. Jeya is an intuitive girl, and she knew this would be our last contact this side of heaven. It was a lovely day and I was not allowing any thoughts of an untimely death to invade my mind. I just thought this was another of those occasions when her emotional Indian temperament took over. After checking in her luggage, Jeya clung on to me, sobbing. Elisabeth gave her a handkerchief with which to wipe her wet face.

Jeya took a couple of deep breaths and quietened down a little. As we approached the barrier she clasped my hands in her own and said, 'God has told me that he is going to give you a special blessing in glory.'

She meant I would be rewarded in heaven for experiencing a short life. A sense of calm came over the four of us as Jeya walked off to the plane. Mike, Elisabeth and I gave each other a knowing glance. It was a look that said, 'Who knows? Perhaps she's right.'

From then on, my attitude to death changed. I could no longer carry a vague acceptance that for me life would be brief. I knew I would die young. And within me came a firm, almost tangible excitement at the thought of meeting my Lord Jesus face to face.

Hundreds of daffodils line the roads of Salisbury each spring. They were there like a welcoming committee when I came home in 1992 and provided a vibrant sign of hope to me the following year. How uplifting to see their glorious yellow show again as I was taken out for a treat to mark the second anniversary of my return from Africa. The doctors had not expected me to live this long. Now Mum, Dad, Pearl and I were lunching in a restaurant, celebrating the fact that an extra twenty-four months of life had been granted.

Pearl had never been supportive of my desire to work overseas. Nor had she experienced the Christian faith in the same way as other members of the family. When I contracted AIDS she became bitter and resentful. There were arguments and tears. The gap of understanding between my sister and the rest of us widened into a great chasm.

My mother is a level-headed person—an ordinary house-wife who is not prone to vivid imaginings. During the meal she announced, 'I had a dream—or rather a vision. It was so real I know it came from God. It means I mustn't worry about what happens to Joy.' Dad and I were told about this earlier in the day. Pearl looked up from her plate aston-ished, fork poised halfway to her mouth.

Mum's eyes, always big and bright, grew even larger as she described what she had seen. 'I was in the most lovely garden with Joy. There were flowers everywhere. We walked by a great mass of roses. Red, white, yellow, peach, pink—every colour you could think of. Each bloom was perfect. Their combined scent was overpowering. Jesus was there and he came and stood between us. He held one of our hands in each of his own, so we were one either side of him. Then everything went black.'

We all carried on eating for a few moments. Sniffing back a couple of tears, Dad dabbed at the edges of his mouth with a napkin. Mum leaned over to Pearl earnestly. 'I think Joy will be taken before long. But it's all right, because I've been given a glimpse of where she's going.'

'Yes, I believe you have,' replied Pearl thoughtfully. She accepted the statement without question, knowing our mother could never concoct such a story.

After this, Pearl began to visit us more often. She came to stay at the house, to be with me while our parents took a holiday together. We became much closer and even prayed together during that week, which meant a great deal to me.

It was necessary to have someone around, for my eye-sight was becoming steadily worse. I first noticed the upper and side vision in the right eye had gone one Sunday morning in church. Pentecostals go in for a lot of hand raising: it is a Jewish custom St Paul helped to perpetuate by saying he wanted 'men everywhere to lift up holy hands in prayer' (1 Timothy 2:8). So we can often be found with our arms held high. On this occasion I realised I could not see my right arm at all.

In addition, breathing difficulties were starting to return; I quickly became breathless when walking. And oral thrush had developed. Time for a visit to the hospital in Southampton. Too weak to walk from one department to another, I was pushed around in a wheelchair. It was humiliating to think how my freedom was slowly being taken away. All the time I was there, my constant prayer was, 'Lord, please preserve the sight in my left eye.'

Bad eyesight or not, I could see that the ward I was in had not been cleaned properly for some time. With the aid of a magnifying glass I wrote out a formal complaint. It took some time. The domestic supervisor and her superior appeared by my bedside.

'Only the bed table is done by the cleaners. The cleaning of the TV table, locker tops and mirror shelf is not our job,' I was told.

'Oh, so who cleans those surfaces then?' I asked.

'The nurses!'

The pair bustled off, giving the impression that a fuss was being made about nothing. However, the next day, when I came back from having an X-ray, my area was spotlessly clean. I have no idea which of the staff was responsible.

The balance between domestic and ward responsibilities is an age-old problem encountered at most hospitals. Unfortunately dust and grime hold germs, and someone has to wipe them away or else patients may be at risk to infections.

There was good news about my eyes. While the doctors admitted there was an advancement of sight loss, they said the virus was now under control. No further deterioration should occur. Apparently the PCP left a weakness in the lungs. An aromatic treatment of menthol and eucalyptus was prescribed for my chest. And I was given something for the thrush before being allowed home.

It wasn't long before the bad headaches returned. This time, though they resembled migraine, they were much worse. The pain extended down the sides of the face to the gums, and was particularly bad around the eyes. With the headaches came nausea, resulting in a loss of appetite. Then the sight in my right eye began to flicker, like a light being switched off and on.

One morning I awoke from sleep with my head on the left, with the good eye closed against the pillow. I could see nothing on the right. I was completely blind on that side. The medics had been mistaken; the virus was not beaten. Terrified at the thought of going absolutely blind, my mind filled up with all kinds of imaginary scenarios. If my parents died, would other members of the family be able to care for me? What if I had an accident, or started a fire while they were at work?

Suddenly, I understood how Peter Griffiths must have felt when his thoughts took off in all directions. Once more I prayed for God to keep my left eye safe and in good working order.

Summer clothes were packed away and out came the warm
sweaters and trousers. How I hate having to change my
wardrobe twice a year. I miss the African sunshine. This
time, as I carefully folded up my pretty cotton dresses, I
wondered if they would ever be needed again.

Once more I was admitted to hospital in Southampton.
The retina of my right eye had become detached, and that
was the reason for the blindness. Nothing could be done
to restore the lost sight. There was more concern about
my breathing difficulties and the fact that I had lost
weight. A cough had developed too. I was put in an
isolation ward.

As I lay in bed, receiving frequent attention from the
nurses, I remembered some of the advice I used to hand out
to carers.

'Sit the patient up, raising the head on pillows to assist
breathing. People tend to panic when they can't breathe
properly, and that makes them even more wheezy. During
panic attacks, stay by their side, encouraging them to stay
calm and take regular breaths.' Now people were doing the
same things for me. I couldn't help but smile.

Far more visitors came than I could cope with. Sometimes I had to ask them to wait outside while I took a nap.
Debbie Brown came over on furlough and it was a real
tonic to see her. We joked that I was so weak I should be in
geriatrics. It was good to learn that since my departure

from the Mission hospital at Katerere, new regulations had been made to protect staff against HIV infection.

'Nowadays we go into the operating theatre dressed for a moon walk!' she told me.

'Well, I'm sure it's much safer that way. If only I'd been more careful, perhaps . . .' Unexpected feelings of sadness and anger washed over me.

'You mustn't blame yourself.'

'Yes, I must. I was in charge—of myself and the rest of you. This is the price I've had to pay for my negligence.' I started to cry. Tears of bereavement for the loss of my own life.

It was an entirely appropriate moment for a doctor to arrive and tell me I would soon be discharged. Apart from making my last months as comfortable as possible with the help of drugs like morphine, there was little more that could be done to combat the HIV in my body. I was being sent home to die.

My story had previously attracted the attention of the Christian press. On release from hospital, Mum and Dad contacted a secular news agency. Journalists began queuing at the front door; photos appeared in the national press; interviews were given for radio and television. What a way to become famous!

Hundreds of cards, letters and presents arrived from all over the globe. So many, it was not possible to reply to everyone who sent them. From closer to home came a request from the new Bishop of Salisbury, the Right Reverend Dr David Stancliffe. He wanted to know if I was strong enough to receive him as a visitor. I said 'yes'.

Before he arrived, I indulged in a few musings as to what he might be like. Perhaps he would wear special robes and speak perfect English in a sing-song voice. Would he expect me to call him 'My Lord Bishop' I wondered? All these ideas were quickly dispelled when he arrived in a businesslike suit, with clerical shirt and collar, and announced, 'Hello, I'm David.'

We sat down together. He was easy to talk to, and listened with interest as I told him something of my calling and work in Zimbabwe. He seemed genuinely moved.

'When a bishop is appointed, it is customary for groups of colleagues and parishes to give various items of episcopal insignia as gifts. If it were not so, it would be difficult to make ends meet. Members of the Liturgical Commission—of which I recently became Chairman—said they would like to present me with something.'

He had already been given a fine bishop's ring by the Bishop of Portsmouth, but said he would very much like to have a smaller and more discreet one which could be worn when not on official business.

'A reasonably simple gold band was found, like a man's wedding ring. The hallmark on the inside showed the year I was ordained to the priesthood. It was inscribed in Carolingian script *IN TE DOMINE SPERAVI*: "In thee, O Lord, have I put my trust." This is a quotation from the last verse of the *TE DEUM*, which forms part of the Anglican Order for Morning Prayer.' Leaning forward, he took the ring he was talking about from his own hand, to show me the words. I could just about see them with my good eye.

He explained, 'I chose this motto because it is all too easy for bishops as well as other people to start putting their confidence into management exercises, or new schemes, or the institutional church, or whatever, instead of in God.'

I nodded, adding that he could include medicine in that list.

'Joy, there is a sense in which a bishop is married to his diocese, taking on its concerns, its parishes and people. When I was consecrated I received special responsibility for outcasts, the poor and those who cannot help themselves. I have little to share with you, except my care for the poor. You have sacrificed your life for their sake. I want to be identified with that sacrificial quality; that giving of oneself regardless of the cost. So I want to give you this ring. It will be a link between us. Will you accept it?'

I had already been impressed that a Church of England bishop was taking an interest in the trials of a Pentecostal. Now a lump came to my throat as I took the precious possession from him.

'I will be proud to wear it, and encouraged by the message it contains.' He seemed quite humbled. A look of understanding went between us; a bond of acknowledgement had been formed that we were both servants of the same God.

I have worn the ring every day since. It is a little large for my slender fingers. Mum wound some embroidery silk around the inside edge, to ensure it does not slip off.

At the beginning of December each year there is World AIDS Day. In 1994 I used my newsworthy status to obtain more publicity for this event. Some of the stories used the angle that I would be dead by Christmas. Spurred on by the challenge to prove the media wrong, I not only lived through the festive season, but also enjoyed it. I even put on a little weight in the process.

I did miss out on the carol services, though. It is not possible for me to attend church any longer. I am too weak, and can only walk a few steps around the house before becoming tired. Instead, Mum stays home with me on a Sunday and we worship together. Sometimes other members of the family or friends come over and join us. These are times I really enjoy. I still have my voice, and can sing the old hymns and modern choruses as loud as I like.

Early in the New Year someone interviewed me and said

the number of AIDS cases worldwide had risen to more than a million. My reply was that it can only get higher. As yet there is no vaccine, no cure. I was also informed that four other nurses have contracted the disease in the same way as myself: victims of their patients.

As Britain moved into a winter of torrential rain, with people being stranded in dreadful floods, one of my worst nightmares came true. The sight in my left eye failed. I am now totally blind. It is so hard to accept. But even this disability has brought unexpected blessings. My hearing is so acute I can hear the smallest sounds. I love to have the bedroom window open and listen to the birdsong. I never really noticed they were there before. It is a mystery to me how such tiny creatures can make such lovely music. I will not be able to see the golden daffodils this year. However, when flowers arrive for me, I can take pleasure in gently running my fingers over the petals. They are so soft and fleshy in a way nothing else is.

The pains in my head and feelings of sickness would be constant and unbearable now if it were not for the morphine intake, which has been increased. It turns me into a giggling girl, but it works. My appetite is extremely poor. I eat less and less. I have become all skin and bone. Every little movement hurts.

Lying still in bed, with nothing else to distract me, I feel God is close all day and night. He is here when the District and Macmillan nurses come to give treatment; when Jacquie relieves Mum or Dad at my bedside; as Roy is heard cutting the back lawn. I pray out loud, 'Lord send someone to make me comfortable.' It feels as if my bones are on the outside of my skin.

Good Friday 1995. The family have church around my bed. It is lovely. I am so full of praise, my arms go up in the air and I shout, 'Hallelujah!' I know I will not live to experience my birthday next week. I do not care. I will be in a better place.

Drifting in and out of consciousness now. Dreams and visions of heaven. Or are they real? I hear Dad say, 'She's going.' Then all my pain disappears as I leave my earthly body behind. My soul is released into the next world. I leave behind me no offspring. This book is my legacy for all those who are children of this age of AIDS.

Note

The risk of HIV infection from social contact or normal day-to-day activity is effectively non-existent. However, health care workers are regularly exposed to risk through accidents with needles, operating instruments or through blood contamination of their own wounds. Despite this, the risk of transfer of HIV from an infected person is still far less than for, say, hepatitis B. For example, an injury from an HIV contaminated needle will result in infection only one time in 200 accidents, compared to 1 in 5 from hepatitis B. Joy may have been accidentally exposed to HIV many times as she worked in an area where the number of carriers is very high. Health care workers can greatly reduce risk of infection by following normal infection control guidelines.

Dr Patrick Dixon MA MBBS
Founder of ACET (Aids Care Education and Training)

Epilogue

Eunice Joy Bath died in the early evening of Easter Saturday, 15th April 1995, two days before her forty-fifth birthday.

On 26th April her funeral service was held in her own beloved Elim Church in Salisbury, attended by almost 300 people: family, church friends, nursing colleagues, school and college associates. Interment followed in Salisbury Cemetery.

Three weeks later a celebration of thanksgiving for Joy's life took place in Salisbury's Playhouse Theatre, attended by over 450 people from all over the British Isles and Africa. Appreciations were given by Mrs P. Rycroft—immediate past Mayor of Salisbury; Doctor R. Drew, Sister D. Brown and the Revd P. Munembe—all from the Elim Mission at Katerere in Zimbabwe; the Revds W. Lewis and B. Edwards—both of Elim Executive Council, and G. Ladlow and M. Hathaway of Salisbury Elim Church.

It was Joy's wish that the inscription on the headstone of her grave should read: 'Greater love has no one than this, that he lay down his life for his friends' (John 15:13).

The Bath family cannot personally reply to all correspondence. Enquiries about Joy, overseas work undertaken by the Elim Pentecostal Church, or questions about the Christian faith, should be directed to:

Elim International Missions
P.O. Box 38
Cheltenham
Gloucestershire
GL50 3HN
England

LIVING UNDER THE VOLCANO

Living Under the Volcano

CHRISTINE HAILES PERILLO
with VIVIEN CULVER

KINGSWAY PUBLICATIONS
EASTBOURNE

Contents

Acknowledgements

The work of the Philippine Outreach Centre depends first and foremost on the Lord, without whom I can do nothing, and then on all the people who faithfully help in so many ways. Of these, special thanks are due to the trustees who work for the Philippine Outreach from the UK; to my parents and Nanna Jean, for their wisdom and understanding and the many sacrifices they have made; and chiefly to my husband and children, whose support and patience mean so much when, as often happens, our work causes us to spend a lot of time apart.

Of those who have helped in the making of this book, thanks are especially due to Kevin Nicholas, for many hours spent helping to arrange the material; to Rita Fenwick, for the speed and efficiency with which she typed the manuscript; and to Fiona Gray, for drawing the map.

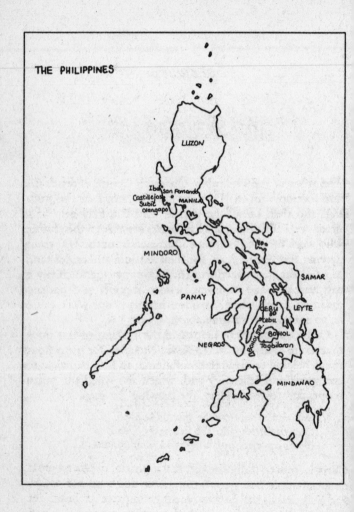

THE PHILIPPINES

LUZON

Iba   San Fernando
Castillejos   MANILA
Subic
Olangapo

MINDORO

SAMAR

PANAY   LEYTE

CEBU
Cebu   BOHOL
Tagbilaran

NEGROS

MINDANAO

Foreword

by the Revd Canon Noel Proctor, MBE
Former Chaplain of HM Prison,
Strangeways, Manchester

After arriving to take the post of Prison Chaplain at Strangeways, Manchester in 1979, I was introduced to a music group of young people from the Altrincham area. They were a talented group, but one young lady reminded me of the following poem:

> Two frogs fell into a deep cream bowl,
> The one was wise and a cheery soul.
> The other one took a gloomy view
> And bade his friend a sad adieu.
> Said the other frog with a merry grin:
> 'I can't get out, but I won't give in;
> I'll swim around 'til my strength is spent,
> Then I will die the more content.'
> But as he swam, though, ever it seemed
> His struggling began to churn the cream
> Until on top of pure butter he stopped,
> And out of the bowl he quickly hopped.
> The moral, you ask? Oh, it's easily found:
> If you can't get out, keep swimming around . . .

Chrissy, in everything she did at the prison, displayed great determination. She played the guitar and sang her songs, and she used all her gifts to reach the inmates for Jesus. Yet her gifts of music and singing were only a means to an end to get the ears of the men. This was followed by her

9

directness with the gospel, which seemed somehow unexpected from such a slight figure of a girl.

She clearly knew that God's Holy Spirit was using her to win men for Jesus, so she was invited to come to the prison on a regular basis to share in groups and services. Early on she spoke of her firm conviction that her ministry would involve prison work, but as I pointed out to her, she was very young; she was also attractive and perhaps her naive and trusting nature could be easy prey for the 'con men'. Furthermore, I knew that in the British prison chaplaincy at that time, there was no possibility of her coming into a full-time ministry.

We talked about this, but she did not seem discouraged. And as we prayed for each other, the Lord began to show me that Chrissy had more than enthusiasm, a nice voice and an attractive personality. She had that wonderful gift of 'stickability', and I concluded that wherever the Lord would finally lead her, she was determined to trust him until the doors would open.

The remarkable quality which stands out in Chrissy's character and personality is her deep love for the Lord Jesus Christ, and her almost hungry desire to introduce others to him. This commitment has given her the determination and resolve to press on against seemingly insurmountable difficulties, and to prove her Lord in every situation.

The following story is so remarkable that it reads like a novel, and I know you will be blessed by it. It is also a real challenge to young Christians, to seek God's will for their lives, and to launch out into the deep waters for the 'catch' which only God gives.

1

'You Shall Receive Power'

'Every one of you will be baptised in the Spirit tonight.'

This statement by our visiting preacher at church that evening was made with a confidence that astounded me. 'All of us?' I thought. 'Surely that can't be true.'

The speaker was Lewis Cardno, a retired fisherman from Peterhead who travelled all over Britain singing and preaching Christ. He had impressed me as being the most joyful person I had ever met – not with a superficial joy, but one that was deep and genuine. He'd been speaking about the power of the Holy Spirit, emphasising how vital it was for all Christians to receive this power in order to live lives that were truly pleasing to God. When he'd finished, he had asked all those who had not yet been baptised in the Spirit to raise their hands. Several of us had done so and it was to us that he addressed those words which so amazed me: '*All* of you. . . .'

My surprise was not due to any doubt about baptism in the Spirit; my father (who was the pastor of the church), my mother and many of my fellow church members had already had this experience. It was due rather to the fact that I was only thirteen. I had mistakenly gained the impression that some Christian experiences were only for adults because my parents had not yet allowed me to be

baptised in water as a believer, even though I'd been a
Christian since the age of seven. Mum and Dad never tried
to force the pace of my development as a Christian; they
saw it as their task to teach me the way I should go and to
leave the rest to God. When they said I was too young to
understand the purpose of baptism in water, they, of
course, were concerned only about my ability to grasp its
significance, but I imagined that what mattered was my
actual age. If I was too young to be baptised in water, how
could I be baptised in the Spirit?

Now suddenly, Lewis' words took hold of me. I became
certain I was included and I was filled with a sense of
excitement and expectancy. There was no doubt in my
mind that I would receive the Spirit that night. And I
did. All of us who raised our hands were baptised in the
Holy Spirit and began to speak with other tongues.

Would this be a passing sensation born of emotional
excitement, or a life-changing experience that would rad-
ically transform my relationship with God and enable me to
translate my faith into action with a new power? Time
would tell.

From early childhood I had seen in my mother's life what it
meant to put Christian faith into practice. Mum became a
Christian at a Billy Graham crusade in Manchester in 1961,
the year before I was born. Her own mother ('Nanna
Jean') became a Christian at the same time.

Nanna Jean worked as a cook in a probation hostel for
boys and would often talk over with Mum the sad stories
these boys had to tell. She felt their troubles deeply and did
everything she could to show them the love of Jesus. She
would bake them special treats and spent hours listening to
their problems and telling them about the love Jesus had
for them in spite of the things they had done. Mum became
as concerned as Nanna and because it was always impossible for her to keep God's love to herself, she had to do
something practical for these boys who seemed to have
been abandoned by society.

One of them, Derek, didn't want to go home when his time at the hostel came to an end. He was afraid that he would soon slip back into crime if he returned to his old haunts. And so, when I was just three years old, my parents invited him to come and live with us in our small three-bedroomed house. Mum's aim was to show Derek the love of Christ so that he might accept Christ for himself. It was different for Dad, though. He wasn't yet a Christian and didn't relish the thought of rebels like Derek invading the privacy of his home. However, he did want to please Mum and he knew she felt that this was something God was calling her to do.

In order to make room for this new member of our family, I had to squeeze into the smallest bedroom with my two brothers, Stephen, who was nine and Paul, five. This was fun for a while, but it didn't take long for war to break out. And the changes weren't over yet.

One afternoon, Nanna Jean was having one of her talks with Mum about the problems of the boys at the hostel. 'You see, Mary, once they get out they have nowhere to go. No one wants to help boys like them. What they really need is a home or some sort of centre. But who would do it?'

Dad looked at them over his newspaper and said, 'If you're so concerned, why don't you do it?'

Even though Dad wasn't a Christian, God used him to plant the seed of a vision in Mum's heart. She knew God was challenging her to provide a home not only for Derek but for other young lads in need. It was obvious that our house just wasn't big enough, so straight away Mum began to look for somewhere more suitable. She had no success for a while, and once again it was Dad who eventually pointed out the right direction. Looking through the newspaper one evening, he called out to Mum, 'Here's the house you need – 52 Barrington Road.'

This was a large house which had been a doctor's surgery; it had sixteen rooms, including nine bedrooms. Dad wasn't really serious. He showed Mum the picture and promptly forgot about it. But the next day, at his office, he received a phone call.

'Les, it's me. I'm in it.'

'What are you in, Mary?'

'The house.'

'What house?'

'52 Barrington Road.'

Such a large house wasn't at all Dad's idea of a family home, but he wasn't too worried because there seemed little chance of ever having to move there. Not only was it well beyond their price range but there was also a prospective buyer, a doctor. Mum wasn't at all daunted by this and confidently told the estate agent that God wanted her to have the house. Within a week she was proved right. The doctor changed his mind, and Mum and Dad were able to buy the house for £3,500 instead of the original price of £6,250. Dad had no option but to surrender and admit that God really did seem to be on Mum's side.

So in 1966 we moved the four miles from our small house in Sale to Barrington Road in Altrincham, leaving behind our unremarkable, average way of life for one that could hardly have been more different. In the years that followed, our extended family included many young lads who came to us homeless, jobless and with a history of being in trouble with the police. Sometimes whole families came if they were going through a difficult patch, and stayed until they were on their feet again. One of our most memorable guests was a tramp called Paddy, who was literally white with lice when Mum took him in and cleaned him up. She carefully warned me to keep out of his way, in case I caught lice too. Paddy, however, took a shine to me and often asked me to sit on his lap, and despite Mum's cautions I never had the heart to refuse, though I was always scared to death as I sat there.

A year or so after we moved, Mum invited Brian Smithyman to take a meeting in our home. Brian was an evangelist

from a Pentecostal church in Wolverhampton; who had felt
God call him to hold meetings in the Altrincham area. That
meeting was the first of many and it was through Brian's
ministry that Mum received the baptism in the Holy Spirit
early in 1969.

It was now, too, that God began to work in Dad's heart,
and shortly afterwards, alone in his bedroom, he had a life-
changing experience. On the same night he was born
again, baptised in the Spirit and healed of a painful injury
to his spine, the result of a fall a year earlier. He was
completely transformed. Instead of being glued to the
television, he became totally absorbed in his Bible. Whereas
before he had found satisfaction in a successful business
career, he was now hungry for the word of God. He spent
every spare moment in reading and studying. He didn't
realise at first that in this way God was preparing him for a
ministry of his own.

But within weeks, God had spoken separately to both
Mum and Dad, directing them to go and see a Christian
couple whom they hardly knew. Through this couple, God
showed Mum and Dad that they were to begin to form a
church at 52 Barrington Road, with Dad as pastor. So one
of the bedrooms was cleared out and before long the
Upper Room Christian Fellowship came into being. We
had all kinds of people attending – families and quiet
elderly folk mixed happily with former drug addicts and
ex-prisoners.

And then there was the Sunday school, which was
Mum's special work. Every Sunday afternoon, the peace
and tranquillity would be shattered when a hundred or
more children came bursting through the doors – and in
a sixteen-roomed house, that's a lot of doors. Dad would
go off to his study while Mum, in her element, spent the
afternoon telling the children about the love of Jesus.

This was no ordinary, run-of-the-mill Sunday school.
Along with the youngsters from Christian homes there
were the ones whom Mum, quite literally, fetched in off

the streets. She would drive a minibus through the roughest areas inviting them to join, and they came in large numbers – some from broken homes, some whose fathers were in prison, others whose parents were alcoholics. But to Mum, whatever their background, they were all just children who needed to know they were loved by the same Lord Jesus Christ.

Of course, I joined them in Sunday school, and when I was seven I gave my heart to the Lord. I had the advantage of a Christian home, I was brought up on the teaching of God's word and from early childhood I had seen faith in action all around me; so though I was very young, I understood that I was a sinner and needed a Saviour, and I believed that Jesus had died for me to save me from my sin and its consequences. I really did love the Lord, and I knew that I should show this by the way I behaved. But as time passed, I had to admit to myself that I was failing to live a life that was pleasing to God. The problem was that I had entangled myself in a situation where my love for God was in conflict with my need to gain acceptance and admiration from my school friends.

When our home was first opened to the lads from the hostel, I was a very cute three-year-old, and for several years I was a great favourite with them. Later, as I grew bigger and fatter, they noticed me less and less and I felt lonely and ignored. I often wished I had a sister, but since I hadn't I decided that if I didn't want to be lonely I had to become one of the lads. I thought that if I shared their interests and their habits they would notice me again, and so, unknowingly, I embarked on a course which led me into a lot of confusion and unhappiness.

It was one thing to compete with the boys on equal terms at football, but unfortunately I didn't stop there. I carried my search for a new identity into school, where I became very unruly and was often involved in fights with other children. I found I could hold my own against anybody – in fact I thought it was beneath me to fight with girls and only fought boys. I took pride in the fact that while my opponents were often reduced to tears, I never allowed myself to cry, however badly I was hurt.

In my heart I was ashamed of my behaviour and took care to hide it from my parents and church friends. I still loved attending church meetings and even sang an occasional solo, but all the time I knew my life was at odds with what I believed. By the time I was twelve I was living what was virtually a double life, and though I didn't want to be a hypocrite I felt powerless to change the pattern in which I was trapped.

When I moved on to secondary school, it wasn't long before many of my teachers had given up on me, I was so badly behaved. None of their punishments had any effect and within a year they had more or less written me off as hopeless. Because my life was such a mess, I never spoke to my classmates about the Lord; I wasn't ashamed of him, but I was ashamed of myself. I knew that people would expect much better of me if I professed Christ and I was afraid I would never be able to live up to their expectations. All my school friends lived a long way from my home and didn't even know I went to church, much less that I was a pastor's daughter.

I was desperately unhappy about my inability to be a good witness for the Lord. Despite my behaviour, I did love him and longed to be faithful to him. I couldn't do it in my own strength, but thankfully God's faithfulness to us always far exceeds ours to him and he granted me the desire of my heart that night when I was baptised in the Spirit.

I began now to experience in my own life the fulfilment of Jesus' promise. 'But you shall receive power when the Holy Spirit has come upon you; and you shall be witnesses to Me . . .' (Acts 1:8). I found I had a new boldness in telling people about the Lord Jesus and what he had done for me, and I was no longer worried about living up to their expectations because I had the power of the Holy Spirit to help me.

My school friends were not slow to notice the change in me. One day soon after Lewis' visit, one of the boys at school pushed me over, knocking me to the floor. Anticipating my usual reaction, he instinctively dived out of my way and was dumbfounded when I just picked myself up and didn't respond to his challenge. I hadn't even had to struggle to overcome the impulse to retaliate – it simply wasn't in my nature any more.

My attitude in class changed out of all recognition. My domestic science teacher, for example, who had been the target of some of my worst and most unco-operative behaviour, could hardly believe it when I voluntarily rewrote my notes for the whole year, so that they would be neat and tidy. Even more amazed was my PE teacher. Having struggled for so long to get me to move so much as a muscle, she now saw me becoming one of the most active in the class, running the cross-country course and eventually winning a place in several school sports teams. The joy of my new relationship with the Lord spilled over into everything I did, so much so that my English teacher took me aside and warned me that if I wanted to pass my 'O' level, I had to stop writing about my religious beliefs in every essay. But when he told me to write about my experiences, what else did I have to write about? Jesus was my life. I continued to write about the Lord, even in the exam (which I passed).

I worked hard at everything. Teachers were no longer my enemies but my friends and my mission field. I would never miss an opportunity to speak about the Lord. I would invite them to meetings and one or two even came along.

The baptism in the Holy Spirit was the beginning of a new and wonderful relationship with Jesus. I really wanted him to reign in my life and I was hungry to know more of the things of the Spirit. My father often entertained visiting preachers, with whom he would have long discussions and debates concerning doctrine, and I used to sit and listen whenever I could, silently soaking it all up. My father is a man of great spiritual insight and I loved to hear him speak of the deeper things of God. I never realised at the time how much the Lord was teaching me through these conversations.

God also had things to teach me directly. I wanted him to reign in my life, I wanted to do with joy anything he asked of me. In the summer of 1976, when I was fourteen, I learned a small but significant lesson about the meaning of obedience. Mum and Dad had taken me to a Christian camp run by the Hollybush Christian Fellowship in North Yorkshire. During one of the evening meetings, I became aware that the Lord had something particular to say to me that night. As I waited for him to make his will known to me, I had a strong sense of his presence, which continued long after the meeting was over. While other people were leaving, my parents stayed behind with me in the marquee, but didn't attempt to intervene as they realised that the Lord was dealing with me. At last, at around midnight, when the marquee was almost empty, he spoke to me: 'Christine, I want you to burn your records.'

Mum and Dad had bought me a record player the previous Christmas and I'd started to build up a collection of pop records which I'd hoped would one day match my brother's collection. I hadn't seen anything wrong in this before, but there and then I made up my mind that I would burn them and that I would not allow anything to alter my decision. It was a small sacrifice, I thought, and I didn't intend to exaggerate it; but obedience even in small things is important, and this seemed to be the least I could offer to the One who had done everything for me. I've since been asked how I knew it was the Lord speaking, but to me it was a simple matter: '. . . the sheep follow him, for they know his voice . . . they do not know the voice of strangers' (Jn 10:4–5). I knew his voice as surely as I knew my parents'.

The return to normal life after the excitement of a camp or convention is always an anticlimax. Away from the atmosphere of faith and expectation in the company of other Christians, I knew it would be easy to let my determination fade – I had seen this happen to other people. When we arrived home from Hollybush, I was already missing the fellowship we had shared with our friends there, and I certainly didn't have the same feelings as I'd had on the night when the Lord spoke to me. However, my father had taught me to live the Christian life by faith, not feelings, so I went straight to my room, gathered up my small collection of records and headed for the back yard. On the way, I met several of the young people from church, who wanted to know what I was doing. When I explained, they tried to persuade me that I should give the records to them. 'You'll still be getting rid of them,' they said. 'That's just the same as burning them.'

I felt terrible. I couldn't do what they asked, but I didn't want them to think I wasn't prepared to let anyone else have the records just because I couldn't keep them myself. But it wouldn't be the same; God hadn't told me to get rid of them but quite definitely to burn them. So I went ahead and did it. My parents didn't interfere, not even to praise me for being obedient. I have always been grateful for the fact that they never encouraged spiritual pride in me, and taught me instead that to be obedient to the Lord – to be a living sacrifice to him – was just my reasonable service.

Giving up my records was a small sacrifice, yet after I had done it I began to appreciate that by asking it of me the Lord had saved me from much that would have been harmful. Soon after, a school friend invited me to a party at her house. In the past, I'd accepted her invitations without a thought, but this time I had to refuse. 'God spoke to me and told me to burn my records,' I explained, 'so I'm sure he doesn't want me to dance to someone else's.' To my surprise, she respected my position and even continued to invite me to her parties, though she knew I wouldn't accept. I was grateful for her kindness, because no teenager likes to be the only one without an invitation, which became mostly true for me once my views became known.

Even though I never went to parties, I couldn't help hearing them talked about at school. Gradually, I found out what I had been too naive to realise before – that while I'd been enjoying the dancing in one room, other things were happening elsewhere. I learned that girls as young as thirteen and fourteen were getting drunk and losing their virginity as a consequence. I was so thankful to the Lord for saving me from that, and I realised that his salvation extended not only to forgiving the sins I had committed but also to keeping me from situations which could lead me into sin.

I once debated this subject with my eldest brother. Before giving his life to the Lord at the age of twenty-one, he had had some experience of the world and the sort of pleasures which it offers. He reasoned that the testimony of a person who had been rescued from the grip of such pleasures was more dynamic than that of someone who had never known them. I understood his point of view because testimonies of that kind do have a dramatic appeal. However, I knew that the only difference between a drug addict who had been saved by grace and someone like me was that whereas God's grace had set the addict free from addiction, that same grace had saved me from ever being ensnared in it. Either way, it was all due to grace.

Grace – and, by the power of the Holy Spirit, a new freedom to do what was right. I had so much to be thankful for. And so much still to learn.

2

'The Day of Small Things'

Nick was the leader of our church youth group, as well as of our singing group, which we called Psalm One-Fifty. More than this, he was also a gifted and dedicated evangelist, wholly committed to taking the gospel to the people of Altrincham. Every Thursday, whatever the weather, he would go out onto the streets with his Bible, a bag of tracts and his guitar. Occasionally, other members of the church would go with him, but not all of them had the same enthusiasm as Nick when it came to standing in the pouring rain, and some of them had other responsibilities which had to come first; so Nick often went out alone. But this never discouraged him. Week by week, with or without helpers, he went cheerfully on with his work. I really admired his faithfulness.

Then my admiration turned to conviction. Why was I just feeling sorry for him when I could go with him myself? Hadn't I been learning that the Christian life meant obedience and sacrifice? Well, here was another area where God was calling me to obey. The prospect filled me with fear, because my only previous experience of open-air evangelism had been as a member of a large group. It would be very different with just the two of us, but I knew I couldn't

let my fear get in the way of my obedience, so I told Nick
that I wanted to join him.

Every week, before we set out, Nanna Jean would pray
for us and Nick would ask the Lord to direct us as to where
we should go that day. It might be the bus station, the
railway station, a pub or the middle of a crowded shopping
centre. Nick had no fear of anything or anyone. By preaching and through songs given to him by the inspiration of
the Holy Spirit, he boldly declared the good news of salvation through Jesus Christ.

At the beginning, I just tagged along in Nick's shadow,
but gradually the Lord used him to train me in evangelism.
Soon, as well as sharing in the singing, I was able to take
my first steps in speaking to the passers-by. Though I was
quaking inside, I learned to trust the Holy Spirit who was
always faithful to give me the words I needed and bring to
my mind the Scripture references which were appropriate
in each situation.

Of course, as I'd foreseen, there were difficulties and
discomforts to face. Sometimes it was rain or freezing
cold; sometimes our pride was wounded when people
laughed at us. But these were only physical and temporal
discomforts. Through them all, we had the assurance of
God's word that those who sow to the Spirit (Gal 6:8) will
have a harvest that is not temporal but eternal. By helping
Nick I was discovering that if in spite of our fears we step
out and rely on God, he will use us however inadequate we
feel. This truth was brought home to me even more by an
experience which followed from my frustrating struggle to
learn to play the guitar.

My interest in playing began when Mum and Dad
bought a guitar as a Christmas present for my brother
Paul. I was constantly borrowing it even though I knew
it annoyed him – I so much wanted to learn to play. I asked
Nick to help me, but somehow I didn't make much progress. All my attempts to discipline my fumbling fingers
ended in failure. So I made a covenant with the Lord, that

if he would help me I would play only for him and for his glory. I wasn't conscious of the Lord speaking to me about this, but he was very gracious and granted me my request, and before long I could play enough for a solo accompaniment. For my part, I resolved to play only for him.

By this time Dad had been involved in introducing the Full Gospel Business Men's Fellowship International (FGBMFI) into Britain, and was President of the Altrincham branch. Psalm One-Fifty, of which I was a member, were often asked to lead the worship at FGBMFI meetings, which might be either evangelistic events or opportunities for Christian men to have fellowship with each other.

On one occasion, when I was fifteen, there was a large FGBMFI convention in Blackpool. One of the items on the programme was the women's luncheon meeting, at which the speaker was to be Jean Darnall. As many of the men too were keen to hear her, Milicent Spilman, who was responsible for the meeting, had invited them to join us. This would make it a very big gathering – over a thousand were expected to be there. At the beginning of the conference, Milicent approached me with a request that almost stopped my breath: 'Will you minister in song at the luncheon meeting?'

My heart thumped and my mouth dropped open. I knew that I'd promised the Lord I would sing for him whenever the opportunity arose, but surely she couldn't mean me? Not on my own, in front of all those people? Milicent could see how nervous I was, but she didn't offer me an escape route. Instead, she encouraged me: 'You can do it; the Lord will anoint you.' Scared and reluctant, I agreed.

As the conference got under way, I became more and more afraid. Others who were to play and sing arrived with all their expensive equipment and backing tapes. They sounded so professional. I began to tremble at the thought of standing in front of so many people, just me and my acoustic guitar. But I couldn't back out; I knew, despite my inadequacy, that this was something God was asking of me.

I went to the Lord in prayer. I didn't ask him to give me a sweet voice or to help me avoid mistakes. As Milicent's words had indicated, it wasn't technical skill that I needed, but his anointing.

When the time came for me to sing and I heard my name announced from the platform, my whole body began to shake. Making my way unsteadily to the front, I encouraged myself with the promise of Philippians 4:13: 'I can do all things through Christ who strengthens me.' But the real battle hadn't started yet. As I began to sing, a voice whispered in my ear: 'You see, all that worry was for nothing. Look, they really like you.' I looked and, true enough, people did seem to be enjoying the song. 'You see,' the voice went on, 'you do sing well.' Then I knew that this was not the Lord's voice – he wouldn't use flattering words or encourage pride – but Satan's. Internally, I rebuked him. 'You were never anything but a liar. Without Jesus I can do nothing, and if I have any talent it's only because he has chosen to give it to me. Be gone, in the name of Jesus.'

By the time the battle was over, so was my song. I had no idea how I'd managed to get through it. I realised that the Lord had allowed this experience so that my motives for singing in public might be tested. Whose approval did I want? Was I doing it to gain attention for myself or, as I'd promised, for his glory? I thanked him for giving me victory in this temptation and for enabling me to reject Satan's lies and recognise that I no longer needed to be accepted by men. He had made me 'accepted in the beloved' (Eph 1:6), and that was all that mattered.

That afternoon, a group of us went out onto the streets of Blackpool to share the gospel. When we'd finished, I went for a walk with a friend along the promenade, where there were horse-drawn carriages waiting to give rides to holiday-makers. The driver of one of these, seeing my guitar, shouted to us and asked me to sing him a song. I

knew he was joking, but remembering that I'd
sing for the Lord at every opportunity, I stop
to him. He had a girl in each arm and when
only sang songs about Jesus, all three of them
ing fun of me. Thanks to Nick's training I was no stranger
to facing insults, so I stood my ground and started to sing.
Almost immediately, the driver silently took his arms from
around the girls and began to listen. He was obviously
moved and after the song my friend and I spoke to him
about the gospel. He didn't receive Christ as his Saviour
there and then, but it was impossible to mistake his genuine interest, which could only be the result of God's
anointing on my singing. My natural ability was nothing
very special; but talent alone could never carry the truth of
the gospel into a person's heart.

I remember once hearing a preacher say, 'God does little
with much, much with little and everything with nothing.'
The challenges I met at Blackpool may have been small
ones, yet they were designed by God to impress this principle on my mind. Focusing on our own abilities leads to
pride and deception; we should be less concerned with the
extent of our gifts than with dedicating them, however
insignificant, to the One who can do everything with our
nothing. Sterner trials would come later, but in the meantime, like a soldier whose first taste of battle comes in a
minor skirmish, I'd had the opportunity to prove my weapons in the face of the enemy.

It was often at a conference or convention that God
spoke to me. Shortly after the Blackpool convention I
went with Mum and Dad and a group from the Upper
Room to a conference arranged by International Gospel
Outreach (IGO), an organisation with which Mum and
Dad had regular contact. While I was there, God spoke
to me directly once again: 'Christine, I want you to stop
watching television.'

I didn't understand why the Lord was asking this of me;
after all, even Dad watched television, so why shouldn't I?

wever, it wasn't necessary for me to understand, only to obey. From the moment I returned home, I avoided watching television and when Tuesday evening came round Mum and Dad were both pleased and surprised to notice me getting ready for our prayer meeting at the Upper Room. The fact was that even after being baptised in the Holy Spirit I'd never attended a single prayer meeting, excusing my absence on the grounds that I had homework to do. This was true as far as it went, but a much bigger factor was that on Tuesdays *Dallas* was on television.

But now that television was out of my life, there was nothing holding me back. I saw then why it had been necessary for the Lord to ask me to give it up; in itself it wasn't wrong, but my priorities were. Without realising it, I had neglected the commandment to love God above all else. From then on I attended prayer meetings whenever I could, even when the Lord gave me freedom to watch television again after a few months. I'd learned my lesson, and ever since I've always been careful to make sure I control my viewing habits rather than allow them to control me.

No area of life is too insignificant to be God's training ground. Minor challenges that have been overcome prepare us to meet bigger ones; a small act of obedience can give a clearer understanding of the first and great commandment. Let's not despise 'the day of small things'.

3

'Your Right Hand Shall Hold Me'

In a number of areas I had made progress as a Christian and in some ways was quite mature for my age. But there was one part of my life where quite the opposite was the case, and this was in my relationships with boys. The problem was in knowing what was the Lord's will for me, and I wasn't helped as a young teenager by receiving so much well meant advice from others in the church. It seemed that every time I formed a relationship, someone would come and tell me that this was not God's will for my life, and as I didn't want to risk stepping outside his will, I would break off the relationship, leaving the boy almost as confused as I was myself.

When I was seventeen, I started going out with Stuart and of course it wasn't long before someone told me that he wasn't the man God intended for me. The advice was more than usually unwelcome since I already felt deeply for Stuart. And besides, I could see no obvious objection to our relationship; he was eighteen – exactly a year older than me to the day – he was a member of the church and to me we seemed so well suited. I prayed and asked the Lord to show me whether the advice I'd been given was right, but my feelings made it difficult to distinguish between his will and mine and I had no assurance either way. However, my biggest fear was of failing to fulfil God's purpose for me, so the following day, in floods of tears, I told Stuart our relationship had to end. I was wretchedly unhappy.

Despite what I'd said to Stuart, I wasn't fully reconciled to losing him and continued to ask God to give me a clear indication of his will, becoming more and more bogged down in a morass of uncertainty. Eventually, Dad decided it was time to intervene, and gently suggested that I shouldn't worry so much about trying to conform to other people's ideas of God's will for me. This was sound advice which often stood me in good stead – even though in this particular case Dad was later to have cause to regret the effect of his words.

As a result, Stuart and I resumed our relationship and within a year were engaged to be married. The perfect ending; apart from just one thing. Though Dad had given his consent to our engagement, I knew he was beginning to have serious doubts about Stuart and me and was unhappy at the changes he'd seen in me. To me it seemed natural that my world should revolve around Stuart. But what Dad saw was his daughter spending virtually no time at home, neglecting her school work and giving up her plans to be a teacher in order to begin earning enough money for an early wedding.

I loved my father very much and wanted to remain close to him whether I was married or not, so I tried to set his mind at rest. I assured him that God and his will for me were more important to me than anything or anyone, even Stuart. Never thinking that I in my turn would regret what I said, I pointed out that God, knowing I wanted to please him, would sovereignly intervene to end the relationship if Stuart were not the right man for me to marry.

Having done my best to comfort Dad, I felt I could now enjoy my future prospects without a care in the world. As well as my forthcoming marriage, I saw a vista of exciting new opportunities to serve the Lord begin to open up before me. Soon after our engagement, I finished school and went to work for a large company as a trainee civil engineering technician, doing technical drawings for a power station project. Once a week I went to college to study for a HTC (Higher Technician's Certificate).

I took care not to repeat the mistake I'd made at school and on my first day at work I let everyone know I was a Christian. The company had a Christian Union, which I joined straight away. There were just four of us, out of a workforce of several hundreds, and we took it in turns to prepare a short talk, which was my first experience of expounding the word of God. I seized every opportunity to speak for the Lord in the office and was privileged to play a small part in two of the men becoming Christians.

Then there was the excitement of another FGBMFI convention at Wembley, where the speaker was to be Demos Shakarian himself, the founder of FGBMFI. I had heard Demos once before at the first British convention in Glasgow and the memory of that meeting was very precious to me because after Demos had spoken, the Lord had given me a vision that I would one day be used to minister to many people. I'd wept before the Lord, knowing I was unworthy but longing for him to use me. I went to Wembley fully expecting that he would speak to me at this convention too.

One of the speakers at Wembley related his experience of ministry in prisons and on death row. It wasn't the first time I had heard such a talk, but before I'd merely found it interesting. This time was different; I knew for certain that God was telling me that I too was going to be involved in prison ministry. It wasn't until the following day that I plucked up courage to tell anyone; I was afraid people would think I just wanted to do something sensational like the speaker the previous evening.

The first person I told was my father. 'Dad,' I said, 'the Lord has spoken to me and told me what my ministry is.'

'Oh, yes, and what's that?'

'Prison ministry.'

I half expected him to laugh. I was eighteen years old and five feet one inch tall; hardly, on the face of it, prime material for such a ministry. Dad's only response, however, was to hand me a leaflet from his inside pocket. It was all about prison ministry. He'd picked it up after the meeting the previous night.

True to his principles, Dad wouldn't interfere in what the Lord was doing and saying in my life, and nothing more was said. Sometimes I found this reticence frustrating; I trusted his wisdom, and his advice would have reassured me. But Dad knew what I really needed and always encouraged me to look to God, not man, for guidance, just as he and Mum did. And God has his own ways of preparing and directing us, often ways we don't expect.

A while after the Wembley convention, Psalm One-Fifty were invited to sing at Christian World, the largest Christian bookshop in Manchester, which ran monthly meetings for worship and teaching in its basement coffee shop. To my great surprise, the guest speaker was Noel Proctor, Chaplain of Strangeways Prison. Perhaps it was through him that I would be given a chance to begin prison ministry, I thought, so after the meeting I spoke to him about my call and asked for his advice.

His response wasn't what I expected. He suggested I should consider training as a prison officer.

'I don't mean that I feel called to minister in women's prisons,' I explained, 'but in men's.'

'Well,' he replied, 'I don't think it would really be wise for a young girl like you to be working in men's prisons.'

I was disappointed, but I couldn't blame Noel. From his point of view, his advice was sensible. He'd only just met me and I couldn't expect him there and then to share my certainty that God had spoken to me. I would just have to wait for God's time: if he had called me, he would open the right doors.

In fact, I didn't have too long to wait. One night, full of excitement, Nick called Psalm One-Fifty together to tell us that Noel had invited us to take two services at Strangeways. At Nick's request, I agreed to do a solo. As usual, I felt nervous, but I was still bound by my promise to sing for the Lord.

The day came and we were waiting in the chapel to begin the first service, which was for remand prisoners. We were all tense and keyed up, especially the girls, as the men filed in. They began eyeing us up and down and soon they were whistling and calling out to us. Their comments were unrepeatable and I could feel myself growing hot with embarrassment. I began to appreciate the soundness of Noel's earlier advice.

However, we made it through the first service and by the end we really sensed that the Spirit was at work. But we still had to face the second service for the convicted prisoners. Once again, the men filed in and we suffered a repeat performance of looks and comments, followed by whistles, clapping and stamping when Noel introduced us. When it came to my solo and I faced this cynical, jeering crowd, I prayed that the Lord would speak to them through me. My song was called 'Jesus, will you go?' and told the story of how Jesus consented to leave the splendour of heaven to die for those who would mock and spit on him. When I finished, there was complete silence. Later we had many more invitations to Strangeways and my singing was never again received in quite this way, but on this one occasion it was as if the Lord was confirming to me, and to Noel, that he wanted to use me in this ministry.

I was so happy with the way my life was going when suddenly my whole world fell apart. Without warning, Stuart broke off our engagement and I was devastated. The words I'd spoken to Dad almost a year ago now carried a bitter significance. I'd acknowledged then that God was sovereign and would end the relationship if it were wrong for me; I acknowledged it still with my mind, but it didn't make any difference to the hurt I felt. Why did God's will have to be so painful?

I revolved this question endlessly in my mind as I struggled to make sense of my shattered hopes. Had I not been too distressed to think rationally, it would have been obvious that pain is inevitable when the desires of fallen human nature have to be denied in order to conform us to the will of God – the Spirit and the flesh are constantly at war with each other and in war the loser always gets hurt.

I knew in my heart that if Stuart were not the right man for me, then God must have a plan which was even better. However, this didn't satisfy my flesh. I didn't want the 'better'. I wanted what I'd had, what Stuart and I had planned together.

To some extent, I came to terms with the situation. I had to. But in my heart a seed of rebellion was sown. I took my eyes off God's plan for me and started to make my own. In my unhappiness I began to look for something that would restore my self-esteem and make me feel better about myself. I was rather plain and always a bit overweight, so I decided to change my appearance, make myself more attractive and, if possible, win Stuart back. I didn't recognise these intentions as rebellion – Satan is very subtle – and carried on as usual at church and in my music ministry.

My first move was to set about reducing my weight. I wouldn't need to lose much, so I didn't anticipate any big problem, and from reading magazines I already knew all the latest diet trends. I didn't actually eat a great deal to begin with: at home none of us ate breakfast and I often skipped lunch, a habit I'd acquired at school when lunchtime was taken up with sport. My main meal was in the evening and this became the target for my diet.

I knew salads and vegetables were safe, but what else? The fibre diet was popular just then and I knew I needed protein, so I thought I'd found the perfect solution when I hit on the idea of canned kidney beans. I ate a large can every day. At work I spent my breaks poring over magazine articles on diet and refusing biscuits and sweets, which, together with the fact that I wasn't really fat at all, earned me the nickname 'Podge'. Of course, I had to hide my peculiar eating habits from my family and this meant inventing excuses for eating at different times from everyone else. After a while, though, I found I couldn't completely do without sweet things and as ice cream seemed to have the fewest calories I added that to my diet too. Not being an obvious diet food, it also helped me to hide what I was doing from Mum.

However, perhaps because the rest of my diet was so unbalanced, the fat in the ice cream began to make me sick. I was actually pleased about this, as it meant I could eat more of it without gaining any weight. Satan had really deceived me in all this, though it was my rebellion which gave him the opportunity.

After a while, I was forced to admit to myself that things were getting out of control. My system became so upset by constant vomiting that my body began to reject everything I ate; even half a biscuit made me sick. I still managed somehow to keep my family in ignorance, but I couldn't fool myself any longer. I knew now that what I was doing was wrong, but I was powerless to change it. I stopped eating ice cream, but the vomiting continued. As with all sin, I'd started off in the driving seat but now I had no control over it.

My health began to suffer and I was an easy target for viruses and infections. One day I felt so ill with what I thought was flu that I couldn't go in to work. That morning I stood in the kitchen glancing over into the breakfast room where Mum was watching a chat show on television. Gradually I became transfixed by the programme as, one by one, a series of young girls described the symptoms of their illness. It all sounded dreadfully familiar: 'I used laxatives'

. . . 'I made myself vomit every day' . . . 'I never wanted to eat with the rest of the family.'

I suddenly realised that what I had wasn't flu. I had the same disease as these girls: anorexia nervosa. Some of them were literally wasting away. There were mothers, too, who told how they had lost their daughters to this modern slimmers' disease. I was horrified.

During the next few days I went through agonies. How could I do this to Mum and Dad? Stronger than ever, I felt the Holy Spirit convicting me: 'Christine, you know this is sin before me.' I did know, but I felt so helpless. Since watching that programme, I knew that facing the truth about my illness would be the first step to recovery, but then Satan would whisper: 'Do that and you know what will happen. You'll get fat again.' I would retreat in panic, thinking it was better to be ill and slim than healthy and fat, only to find myself faced once more with God's absolute demand that I repent. Finally, I surrendered to the Lord and made an appointment to see the doctor.

He was puzzled by my symptoms, as little was known then about anorexia and even less about bulimia, but when I told him about the girls I'd seen on television he immediately arranged for me to see a specialist.

When I kept the appointment, I was astounded to discover that the specialist was actually a psychiatrist who, after asking a lot of questions, began trying to convince me that my problem was due to an unhappy home and family life. Nothing could have been further from the truth and I knew that this man couldn't help me. As soon as I could, I escaped, resolving never to go back. It was just me and the Lord now, I thought.

The vomiting got worse over the next few weeks, but then I was given another appointment with a different doctor – completely different, in fact. This one spent time putting me at ease and then just listened as I described my symptoms. He made no judgements, and when I'd finished, as I'd expected, he confirmed that I had anorexia.

But he insisted that next time I saw him Mum had to come too, and he would tell her the truth.

Between then and the next appointment I ate less than ever, worrying about how Mum would react. I hated myself for doing this to her. So far, she only knew I was having trouble digesting food, which was all I'd been able to tell her.

Too soon for me, the day of the appointment came. The journey to the hospital was a nightmare, and then we were sitting in the doctor's office as he pronounced the words I'd dreaded. 'Mrs Hailes, your daughter has anorexia nervosa.'

I looked at Mum. Her face registered total horror and disbelief. She didn't hear a word the doctor was saying about his plans for my treatment.

Afterwards, I tried to comfort her: I would be visiting the hospital weekly as an outpatient and my decision to seek help was a sign of my determination to get better. As I said this, I felt a faint twinge of uneasiness. However, I kept all my appointments. (This, of course, meant I had to tell people at the office about my anorexia, in order to explain my absences, but I told very few others.) Between appointments, I had to write down everything I ate, which in fact resulted in my eating less, as I couldn't be bothered to write down 'half a biscuit' or 'a bite of Mum's apple'. It was easier to cut them out.

The goodness of God is amazing. Though my eating habits were no better at all, I noticed my weight never once went below 7st 2lb. This was a miracle, as I was eating much less than other girls who weighed 5st, and was vomiting what little I did eat. It was clear evidence that the Lord was upholding me throughout this ordeal. I marvelled at his faithfulness to me in the face of my rejection of his will. I found, like the psalmist, that I couldn't run away from the loving hand of God:

Where can I go from Your Spirit? Or where can I flee from Your presence? If I ascend into heaven, You are there; if I make my bed in hell, behold, You are there. If I take the wings of the morning, and dwell in the uttermost parts of the sea, even there Your hand shall lead me, and Your right hand shall hold me (Ps 139:7–10).

Even in my rebellion, he was there all the time. He didn't give up on me; even more, he was still prepared to use me.

4

'Are You Willing?'

A visiting missionary speaker at the Upper Room was nothing unusual. We had them often, and one of the most frequent and popular visitors was the Revd David Nellist. David was an independent travelling preacher and evangelist, well known and respected in International Gospel Outreach circles and among the many people who went to the Hollybush camps in North Yorkshire. Since the late 1970s, he had been making short missionary visits to the Philippines a couple of times a year, working among tribal groups such as the Negritos and Aetas. His vision was to train Filipino converts to evangelise their own nation and he had established a work in the village of Cabalan in the Subic Bay area of Luzon, which is the largest of the Philippine islands.

As David's own ministry took him all over the world, the work in Calaban was staffed permanently by two other English missionaries, one of whom, Dorothy, came with him to the Upper Room one weekend in the spring of 1983. I watched and listened while Dorothy spoke about the work and showed her slides. I was interested and impressed, but nothing more. Then David stood up to preach. As usual, he gave a powerful challenge concerning the urgent need for foreign missions – but that was for other people, I thought. I was happy with the prison ministry I already had and was visiting prisons fairly regularly by now with Psalm One-Fifty; we had just made an album and were receiving plenty of invitations.

At the end of his talk, David made an appeal: 'If you are willing to go to the foreign mission field to serve the Lord, I want you to step forward tonight. I'm not saying that you will certainly go, but are you willing?'

At that moment, the Lord spoke to me. I knew that he was calling me, not simply to be willing but, clearly and definitely, actually to go to the Philippines. How many times in the past had it been easy just to say, 'Yes, Lord'? But not this time. I loved and feared the Lord too much to say 'no', yet I couldn't bring myself to submit to this request.

A few people began to get up and go to the front. I huddled in my chair, wishing that the ground would swallow me up, and hoping desperately that no one was looking at me. I was sure that guilt and embarrassment must be written all over my face for anyone to see. I couldn't wait for the service to finish and stayed rigidly in my seat until it was all over. Afterwards, I quickly started talking to my friends about other things in an effort to take my mind off what the Lord had asked. Though I couldn't say 'no', neither could I say 'yes', so I fought to avoid answering at all. It would be a relief to get back to work, where I wouldn't have to think about it. Or so I thought.

Next day, at the office, I discovered my mistake. The Lord wasn't to be put off; he wanted an answer, and I had to make a choice. Doggedly, I tried to concentrate on my work and refused to commit myself. I survived Monday, but Tuesday was worse. Instead of my drawings, all I could see were Filipinos running off the edge of a cliff into a Christless eternity. The Lord's voice was insistent: 'Christine, they need you to tell them.'

I thought about my present ministry, and how much I enjoyed it; I didn't want to give it up, even for a little while.

Then I tried to imagine myself working among primitive tribes. How could the Lord ask this of me? What about the prison ministry he'd given me? I tried another tack. 'Lord,' I said, 'I've never been to Bible school; and what do I know about preaching?'

'Christine, all I'm asking you to do is love the people. Can you love the people?'

This cut through all my evasions and defences. It was the sort of question my dad had a knack of asking. I began to see where he got it from. It put me in a no-win situation. If I said 'no', I'd be denying the power of the Holy Spirit within me. I'd often sung a song based on Romans 5:5 and knew very well the truth that 'the love of God has been poured out in our hearts by the Holy Spirit who was given to us'. But if I said 'yes' . . . .

'Yes, Lord. I can love the people. I surrender.' I put down my draughting pen and made an announcement to the lads in the office: 'Guess where I'm going!'

'Where are you off to now then, Podge?' asked Norman, obviously expecting me to tell him about one of my prison visits.

'The Philippines. God's called me to go there.'

'Come on, Podge! Don't be stupid! You can't even eat in England, let alone the Philippines. You'll end up coming back in a box, and I'm not buying flowers.'

With everything else on my mind, I hadn't thought about my anorexia which, despite all my visits to the hospital, was still no better. Somehow, though, it didn't seem important. 'If God has called me, then he'll heal me,' I said.

'What about money, then?' Norman asked. He knew I'd been struggling to find the money for my summer holiday in Spain with friends from church.

'If God wants me to go, he'll provide what I need.'

'But where will you stay when you get there?'

By now, he must have been anticipating my answer. 'God will give me somewhere to live.'

The others in the office remained silent, listening intently. They could tell I meant what I said. I hadn't spoken lightly and there was no doubt in my mind that God was going to meet all my needs – even though I would have preferred him not to.

When I got home that evening, I told my parents. They didn't say much, which didn't surprise me. I knew them well enough by now not to expect them either to approve or try to dissuade me. Straight afterwards, I phoned David Nellist, as he was my only contact with the Philippines, to ask for his help. At this time, I had one more year of my HTC course to complete, so I told David that I'd like to spend the summer, while college was closed, working in the Philippines. However, he explained that summer wouldn't be a suitable time to go, because it would be the rainy season, when the work was often hampered by the rains and even fierce storms and typhoons. His advice was that it would be better to go in September.

It dawned on me at this point that I had never even asked the Lord how long I was to stay in the Philippines. I had just assumed it would be a month or two. But if I were to take David's advice and go in September, I would have to miss college, and in that case I might as well take the opportunity to stay for ten months until the next rainy season and pick up at college the following September. When I told David what I was thinking, he invited me to become part of his own small mission, working alongside Dorothy and her colleague, Linda.

So within a day everything was settled: I would be flying out to the Philippines in just three or four months' time. Not long afterwards, someone asked me, 'Where are the Philippines, anyway?' It came over me afresh just how little concrete planning I'd done; I didn't even know exactly where I was going. I went to find a map. 'Australia, up a bit, left a bit,' I answered.

I didn't know anything about this place. At this point I still thought it was populated entirely by tribal peoples, as it was with these that David's mission was particularly concerned. But now that I'd committed myself I was no longer troubled by this prospect; I was willing to go wherever the Lord sent me. Only two things remained to be sorted out: my fare and my anorexia. God dealt with my anorexia first.

A few weeks later, I attended a FGBMFI breakfast meeting, where the speaker was Allan Jones. After he had given his testimony, he began to speak out some words of knowledge which the Holy Spirit had revealed to him. 'There's someone here with a serious digestion problem.'

'Gosh,' I thought, 'that's what I used to call my anorexia.'

'If you will come out to the front here this morning,' Allan went on, 'God will heal you.'

I knew this word of knowledge was for me. And then the full significance of it hit me: God would heal me *if I went out to the front*. He was requiring something of me. Satan, as ever, was there immediately, trying to sow confusion and tempting me to disobedience with the same words he'd used before: 'If you do that, you'll get fat.'

I recognised this temptation for what it was, but I really didn't want to get fat. I couldn't make myself go forward; I felt as if my feet were glued to the carpet. In a moment of painful insight, it became clear to me that although I'd thought my willingness to go to the doctor was a step towards recovery, the truth was that I didn't want to get better. I wanted this illness because it kept me slim.

Then the Lord spoke to me, very solemnly and sternly: 'Christine, it's now or never.'

I felt as if I'd been brought out of a daze by a blow in the face. I knew that it was only by God's grace and forbearance that my weight had so far never fallen below 7st 2lb; and now he had delivered an ultimatum. If I continued in rebellion, he would withdraw his protection, the anorexia would run its course and I would lose my life. But still I stayed rooted to the spot. And then I remembered my commitment to the mission in the Philippines. If I jeopardised my health it would be impossible for me to go. By refusing to be healed I was in effect going back on my promise.

At that, I quickly shuffled my way to the front and joined the others already standing there in response to other words of knowledge that Allan had given. Allan prayed for us all and though I felt nothing, I knew in my heart that I'd stopped rebelling against God. I was utterly free. I went home and ate a good meal, and for the first time in almost a year I didn't have to go to the bathroom afterwards to vomit. From that time, the vomiting stopped and I never went back to the hospital. I was completely healed.

That left the other problem – my fare. I was well aware that Dad wouldn't pay. In accordance with his principle of never interfering in my dealings with the Lord, he would expect me to look to God to confirm his call by supplying my needs. And God's confirmation was particularly important this time – we've always been a very close family, and Mum and Dad hated the thought of us being separated just as much as I did. They wouldn't offer me any encouragement in a venture which would take me thousands of miles away unless it was undeniably the Lord's will. I would simply have to pray about it.

My prayers were answered on my twenty-first birthday, which fell on 15th June 1983. Mum had organised a party for me with all our friends at church and I was really touched by all the love and kindness everyone showed me. I had so many lovely gifts, most of which had been chosen with the Philippines in mind. There were suitcases and sundresses, and one lady, Alice, had decorated my cake with a plane flying away from a map of England.

Then one of the couples in the church, David and Anne, slipped an envelope into my hand as they wished me a happy birthday. It contained £500 – more than enough for a return ticket – which the Lord had told David to give me. I knew then that although I would have no fixed income while I was away I could trust the Lord to provide for me. (And in fact, although I hadn't asked for financial support, the congregation at the Upper Room subsequently decided to take up a special collection for me once a month.)

Mum and I almost cried our way through the next two months; we could hardly bear the prospect of being apart for almost a year. How little we knew! If we'd realised then what the future held, neither of us could have coped. By now I was totally secure in the fact that this step was the Lord's will, but he graciously gave us many words of encouragement and confirmation during those two months.

Another blessing I hadn't counted on was a companion for the journey. Through Jonathan, who had been working as co-pastor with Dad at the Upper Room, I was put in touch with a girl called Lesley Keenan. Lesley was due to fly out to work as a nurse with a mission based in the same part of the Philippines as David's (though not connected with it). We booked our flights to Manila for the same day in September.

Shortly before I was due to leave, David Chaudhary, a missionary and preacher whom my parents knew through their contact with International Gospel Outreach, prayed for me, asking the Lord to give me favour with the authorities. It struck me as an odd thing to pray for; what 'authorities' would I encounter in a tribal situation? But I stored it away to meditate on.

On the day of my flight, after a painful parting from the rest of the family, Dad drove me to the airport with Mum and Nanna Jean. We cried throughout the entire journey. Even Dad's vision must have been blurred by a tear or two, because we suddenly realised we were heading for the wrong airport; we were on the way to Heathrow, and my plane was departing from Gatwick.

'Gatwick?' yelled Dad. 'We'll never make it.' Suddenly,

the problem of getting there on time pushed everything else into the background. We arrived at Gatwick with only minutes to spare. In a way it was a good thing that we were so late; there was no time for long, tearful goodbyes – nor was there time to weigh my luggage, which was hugely over the limit, with my guitar, books, Bibles, clothes, teddy bears and a good stock of my favourite chocolate.

After a brief farewell, I had to hurry straight onto the plane, and thankfully took my seat next to Lesley. She was about my age and I could tell that she too was upset at leaving her family, so we waited until our emotions had subsided a bit before starting to chat to each other. We hadn't been in the air very long when a stewardess came up to me.

'Are you Christine Hailes?' she asked. I immediately thought something awful had happened to Mum and Dad.

'Yes,' I replied, apprehensively.

'You dropped your passport at Gatwick. What do you want to do? Do you want to disembark at Frankfurt or take a risk and go on to Manila?'

I realised she needed an immediate decision, and I found that I was able to answer, as calmly as if she'd asked where I wanted to take my tea, 'Um, I think I'll just go on to Manila, thank you.'

As I sat there, I laid the problem before the Lord. 'Lord, it's all up to you now. You'll have to find a way of getting me into the Philippines without a passport.' With that, I left it in his hands.

'How long do you plan to stay in the Philippines?' Lesley asked.

'Just ten months.'

'Gosh,' she exclaimed, 'how can you manage that long?'

'I don't really know. The Lord will have to do something. How about you?'

'Only six months,' she replied, little knowing that her future too contained some surprises. Fourteen years later, she is still ministering in the Philippines.

After a seemingly endless twenty-one-hour flight we finally arrived in Manila. Getting there, however, was the easy part; my problem was going to be staying there without a passport. As I queued at immigration I prayed, 'Well, Lord, you've got me this far, and I trust you to get me through this.'

'Passport, please, miss.'

The immigration officer listened carefully as I explained what had happened and then disappeared for several minutes, asking me to wait. Lesley went on ahead while I continued to pray quietly. When the officer returned he was accompanied by several others who were obviously of higher rank. I went through my story again and one of them left to make a phone call. They all seemed very grave and it was plain that they were considering asking me to take the first plane back to England. I discovered later that security was particularly tight just then; only three weeks earlier, Benigno Aquino, the chief political rival of the President, Ferdinand Marcos, had been shot dead at that very airport. Had I but known it, I was entering a country which at that time was beset by political strife, instability and other evils resulting in large part from Marcos' repressive regime.

However, still happily ignorant of all this, I waited again. I knew that the God I believed in was a God who specialised in doing things which seemed impossible, but it was still with a profound sense of relief that I eventually heard that my passport was already in transit and that provided I returned to collect it in a few days' time permission had been granted to allow me through. 'Thank you, Lord!'

I was finally able to rejoin Lesley, whom I found patiently waiting along with Dorothy, who had come to meet me. The three of us were staying overnight together in Manila. On the short taxi-ride to our hotel, I was too exhausted to do more than register the fact that, at least here in the capital, I wasn't in an undeveloped tribal area.

And the hotel itself was as luxurious as anything I'd encountered in England.

Comfortable as it was, though, I didn't spend much time sleeping that night, in spite of my tiredness. I was sharing a room with Lesley and Dorothy and, not wanting to disturb them by switching on the light, I spent several hours in the bathroom writing letters home. I was already homesick and I couldn't hold back my tears. Reflected in the mirror I saw a twenty-one-year-old girl clutching a teddy bear and crying for her mother.

'What can the Lord possibly do with me?' I thought. 'Can he really have a purpose for me here?'

5

'*I Was in Prison and You Came to Me*'

Next morning we said goodbye to Lesley, who was flying north to Baguio City on the way to join her mission in San Fernando. Dorothy and I were also going north, but by road up the west coast of Luzon to Subic Bay. We had a long journey ahead of us, which began with a taxi-ride to the bus station. As we climbed into the taxi, I thought privately that it looked ready to fall apart, but I said nothing, not wanting to betray my inexperience. As soon as we set off, I realised why the taxi was in such a state. 'He drives this thing into the ground,' I said to Dorothy.

'Oh, Chrissy, this is nothing. Wait until he really gets going!'

As we drove, I began to get a fuller picture of Manila. A few minutes away from the opulent area around the hotel, we encountered one of the hundreds of shanty towns which house the poorer section of the population. I'd never seen real poverty before and nothing had prepared me for this. Of course, I'd seen television documentaries about third-world poverty, but the images of blue skies and sunshine, so attractive to English eyes, had distracted me from the grim reality. And besides, television reaches only two of the five senses. Here, I could actually experience the intense heat that these people were living in and feel my energy draining away in the humid atmosphere. The smell was nauseating; there were piles of garbage anywhere and everywhere. Half-dressed toddlers were wandering around unsupervised, while older children scurried in and out of the traffic trying to sell anything from sweets and cigarettes to floor mats. When the traffic halted, small children would lead their blind or disabled parents from car to car, knocking on the windows and begging for money.

The moving traffic was absolutely chaotic. It made London in the rush hour seem like a quiet Cornish village. Though there were only four lanes officially, the drivers managed to squeeze in another two, recklessly weaving from one to another at frightening speed. Ancient buses billowed out dense black fumes which, combined with the stifling heat, made it almost impossible to breathe. 'How can people live and work in these conditions?' I asked myself.

Manila is a city of extremes; alongside the starkest poverty lies the evidence of immense wealth. Beyond the shanty town I saw shopping malls larger than anything I'd encountered before, as well as enormous, imposing skyscrapers and exquisite houses. My preconceived ideas of the Philippines as a country at a tribal stage of development were undergoing a rapid readjustment.

In actual fact, the process of modernisation under western influence began as long ago as the sixteenth century, when the Philippines became a Spanish colony; it was accelerated from the end of the nineteenth when America took over the islands from Spain. One lasting result of Spanish influence is that most Filipinos are (nominally at least) Roman Catholic. Full independence was gained in 1946 (though America maintained military bases in the Philippines until 1992). The economy is both agricultural and industrial but it has been badly disrupted by political and social unrest, resulting in widespread poverty and unemployment. The tribal peoples, who I'd thought made up the whole population, really make up less than three per cent!

When we got out of the taxi at the bus station we were immediately surrounded by a crowd of men, all insisting loudly that they would carry our luggage. I thought it was very kind of them and was surprised when Dorothy refused so firmly. She explained later that the men, taking us for rich American ladies, would expect to be handsomely rewarded for helping us – and there was a strong chance of losing an item or two if we lost control of our things.

The coach which was to take us as far as Olongapo, 120 miles to the north, was comfortable and air-conditioned, and for the next four hours I slid back into the world I knew. It was like watching those television programmes, observing without feeling. During the long, quiet journey, homesickness began to creep over me again, but I cheered up as we neared Olongapo and the road began to climb. The country was hilly and green and reminded me of the Welsh village where my parents had their holiday home.

At last Dorothy announced that we were actually in Olongapo City. 'This is a city?' I thought. 'It looks more like a big shanty town.' There seemed to be no pattern or order to anything. There were open-front car workshops, bakeries and a market place all crowded together, and shops whose window displays were so crammed and chaotic you could hardly make out what was for sale. Everything looked grey and dirty, even though the sun was shining.

However, there was no time to look around. We still had another six or seven miles to travel to Subic Town, our final destination. On this last stage of our journey we rode in a jeepney, which is the most common form of public transport in the Philippines and resembles an elongated, open-sided, windowless jeep embellished with highly coloured decorations and providing bench seating for about sixteen passengers. There are no predetermined stopping points; the jeepney stops to pick up passengers or allow them to alight anywhere along the route. After about half an hour, Dorothy called out to the driver: '*Para na ho*' ('Stop now, please') and the jeepney screeched to a halt.

'Chrissy, we're home now.'

Home. For the next ten months I'd have to get used to thinking of Subic as 'home'. Still entertaining the notion that I was destined to work in a tribal situation, I'd been surprised, when we first entered Subic, to find myself in such a built-up area. It had been a pleasant surprise, however, because this promised a less drastic change of life style than I'd anticipated.

Subic is a small coastal town with a population of about 60,000, one of several towns and cities which together form the Subic Bay area. My first impression was that it had a curiously half-finished appearance, which was due to the fact that the inhabitants had to build and develop their houses at a pace dictated by their limited incomes. Even a completed house might remain unpainted or unglazed for ages. It was a bit like a huge building site. Everywhere there were heaps of rubbish, especially in the area by the shore, right next to the market; this presented an odd contrast to the people themselves, who all looked so clean.

I'd been surprised, too, to notice a number of American GIs walking around. I hadn't realised there was a large US naval base nearby in Olongapo. I was less surprised, after experiencing the shanty town in Manila, to see so many blind and disabled beggars sitting in the streets, or to observe the street kids hanging around waiting for small jobs.

Dorothy and I got out of the jeepney and I found myself in front of a row of small terraced houses situated in a fenced area known as a compound. Out of the house at the end of the row came two young women, one English and one Filipina, who ran to meet us and help us with our bags. I was introduced to Linda, Dorothy's missionary colleague, and Redemia, their helper and interpreter. Redemia was a Negrito (one of the minority tribal groups). She was tiny –

less than five feet tall – and extremely pretty, with long crinkly hair and skin much darker than the more common brown of the majority of Filipinos.

They led us into the house and from bright sunlight I was plunged into what seemed like total darkness. Too many windows were not a good idea, I was told, as they let in heat as well as light. I saw the point of this when Linda took me upstairs to see the two small bedrooms, which in the daytime were very light but almost unbearably hot. Dorothy and Linda wanted to give me the most comfortable bed, but eventually I persuaded them that Redemia and I, being several years younger than they, should take the metal-framed bunks in the smaller room, where there was just space also for a wardrobe (and, as I later discovered, a rat).

Downstairs again, Dorothy decided to take a shower and disappeared into the bathroom next to the kitchen. 'Kitchen' is perhaps a bit of an overstatement, as the ground floor was an open-plan area with a tiled work top and a sink in one corner. Under the sink was a small cupboard for pans – and cockroaches (which proved impossible to eliminate, despite Dorothy's insistence on meticulous attention to cleanliness); on the wall was another small cupboard for cockroaches and cans, etc. The cooker was a Calor gas camping stove.

The rest of the furniture was just as basic: a Formica-topped table, a very small plastic-covered sofa, a couple of hard chairs, a chest of drawers and a small black and white television. As in many ordinary houses in the Philippines, the floor was of cement and was painted red.

Dorothy emerged from the shower and I took my turn in the tiny bathroom. Again, I saw that 'bathroom' was something of a misnomer, as there was no bath – only rich people have baths in the Philippines – just a toilet, a wash basin and the 'shower', which consisted of a shower head sticking out of the wall. The water obviously drained away through a grid in the floor. 'Ah, well,' I thought, 'it could be worse.' Then the truth hit me. There was no hot water.

I'd never taken a cold shower in my life, not even after a hard game of squash. Hesitantly, I turned on the tap and flinched at the temperature of the water. 'No hot water! No bath! How can I bear it?' I muttered. Then, reminding myself that I ought to be grateful that we had running water at all, I gritted my teeth and shivered through my shower.

And really, cold showers began to assume the character of a minor inconvenience when I learned what Dorothy and Linda had endured in the past. Once I'd unpacked and settled in, it was time for me to catch up on their news and assess the situation; circumstances had changed since that weekend earlier in the year when Dorothy came with David to speak at the Upper Room. The work Dorothy had described on that occasion was based in Cabalan, a village just south of Olongapo. The hills surrounding the village were populated by tribal peoples whom Dorothy and Linda would visit regularly, travelling miles on foot and preaching the gospel as they went. Those who responded were invited to Dorothy's home for Bible school training every day. Redemia had been one of their students and had progressed so well that David had sponsored her through a further course at a Bible school in Manila.

Dorothy had moved into Cabalan alone five years previously. Before that, she had spent a year in the Philippines with another mission and at the end of it she'd felt a strong desire to return. David, whose wife was a close friend of Dorothy, had been able to enlist the help of a local pastor in Cabalan, whom he'd met on one of his own missionary visits. This pastor had helped Dorothy set up the work and had provided her with accommodation. Linda had joined her a couple of years later, having received a call to the Philippines after hearing David speak at the Bible college in Scotland where she was studying.

Together they continued the work, seeing many converts among the Aetas and Negritos who, through the teaching they received in the small Bible school, were firmly established in their Christian faith. (Today, a number of them are conducting successful ministries in evangelism and pastoral work among their own people.) Then suddenly, without warning, the local pastor asked them to leave their accommodation and they were forced to move into a rented house, made of wood and full of rats and termites and without running water. For a while they struggled on with the Bible school, but finally the house became impossible to live in and the school had to close. Dorothy and Linda were then faced with the need to rent new accommodation in time for my arrival and had only just settled in Subic themselves. Our present house, they assured me, was luxurious compared to their previous one.

As I listened, I felt very privileged to be able to walk straight into a situation where all the practical arrangements had been made and where I could draw on Dorothy's and Linda's experience. I particularly admired Dorothy; I couldn't imagine myself being able to start from scratch, all alone, as she did.

Having hurried to prepare a place for me, Dorothy and Linda had had no time to consider their own future plans. But at David's request, they had made some preliminary enquiries and arrangements on my behalf. Having learned from David of my prison ministry in England, Dorothy had contacted one of the local jails and received permission for us to visit.

I remembered how my dismay at the thought of giving up my prison ministry had made me so reluctant to come to the Philippines; how I'd questioned God's ways in opening up this ministry for me only to call me to do something entirely different, as I'd thought, halfway across the world. I saw now that though God's purposes are not always clear to us, we can trust him to work them out in our lives. I'd thought my prison ministry and my call to the Philippines were mutually exclusive, yet here I was, about to visit a Philippine prison.

Not immediately, however. I'd arrived at the tail-end of the rainy season and for a couple of weeks the bad weather returned, making it impossible to venture far from the house. This gave me the opportunity to recover from jet lag and familiarise myself with my immediate neighbourhood.

As the house was part of a terrace, we were very close to our neighbours. In fact, two steps out of the front door and we were already in the next house! Most of the houses in the compound were owned by members of one extended family, one of whom was our landlord. Some of them were very poor, others rather better off, but all were friendly and later we got to know many of them quite well.

At the back of the compound was a small piggery and beyond that a boggy area of stagnant water where I was amazed to see children swimming. You didn't have to walk far before encountering a rubbish heap – a circumstance which rather undermined our own efforts to maintain hygienic surroundings. Mice, and even rats, proved an ineradicable problem. The mice didn't even wait for us to finish a meal before appearing to claim their share. Bowing to the inevitable, we ended, like Cinderella in the Disney film, by making friends with them. I never got used to the rats, though.

Right alongside us was the Municipal Hall, the equivalent of a Town Hall, where the mayor's office, the post office and Subic Jail (not the one we were due to visit) were located.

Eventually better weather arrived, and with it the moment I'd been waiting for – the day of our first visit to the jail. Camp Maquinaya was a fifteen-minute jeepney ride from our house, on the road to Olongapo. It was a Friday morning when the four of us – Dorothy, Linda,

Redemia and I – set off, none of us having very much idea of what awaited us.

We presented ourselves at the padlocked gate, which was opened for us by a police officer who had a desk by the entrance (prison officers are also police officers in the Philippines) and we were led into a compound surrounded by a barbed-wire fence. Within the compound were two separate cell blocks called Alpha and Bravo. The officer indicated a spot in the compound where we could hold an open-air service and then left us to return to his desk.

Security seemed very lax, the barbed-wire fence being the only apparent barrier to escape. Later, we understood prison security better. Escape attempts were few because all the guards were armed and would simply shoot anyone who tried it. A warden once remarked to me concerning a particular prisoner: 'This inmate's mother was very grateful to me. When her son tried to escape, I ordered him to be shot in the leg. Others would have given orders to kill.'

I looked round the compound. This was nothing like Strangeways. No chapel, no seats, no organ; and above all, no guards to ensure our safety. We soon learned that the guards remain outside the jail most of the time and that visitors who enter do so at their own risk. To all outward appearances we were at the mercy of the prisoners.

In the late 1980s, the world was horrified by the news that a group of western missionaries had been raped and murdered in a Philippine jail in Davao City on the island of Mindanao. The news prompted many people to ask me whether I was ever afraid to minister in the jails. I always replied that every time I went in, I went with the assurance that my life was not in the hands of the inmates, nor in my own, but in God's. I know that no harm can come to me unless God allows it; and should he allow it, then I believe that it will be ultimately for my good. 'All things work together for good to those who love God' (Rom 8:28);

and 'whether we live or die, we are the Lord's' (Rom 14:8).

I picked up my guitar and started to play. Immediately, a group of inmates began to gather round us and as we sang some of them even tried to join in. After the singing, we gave a simple gospel message which Redemia translated into Tagalog, the local dialect of the area and also the main national language of the Philippines. Dorothy knew quite a lot of Tagalog, but wasn't fluent enough to preach, and though English is the second national language, many uneducated people can't understand it at all; and of course, the jails contain a high percentage of uneducated people. But they all listened intently to every word and at the end we were thrilled when a number of them professed a desire to accept Christ as Lord and Saviour.

After the service, some of them invited us inside their cells. This would remove us even further from the possibility of help but, not wanting to rebuff their overtures of friendship, we accepted. Within the cell blocks there was no individual accommodation, just large communal cells. The inmates had secured a measure of privacy for themselves by constructing bedroom areas out of papier-mâché and string. For wallpaper, they used old magazines and newspapers. Though one or two had folding sun-loungers or bare wooden beds, most had no beds at all. There was no running water and no toilets.

Nevertheless, they were eager to show us what hospitality they could and bought us soda and crackers from the prison tuck shop, and while we ate and drank they began to talk about their lives. They all wore civilian clothes, for the most part completely threadbare. They were given no clothes, they explained, nor any soap or toothpaste. If their families were unable to supply these necessities, they either had to do without or find some way of earning a little money to buy them. These conditions apply in jails throughout the Philippines and in each the inmates try to develop skills in various crafts, producing artefacts which are offered for sale to visitors. In Camp Maquinaya, it was mostly woodcarving. The tiny income this generates also enables them to supplement the low quality prison diet with food from the vendors who visit daily.

We were staggered to learn that many of the men had endured these conditions for up to ten years without yet having been convicted. Like almost all Philippine jails, Camp Maquinaya was a remand prison. After conviction and sentencing, prisoners were transferred to the main prison in the Muntinlupa district of Manila; any who were acquitted would receive no compensation for the years spent in jail.

The majority of Camp Maquinaya's inmates were being held on charges of murder or drug-related offences, and while their guilt or innocence had yet to be established, there was no doubt that we were in the presence of men who were capable of hideous violence. The two cell blocks Alpha and Bravo reflected the need to separate two rival gangs among the inmates, between whom existed the bitterest rivalry and hostility. Given the opportunity, this might at any time erupt into violence and it was not unknown for quarrels arising from the most trivial causes to end in murder.

One visit was more than enough to confirm to us that the grace of God alone could bring light into this dark place. There was a work for us here. The warden in charge of the jail raised no objection to our request to visit every Friday, and this became part of our normal schedule.

Life began to assume a regular pattern. On Sundays, of course, we went to church. Dorothy, Linda, Redemia and I all attended an Assemblies of God church in Olongapo, where Dorothy taught adult Sunday school. The congregation of about 100 members were of all ages and were mainly Filipino, though quite a number of US military service men and women also attended as the pastor spoke excellent English. The sermons were given in 'Taglish', a mixture of Tagalog and English.

A month or so after our first visit to Camp Maquinaya, we obtained permission to visit the small jail in Subic Town. As this was situated in the Municipal Hall next to our house, the inmates were literally our neighbours. Every Monday night we conducted services for them along similar lines to those at Camp Maquinaya. This growing prison work had been initiated as a result of my own previous experience, but the other three girls were unstinting in their efforts to promote what was to them a very different area of ministry from the one they had known before.

Almost unwittingly, we also found ourselves developing a ministry to the children of Subic. Redemia had a beautiful voice and she and I would often sit outside the house singing together as I played my guitar. I've always found a guitar to be an effective crowd puller and we quickly gathered an audience of local children. It seemed natural to speak to them about the gospel, and before long all four of us were involved in organising simple Bible instruction for them every Thursday afternoon. Very soon we moved further afield and began children's outreaches in other *barangays* (village-like subdivisions) of Subic Town. I'd only just started to learn Tagalog with Redemia, so mostly all I could offer was my guitar, a song and a smile: just loving the kids.

Linda felt a particular call to the children's work and she began to head up this side of our ministry. The work nearest my own heart was the prison ministry. Our visits were a real source of joy to me and before long I found myself going along on my own, aside from our scheduled services, just to spend time with the inmates. At their request I helped them learn the songs we sang in the services and bought them a guitar so that they could participate themselves. From being my ministry, they were becoming my friends.

Later, when I'd had more experience, I realised that Camp Maquinaya was one of the worst jails in the Philippines. On some occasions, while we were holding a service in one room, other inmates who didn't attend the services were having a drunken orgy in the next cell. Alcohol, drugs and prostitutes were all available at a price. Guards would turn a blind eye – but expected to be rewarded in return.

Gradually I became involved in helping the inmates in other ways. Several of them asked me to lend moral support by being there in court when their hearings came up, or by accompanying them on visits to their lawyers. One of these was Rhey. He was the 'mayor' of Alpha group (the mayor was the acknowledged leader of the group and commanded unquestioned obedience). Rhey was one of the most hardened criminals in the jail yet, such is the grace of God, he was also one of the most responsive to the gospel. His conversion, which was deep and lasting, was one of my greatest encouragements. As a Christian he retained the respect of the other inmates and his habit of command. I learned later that the reason our services were so well attended when he was mayor was that he made attendance compulsory.

I'd never questioned him about his criminal record. I decided right from the start that I would always wait for a prisoner to confide in me. So when I first went with him to a court hearing I received a shock. Rhey had killed a man with a pair of scissors. But shock was quickly swallowed up by compassion. Many of the inmates were guilty of horrific crimes, but the reason I had come to the Philippines was to reach out to those who were rushing headlong down the road to destruction, and to tell them of their need for a Saviour.

I thought back to the time when I was still working as a technician and my colleague Norman had questioned me about my prison work in England: 'Why do you waste your time on a bunch of convicts when there are people so much more deserving?'

But isn't it good that God doesn't give us what we deserve? If he did, none of us would have any hope. We're all sinners dependent on his mercy: 'But God demonstrates

His own love toward us, in that while we were still sinners, Christ died for us' (Rom 5:8). The recognition of my own unworthiness was sufficient reason for not rejecting Rhey.

The passage of Scripture which spurred me on perhaps more than any other was the parable of the sheep and the goats. To those who inherit the kingdom of heaven, Jesus says:

> I was naked and you clothed Me; I was sick and you visited Me; I was in prison and you came to Me . . . Assuredly, I say to you, inasmuch as you did it to one of the least of these My brethren, you did it to Me (Mt 25:36, 40).

6

Eddie

Almost before I knew it, Christmas was approaching and inevitably my mind turned towards home. I thought about the huge family celebration I'd be missing this year and a great wave of homesickness swept over me as I contemplated the prospect of spending Christmas so far away from those I loved.

I was rescued from these gloomy introspections by the realisation that, in the prison inmates who had come to mean so much to me, I had a family right here in the Philippines. I remembered too that a large part of my mother's preparations for Christmas consisted of ensuring that every poor family she knew received a gift on Christmas day. What could I do to make Christmas special for the inmates? Unlike British prisoners, who are provided with entertainment and a traditional Christmas dinner, inmates in the Philippines would spend Christmas day much like any other.

My first thought was to do some baking, but on a Calor gas stove that was impossible. I couldn't afford to buy gifts for all the inmates and it wouldn't be fair to single out a few. Materially, there was little I could do. I decided to ask the youth group at the church we attended in Olongapo if they would be willing to take part in a special service at

Camp Maquinaya just before Christmas. None of them had
ever been inside a jail before and not unnaturally some
found the idea daunting. Nevertheless, they all agreed
and together we began to devise a programme of good
Christian Christmas songs and a short narration of the
nativity story.

As I immersed myself in the preparations I found myself
eagerly looking forward to Christmas instead of dreading
it, as I pictured to myself the inmates' pleasure at seeing
such a large party of young people. I solved the problem of
presents by buying a big tin of biscuits for each of the cell
groups, as well as a few small gifts for one of the inmates
who was being transferred to Muntinlupa. The 23rd
December was going to be a truly special day.

A week before the Christmas presentation, Dorothy,
Linda, Redemia and I paid our usual Friday visit to
Camp Maquinaya. Attendance at the service was unusually
low that morning, and I was particularly surprised by Eddie
Lazaro's absence. It wasn't like Eddie to miss a service;
he'd been one of the first to respond to the word of God
and I'd been greatly encouraged by his spiritual progress.
He'd developed a genuine friendship with all four of us and
often referred to me as his adopted sister. The reason for
the absences was explained by one of the other inmates,
who told me that a large group had been summoned to
attend court hearings. Things were moving pretty fast in
Eddie's case: he'd only been in the jail for six months. He
was being held on a murder charge but consistently maintained that he hadn't intended to kill his victim and was
hoping that the charge would be reduced to manslaughter.

During the closing part of the service the absentees
returned. As they were led through the gate I saw Eddie,
his face split by an enormous smile. The whispered news
spread rapidly: Eddie had been completely acquitted.

We finished the service quickly and joined the lads from
Alpha in their cell sitting room where, as they often did,
they brought us drinks as we sat and chatted. Eddie joined

us and asked if I could help him obtain his release papers. Before a detainee is released he has to pay a fee (about five pounds) for the processing of his papers. Failure to pay means that release is deferred. Eddie had no money and naturally I was willing to help. However, I'd made it a firm policy not to hand over cash to the inmates, and so arranged to meet him at the jail the following Monday, his expected release date.

I was almost as thrilled as Eddie himself at the decision and it was with great excitement that I set off for Camp Maquinaya on Monday morning, taking my camera so as to capture the very moment of his first steps to freedom. I hadn't anticipated any difficulty over the formalities, but as we waited with growing impatience for the papers to be produced the minutes turned into hours. I began to worry about my preparation for our Bible study at Subic Jail that evening, so when Eddie suggested that if I would leave the money with him, he would call round later to bring me a receipt, I reluctantly agreed. It wasn't just the money; I didn't want to miss seeing him pass from one side of the barbed wire to the other. I returned home full of disappointment.

Shortly before 4 o'clock, I heard my name called out and saw Eddie's face peering through the mosquito screen on the front door. I invited him in and offered him a snack, but he was far too excited to eat or drink. Proudly he presented me with his papers and then for the first time began to tell me the full story of his crime. I'd never pressed for details before.

Eddie had worked as a house-boy/yard-boy, doing work around the house and cleaning his employer's car. Like many others similarly employed, he'd been treated with harshness and contempt. 'He treated me as if I were an animal,' was Eddie's description. One day his employer had pushed him too far and Eddie's temper snapped. Never dreaming that his impulsive action would be fatal, he picked up a bottle and hurled it at his employer. The bottle found its mark and the man was killed. Eddie was charged with murder and his best hope had been that a plea of manslaughter would be accepted. Either way, he had expected a long sentence.

I shared his amazement at his acquittal, for which I could see no grounds in the story he had told me. I believed Eddie had not intended to kill, but he had confessed to causing his employer's death. Eddie explained that his acquittal was due to the fact that the dead man's family had dropped all charges against him. This puzzled me even more, but I didn't want to knock the bloom off Eddie's joy by interrogating him. I tried to keep my manner easy and relaxed, yet underneath in my mind flowed an uneasy stream of questions.

Why would any family drop charges like this? Why would they not want justice meted out to the man who had killed their father, husband, brother or son? As a missionary – and a missionary to prisoners at that – I was called by God to reach out and help criminals, but in a similar situation I would none the less want to see justice done. I would endeavour to love the killer with the love of Christ, to forgive him and long for his repentance, but there are laws which Jesus himself respected. The thief who hung on the cross beside Jesus received forgiveness and the promise of entry into paradise, but Jesus didn't save him from the punishment he'd incurred by breaking the law.

I stilled my doubts as best I could. Maybe the family had been motivated by the fact that Eddie had been severely provoked. The important thing now was to make sure he made good use of his freedom and for this I had to maintain contact with him.

Our church in Olongapo was holding a Christmas party that evening, so before he left I invited Eddie to join us. I wasn't sure he would want to spend his first night of freedom at a church party where he knew so few people, but to my surprise he accepted with alacrity. My anxiety not to lose touch was not based on any doubts as to the reality of his profession of faith nor the sincerity of his good intentions, but I'd learned through Mum's work with juvenile offenders that there are those who, having become Christians, wander away from God when they return to normal life.

As I made my way to the party after the Bible study I was half-prepared for the possibility that he might have changed his mind. Imagine my delight when, as soon as I arrived, I saw that not only was Eddie already there, but he'd also brought a friend. I recognised the friend; it was Jake, one of the pleasantest of the prison officers at Camp Maquinaya. He came from the same *barangay* as Eddie, though I hadn't realised they were friends. Jake couldn't stay long – he was on duty that night and he felt somewhat conspicuous because of the gun he was carrying. He certainly looked like a fish out of water among all the innocent-looking young people.

While poor Jake did his best to efface himself, Eddie threw himself into the fun with enthusiasm and settled in as if he belonged there, joining in all the games and enjoying himself immensely. If the church members were apprehensive on account of his past record, they hid it well. I relaxed a little. Eddie was going to be OK.

Before the party ended I went to say goodbye to him; I had to leave early as I was setting off first thing on Tuesday morning for Manila, where I had to make some official enquiries concerning my prison ministry. I'd be staying the night with some friends of Dorothy and Linda, members of a church founded by David Nellist. Eddie wanted to accompany me on my trip, but I assured him I would be fine. In that case, he said, as he was enjoying the party so much he'd stay to the end and escort Dorothy, Linda and Redemia home. He hoped to call and see us sometime during the week, but couldn't fix a time because he'd be looking for a job in Olongapo. However, we could count on his being at Camp Maquinaya for the service on Friday, as he was looking forward to the youth group's

Christmas presentation. I thought it would have been natural if he'd never wanted to set foot in the jail again, and was encouraged by this indication of his determination to go on with the Lord.

I completed my business in Manila on Tuesday and as soon as I returned on Wednesday I checked with the other girls whether Eddie had called. He hadn't, but then he had warned us he would be job hunting, so I didn't feel too let down.

Thursday came, and still no sign of him. At every knock on the door, Redemia and I leaped up, hoping it was him, but he didn't come. We consoled ourselves with the thought of seeing him the following day.

At last it was Friday the 23rd, the day of our Christmas programme. The tins of biscuits were wrapped, the programme sheets were all prepared for the young people and everything was in place. The four of us set out in the jeepney, accompanied on this occasion by Steve Dulwich, an English minister, and his wife, who were friends of David, working in the Philippines for a few months.

As soon as we arrived at Camp Maquinaya, I was greeted by a young woman, the wife of one of the prison officers: 'Hi, Chrissy. Merry Christmas. Have you heard what happened to Eddie Lazaro?'

'Yes, he was released on Monday.'

'You don't know? He was shot and killed on Tuesday.'

This couldn't possibly be true. Why would anyone shoot Eddie? I felt hollow with shock. The woman was still talking, telling us that according to the story that was circulating, Eddie had been in a restaurant on the main street of Olongapo leading to the naval base (the area where he'd planned to look for a job) and had stolen a watch from an American customer. The police were summoned, Eddie resisted arrest and was shot.

I was quite certain that Eddie would never have done such a thing. No one would be foolish enough to attempt theft in so public a place so soon after being released from

jail – much less someone like Eddie, who was determined
to put his life right and go on with Christ. Only the night
before, at the party, he'd asked the pastor if he would be
willing to give him some private Bible instruction, as he
had so much to learn. Eddie hadn't committed the crime
he was accused of, I was sure of it. And yet he was dead.

I felt ready to sink under a welter of confused emotion. I
wanted to scream and cry out to the Lord. But all of this
had to be held in check. I had responsibilities to the
inmates who were looking forward to the service, and to
the young people who had worked so hard to prepare it.
No one else appeared to be as devastated as I was; there
was some shock and a little distress, but not the turmoil I
was experiencing. Only Steve Dulwich seemed to realise
what I was going through and put his arm gently on my
shoulder.

Inside the compound, we discovered that the young
people hadn't yet arrived, which afforded me a brief respite
– a few minutes on my own to pray and lay my troubles
before the Lord. Alone outside the camp, I struggled to
come to terms with what I was feeling. Mixed with my grief
at the death of a close friend was a suspicion which was
quickly hardening into certainty. During the past few
months of working in the jails, I'd often heard the inmates
mention 'salvage' (the word is the same in Tagalog and
English: an example of Taglish). At first I hadn't understood the term; the contexts in which it was used didn't fit
the usual meaning of the word. I later learned that in the
Philippines 'salvage' has quite the opposite meaning to
saving or rescuing: it is used to refer to the unlawful execu-
tion of criminals by the police or others in authority. I
became convinced that Eddie was a salvage victim.

As I saw it, this would explain why the family of Eddie's
employer had dropped the charges against him. Had he
been convicted and given a life sentence this would not
have satisfied their desire for revenge. They wanted him to
pay with his life, a result they could ensure by dropping the

charges and colluding with the police to have him shot on his release. (At the time of Eddie's death, such corruption among the police and the military was commonplace. Since then, power has changed hands twice and the present government is working hard to remedy these abuses.)

I felt full of bitterness towards the police. It was like a physical pain in the pit of my stomach. At the same time, I was conscious of the Holy Spirit reminding me that bitterness is not of God and must be cast out and replaced by love. My human nature tried to justify my anger and rebelled against the conviction of the Spirit. But the word of God requires us unequivocally to love our enemies and I knew I could not allow sin to reign in me. I began to pray in the spirit, speaking in tongues, as I asked the Lord to help me.

As I prayed the pain in my stomach faded away and I knew the victory was mine. Sorrow remained, sorrow for the loss of Eddie, but now I was able to receive the comfort of the Holy Spirit. Most importantly I was free of bitterness, which is so destructive, and ready to take part in the service. I could face the police without hypocrisy. Just then a jeepney drew up, bringing the youth group. I thanked the Lord for his perfect timing.

The inmates gathered for the service were somewhat subdued by the news of Eddie's death, but, as I'd anticipated, it was obviously an encouragement to them to see so many young people willing to come into the jail to bring the Christmas message to them. I was proud of the way the youth group played their part, especially as they had much more to contend with than they'd expected. The police had never guarded our services before, but this time a row of officers, and even the warden himself, stood over us with folded arms and grim faces. They knew I'd been a close friend of Eddie and seemed to suspect that I was unhappy about the circumstances surrounding his death. It was clearly their intention to intimidate me. I did feel a little afraid, but I hung on to the victory I'd won in prayer as I stood up to close the service with the song 'Oh, how he loves you and me'. While I was singing, my eyes met the warden's. At that moment, the Lord gave me his love so that I in turn could look at that man not with hatred but with love. Either embarrassed or ashamed, the warden looked away.

Afterwards, Eddie's friend Jake offered to take Steve Dulwich and me to Eddie's home nearby, where his body was laid out. I wasn't really prepared for what we found there. It was the first time I'd ever seen a dead body and it didn't look like Eddie at all. I wished I hadn't seen him that way. There were no wounds visible so I asked Grace, Eddie's mother, where he had been shot.

'He was shot four times in the back and neck,' she replied.

This added further confirmation to my suspicions.

I'd never met Eddie's family before. There was Grace, his sister and his son Carlito, who was just three years old. Carlito's mother had abandoned him as a baby and Grace had brought him up as her own. The house was full of visitors, so we couldn't talk much, but I visited Grace again and we talked a little about what had happened. She seemed very reluctant to discuss the events surrounding Eddie's death and I suspected there was more to this than simply the pain of bereavement.

'Why don't you try to find out the truth of what happened?' I asked.

'Chrissy,' she replied, 'I still have my daughter and Carlito. If I take any risks, I might lose them too.'

I wasn't the only one to feel intimidated by the police.

Several days later, the newspaper carried a story purporting to give the details of Eddie's death, and the alleged circumstances were entirely different from those in the first account I'd been given. This time, Eddie was supposed to have stolen money from the restaurant cash register and stabbed the police officer who was trying to arrest him. As he fell badly wounded to the ground, the officer managed to shoot Eddie. I found it impossible to believe that a man in that condition could have placed four bullets so neatly and accurately in Eddie's back.

For many weeks afterwards, officers would stand guard at our services in Camp Maquinaya and in order to safeguard our ministry we affected to be unaware of the reason for their presence. The Lord continued to give us love for them, and indeed we recognised that their need of Christ was as great as that of the inmates.

Grace never was able to search for the truth. For myself, I would have been willing to risk taking the matter further, but I couldn't jeopardise her safety or that of the children. So I managed to avoid a clash with officialdom over Eddie; but it was a different story with Danny.

7

Danny

Gunshots rang out through the night. They sounded quite close, though I couldn't be sure. No one else seemed concerned, so perhaps it was just firecrackers after all. They could sound remarkably like gunfire. Anyway, we were right next door to the jail and the police station in the Municipal Hall, so we'd be safe enough.

Redemia and I were leading a Bible study in the home of Simon, one of our neighbours in the compound. The idea of beginning a Bible study had come from Simon's cousin-in-law Francisco, who had simply knocked on our door one day and asked us to start a study group for him and several others. He rounded up a number of young men and women, his friends and neighbours, and we'd been meeting with them regularly. Francisco had become a Christian and the level of interest among the others was high.

The following day I discovered that the feeling of security I'd derived from being close to the Municipal Hall had been completely unfounded: the shooting had happened in Subic Jail itself. One of the inmates, a boy called Danny, had been shot in the face by a police officer. I'd been in the Philippines for eight months now, long enough not to be easily shocked by such an incident, especially after Eddie's

73

death, but still it was horrifying to think of it happening to someone we knew.

Danny had been in Subic Jail ever since we first began to visit. He was charged with assaulting a policeman, but his case had not yet come to court. He wasn't a troublesome prisoner; rather the reverse. For some time he'd been a trusty (a well-behaved prisoner granted special privileges), which meant he was allowed to work outside the jail in other areas of the Municipal Hall and often ran errands for the officers. This made it all the more surprising that he'd been shot; it was unlikely he'd been trying to escape.

My surprise receded somewhat when I learned that the officer responsible was Patrolman Apin, and that he'd been drunk on duty at the time. Living so close to the jail and visiting often, I'd gained a fair amount of knowledge about the various officers and their characters, and I knew Patrolman Apin had treated inmates harshly before, including Danny. In his drunken state, Apin had pointed his gun at Danny's head as a joke – and then pulled the trigger. Danny's quick reflexes had saved him from instant death, but he was very badly wounded.

Redemia was the first to visit him at the General Hospital in Olongapo and she returned so distressed by what she'd seen that I decided to visit him myself. I felt strongly that I should lay hands on him and pray for his healing. This was my first visit to a General Hospital in the Philippines, and it gave me a real taste of culture shock.

As I walked along the corridors I could hardly believe the evidence of my senses. I remembered the almost aggressive cleanliness of British hospitals, where the smell of disinfectant clings to your clothes for hours after a short visit. The smell here was utterly nauseating. As I glanced into the various wards as I passed, it was like being taken back in time and witnessing the scenes pictured in my school history books about the Crimean War. Chaotic disorder prevailed everywhere, as if the hospital had been overwhelmed by a major disaster. There had been no disaster; this was just the normal state of affairs.

In Britain, there are nurses constantly checking on their patients, but here there were none. Instead, each bed was surrounded by the patient's family and friends on whom devolved the task of comforting, feeding and caring for their sick relative. The heat was almost unendurable even for a healthy person and there were no fans except those provided by the patients themselves. There was a general air of dilapidation; the walls obviously hadn't seen a paint-brush in a long time.

When at last I found Danny lying alone and motionless with no one taking the slightest notice of him, I barely recognised him. His face and neck were swollen to twice their normal size; the bullet had grazed his face as he leaped out of the way, damaging his eye, nose and mouth. None of the staff, when I eventually found them, could tell me whether the damage to his eye was serious, nor whether it would require surgery. Danny had so far received provisional first aid, nothing more. His face was a mass of stitches and was covered with flies. He was still wearing the clothes in which he'd arrived two days ago and since then no one had washed him. His hands and clothes were crusted with dried blood, as was the single sheet on which he was lying. The sheet was rumpled and beneath it I could see the filthy stains on the mattress. I felt like being sick.

Danny was in such pain that he was barely aware of my presence, but as I gazed at his injuries I became convinced that God was going to perform a miracle for him. I laid hands on him and prayed that the Lord would reach down and touch him, and grant him complete healing.

After this first visit, I felt such concern for Danny that I began to visit him daily. Francisco offered to come with me to act as interpreter, as Danny knew no English and I wasn't yet proficient in Tagalog. We brought an electric fan which, though it didn't have much effect on the heat, at least helped to keep the flies away. We also provided clean sheets and a set of Francisco's clothes for Danny to wear while we took his own away to wash them.

At first Danny was unable to speak, but I was buoyed up by my inner conviction that God was going to heal him. And within a few days we began to see an answer to our prayers as the horrific injuries started to heal and Danny's speech was restored. There still wasn't much medical care, but at least he'd been put on a dextrose drip, which was something. Yet God was doing a greater work in Danny than his physical healing.

Through Francisco, I talked to him about God's love, explaining from Scripture how the Lord Jesus Christ had died in his place. It was wonderful to see how, in such a desperate situation, the grace of God evoked a response in Danny's heart, bringing him to the point where, as we led him in a short prayer, he acknowledged his need of a Saviour and surrendered his life to Christ.

One day I arrived at the hospital alone to find Danny's bed empty. My mind full of awful possibilities, I looked around for someone who could tell me what had happened, but of course there were no nursing staff to be seen. As the minutes passed my anxiety mounted and I decided to take a chance that the elderly man in the opposite bed would understand English. Thankfully he did, and was able to reassure me that Danny was fine and had just gone to get himself something to eat. He was a very friendly man and amazingly cheerful in spite of his circumstances. He was waiting to have his leg amputated and his wife was in the next bed suffering from a stomach complaint. It was hard to believe that this man was about to lose his leg in consequence of a simple scratch on his toe. Because of the lack of clean water and poor hygiene, and because he could not afford antiseptics, this small scratch had led to gangrene in the foot, with the result that several of his toes were now missing and what remained of the foot was black with decay.

As I looked at this poor elderly couple who had no

visitors to care for them I reflected on the way in which we in England so easily take for granted the health care provision which is available to us, and how quick we are to grumble about cuts in welfare benefits. We complain about the rising cost of prescriptions, yet a Filipino has to pay a day's wage just to consult the doctor, before he even obtains a prescription. If he is admitted to hospital, he knows he won't be allowed to leave until he has paid his bill. If he can't pay, he has to stay, incurring more debt the longer he remains there. A first-hand experience of third-world poverty in a country which doesn't enjoy the advantage of a National Health Service, and where children die of measles, diarrhoea and malnutrition, certainly makes one appreciate the blessings of living in the western world. No government service is ever perfect, but we do have so much to thank God for.

As if to confirm the contrast, Danny returned with the boiled eggs he had bought from a canteen, having had to carry his bottle of dextrose with him out of the hospital.

It was never my intention to get involved in the politics of Danny's case – I was simply a missionary offering pastoral care and moral support. But circumstances forced my hand.

One day when Francisco and I arrived, Danny already had a visitor, a woman. This was unusual, as apart from us Danny seemed never to have visitors. Not wanting to intrude, we withdrew until the woman had left.

When we returned, Danny immediately launched into an animated explanation. I couldn't understand a word of his rapid Tagalog, but Francisco told me that Danny's visitor was the wife of Patrolman Apin. She had offered to pay for Danny to have plastic surgery on his face and to arrange for him to be released from jail and go to live somewhere in the country. In return, she wanted him to promise not to press charges against her husband.

Although Danny was twenty-one, he was very naive and had taken Mrs Apin's offer at face value, believing implicitly all she told him. However, knowing that very few Filipinos could afford to pay for plastic surgery, and remembering what had happened to Eddie, I was instantly convinced that Danny was being set up. I'd heard stories of other people being taken away to the country – and the arrangement wasn't made out of concern for their welfare but in order to conceal their whereabouts so that they would not be missed if they disappeared suddenly.

It was up to me to do something because Danny had no one else to take an interest in him. I went to see his mother, but she refused to 'waste' her money on the jeepney ride to the hospital. The choice I faced wasn't much of a choice at all: either sit around, do nothing and risk a repeat of Eddie's fate; or put my own safety in jeopardy and fight for justice for Danny. I simply couldn't leave him at the mercy of the police officer who'd shot him, so I began to pray for the Lord's guidance and wisdom, to lead both Danny and me to safety.

What my commitment to help Danny was going to mean in practice, I didn't precisely know; and in the event the need for action arose before I'd had time to seek advice. By now, Patrolman Apin had learned of my daily visits to the hospital and perhaps it was because he was afraid I would interfere with his plans that his wife went to see Danny and told him he'd be leaving that same day. I had no plans of my own ready, so I did the only thing I could think of: I went straight to the hospital director and pleaded with him not to allow Danny to be discharged. 'We need the bed,' he said coldly, and that was that.

Patrolman Apin arrived with his wife in a rented jeepney and poor Danny, suspecting nothing, went without protest. I followed them to the jeepney, wanting to demonstrate that I intended to concern myself with Danny's welfare. As the jeepney pulled away, Danny waved and smiled, such an innocent, trusting smile. I forced myself to smile back, but inwardly I was shaking with fear. I was only twenty-one myself and very inexperienced. Less than a year ago I hadn't even had to worry about paying an electricity bill, and now a man's life might depend on my doing the right thing. But 'God has not given us a spirit of fear, but of power and of love and of a sound mind' (2 Tim 1:7). With this assurance, I rebuked my fear and at once experienced the truth of Christ's promise: 'I am with you always, even to the end of the age' (Mt 28:20).

As quickly as I could, I made my way back to Subic and went immediately to the jail to ask where Danny had been taken. The police were very offhand with me, even contemptuous, though in the past we'd been on the friendliest terms. Danny, they told me, was back in their custody and I was not permitted to speak to him.

I tried again the following day, taking Francisco with me, and this time I was successful. Danny showed me a paper he'd been told to sign. It was an affidavit of desistance; that is, a statement affirming that he did not wish to press charges against Apin. The police had exerted a lot of pressure and repeated all Mrs Apin's promises, and Danny had signed. Gently I tried to make him understand that Patrolman Apin couldn't possibly afford to fulfil these promises and that once he was freed from the threat of prosecution, Danny himself would be in grave danger. I promised that if he wanted to change his mind, I would do all I could to support him.

Danny was pathetically surprised that anyone should be taking an interest in him. He had known so little love in his life and couldn't understand why I, whom he'd known for so short a time, should try to help him when even his mother showed no concern on his behalf. It was the love of Jesus in my heart, I told him, that caused me to care about him.

He thought about my offer for a while. It didn't come naturally to him to suspect people of ulterior motives, but once he'd grasped what lay in store for him – and perhaps for others too, if Apin went unpunished – he decided to ask for the affidavit to be revoked.

My role in persuading him placed me in open conflict with the police, which on the face of it looked like a very unequal contest, especially since, from then on, I was more or less on my own. Only Francisco remained willing to be actively involved and many people, convinced that I was taking too big a risk, tried to dissuade me from pursuing Danny's case. I wasn't sure how far I was risking my personal safety, or my prison ministry, but I did know I couldn't abandon Danny.

The day of reckoning was not long in coming. Early one morning we answered a knock at the door to find one of the Subic policemen bringing a message from his superior officer, Lieutenant Santos: would I please go and see the lieutenant in his office? There was no question of disobeying the summons, so I set off for the Municipal Hall.

When I entered the lieutenant's office, the first thing I saw was Mrs Apin sitting at the far end of the room. Lieutenant Santos began to speak. In the past he'd always been supportive of our ministry, but there was no mistaking the fact that his present purpose was to warn me off. His voice was quiet and his manner sympathetic, but the message was plain: for the sake of my own safety, I should take his advice and drop the matter. I wasn't sure exactly what he was implying, but I replied as firmly as I could that I would help Danny for as long as he wanted me to.

Mrs Apin, who had been simmering with barely suppressed anger during this exchange, could contain herself no longer and erupted with a stream of filthy abuse which even Lieutenant Santos, who was obviously embarrassed, couldn't stem. She was consumed with rage and bitterness against me, accusing me of the most unspeakable things. The tirade ended with her screaming that I was trying to destroy her husband. Though it was disturbing to find myself the target of her virulence, I didn't actually feel any anger towards her. I could understand that she was afraid for her husband. As calmly as I could, I replied, 'No, Mrs Apin. I understand that you are standing up for your

husband, but I have no personal grudge against him. He's
fortunate to have someone who cares for him. Danny has
no one except me and all I want is to stand by him and see
that he receives justice.'

A protracted silence followed. Eventually, Lieutenant
Santos said that the judge who had witnessed the signing
of the affidavit was waiting to see me in his office on the
next floor.

The judge's hostility was less ambiguous than Lieutenant Santos'. In no uncertain terms he told me I had
no business to meddle in the affair and that it would be
greatly to my advantage to keep out of what didn't concern me. 'The weapon of a missionary is the Bible,' he
said, 'and you should stick to that, because the weapons
of the police are guns.' Incongruously he added, 'I'm not
trying to scare you.'

I made no reply and, rightly taking my silence as a refusal
to comply, he began to threaten me more openly. 'I could
make it impossible for you to remain in the Philippines as a
missionary, and then what would you do?'

'Well, sir, I think I'd go to Africa.' I wasn't trying to be
cheeky. I just meant that if I was prevented from preaching
the gospel in the Philippines, then I was sure God would
open other doors.

With that, the interview was over, but I'd left the judge
in no doubt that I wasn't to be intimidated into abandon-
ing Danny. My greatest fear was that I wouldn't have time
to see things through to a conclusion before my ten
months came to an end. My return flight was just a short
time ahead and I knew only too well how protracted judi-
cial processes could be. It had in fact become clear to me
recently that I wouldn't be leaving the Philippines for good
and that God had much more for me to do here. I was
ready for a break, but that was all it would be. However, I
was worried about leaving Danny at this crucial stage.

Thankfully, Francisco was now as committed as I was
and assured me he would take care of everything. Nothing

was settled before I left and I was dependent on Francisco
for news. While I was in England, things moved very fast
(which didn't often happen in the Philippines) and Francisco, true to his word, wrote to tell me the outcome,
which was mostly good. For while no charges were being
pressed against Patrolman Apin, Danny had been acquitted
of the assault charge on which he'd been detained and after
his release had found work in Manila, where he would be
safe.

I was profoundly relieved that Danny's story had ended
so differently from Eddie's. But it wasn't until months
later, after I'd returned to the Philippines, that I received
confirmation of just how real the threat had been.

It took a while for the Subic police to overcome their
hostility, but in the end I regained their friendship and even
an extra degree of respect. Patrolman Apin, however, never
forgave me. Then one day, on a regular visit to Camp
Maquinaya, when I'd been back eight months, I was
stunned to discover that Apin was being detained as an
inmate. Late one night, in a quiet spot not far from Subic
Town, he had forced a nineteen-year-old boy to strip himself naked and ordered him to run. As the terrified boy fled,
Apin shot him in the back.

My blood ran cold when I heard this story. It could so
easily have been Danny. My involvement in his case
brought me a great deal of trouble and anxiety, but I thank
the Lord that I did it.

8

The Vision

I flew back to England in the summer of 1984 both physically and emotionally drained, feeling that the past ten months had provided enough harrowing experiences to last a lifetime. Yet I had a vision in my heart of what the Lord wanted to accomplish through me when I returned to the Philippines.

I saw clearly now that my work so far was only a beginning. Taking the gospel to the inmates in the jails was one thing, but what prospect was there for them when they were eventually released? All they had to look forward to was unemployment, poverty and discrimination. Take Rhey, for example. Rhey, the mayor of Alpha block at Camp Maquinaya, had killed a man with a pair of scissors and though there was no doubt that he had acted in self-defence it was more than unexpected – it was a miracle – that when his case was heard, he was released.

Nothing in his previous experience had fitted him for anything other than a life of crime. Orphaned as a young child and thrown out onto the streets by his stepmother when he was only seven, he had turned to selling drugs in order to survive. It was the only life he knew. He'd been attracted to Olongapo by the possibility which the naval base afforded of earning dollars, and had worked with a member of the US military who imported the drugs which Rhey, with his many contacts, was able to sell for high prices. He made a lot of money and was a well-known figure in the bars around the base, and though the police were aware of his operations he was always able to buy himself out of trouble until he was arrested and charged with murder.

On his release, Rhey faced an impossible situation. Having had no education, he could neither read nor write and so could not even fill in an application for a job, which in any case he'd be unlikely to get, given his record. Drug dealing was the only way he knew of making money, but as a newly converted Christian this avenue was obviously closed to him. How was he to support himself and his family?

When I visited him after he came out of jail, I found him and Ning, his wife, squatting in an empty derelict house entirely bare of furniture and with gaping holes in the roof through which the rain poured relentlessly. They had a few cooking pans but no food; they were using the pans to catch the rain. To add to their problems, six-year-old Precy, the elder of their two daughters, suffered from a congenital condition which rendered her unable to walk, talk or eat solid food. She never communicated with her parents at all and they believed she was also mentally handicapped, though because of her physical problems it was difficult to be sure.

I had spent the whole of those first ten months preaching, teaching and caring for the spiritual needs of those I met in the jails, but now the Lord was showing me that the gospel is more than 'pie in the sky'. Jesus was concerned not only with their eternal well being but also with their physical welfare here and now. It was not enough to have preached the gospel to people like Rhey – they needed help to become established in their new life with Christ once they faced the harsh reality which awaited them on the other side of the barbed wire. Thus was planted the seed of my vision of a rehabilitation home for ex-prisoners, their wives and their families.

Equally urgent were the needs of the children in the Subic area. Under Linda's leadership, the four of us had extended our children's outreach work to many of the surrounding villages, but so far we had dealt only with spiritual and emotional needs. I now envisaged, in addition to the rehabilitation home, a children's refuge home to cater for two different classes of children.

First, there were the many youngsters who were deprived of education because their parents couldn't afford to send them to school. Elementary education was really quite cheap, but parents often failed to enrol their children if they couldn't afford to buy them decent clothes or if they needed them at home to take care of younger brothers and sisters while they tried to find work. Some of the poorest, who couldn't even feed their children properly, saw no point in encouraging them to study on an empty stomach. Kids like these would remain trapped in poverty all their lives. Short of a miracle, the only way out lay in education.

The other group were the children of inmates in Camp Maquinaya. Unbelievable as it sounds, some of these children actually lived with their parents inside the jail, where they regularly witnessed drunken brawls, drug abuse, prostitution and homosexuality. To have a child growing up in this environment, which the inmates themselves called 'this dark place', was a situation no parent would willingly countenance, but these parents had no choice. For them it was the only alternative to allowing their children to starve alone on the streets. God had given me a burning desire to reach out to them and provide them with a home where they would receive love, stability and an education. Above all, I was mindful of his word: 'Train up a child in the way he should go, and when he is old he will not depart from it' (Prov 22:6).

The final strand of my vision related to the particular

difficulties which newly released prisoners found in becoming part of a worshipping community. Shortly after his release, Rhey went with us to church. With his scruffy clothes and unkempt hair he looked very out of place. I felt uncomfortable at the way people stood aloof from him, though in truth Rhey's rough exterior, his body covered in tattoos and his scarred face presented an alarming appearance to anyone who didn't know him. People like Rhey needed a spiritual home where they could feel accepted, and I believed God was calling me to create a place where they could worship freely. I was concerned also about our neighbours in Subic Town who needed Christ and for whom there was no nearby church where the gospel was preached.

This was the vision I carried home. A rehabilitation home; a children's refuge; a place of worship: a work which would be called the Philippine Outreach Centre.

During my three months in England a number of churches invited me to speak about my work and I took the opportunity to share my vision for the future. After many of these visits I came away very encouraged by the enthusiastic response of the many people who wanted to be kept informed about the Philippine Outreach Centre.

It was in England that I had my first serious encounter with culture shock. Apart from the General Hospital at Olongapo, I'd absorbed the impact of my environment in the Philippines without much trouble, adjusting quite easily to the lower standard of living and to sharing my home with insects and other forms of wildlife. But when I walked around Manchester and saw people who had spent more on the clothes they wore than many Filipinos have invested in their homes, I was struck by a deep sense of the unfairness of things. As I wandered round the huge, spotless supermarkets I recalled shopping trips in Olongapo, where I'd seen mice, and even rats, scurrying along the floors of the grocery stores. 'Excuse me,' I'd said to one store owner, 'but you have a rat on your bags of sugar.'

'Oh, yes,' she'd replied, 'we have a lot of those.'

In the meat section of the supermarket, I remembered my first visit to a Philippine meat market: row upon row of stalls where the meat hung sweating through the heat of the day. The vendors waged a continual but hopeless war against the flies which buzzed around in clouds. Add to this the fact that the most popular meat was pork, and you've got a paradise for bacteria. It was a world away from the hygienic refrigerated packages in front of me. And the prices! In the Philippines our weekly budget for rice, fish and vegetables was only 100 pesos (the rate of exchange then was 18 pesos to the pound) and pork and chicken were luxuries.

The comfort – the opulence, even, as it now appeared – of my own home and those of my friends made me uneasy, and once, when I was taken for a meal at an expensive restaurant, I was so upset by the prices that my friend and I had to leave and find somewhere with a more modest menu. Culture shock was in danger of turning into resentment of all this western affluence, until God began to show me that it is not necessarily wrong for Christians to have money; in fact, my own work had benefited from the generosity of his people. And just as I shouldn't condemn Filipinos for their poverty, neither should I condemn the British for their prosperity. Like St Paul, I had to learn to live both with humble means and with plenty (Phil 4:12). None the less, my return in September to the little house in Subic felt like a return to normality.

When my plane landed in Manila, I was welcomed not only by Dorothy, Linda and Redemia but also, to my delight, by many of the young people who met for Bible study in Simon's house. It was good to be reunited with the other three girls, but I wasn't actually going to be living with them for much longer.

David Nellist had been very enthusiastic about my vision for the Philippine Outreach Centre and encouraged me to go forward with it, but at the same time, his own long-term vision was still to train Filipinos to evangelise their own nation. We therefore agreed together that my work and his should become separate, developing on independent lines with mutual love and respect. I would never forget how the Lord used David to call me to the Philippines, nor how he helped me take my first steps as a missionary.

Though I felt sure the decision to pursue separate ministries was the right one, it meant I had to pioneer the Philippine Outreach Centre alone. When I first conceived my vision, I'd thought in terms of continuing under the umbrella of David's mission, but I now began to pray and seek God's will as to the way forward on my own. I rented a small bungalow not too far away and prepared to move in. I'd be on my own, but only for two weeks because Mum was coming out to visit me and spend Christmas in the Philippines.

Just two weeks. That was all Satan needed to draw me into a situation which laid waste all my hopes. Ironically, the trouble had its roots in the Bible study group at Simon's house, which Redemia and I had resumed on my return.

Simon lived alone, as his wife was in America at the time. This sort of arrangement is not uncommon in the Philippines; it's the ambition of many Filipinos to reach America in search of a better way of life, and if one partner in a marriage succeeds in obtaining a visa, he or she will emigrate alone in the hope that the other will be able to follow later. Simon, however, was finding it difficult to cope with his loneliness and began to get very depressed. His wife's cousin, Edwin (who was also a member of the Bible study group) used to visit him often, but all his attempts to shake Simon out of his depression failed. Simon lost interest in everything, became increasingly lethargic and didn't even bother to eat.

While I was still living with Dorothy, Linda and Redemia, we began inviting him round for meals from time to time. He'd become a friend, and we were concerned at the state he was in. Then, when I moved into the bungalow, Simon started to visit me there, bringing questions about the Bible study and asking my advice about spiritual things.

I was still only twenty-two and very naive. I was also ignorant of many aspects of Filipino culture and was unaware that to a Filipino, a single woman who opened her door to him was also opening her heart. It took a while for me to realise that Simon's feelings for me were much more than those of a friend, but when I did, I was horrified and made it clear that the sort of relationship he wanted was not an option. But Simon, though a very gentle man, was also very persistent; and I, on my own for the first time in my life, was very vulnerable. Simon took advantage of my vulnerability and before I knew it, I was emotionally involved with him. It never went further than that, but I knew it was wrong and I knew I had to end it, yet I lacked the will to act. Guilt and remorse tormented me, but I was unable truly to repent and confess my fault. The struggle was sharp but mercifully brief and when I finally turned to the Lord in repentance his grace and forgiveness were instantaneous.

On the day my mother arrived, Dorothy came to pay a farewell visit. Her time with David's mission was over and she was leaving the next day. As we were talking, Edwin called and asked to speak to me outside. As soon as we were alone, he dropped his bombshell: he'd found out about my involvement with Simon and intended to make his knowledge public unless I agreed to marry him. Still reeling under the shock of discovery, it never occurred to me that he thought things had gone much further between Simon and me than was actually the case. I felt so guilty anyway that I never thought to go into details with him. Pulling myself together, I told Edwin that I couldn't possibly marry him, whereupon he threatened to tell his cousin

(Simon's wife) about me and assured me that his family would take revenge on me. Somehow I managed to get rid of him and the rest of the day passed in a blur.

The following day Edwin returned. He had obviously been taking drugs, something I'd never known him do before, and, in front of my mother, repeated his threats and his demand that I marry him. Of course, Mum told him it was out of the question, so after raging and shouting at us Edwin went home and phoned his cousin in America.

Poor Mum. I'd done it to her again. She was still suffering from jet lag and culture shock, and here she was facing the situation all mothers dread. She'd assumed from Edwin's account that I'd had a sexual relationship with Simon and of course she was devastated. Not realising her mistake, I naturally didn't disabuse her. Her anger and disappointment seemed perfectly justified by what I had done and it was quite some time before the truth came out.

Despite her anger, Mum's chief concern was for my safety. We were both worried by Edwin's threats of revenge, which we soon discovered were not idle. On several consecutive nights, as we lay in bed, we heard footsteps and furtive whispers outside our window. The sense of being spied on was terrifying. A few days later, we returned from shopping to find crosses painted in blood all over the walls of the house and the initial 'C' scrawled in blood at the doorway. We couldn't doubt that Edwin was responsible, though we never saw him, until, on Christmas Day, I had an accidental meeting with him and his sister in the street. As soon as he saw me, he sprang at me, punched me in the face and began beating me up until his sister dragged him off. I staggered home wondering how much more I could take.

One of the worst aspects of this nightmare was that we felt unable to ask anyone for help. Dorothy had gone, and to involve Linda would only make her afraid too. We were too ashamed to tell the people at church. Occasionally we took refuge with Phil and Audrey Houghton, an American missionary couple who ran the Military Mission for US servicemen in Subic. They had become good friends to me and though we didn't confide in them, it was a relief just to have fellowship in an atmosphere of peace and sanity.

We no longer felt safe in our own home. Mum had never liked the house anyway (it was very bug-ridden), so we decided to move. We found a bungalow in another *barangay* of Subic called Pamatawan which, being on the outskirts of the town, put both physical and psychological distance between us and our problems.

Throughout this trial, Mum and I struggled to keep the prison work going with Redemia's help. I avoided going to Subic Jail because it was so near to where Simon and Edwin lived, but in addition to Camp Maquinaya I was by now making weekly visits to Iba Jail at the request of a local pastor. Iba lay a one-and-a-half-hour bus ride to the north of Subic. I often wept as I sang and preached to the inmates, knowing that my words about sin and repentance were for me as much as for them. I'd let the Lord down so badly and jeopardised my whole mission. I knew that gossip about me was rife – Edwin had fulfilled his threat there too – and I had foolishly given room for it.

With all the stress I began to lose weight and looked so very pale and ill that finally Mum insisted that I go home for a break and allow her to continue the ministry in my absence. We booked a flight a few weeks after Christmas and I flew home in despair. I hadn't told Mum that I had decided never to return to the Philippines.

9

'My Grace Is Sufficient'

When Dad met me at the airport he didn't recognise me until I spoke to him. He was visibly shocked to see me looking so pale and thin. I'd dreaded facing questions from people at church, but in fact no one asked any. My physical appearance seemed reason enough for my early return. However, I wanted to be honest, so I let it be known, without going into details, that I'd failed the Lord.

I was so sure he'd never be willing to use me again on the mission field that almost as soon as I arrived home I began looking for work. I found a job in a technical drawing office and tried to pick up the threads of my former life. As I sat at my desk, my heart and mind were in the Philippines, but I never spoke to the Lord about it. I'd repented and he had forgiven me, but I would never dare ask for a second chance.

Mum wrote telling me that Remedia had moved in with her and that the two of them had begun attending a small church in Olongapo, called the Born-Again Christians' Den, whose pastor, James, was helping them with the prison ministry. James was an ex-prisoner himself and related easily to the inmates. Mum had also started a new children's outreach in Pamatawan, and, as if all this were not enough, had established an evangelistic work of her own among Filipina women in the remote rural districts around Subic. While I rejoiced at what God was doing through Mum, it made me even more keenly aware of what I had lost. My own life seemed like a pointless succession of empty days. I wondered what I would do with the rest of my life.

The graciousness of God never ceases to amaze me. One Sunday morning in church, when I'd been home about six weeks, I had a fresh experience of his love and received from him the assurance that his power had redeemed all my failures. He spoke to me in the words of 2 Corinthians 12:9: 'My grace is sufficient for you, for My strength is made perfect in weakness.' I had an overwhelming sense of his grace in my heart and I knew he was giving me the second chance I hadn't dared ask for. Full of thankfulness, I renewed my vow to serve him in the Philippines.

After that, things moved quickly. A few weeks after Mum came home in February, I was ready to go back. In preparation for my return, I meditated on the events of the past few months, knowing that God works through trials for our good and that there were lessons for me to learn from my failure. Painfully, I recognised that I had glibly assumed that as a missionary I was somehow immune to the temptations which beset other people. For all the fact that I was so frequently engaged in preaching about the seriousness of sin, I never really reckoned with the possibility that I would fall into sin myself. I'd allowed myself to become spiritually proud and self-righteous, too sure of my own strength. I believe God permitted me to fall from his grace for a short time so that I would learn the full extent of my dependence on him. It is easy to say, 'Without God I can do nothing;' it is much harder to grasp the reality. I thanked the Lord for teaching me this so early in my ministry.

I returned to the little bungalow in Pamatawan in March 1985, chastened and humbled but with a renewed vision for the work ahead. I didn't expect it to be easy. With my reputation in tatters as a result of the gossip spread by Edwin, I had to be prepared for hostility and mistrust. It might take years to re-establish my credibility before I could even begin to think of setting up the Philippine Outreach Centre.

I was so grateful to Remedia for standing by me. She had decided to join me permanently and together we resumed the familiar pattern of children's outreaches and prison work. We concentrated on Iba Jail and Camp Maquinaya, adding weekly Bible studies to our regular services in both places. This meant making four trips a week to Camp Maquinaya, as for security reasons Alpha and Bravo blocks were never now opened on the same day, and each group had to be visited separately.

It was satisfying to be back where I felt I belonged, doing the work I knew was mine, but how hard it was to react calmly to the cold stares and contempt of those who had believed Edwin's gossip. Phil and Audrey Houghton at the Military Mission were always there for me and their friendship helped me find the courage to go on. Making light of the demands of his own work, Phil made time to come with us to the jails from time to time. He and Audrey treated me like a daughter; to me they were (and still are) 'Mom and Pop Houghton'.

Simon's wife had returned from America and the couple were immediately reconciled. I met her one day in the market and asked if we could talk. It was only then that I discovered that Edwin had told her (and others) that I was pregnant. I explained that this was impossible – that Simon and I had not had a physical relationship. I apologised to her for what had happened and assured her that Simon's feelings for me had only arisen as a result of his missing her so much. Shortly afterwards she and Simon left the Philippines to go to America together.

Not long after this, Edwin took to cycling past our house and I schooled myself to return a polite greeting to the insults he hurled at me. This had its effect and eventually I was able to have a reasonable conversation with him. He admitted that it was he and his friends who had spied on Mum and me and that they had painted the walls of our house with expired human blood which Edwin had taken from the medical lab where he worked on the US naval base. He still insisted he wanted to marry me, but the firmness of my refusal finally convinced him and he accepted it. Later, when he was married to someone else, we were able to meet as friends.

These encounters went some way towards resolving the situation, but what really helped me to put the past behind me was a visit I made to a group of small islands in the southern part of the Philippines. I couldn't have afforded the trip had it not been for the fact that when I flew back in March, a special promotional offer entitled every international passenger on Philippine Airlines to an internal flight at half price. Through a network of mutual acquaintances, I'd received an invitation from a Pastor Thomas on the island of Bohol to visit him and take part in his prison ministry. The cheap ticket appeared to be God's provision, and confirmation of his will that I should go.

From Manila I flew first to the island of Cebu, where I stayed for a few days with some English friends of Linda who ran a children's mission called Sunshine Corner, before flying on to Bohol to spend a fortnight with Pastor Thomas.

I knew that Thomas had founded a church and a Bible school and that he led his students in various forms of evangelism, especially in the jails, but I'd never met him and I wondered, as the small aircraft flew across the Bohol Strait, how I would recognise him when we landed. However, all uncertainty dissolved when I stepped off the plane at Tagbilaran airport (airport? it looked more like an ordinary bus shelter back home) and saw a huge Filipino surrounded by a group of young people carrying a banner emblazoned with the words 'Welcome, Sister Chrissy'.

Thomas placed an enormous garland of exotic flowers round my neck and I felt instantly at home.

Bohol was a tiny island paradise, largely untouched by western influence. There was a hotel for foreign holiday-makers, but its guests can't have ventured far: in my two weeks there, I met only Filipinos. The island had few modern amenities, but everything was so clean. After the dirt, the squalor even, of Subic Bay, I was entranced by the golden beaches, the greenness of the dense vegetation and the purity of the air. The freshness of the scene felt like a new start in itself.

Thomas' house in Tagbilaran, where I stayed, was made of *kawayan* (bamboo) and *nipa* (palm leaves) and was as clean as everything else. I was delighted with it, despite Thomas' tendency to apologise for its lack of modern facilities.

On my first evening (Filipino Christians don't believe in wasting time) I was the speaker at a service in Thomas' church. The Holy Spirit's presence among us was unmistakable and as I saw the many young people in the congregation eagerly responding, being challenged to take part in prison outreach, my own heart overflowed with gratitude to the God who was still willing to use me as his instrument to speak to others.

It was the beginning of a very precious time for me. In the following days, as I visited Tagbilaran's two jails with Pastor Thomas and his young people, I discovered a new joy in serving the Lord and, freed from the problems which dogged me at Subic, I was able to appropriate the full reality of my restoration. The Lord was with me as I sang and preached to the inmates, and I had the privilege of seeing many profess the desire to receive Jesus as their Lord and Saviour.

One incident in particular remains with me, and this concerned not an inmate but a police officer. Unaware that he'd even been listening to what I was saying, I was first startled, then thrilled, when he indicated that he too wished to become a Christian. This was the first time either Thomas or I had been able to lead a policeman to the Lord; they were notoriously harder to reach than even murderers and drug addicts. It seemed like a special pledge that God was with me in my work.

I returned to Subic with my confidence renewed, sure now that if I only trusted him, God would use me in some way, even if the Philippine Outreach Centre lay far in the future. For now, I was glad to be back and visiting Iba and Camp Maquinaya again. I had enjoyed my time on Bohol, but the inmates here were my family and I had missed them.

At Mum's suggestion, I'd joined James's church, where Remedia was already a member. Because it was situated near the main gate of the naval base in Olongapo, the Born-Again Christians' Den was often visited by service people, but the members, who included a lot of young people, were mostly Filipinos, as was James. It was a small fellowship which James himself had started, and the services, which were relaxed and informal, were conducted in Taglish. James's own ministry with the church kept him fairly busy, but he continued to help Remedia and me in the jails, and from time to time some of the young people came along too. It was good to belong to a church that was so supportive of my ministry and I was very happy there. And it was there too that I first met Dondie.

10

Stepping Stone

Good news: Jason was to be released from Iba! When we first met him, Jason was being detained at Camp Maquinaya because of his drug abuse, and at that time he made it plain that there was no room for God in his life; but when he was later transferred to Iba a marked change came over him. The preaching of the gospel began to penetrate his indifference and it was not long before he gave his heart to the Lord.

Jason was only twenty-four, and on his release he went to live with his mother. Though not rich by any means, the family was moderately well off compared to those of most ex-prisoners, so this seemed a hopeful arrangement. James and I invited him to join us at church on Sundays and he came faithfully for several weeks, fitting in well with the others of his age group, who did their best to make him feel accepted.

One Sunday he appeared distressed. He approached me and asked me to pray for him. 'I need a place to stay,' he said. 'The problem with staying at my mother's is that all my old friends know where I am and keep trying to get me back onto drugs. Sister Chrissy, I don't want to go back to that kind of life.'

Twenty years ago a similar plea for help had set my

mother on the path to creating a refuge for young offenders. Now, incredibly, I sensed the Lord reminding me of my own vision of a rehabilitation home. I heard his voice say: 'The time is now.'

'Lord, you can't really mean that!' We were not yet ready for a rehabilitation programme. I'd been so sure that it lay far in the future and felt miserably unprepared and inadequate. Then I remembered: 'My grace is sufficient for you, for My strength is made perfect in weakness.' The time was now.

I talked it over with Redemia, who was instantly enthusiastic and eager to go ahead. But one thing was immediately obvious: we couldn't do it with just the two of us. It was impossible for two young girls to run a rehabilitation home for ex-prisoners; there would have to be a man to oversee the work.

Straight away I thought of Dondie, who often helped James at church, taking Bible studies and leading adult Sunday school. He'd been with us on prison visits a number of times and was always keen to help with any kind of evangelism and outreach. Dondie was working very successfully as a freelance land agent, earning commission on the plots of building land he sold, and was clearly very intelligent and capable. His spiritual maturity was plain to see in the way he taught the Scriptures. He seemed suitable in every way and I was sure he was the right man for the job.

I had learned caution, however, and I admitted to myself that in the few months I'd known him I had come to like and admire Dondie a great deal. He was one of those people whose personalities make them the centre of any group of which they're a part, but his popularity hadn't made him conceited. At thirty-one, he was slightly older than most of the young people at church and was often on the receiving end of jokes about his age and the fact that he was still single. He took this with perfect good humour, as he did when they teased him about his deep voice and his height (he was quite short). If Dondie were to join us in the work, it had to be in response to a call from God, not because I wanted it, so when I approached him I would have to exclude the least hint of persuasion on my part. When, therefore, I asked Dondie to pray as to whether it were God's will for him to work in the Philippine Outreach Centre rehabilitation home, I was careful to spell out the level of commitment that would be involved. It would be his job to live in the home with the ex-prisoners and conduct daily Bible studies with them. 'There'll be no salary,' I explained, 'but we'll give you what we can, according to what God provides.'

Good jobs were not so plentiful that a Filipino would lightly give up his career prospects to take on such hard work and responsibility for no salary. I had done my best to ensure that Dondie would accept only if he believed God was calling him. He agreed to pray.

Redemia and I, meanwhile, wasted no time and began to look for suitable premises. We had very little money. I was still receiving my regular support from the congregation at the Upper Room and had been given an extra gift of £1,000 by a friend of my mother, but that had gone towards the purchase of a small car – a twenty-year-old VW Beetle – which we increasingly needed as the work expanded. We decided that Redemia should be the one to search for a property, as Filipinos always ask higher prices from foreigners, imagining them all to be rich. I stayed at home and prayed.

On the first day, Redemia returned wearily after several hours, having had no success. Rents in Subic were very high. So many US servicemen from the naval base were renting houses in the town that property owners were able to demand exorbitant amounts. Redemia asked whether I would consider having the rehabilitation home in Castille-jos, a small town just to the north of Subic. It was only a ten-minute jeepney ride away from our bungalow in Pama-tawan, which, being on the edge of Subic, was as close to

Castillejos as it was to Subic town centre. It seemed a possible solution, so I agreed.

Next day, Redemia returned home beaming. 'Chrissy, I've seen just the place, a bungalow in Castillejos, and the rent's only 400 pesos a month!'

When I went back with her to look at it, I could see why it was so cheap. It had been empty for quite a while and looked very dilapidated. There was no guttering or drainage, no running water, and the roof needed repairing. But it was only 400 pesos, and I always enjoyed a challenge. Inside, there was a good-sized living and dining room, one large bedroom, three smaller bedrooms, a typically Filipino kitchen with a sink but no running water, and a bathroom with nothing in it except a toilet and a hole in the floor for drainage.

We went home and prayed about it. I had no specific, audible word from the Lord, but as we prayed I felt an inner conviction and peace that he was guiding us to Castillejos. At the same time, I knew that it would be a temporary location; not the accomplishment of my vision but a stepping stone towards it.

When I began negotiating with the owner of the bungalow, he was initially unwilling to do any maintenance work on the property, as the rent was so low, but after some persuasion and the offer of a slight increase in the rent he changed his mind and agreed that responsibility for maintenance would be his. Things were falling into place. When Dondie came and told me he believed he was being directed to accept the job, this seemed further confirmation that we were truly in the will of God.

Now that I had a definite prospect to offer them, I went again in search of Rhey and Ning. They had moved from the derelict house where I'd visited them before and were now living in one small room in someone else's home. Ning was expecting another baby and was several months into her pregnancy, but as there was no free ante-natal care available, she would only know for sure when the baby was due on the day she actually went into labour.

I'd brought some sweets for Nina, the younger of their two girls. Precy, because of her illness, was fed only on condensed milk. As I leaned over to offer some *banana-que* (like toffee apples, but made with bananas) to Nina, Precy suddenly grabbed it and in a few seconds had eaten it all. She was obviously ravenous. Gently, I asked Rhey and Ning how they were managing to feed Precy. They looked at the floor and in a halting voice Rhey told me that they frequently had no money for food, even ordinary food for themselves, and milk was so expensive they could rarely afford it. While there was usually a neighbour willing to give them a bit of rice, getting hold of milk was not so easy. Rhey loved Precy very much. Though she was now about seven, he still referred to her as his baby and I could hardly imagine the pain it must be causing him to see her so hungry.

Glad to be able to bring a little hope into their grim situation, I told them the good news about the rehabilitation home. They were elated at the prospect of security and regular food for the children. When I left, I asked Rhey to walk with me to the town centre, where I could buy him a supply of milk for Precy.

The image of the frail, starving child haunted me, and when, a few days later, Rhey came to see me I knew before he spoke what he was going to say. 'Sister Chrissy, Precy is dead.'

I tried to comfort him, reminding him that his innocent little girl was safe in the Lord's hands and would never suffer again. For Ning, who was not yet a Christian, there could be no such consolation. I wept for them both.

Rhey also faced difficulties in arranging the funeral, for which he had no money. I gave him what I could and agreed to conduct a short service for Precy. We were into the rainy season and on the day of the funeral, the downpour was torrential. Several of Rhey's relatives, whom I'd

never met before, came to the service at his sister's house
and when it was over we set off on the long walk up the
mountainside to the cemetery. Public cemeteries, where
the poor can be buried free of charge, are mostly situated
a long way from the main roads, as land is cheap there.
Ning's pregnancy was too advanced to allow her to make
the journey and I walked at Rhey's side, weeping with him
for his loss, but also for joy that Precy's suffering was over.
The rain mingled with our tears as we climbed.

Meanwhile, the contract for the house at Castillejos had
been signed and we began the task of turning the building
into a home. The young people at church eagerly volunteered to form a cleaning party and turned up in a laughing
crowd, wearing their oldest clothes and with handkerchiefs
on their heads, all ready for work. They tackled the scrubbing and sweeping with determination and my heart lifted
as I worked alongside them, feeling how good it was to be
part of a fellowship where we were friends and not just
members of the same church. In a remarkably short time
the accumulated dirt and grime were gone and once a coat
or two of paint had been put on, the place began to look
habitable. Apart from the fact that there was no furniture.

Mom and Pop Houghton had introduced me to a number of Christians on the naval base, and one of these, who
ran a Bible study group, invited me along to give my
testimony and talk about my work. I told them of our plans
for the rehabilitation home, and the generous people on
the base donated several pieces of furniture and lots of
other household goods. Mom and Pop also put me in
touch with a Christian carpenter who had done work for
them at the Military Mission, and he made us some bunk
beds and a dining table. By September we were ready to
go.

We fixed a day to celebrate the completion of the home
with a thanksgiving service. I invited Pop Houghton to
speak and to dedicate the building to the Lord, and as
always he was full of words of encouragement. At the

end of the day, we all shared a typically Filipino feast. There was rice (there was always rice!), chicken cooked with black pepper, bay leaves and potatoes, and barbecued fish stuffed with tomatoes and onions. We lingered over the food, enjoying the fellowship and talking over our plans for the future.

Rhey and his family moved in immediately, as did Jason, along with Dondie as overseer. Every day they met for Bible study, at which Dondie and I shared responsibility for the teaching, and for discussion of their spiritual needs. On one occasion, Rhey told us that he was praying that the expected baby would be a son; he'd promised the Lord that he would 'go straight' for the rest of his life if the Lord would grant his request.

One Sunday after church a few weeks later, I went with Dondie and Jason to the rehab (the rehabilitation home had become 'the rehab' to all of us) to find that Ning was just delivering her baby right there in the house. The local midwife was helping her. Rhey came rushing out to us, yelling, 'It's a boy, it's a boy!' before dashing back inside. Meanwhile, the midwife was telling Ning not to stop pushing, as there was another baby to come. Ning had had no idea she was carrying twins. Minutes later Rhey ran out again, 'It's another boy, another boy!' Needless to say, he was euphoric. The Lord had given him not one son, but two!

More than ten years have passed since then, and Rhey has never forgotten the promise he made to the Lord. For him this has meant living with poverty, but he has never considered returning to the drug dealing which once made him a rich man. He is a living testimony to the grace of God.

In order to encourage Rhey and Jason to share their faith, I began to involve them in the prison outreach. I didn't take them to Iba or Camp Maquinaya, as I judged they were not yet ready to visit the jails where they had been inmates themselves. However, I occasionally made trips to the big main prison at Muntinlupa, Manila. During my first ten months in the Philippines, friends in England had put me in touch with a remarkable American woman who had been working with the inmates at Muntinlupa for thirty years. Her name was Olga Robertson, but she was known to everyone as 'Mammie Olga'. An account of her experiences would fill volumes.

Muntinlupa is actually a district in Manila, but the name has become synonymous with the prison located there. It is the most notorious prison in the Philippines and consists of a vast campus on which are sited three separate prison buildings housing up to 12,000 inmates. The maximum security prison is called New Bilibid and the medium security, Sampaguita, and it was in these two that Mammie Olga worked; there is also a minimum security facility. The campus is almost a self-contained community, comprising, along with the prison buildings, houses for those who work in the prisons (Mammie Olga had one of these), schools, and churches established by both Roman Catholics and the various Protestant denominations. There are also churches actually within the prisons themselves. Mammie Olga had founded churches for the inmates in both New Bilibid and Sampaguita and over the years had seen many of them become Christians. She would train the converts to take responsibility for the preaching and pastoral oversight of the congregations, and after finishing their sentences several of them stayed on to help her with the work.

Mammie was greatly loved by the inmates and her long and faithful service had earned her the respect of all the prison officers. Though security at Muntinlupa was much stricter than at Camp Maquinaya, the mere mention of her name was enough to secure admittance. Mammie was (and still is) a source of inspiration to me, and I loved the opportunity to share in her ministry when I visited.

The first time I took Rhey and Jason with me, even Rhey confessed he was scared. Muntinlupa is exclusively for convicted prisoners and contains some of the worst criminals in the Philippines. But after meeting the Christian inmates and seeing some of these very men now making an uncompromising stand for Christ and even learning to be pastors and teachers, both Rhey and Jason came away with an increased faith that they too could put the past behind them and live for Christ. Ministry among ex-prisoners isn't all about happy endings, however. Our requirement for admission to the rehab was not conversion to Christ, simply a desire to forsake crime, but we found that those who had no interest in the things of God usually left of their own accord before long, unable to resist the lure of their former lives. One such was Danilo Cruz.

Danilo came to us in November, a few months after the rehab opened, just as I was due to leave for a three-month furlough in England. My next news of him came in the shape of a letter from Dondie some six weeks later. It seemed that Danilo, though he had professed interest in the gospel, had found the pull of the world stronger than his desire to be reconciled to God, and had left the rehab after a couple of weeks. Three weeks after that, his head was found in a box on a bus, with a stick of marijuana stuffed into his mouth. We never found out who did it, or why.

If only men would realise how transient are the pleasures of the world, while the consequences of rejecting Christ are for ever. And what an urgent task we have as Christians to warn them. Serving the Lord can involve suffering, but with eternal issues at stake can we allow it to deter us?

11

Confusion

By the time I returned to England in November 1985, Dondie had become quite special to me. We spent a great deal of time in each other's company, both at the rehab, where we shared the Bible teaching, and in the jails, where Dondie now did much of the interpreting for me. Since, however, I had no reason to think he returned my feelings, I'd kept my own well hidden. I wrote to him a few times while I was away, but apart from his letter telling me about Danilo, which was quite impersonal and businesslike, I didn't hear from him at all. I decided I would have to accept the fact that Dondie had no interest in me except as a colleague.

At the same time, I'd been seeing rather a lot of Stuart. Despite our broken engagement four years earlier we had remained friends and he had been very supportive of my work. He was much more stable spiritually than in our teenage years and was now an elder and assistant treasurer at the Upper Room.

As on my previous furlough, I had received many invitations to speak about my work, and Stuart often volunteered to drive me to these engagements, which took me all over the country. He was kind to me in other ways, taking me out for meals or to the theatre, wanting me to enjoy for a short time some of the things I'd given up by going to the Philippines. It was impossible not to enjoy being treated with such consideration, but my pleasure in Stuart's company was disturbed by the uneasy awareness that spending so much time with him was beginning to reawaken the feelings I'd had for him before, especially when, as we inevitably did, we talked about the time when we had been engaged. I was troubled by the unexpected turn my emotions were taking and wondered what was going on in Stuart's mind, though, overtly at least, the understanding was that we were just friends. Until the week before I was due to go back.

We were reminiscing about the past, swapping memories of our courtship, when Stuart said tentatively, 'We could still get married if you wanted to.'

Hopes I'd thought were long dead rose up again to dazzle me. Everything I had wanted, everything I had wept for when our engagement ended, was being offered me; all the broken dreams which had driven me to dieting and anorexia could be made whole again. How desperately I longed to snatch at this chance of happiness. But even while part of me reached out with delight towards the future which my imagination was already busily painting – flowers, romantic walks in the park, returning from an exotic honeymoon to a beautiful home of our own – I felt again the sharp tug of unease. What about my vision for the Philippine Outreach Centre? How could I marry Stuart without renouncing the work to which I knew God had called me?

Tearfully I told Stuart it was impossible. Our lives were moving in different directions; mine to the Philippines, his towards the managing of his own very successful engineering company. Of course, Stuart could see perfectly well that I was refusing him because I felt I ought to, not because I didn't want him, and he himself saw no difficulty in reconciling our marriage with my call to the mission field: I would spend three months every year in the Philippines and his business would pay for my trips and finance the ministry. He was so sure it would work, and I wanted to think so too. But was it what God wanted for us? Satan had tried so many times to deflect me from obeying God, and I had no assurance that this was his will for me. I told Stuart I couldn't make any commitment to him until the Lord confirmed that it was right.

I tried hard in the days that followed to convince myself that it was, but all my efforts failed to stifle a deep-seated sense of misgiving. Our time together was almost over. Even before I left, Stuart was flying to Switzerland for a skiing holiday. He remained full of his plan, confident that God would confirm it, and as we talked it seemed to grow more plausible. But I still had no assurance from the Lord.

On one of our last days together, Stuart suddenly said, 'Why don't we go and look at rings?'

I knew I shouldn't allow myself to be drawn so far towards a commitment to him when I was so confused, but he persuaded me that if he bought me a ring, I needn't wear it until I was certain our relationship was right. He would be willing to wait and we could postpone any announcement of our engagement until I was sure. I found myself standing beside him in the jeweller's shop, trying on a beautiful diamond ring. As I looked at my finger where the stone flashed and sparkled, I felt like the star of a Hollywood film. That was the trouble. I had the sense of being caught up in all the romance and all the unreality of that celluloid world.

When Stuart left for Switzerland I went with him to the airport and cried uncontrollably all the way. I couldn't tell him of my fears that my dreams would come to nothing.

Days later I returned to a different world. Which was to be the real world for me? That of expensive clothes, dinner dates, carpeted churches and Sunday roasts? Or was it to be heat rash, perspiration, hard wooden benches and fish with rice? Could Stuart be right – was it really possible to achieve a compromise, to keep a foot in both worlds?

By the time I'd been back a few weeks, Stuart's plan had lost much of its plausibility. I began to fear that my ability to accept the conditions in the Philippines depended on regarding them as the norm. If I spent nine months of every year in England, my time in the Philippines would become an unnatural and unwelcome interruption of my accustomed way of life and I could end up resenting both the people and the place. My work would be impossible under those circumstances. How could I reach people for Christ if I couldn't enter fully into their culture and identify with them? Yet marriage to Stuart represented everything the woman in me had ever hoped for.

Even though I was incapable of reaching a firm decision, I felt I had to tell Dondie about the possibility of my engagement, because it would affect the future running of the Philippine Outreach Centre if it ever became reality. He took the news quietly, though I had the distinct impression that he disapproved, which naturally did nothing to ease my turmoil. My indecision was compounded when the reason for his disapproval emerged a few days later, as we were on our way to one of the jails in the old Beetle. The car broke down and as we waited for the mechanic, the topic of my engagement came up again. Dondie stunned me by saying, 'Well, I have feelings for you too.'

Here was something else to add to my confusion! Why hadn't he spoken earlier? (It was a long time before I had the answer to that one.) And what did 'feelings' actually mean? I didn't feel up to tackling these large questions and instead seized on something more immediate and concrete. 'Then why didn't you answer my letters?' I asked.

It turned out that he'd never received them and the letters he'd written to me must also have gone astray. What a muddle it all was.

Dondie and I said no more on that occasion, but I

brooded endlessly on the possible significance of his revelation. Could it be that the Lord was telling me that Dondie had been brought into my life to be more than just a co-worker? Was this why I had no assurance about Stuart? I began to feel I had been unfair to Stuart in allowing him to commit himself to waiting for me. Yet the alternative was to give him up completely. . . . My thoughts ground on like a remorseless treadmill, going round and round but getting nowhere.

Competing for my attention with the seemingly intractable problem of my own future was my anxiety about Redemia's. Several months previously Redemia had met Sammy, a young American serviceman, and they were instantly attracted. By the time Sammy had to return to America two weeks later, Redemia was head over heels in love. They wrote to each other every day and soon Redemia was talking about marriage. But Sammy wasn't a Christian. She'd met him when he was visiting the home of our landlord, who lived in the house next to ours and was himself, though a Filipino by birth, a retired US serviceman.

For the first time, Redemia and I had a serious disagreement as I tried to convince her that it would be wrong to marry a man who was a non-believer. From my own bitter experience with Simon, I knew what it was to be swept along by emotion into a wrong relationship, and I didn't want Redemia to make the same mistake. But she was adamant, and by the time I returned from England in February plans for her wedding in America were well advanced. Now I had to come to terms with the fact that I was soon to lose Redemia, my closest friend on whom I'd depended for so much.

Meanwhile, work had to go on. We were visiting Camp Maquinaya twice a week now and Iba once, on top of running the rehab where adult residents now numbered five, including Rhey, Ning and Jason as well as Rhey's three children. Every morning after an early breakfast, while Ning cleaned the house and cared for the children, the boys would go off to spend the day working on the plot of land we had leased nearby. They were growing various kinds of fruit and vegetables, which was both a healthy occupation for them and a useful contribution to the domestic economy of the rehab. In the evenings I usually joined them for prayer and Bible study, and of course we all went together to the Born-Again Christians' Den on Sundays.

Shortly after my return, we added pig-keeping to our activities – an enterprise made possible because the owner of our vegetable plot offered us the use of his pigsties. We started off with just a few pigs, two of which represented a very special gift I'd received while in England. A number of the churches and fellowships to whom I'd spoken about my work had begun to support me financially, and among these was a small group of elderly women in Sale, near my home town of Altrincham. One of them, Amy, had taught herself to knit and made dishcloths which she sold to raise funds for us. 'I know this can't do much,' she said, as she handed me the money she had raised, 'but I hope it will help.'

'You mustn't think that. With this amount we can buy a pig,' I replied. The idea of buying us a pig appealed to her enormously and prompted her friend Alice to ask me to use her money to buy a pig too.

I named two of our first pigs Alice and Amy and we kept them as breeders, raising others to provide meat for the rehab kitchen. In succeeding years, Alice and Amy's off-spring continued to supply us both with food and with piglets to sell when money was tight.

I received another invitation to Bohol, to speak at the annual convention at Pastor Thomas' Bible school in Tag-bilaran. As I'd done on my first trip to Bohol, I planned the journey so as to include a short visit to the children's mission at Sunshine Corner on the island of Cebu. I'd promised Jason that he could come with me on my next trip and since it would offend Filipino notions of propriety for a single woman to travel alone with a single man of similar age, Dondie came with us too. I was apprehensive about spending so much time with him (we'd be away for two weeks), but unless I were to disappoint Jason, who was very keen to come, there was no other way. Besides, though I was reasonably proficient in Tagalog by now, I still needed an interpreter for preaching, and Dondie's presence meant we would be able to take any opportunities that offered of visiting the jails.

As flights for three of us would be too expensive, we had to travel by boat, so on the day of our departure we set off for Manila Bay, leaving Rhey to oversee the day-to-day running of the rehab and Redemia to supervise the Bible studies. Seen from the land, the boat on which we were to make the twenty-four-hour journey to Cebu looked like a typical, if ancient, cross-channel ferry, but once on board the resemblance ended abruptly.

'Dondie,' I asked, 'what are we supposed to sit on?'

'Oh, there are no seats, just cots.'

Cots? Cots were for babies, I thought. When we went down to the dormitories I had my second taste of culture shock in the Philippines: the 'cots' were actually double bunk beds. Travelling alone, I might have ended up sleeping next to anyone. 'Imagine writing home,' I thought, 'and telling them I'd slept with all these people. What would Mum think if I told her I'd slept with Dondie and Jason? Anyway, I don't care! I'd rather sleep with someone I know next to me than a perfect stranger.'

Being the only white person in the dormitory, however, made me very conspicuous and earned me an embarrassing amount of attention from the other passengers. How could I lie down and sleep with everyone watching me? I hung on to my dignity for as long as possible, but tiredness won in the end and I stretched out on my bunk to get what rest I could. At least we were travelling second class; the third-class passengers ate and slept in the aisles, so there were bodies everywhere.

My discomfort increased as the journey went on. The food available on the boat was both expensive and badly prepared, so most people had brought pots of rice, fish and vegetables, whose mingled smells hung heavily in the air, becoming more and more unpleasant as the food began to go off. I was glad I had decided to stick to sandwiches. Towards the end, we were almost suffocated by the stench of sweating bodies, dirty bathrooms, babies' nappies and rotting food.

But the few days we spent at Sunshine Corner more than repaid the effort of getting there. Sunshine Corner was in the city of Cebu (the island and its main city share the same name) and was a mission for street kids. When it opened its doors at 5 o'clock each evening, anything between twenty and forty dirty, tired, hungry children would come streaming through. Well acquainted with the routine, they headed straight for the bathroom, where one of the workers would check that they were scrubbed clean, delousing them where necessary, while another collected all the dirty clothes, which went immediately into the washing machine.

Then, dressed in fresh Sunshine Corner clothes, the children waited for the call to dinner. I've never seen kids run as fast as they did when the summons came. Huge piles of rice, corn grits, fish and fresh fruit were demolished in short order and every plate scraped clean. Bible hour followed, then prayers, by which point the younger ones had already drifted off to sleep and by 8 o'clock the mats were brought out and all the children settled down for the night.

Early next day, after morning prayers and a huge breakfast, their own clothes were returned to them clean and dry, and they were ready for another day on the streets. To my mind, the great virtue of this mission lay in its willingness to respond to the kids' needs: the streets were their life and they would never have submitted to the discipline of a conventional children's home. Sunshine Corner took the gospel to children who could be reached no other way.

Our visit to the larger of Cebu's two jails turned out to be a memorable occasion. When we went to request permission to conduct a service, we took with us one of the Sunshine Corner workers, Luke, who had once been detained there himself. We had no trouble obtaining the warden's consent, but we were made to wait for a long time before being admitted; the inmates were preparing for us, the guards explained. When at last we were allowed in we were greeted by the sight of 700 men jammed shoulder to shoulder on the jail's basketball court: every single inmate had wanted to be present. This was, and still is, a very rare occurrence.

Luke spoke first, weeping as he told how, in that very jail, he had heard of the love of Christ and accepted him as his Saviour. A stillness that was almost palpable came over the men as they listened, and when I stood up to preach from the Scriptures the quality of their attention was such that I felt I was speaking directly to each member of that tightly packed crowd. Dondie closed the service by asking any who wished to accept Christ to raise their hands. Literally hundreds responded. I just stood and wept, my mind going back to the FGBMFI convention in Glasgow many years ago when the Lord told me I would one day be used to minister to many people. I won't know until I meet him how many of those men stood firm for Christ, but it was a joy to bring them God's word that day. And a good note on which to end our time in Cebu.

Another boat – but only eight hours this time. However, as the journey to Bohol was shorter, both the boat and the cots were correspondingly smaller. Eight hours can seem a long time.

On arriving at Tagbilaran, we were introduced to 'Mammie Ruth', a lady in her fifties whom everyone seemed to know. I gathered that she was the Mammie Olga of the southern Philippines. Mammie Ruth was also a guest speaker at Thomas' convention and I was to share a room with her.

Introductions over, we were set to work at once in true Filipino fashion. As we battled through a hectic programme of church services, prison visits and meetings at the Bible school, the load was lightened for me by the ease with which Dondie and I worked together. We made a good team. We often sang together before I preached and he interpreted. Sometimes, to give me a break, he would take on the preaching himself. But what I lacked was someone to share my emotional burden.

While we had been away from the rehab, Dondie had opened up a little more about his 'feelings' for me, and in spite of his natural reserve I could no longer doubt that what he felt was genuine love. For my part, I was coming to enjoy being with him more and more, not just because of the work we shared but for himself.

These sensations troubled me deeply and I suffered terrible pangs of guilt whenever I thought of Stuart. I was a mystery to myself. I no longer knew what I wanted, nor, more importantly, what the Lord wanted for me. In desperation I confided in Mammie Ruth who, though she couldn't solve my dilemma, none the less greatly comforted me by her assurance that if I waited patiently, God would show me his will.

I was distracted from brooding on the tangled web of my own emotions by Jason's problems. One night, after giving his testimony at a prison service, he had broken down and confessed he was finding it hard to resist the temptation to go back to taking drugs. As we returned to Subic, I reflected that it might be easier to sort out my future if I had more time for myself.

But if I was hoping that the pace would slacken, I was to be disappointed.

12

A City on a Hill

Just when it seemed I most needed the comfort of familiarity, the pattern of my life began to shift. Redemia left for America to be married, and I hadn't even the consolation of feeling confident that all would be well with her. I should have known that the unwelcome change was part of the larger pattern God was weaving, but at the time I simply felt bereft of an intimate friend and valued co-worker.

Dondie now took over entirely the job of interpreting for me in the jails and the gap which was left in our children's work by Redemia's departure was filled by Freda, a middle-aged lady from Peterhead in Scotland, whom Mum had met through her IGO and Hollybush contacts. Freda phoned Mum one day and, right out of the blue, announced that the Lord had told her to go to the Philippines to help me. Having had a troubled childhood herself, spending most of her teenage years in care, Freda had developed a desire to help other needy children; and the timing of her arrival, just before Redemia left, was perfect. Language would be no problem, as she would have as her assistant a local girl from Pamatawan, a neighbour of mine and Redemia's called Joy who, after helping with the

119

children's outreaches for several months, had recently asked to join us.

The last few months had also seen our ministry to young people extend into local schools, such as San Agustin School in Castillejos, where a number of the children in the neighbourhood of the rehab were enrolled. It was a public (government-run) school and catered for both elementary and high school pupils. (Elementary level is the equivalent of English infant and junior school, and high school of English secondary school.) Public schools in the Philippines don't have daily corporate worship, so we ran a Bible hour for elementary pupils after the official end of the school day, while for the high school students we were allowed to do Bible teaching within the school timetable. Of the youngsters who accepted Christ as a result of our outreach there, several are now being used in the Lord's work in pastoral ministry and leading worship in various churches.

Freda worked with us for several months and she and I became good friends during the time we lived together, the gap in our ages being easily spanned by her warmth and sense of humour. She was great fun to be with, and a great asset in the children's outreaches. As time went on, her vision for children's work grew and she conceived the idea of opening a children's home for the street kids of Olongapo, an idea she was able to realise later that year while I was on furlough in England. The home she established is still flourishing and has given a bright new future to many children.

On my journey back to the Philippines, I was intrigued to notice a young woman on the opposite side of the plane reading *Arise and Reap*, a book which I recognised as being by a Christian woman who went to the Philippines as a missionary. When we stopped over in Dubai, we boarded the bus for the terminal together.

'I couldn't help noticing the book you were reading,' I said. 'Are you on your way to the Philippines?'

'Yes, that's right.'

'Me too. What will you be doing there?'

'I'm going to be a missionary.'

'I'm a missionary too! Where will you be working?'

'Subic.'

Her name was Julie and she'd just graduated from Bible school in Peterhead, Freda's home town. She felt God was calling her to the Philippines, but since she wasn't sure in what capacity she should work, or where, the principals of the school had arranged for her to spend some time with Freda, familiarising herself with the country while she prayed and sought the Lord's guidance.

By some mischance, Freda wasn't there to meet her when we landed in Manila, but the Lord had seen to it that I was and we travelled to Subic together. As it was very late when we arrived, I invited her to spend the night in my bungalow. In fact, Julie continued to stay with me for the rest of her visit since the house Freda had taken wasn't really big enough to accommodate another person.

Meanwhile, the bungalow at Castillejos which housed the rehab was strained to bursting point. Ning's sister had joined us and numbers swelled considerably with the advent of Freddie and Peter, ex-prisoners from Camp Maquinaya; Peter also brought his wife and four children and their fifth child was born in the rehab. I had known from the start that this building was a temporary stepping stone and it began to look as if the Lord would soon be moving us on.

Another consequence of growing numbers was the difficulty of transporting all the rehab residents to the Born-Again Christians' Den every Sunday. My old Beetle was beginning to feel her age and objected to the constant overloading during the forty-minute journey – which would take an hour by public transport and might be lengthened by a further hour of waiting on the return trip, as the bus wouldn't leave Olongapo until it was full.

Could it be that the second phase of my vision was about

to unfold? Was it now God's time to establish a worshipping community for the rehab members? Dondie and I began to pray and seek the Lord, and he gave both of us the confirmation that we should go ahead with the Philippine Outreach Christian Fellowship.

We planned to meet in my home in Pamatawan. In retrospect, it seems odd that I never once considered using the rehab house in Castillejos, which on the surface was a more suitable venue in terms of size, but the decision was undoubtedly prompted by the Lord, who had given me my original vision in and for Subic. Being on the northern edge of Subic, and equidistant from the centre of Subic and Castillejos, my home provided a meeting place both consistent with the vision and conveniently close to the rehab. Its smallness wasn't an insuperable problem: by moving out all the furniture each Sunday and replacing it with bench seating, we reckoned we could manage. A local man in Pamatawan made the benches for us, and we were ready to go.

On the morning of 2nd November 1986, when we held our first service, the house was filled with people. All the rehab residents were there and Joy, who of course came from Pamatawan, had invited several members of her family. A number of local people, whom we didn't know, also joined us. As I welcomed them, my excitement was tinged with nervousness. When the Lord gave me the vision of founding a church, I hadn't expected that I would be its pastor, yet in a short while I would be standing up before these people to preach God's word. I knew he had given me the ability to preach and I was willing to use the gift in obedience to him, but as a woman it felt strange to be doing so in this situation. Dondie had little experience of preaching, but his ability as a Bible teacher would be indispensable in the adult Sunday school which would normally precede the service. Between us we had the necessary gifts to meet the congregation's needs.

After the opening praise and worship and Scripture

reading, I got up and, with Dondie interpreting, began to preach the good news of salvation through Christ. The Holy Spirit was with us that morning and several of the non-Christians responded by surrendering their lives to the Lord. I have a vivid memory of one local woman weeping in repentance while trying to comfort her three-year-old son who was crying in bewilderment at his mother's tears. The new converts were eager to learn and soon we were having church Bible studies and prayer meetings midweek, each as well attended as the Sunday services.

Another of our earliest converts was Joseph, whom I invited to church when he was released on bail from Camp Maquinaya, where he was being detained on charges of possession of drugs and drug pushing. Though he was initially reluctant to come, and despite the unpromising character of his first visit – it was at a prayer meeting, and he arrived thoroughly drunk – there was no mistaking the genuineness of the profession of repentance and faith which he made on his second visit. The evidence was the transformation of his life and his determination to give up drugs for good.

We accepted him into the rehab and I went, as I often did on behalf of prisoners, to see the judge responsible for his case and ask when the hearing was likely to be. I took the opportunity to tell the judge of the change that had taken place in him and that he had voluntarily entered the rehab. When the case came up, Joseph realised that he faced the possibility of ten years in jail, or even longer, and it was therefore with profound thankfulness for the grace of God that he heard his sentence pronounced: he was put on probation for six years and ordered to report regularly to his probation officer. I knew then that God had heard David Chaudhary's prayer that I would 'find favour with the authorities'.

Though we were delighted to welcome Joseph into the rehab, the problem of overcrowding in our 'stepping stone' was becoming ever more pressing. If the work were to expand, we would have to move.

One day towards the end of November, Julie went out walking with Joy, exploring parts of Subic she'd never seen before, and returned scarcely able to contain her excitement. 'Chrissy! We've just seen a building in Calapandayan that could be just what you need – an old empty hospital, really big. Will you come and have a look?'

I had lived in Subic for three years and had never even heard of the existence of such a building in the *barangay* of Calapandayan. I had no idea what to expect, but I was willing to explore every avenue, so I got the car out and drove back with Julie. The hospital was situated right on top of a steep hill so we parked the car at the bottom and started to climb.

As soon as the building came into view, I said, 'This is it. This is the vision the Lord gave me.' When I looked down into the valley below, I could see Subic's 'red-light' district where, in my first months in the Philippines, I'd been shocked to see half-dressed girls running along the street calling to American GIs and trying to drag them into one of the row of dingy bars. A verse of Scripture came into my mind: 'You are the light of the world. A city that is set on a hill cannot be hidden' (Mt 5:14). I prayed that our light would shine in that needy place.

On closer inspection the hospital proved to be truly enormous – bigger even than the General Hospital in Olongapo. It had three storeys and we estimated that there must be close to a hundred rooms. Just opposite was a single-storey building in the shape of a squat 'L', which had been a training school for nurses. It is amazing how different things can seem when viewed through the eyes of faith. To me these buildings were beautiful, though in reality they had lain empty and untended for years and bore the marks of many strong typhoons. They needed literally millions of pesos' worth of renovation.

As we were leaving we met a man who lived nearby and I

asked him if he knew who owned the building. He'd heard that it had been repossessed by a local bank, so I went straight there to make enquiries, only to find that my information was wrong. It hadn't been repossessed and no one at the bank knew the owner. They did know, however, that he had a mortgage and made monthly repayments to the SSS (the Social Security System which, in addition to dealing with such things as pensions, also makes loans to its members). So it was on to the SSS in Manila.

Since Dondie knew Manila better than I, he came with me and successfully located the SSS building where the staff, having consulted their records, gave us the name of the estate agent who dealt with the property. When we reached the agency we discovered that its owner, Mr Cruz, was also the owner of the hospital. What a relief. On asking to speak to him, we were told we would have to wait, and the interval certainly provided food for thought. Every so often, an employee would enter Mr Cruz's office, to emerge minutes later with a shattered expression and sweat pouring down his face.

Satan started to whisper: 'Chrissy, this is one hard businessman and you're making a big mistake.' Another man left the office looking pulverised. 'You're going to talk to him about buying his building when you've no money? You're a fool.'

'Don't you ever give up?' I retorted. 'The Lord can supply all my need.'

Even Dondie was nervous. 'What if he has us thrown out?'

'So what? What do we have to lose? We won't exactly be losing our best friend. Anyway, if God is for us, who can be against us?'

Eventually we were led into the office and introduced ourselves to the formidable Mr Cruz. After a few minutes of preliminary chitchat about England, which Mr Cruz, who seemed to have business interests all over Europe, had visited many times, he invited us to explain the purpose of our visit. Since this concerned my vision, Dondie left the talking to me and I began to tell Mr Cruz about the work of the Philippine Outreach Centre.

'Yes, yes,' he interrupted, 'this is all very nice, but what has it to do with me?'

'We've been looking for bigger premises,' I explained, 'and came across your hospital in Calapandayan. I'm here, sir, to ask how much you're selling it for.'

'How much are you offering?'

'Well, actually, I haven't any money at the moment. I'm . . . .'

My voice was drowned by Mr Cruz's roar of laughter. 'You mean to tell me you've come to buy my building without any money? Who do you think is going to pay for it? The Queen of England?'

'No, sir, the King of kings.'

'You must really be somebody,' he said, puzzled and intrigued rather than sarcastic, 'to come here and ask to buy a building with no money. You must really be somebody.'

I whispered a word of praise to the Lord. There I was, before a millionaire, and he was saying I was somebody. Well, of course, I was nothing in myself, but as I'd learned long ago, our God is a God who does everything with our nothing, takes it and fills it with himself so that the powerful of this world can see that, in him, we are 'somebody'.

'I'll tell you what,' he went on, 'seeing that you have no money, let's not talk about the hospital. There's the nurses' training school. I'll let you have the use of that first. There are thirty-three hectares of land around those buildings that you can use for your pigs and agriculture and any other livelihood projects. If you want to renovate the school, it's up to you; we can talk about the hospital later.'

There had been no mention so far of any rent or leasing arrangement, without which we would not have the security of a contract. Trusting the Lord doesn't excuse us from using the common sense he has given us, so I asked how much the rent would be.

'Whatever you're paying now for your own home and your current rehabilitation home. If you all move into the school you'll have no extra expenses. Come back in a few days to pay the deposit and sign the contract.'

'But I can't live in the rehabilitation home myself,' I objected.

'Well,' he said, easily, 'you can have one of my properties at La Sirena beach. Go and have a look, pick whichever you like. I own the whole beach resort there. Tell my secretary at La Sirena when you've decided; she'll deal with it.'

Could this be the same man who reduced his staff to jelly? The Lord was surely with us that day. Just before we left, however, we caught a glimpse of the hard business-man whose ruthlessness had been in abeyance during the interview so far. 'I must warn you,' he said, 'that I can be your best friend or your worst enemy.' I could well believe it, but my trust was in the Lord.

I left the office completely awed. My intention had been simply to find out how much money to pray for. Instead, I came away with everything fixed for us to move into the nurses' school.

The beach resort at La Sirena consisted of a hotel, a restaurant, sports facilities, and a number of very pretty beach cottages, much like my own bungalow. But it was not really near enough to the hospital. When I mentioned this to Mr Cruz's secretary, she pointed out that he also owned houses at the bottom of the hill, below the hospital; why didn't I ask for one of these?

I returned to Mr Cruz's office a few days later to sign the contract. Emboldened by the success of our previous inter-view, I explained to him that though I had enough for the deposit, we needed all our available funds to renovate the building. Without demur, he agreed to waive the deposit. The secretary dealing with the paperwork was so taken aback that she asked him to confirm that everything was in order. 'He's never done this before,' she told me. 'Our policy is to insist on a minimum of two months' rent in advance.'

Before I left, Mr Cruz, affability well to the fore, asked me, 'Is there anything else you want?'

'Well, there's just one thing,' I replied, feeling a bit like Oliver Twist. 'The houses at La Sirena are lovely, but it's too far from the hospital. I really need something nearer.'

Before I could go on, he broke in: 'At the bottom of the hill there, you will see several houses, all my property. Pick any you want.'

I left the office walking on air.

Preparations for moving began at once as Mr Cruz had insisted on us taking over the properties almost immediately. Julie missed the excitement of the move as she'd gone to Manila to meet David Nellist and spend some time working with him before returning to the UK. As I thought about Julie, I reviewed the events which had led us to the new rehab: Redemia leaving, to be replaced by Freda, because of whom Julie had come to Subic and found the hospital. All strands in God's larger plan.

It would be a wrench to leave my neat little bungalow in Pamatawan, with its bright garden full of flowers which Redemia had planted and carefully tended. My new home, which I would share with Joy, was in a sad state of disrepair, with no glass in the windows, no electricity and no water supply. I had to remind myself of the apostle Paul's instruction: 'Set your mind on things above, not on things on the earth' (Col 3:2). This kind of discipline is particularly necessary in the age we live in, where the pleasures of the world have never presented a stronger temptation to Christians. Without constant vigilance we can be so easily lured away from our calling to live for God and sink into self-indulgence. Of course, material prosperity, if regarded as held in trust from God, to be used in his service, can be a great blessing, but it's up to us to see that we don't turn God's blessing into a curse.

So, setting my mind on the vision the Lord had given me, I was able to turn my back on the comfort and security of my bungalow. Indeed, my loss dwindled into insignificance when seen in the context of all that had to be done at the new rehab. Mr Cruz's insistence on immediate occupation posed enormous problems, as the nurses' school was totally uninhabitable, except by the large ugly lizards, mosquitoes and cockroaches which had colonised it while it lay empty. The interior would have to be entirely rebuilt because every inch of wood had been eaten away by termites. The cement floor was buried under a thick layer of silt washed in from the mountainside every rainy season; spread over an area of almost 500 square yards, that was going to be an awful lot of dirt to clear away. There was no glass in the windows and until all the wiring was renewed, there would be no electricity. More important, it would take a great deal of work to lay on a water supply because the building was so far away from the town's water mains.

My new home, by contrast, though badly in need of repair, could quickly be made habitable at a pinch. Furthermore, there was a natural well nearby, where it would be possible to drill for water, which could be drawn up by a hand pump. Until there was a water supply at the rehab, therefore, though it was a far from ideal arrangement, most of the rehab members would have to be squeezed into the house with Joy and me, apart from a couple of the lads who camped out in the rehab itself.

It took a week of drilling to reach the water level and install the hand pump. We connected a hosepipe to the pump and draped the other end of the pipe through the bathroom window into a large bucket, and after ten minutes of pumping it was possible to have a 'bath'. The water wasn't very clean, though, and was full of long, thin worms, which made bathing an itchy business.

Primitive it may have been, but it was an inexpressible relief after a week in which I had to walk across a field to a nearby well every time I wanted a bath. It wasn't the sort of picturesque well from which Jack and Jill might have fetched a pail of water, either. It was just a point where water sprang up from the ground, in full view of several neighbouring houses. The villagers could hardly be expected not to relish the novel spectacle of a white woman bathing fully clothed by the well – it needed the skill of a contortionist – and the whole thing was an embarrassing ordeal. I much preferred the worms. The water at the house was no good for drinking, of course, but kind neighbours who had a clean supply allowed us to draw water from their well.

While we were wondering what to do about the electricity, it so happened that Rex, one of the inmates at Iba, was released on bail. Rex was an electrician and willingly agreed to do the rewiring. In a remarkably short time my house had the luxury of electric light, and Rex began work on the rehab. Ronnie Castillo was another answer to prayer when he too was released from Iba. Ronnie was acquitted of a murder charge after being involved with several others in a fight in which one man was killed. He'd never shown much interest in the gospel, but he was anxious to find work and as a carpenter he was just what we were looking for. All the wood in the rehab would have to be replaced as and when we could afford it, but Ronnie began by salvaging some usable plywood from the ceilings with which to begin constructing a few temporary bedrooms. He moved into one of these himself, with his wife and three children, having asked to join the rehab a week or so after starting work.

Between the work at the rehab and visits to Iba and Camp Maquinaya, life had never been busier, yet we always made room for our Bible studies and prayer meetings with the rehab members. Though most of them had made a profession of faith in Christ, their knowledge of God's word was at best fragmentary and their eagerness to learn was heartwarming. But my satisfaction with their spiritual progress was marred by the fact that, unlike several other church members, none of the ex-prisoners had received the baptism in the Holy Spirit and seemed not to understand their need of it. Remembering my own inability to live the Christian life prior to baptism in the Spirit, I was only too aware of the struggles they might face in the battle against sin. It never occurred to me that one particularly disastrous failure would shortly pose a threat to me personally.

However, there was no doubt that their faith was increased by the lavish way in which God answered our prayers at this time. The cost of renovation and building materials sometimes stretched our faith to the limits, but the Lord never failed to provide. My network of supporters back home was expanding steadily, so much so that Dad had recently decided to form a charitable trust to administer their contributions. By means of their generous and timely gifts God supplied every single item we prayed for and there was enough to pay a reasonable wage to all those who worked for us.

Looking back over the whole period of renovation, though, perhaps the most remarkable gift came through Mum's efforts. My businessman father was more than a little startled when she took a market stall in Salford and began selling second-hand clothes to raise funds for us. Indefatigable as ever, she single-handedly loaded and unloaded the heavy rails of clothes, and the profit she made was ultimately enough to buy a jeepney, which was invaluable in transporting building materials up the hill to the rehab and which served us for many years afterwards.

Back in the present, meanwhile, there was no lack of employment for everyone. Freddie, Peter and Joseph were all fully occupied and Rhey toiled uncomplainingly up and down the hill carrying water for the reconstruction work until we were able to buy an electric pump for the rehab. The building of a retaining wall to protect against flooding in the rainy season; the construction of new pigsties; the making and installation of a water tank big enough to hold at least a day's supply; the erection of a temporary outside bathroom to serve until we could afford something better: these were just some of the jobs we had to do to make the building viable.

But while all this was still going on, the Philippine Outreach Christian Fellowship had to move into the rehab.

13

'My Times Are in Your Hand'

Because quite a few of the congregation actually lived in Pamatawan, the church had continued to meet there when we moved to the new rehab, first in the home of one of the members and then, because that was too small, in the open air. But soon after we founded the fellowship, another church opened in the same neighbourhood. Its doctrine and practice were fully biblical, yet its existence nevertheless created a problem for us. Many local people drew the conclusion that two separate churches so close together must represent two rival systems. This confusion could only hinder the preaching of the gospel and the obvious solution was for one of us to move elsewhere, but having been in Pamatawan first my natural inclination was to resist being the one to leave. However, as we prayed about it, it became clear that the Lord was directing us to move.

We set about preparing a room in the rehab and I explained the decision to our members in Pamatawan, telling them that they should feel free to join the other church, which would be more convenient for them. To our surprise, most of them elected to stay with us.

Our neighbours in Calapandayan reacted far less favourably than the people of Pamatawan to our presence among them, partly because they felt intimidated by the ex-prisoners, but equally because they knew we were 'born again'. There was beginning to be something of a revival throughout the country in the Protestant denominations and the number of conversions was perceived as a threat by the Roman Catholic Church. Its leader in the Philippines, Cardinal Sin, had recently been conducting a vigorous campaign against the 'Born Agains', with the result that our neighbours viewed being born again not as a life-changing experience of the Lord Jesus Christ, but as a new religion hostile to their own beliefs. We could only pray that in time we would overcome their suspicion and mistrust by love.

After a year of incident and upheaval, both physical and emotional, I was becoming acutely aware of an aching sense of loneliness at the centre of my outwardly busy life. My work in the jails and at the rehab was as fulfilling as ever and it was thrilling to see my vision becoming reality, but though I knew I was liked and respected by those around me I now had no close friend in whom to confide. Dondie was the only one to whom I could talk easily and even with him my relationship was of course complicated by the fact that my dilemma concerning Stuart was still unresolved. Though he never pressed the issue, Dondie had made it plain that he wanted to marry me, while I remained as confused as ever as to the Lord's will. Then came the event which precipitated the breaking of the deadlock.

At about 4 o'clock one morning I was jerked out of sleep by the terrifying realisation that someone had crept under the mosquito net and climbed onto my bed, and as I instinctively opened my mouth to scream, a rough hand covered my mouth. It was Freddie. I tried frantically to push him away, but though small he was very strong – far too strong for me. Joy, who shared my room, slept on oblivious while I kicked and struggled in mounting panic for what seemed like hours, feeling as if I were pinned down by a wild animal under the trap of the mosquito net. Finally, in an effort to pull me closer, Freddie relaxed his hand from my mouth and I let out a piercing scream which brought the rest of the household running. Freddie leapt for the door but was seized by Dondie and the other lads and thrown out of the house.

Really it was all over very quickly, and superficially no great harm had come to me. But for many days I was gripped by fear, which gave Satan a foothold in my life and he tormented me with thoughts of what might have happened if I hadn't been able to scream. At other times, I gave way to the temptation to indulge in self-pity. How could Freddie treat me like that after all I'd done for him? I'd given him a home, a job, even the clothes on his back and he repaid me by trying to rape me.

I became withdrawn and irrational, afraid to go out alone and subject to sudden attacks of claustrophobia as the memory of being trapped under the mosquito net swept over me. Then I grew angry. I had given up so much to come here, and this was my reward. I'd be better off going home than wasting my time on people like this. Mentally I began to plan how I would return to England and find someone to replace me. But at this point Satan overplayed his hand.

'So you're giving up and going home. It was all too much for you, was it?'

I woke up to the fact that through anger and self-pity I had almost fallen for Satan's tricks. What would please him better than for me to give up? I felt faith begin to rise again, and the assurance that it would be Satan, not I, who would be defeated. In God's hands, the snare which Satan set became the means to bring me to a place of victory. My fears fell away and I was ready again for the front line.

Freddie returned to ask my forgiveness and for permission to re-enter the rehab. Though no longer afraid of him, I really didn't like the idea of living in close proximity to a man who had tried to rape me, but I knew I couldn't go on preaching forgiveness if I didn't practise it. Freddie was allowed back, but I made it clear that my forgiveness was not to be taken as condoning his behaviour. I warned him that if ever he was seen alone in a bedroom with a woman or a child, I would personally ensure that he went to jail. The safety of the other residents, especially the children, could not be put at risk on his account.

Perhaps the discovery that there was a hitherto unsuspected stern side to my nature struck him as a challenge. Not many days later, he deliberately locked himself in a bedroom with one of the children, a girl of seven. He didn't harm her and she wasn't even frightened, but the running of the rehab depended on all the residents, not just Freddie, understanding that I didn't make idle threats.

The hostility of the Subic police following my involvement in Danny's case had evaporated by now, and as I was back on friendly terms with Lieutenant Santos I went directly to the Municipal Hall to ask for his co-operation. I didn't intend to press charges against Freddie, I explained, but he needed to be taught that he couldn't flout the rules with impunity. Lieutenant Santos thought for a while and then asked, 'Does he have any tattoos? Most prisoners tattoo themselves in jail, to show which gang they belong to. These gangs are actually illegal and he could be held for a few weeks without an arrest warrant.'

So the police came and took Freddie away. We visited him and took him food while he was in jail, but when he was released I refused to have him back. There were no more chances, I told him. The children's welfare came first.

With Freddie gone, the whole episode was closed, but what remained when I reflected on it was a deep sense of thankfulness for God's protection. Dazed and half asleep, I could easily have been overpowered by Freddie's greater strength, yet the Lord had not allowed it. 'I am with you always,' said Jesus (Mt 28:20). With David, I could reply,

'I trust in You, O Lord; I say "You are my God." My times are in Your hand' (Ps 31:14–15).

The incident also forced me to ask myself how I would have coped if I'd been married to Stuart when it happened. Under the arrangement he'd proposed, I'd be here in the Philippines and he'd be thousands of miles away in England. I had no phone (even if I had, overseas calls were virtually unobtainable) and it would take a month to get a reply to a letter, which would be no substitute for the immediate comfort and reassurance I needed. Though I might never face another rape attempt, ministry to ex-prisoners would always be fraught with difficulties and disappointments. Could a marriage work if my husband were not there to share my concerns and support me through crises? The longer I thought about it, the more unrealistic it looked and the more I felt the need to know the Lord's will before embarking on marriage. One thing was already clear, however: as things stood, it would be wrong for me to commit myself to an engagement.

So when I returned to England on furlough shortly afterwards in May 1987, I gave Stuart back the ring I'd never worn. It was a beautiful ring; as beautiful as the dream it represented was unreal.

After visiting various churches in England to talk about the Philippine Outreach Centre, I'd be spending a month that summer in the United States. A missionary friend I'd met while living with Dorothy and Linda had offered to arrange a speaking engagement at a Fourth of July convention at Pinecrest Bible Institute in Syracuse, New York, and a friend of Dad's was organising an itinerary for the rest of my stay. I knew practically nothing about the people and places I was to visit, which was a sufficiently daunting prospect in itself, but just a few days before my flight to New York I received letters from several of the people Dad's friend had contacted, all regretting that it would not be convenient for me to visit.

That left just two, in Pennsylvania, plus the Bible Institute in Syracuse. At the thought of spending a whole month in the States with only three engagements I almost called the trip off, but somehow I felt that the Lord had a purpose for me in going.

With so few definite plans and very little money in my pocket, I wasn't in the best of spirits when I arrived, late in the evening, at Kennedy Airport, and though I wasn't exactly expecting to be greeted with banners and garlands of flowers, my heart sank still further when I realised that there was absolutely no one there to meet me. An awful possibility began to form in my mind, and a phone call to Pinecrest confirmed it: they weren't expecting me at all. The principal's son, who took my call, told me that my missionary friend had failed to tie up the details of my visit. The young man was very sympathetic and assured me that I would be welcome to attend the convention anyway. I'd have to fly the 200 or so miles to Syracuse, and when I checked the next flight I could afford, I found it didn't leave till the next morning. The principal's son agreed to meet me at Syracuse the following day.

I sighed as I put the phone down. Even for me, whose travels seemed never to be unattended by some such complication as overweight luggage or a lost passport, this trip looked like providing more than the usual quota of problems. I couldn't afford a hotel, so I spent the night in a chair at the airport.

When I finally arrived at Pinecrest everyone was very kind, but there was a look in their eyes that over the years I'd learned to recognise – a sort of who's-this-little-girl look, which by now no longer intimidated me. Just as well, as it turned out. Pinecrest's arrangements for the Saturday night service had fallen through and there was no speaker, so the principal, Wade Taylor, invited me to speak. 'My times are in your hand, Lord,' I thought.

In many ways it was the most imposing audience I'd ever addressed: students, graduates, pastors and academics, many of them authors of recognised works of theology. I couldn't help noticing that their average height was six feet to my five foot one. As I faced them, I felt as Peter must have felt when he took his eyes off Jesus and began to sink into the stormy sea. But the Lord responded to my cry for help and his anointing enabled me to deliver my talk with confidence and conviction. I spoke of the need to advance into the enemy's territory to take back that which belonged to the Lord, instead of being always on the defensive. The Holy Spirit moved in power that night and I believe many were challenged.

I still treasure the memory of my stay at Pinecrest. There were further opportunities to speak and profitable times of fellowship with others attending the convention – among them people working with Teen Challenge or in the New York Bronx. I got to know some of the students too, and one of them, Renee, was to become a close friend. When she discovered that my two other remaining engagements were in Allentown and Bethlehem, Pennsylvania, near to her own home town, she insisted on asking Wade Taylor for time off from her studies in order to take me there. This was an enormous relief, as I'd discovered that there were no buses to either town and I had no idea how I was going to make the 200-mile journey.

One memory stands out from all the rest. Alone in my bedroom, I heard the Lord speak to me; just four words in a still, small voice: 'Dondie is the one.'

I waited for more. I wanted it all explained, and to know exactly why Dondie was the one and Stuart wasn't. I wanted a sign, something more dramatic, to confirm what would after all be one of the most important decisions I'd ever make. 'Is that all, Lord? Do you want me to marry Dondie on the strength of "Dondie is the one"?'

There was no more, just a deep silence, impenetrable yet not empty, as if he were saying, 'It's enough. I've told you what you wanted to know.'

I'd had ample proof in recent months that I could

entrust myself to him. Yes, it was enough. My times – past, present and future – were in his hands. For the first time in over a year I had peace in my heart about my future, and I knew that Dondie really was the one. I'd never before had the confidence to say to anyone that I felt sure about whom I would marry, but next morning I told Renee that Dondie was God's man for me.

Then I wrote to Dondie.

14

The Family Band

I told my parents when I returned to England at the end of what proved to be a busy time of ministry in the States. Renee's parents welcomed me into their home and treated me as one of the family and God opened many doors for me so that I had on average a speaking engagement every other day. The rest of my trip flew past.

Mum and Dad greeted the news of my impending engagement with dismay. For one thing, they had never even met Dondie, and for another, our marriage would rule out any possibility of my ever returning to live in England. It had been hard enough for them to lose me to the mission field for an indefinite term, but this would be final. I could only hope that some of their fears would be allayed once they knew Dondie, and we arranged that they should fly out for a visit the following January. Only Nanna Jean, of the whole family, had no misgivings.

Dondie and I realised that we would be able to do little from the Philippines by way of preparation for the wedding, so we'd agreed that I should do whatever I could while I was still in England. One day while I was shopping in Manchester with Nanna, we found the perfect wedding dress. The pale pink embroidery round the bottom of the wide, hooped skirt of white taffeta lent a Filipino air to the otherwise conventional English design, as did the short puffed sleeves, which were characteristic of Filipino formal dress. Dad, summoned from his office by a hasty phone call, agreed to buy it, though with some reluctance. He saw no need to rush things. There was a whole year before the wedding, in which he secretly hoped I might change my mind.

I returned to the Philippines in September 1987, and a month later Dondie and I were officially engaged.

Renovation of the new rehab was still incomplete, though of course it was habitable by now. At the beginning of December, when we'd been there almost a year, Ronnie Castillo, our carpenter, had a surprise visitor – his brother, Alex, who had been involved in the same murder charge of which Ronnie had been acquitted. Alex and Ronnie, along with several others, had been swindled out of thousands of pesos by a man who claimed to represent a recruitment agency finding jobs overseas for Filipino workers. Having accepted their placement fees, he absconded with the money. His victims tracked him down and in the ensuing fight the man was killed.

Ronnie was delighted when Alex told him he had just been released from jail in Manila and was hoping to stay a while with his brother. When he'd been with us a few days, Alex asked us if he, his wife Marie and their family could move into the rehab on a more permanent basis, and after interviewing him I agreed. It was only then that I found out that he had five children and stepchildren and was also supporting his sister-in-law, Norma, as well as one of his nephews. However, we had room for them all now, and we soon had reason to be glad we'd accepted them. Ronnie had already become a Christian since entering the rehab and now Alex too accepted the Lord as his Saviour.

A few days later, the peace of the rehab was shattered in the dark early hours of the morning by the sound of a jeep roaring up to the entrance. It was the Subic police, come to arrest Alex who, they said, had not been released at all, but had escaped before his case had been processed. Guessing that he would seek out his brother, they had traced him to the rehab. Ronnie was arrested too for aiding and hiding an escapee.

When I visited them in the cells at the police station, Ronnie assured me he had known nothing of Alex's escape, and I believed him. I would do my best, I promised, to get him released. First of all, though, I apologised to Lieutenant Santos for neglecting to check Alex's release papers, something I did routinely with the inmates I knew personally. This was the first time, I explained, that we'd accepted a prisoner from outside the scope of our own ministry.

The officer from Manila who had come to collect Alex turned out to be a Christian and when he learned that Alex was now a believer, he promised to do what he could to get his case finished. It would be in his favour that he hadn't resisted arrest and had been found in a Christian rehabilitation home to which he'd admitted himself voluntarily. When Alex had been taken away, I managed to prevail upon Lieutenant Santos to release Ronnie.

Alex's family decided to remain in the rehab to await the outcome of his case and at every prayer meeting we prayed that the family would be reunited in time for Christmas. Christmas was very close when, one evening as we were praying, we heard noises outside, followed by Marie's loud cry of delight: it was Alex, furnished this time with the release papers that showed he had been acquitted. The anxious weeks of waiting for his case to come up had taught him something of what it means to trust the Lord, and from that time on we began to see a marked change in his character.

It wasn't long before we collected another Castillo. Jim, also an ex-prisoner, arrived at the rehab and asked to join us. He stayed for several months, but unlike his brothers he made no profession of faith in Christ. He made an effort to fit in with our way of life, but it was obviously a struggle, and one which was doomed to failure. There came a night when Alex, incensed by the fact that Jim had made a pass at one of the married women in the rehab, took him to task and their subsequent quarrel erupted into a fight in which Alex cut himself quite badly on a piece of broken glass.

It was a hair-raising scene. There was blood everywhere, Jim was hurling threats and foul language in all directions and most of the rehab members, especially the children, were terrified. My own feelings were of anger rather than fear – anger that Jim should use such words in the home we'd dedicated to the Lord. I ordered him to curb his bad language and leave the rehab for good. I had no scruples about doing this; I knew that his behaviour was not a momentary lapse but an expression of his unregenerate nature. He'd had many opportunities to put his life right with God, but he had taken none of them and clearly had no intention of doing so. In the end he left quietly, and peace was restored.

While Jim was one of our failures, Rhey was a continuing source of encouragement. Spiritually, he'd been going from strength to strength and now felt that he and Ning were ready to stand on their own feet. When they asked permission to leave the rehab, we willingly granted it and gave them some materials to build their own home. Their places were soon filled by Helen Gerez and her four small daughters. Helen, pregnant with her fifth child, had been abandoned for the second time by her ex-prisoner husband, a man I'd known for several years. Their house had recently burned down and Helen had borrowed money from a friend to build another. Since she couldn't afford a proper building plot, the new house was situated by the side of the river and was a rickety-looking structure perched precariously on stilts.

When I visited there for the first time I saw no sign of Helen, only two-year-old Clara, with a runny nose, dirty face and uncombed hair, climbing up the flimsy steps to reach the house. I learned from the neighbours that Helen went out to work at six each morning in order to pay off her loan. Before she left she would prepare breakfast and lunch for the four girls, returning at six in the evening. The three older girls were at school for most of the day, but Clara, who was supposed to be in the care of a neighbour, was often left to wander around unsupervised. My heart went out to the grubby little girl, and to poor Helen. How on earth was she going to manage with another baby? Inviting them to join us was the only solution. They moved in shortly after Rhey and his family moved out. Breathing space was never a notable feature of life at the rehab.

However, much of this was still in the future when Mum and Dad arrived just before New Year's day. Dad could only stay for three weeks, but Mum would be with us till the end of February. I had given a good deal of thought to where they should stay, especially on Dad's account. Mum had been to Subic before and I knew she'd be better at coping with the living conditions, but it was Dad's first visit and I didn't want it to be his last. Neither my own house nor the rehab offered much by way of comfort, and for someone like Dad, who wilted in the heat, the lack of air-conditioning would be a big problem. At least for the duration of Dad's stay, I persuaded them to book into the White Rock Hotel in Subic. I chose it simply because it was the best hotel in the area, often used by the US military to accommodate their visitors and new arrivals, and I had no inkling that my choice would have far-reaching consequences for the Philippine Outreach Centre.

Greatly to my relief, Mum and Dad got on well with Dondie from the start, and as they grew to know him better many of their doubts about our marriage faded, though naturally it would still be hard for them to have me based permanently in the Philippines. They joined us every day in our children's outreaches or visits to the jails and the schools, and then returned to the hotel where they had their evening meal in the restaurant. I joined them most evenings, so it was like a holiday for me too.

As is common in the Philippines, there were always live

entertainers in the restaurant and we noticed that one of the regular groups, The Family Band, sometimes included gospel songs in their performance. This wasn't really so surprising, as the hotel proprietor, Veronica Lorenzana ('Sister Onie'), whom I knew slightly, was a Christian and Pastor of the White Stone Christian Fellowship in Olongapo. The Family Band consisted of two men and three women. One of the men was obviously the father, so we guessed that one of the women must be his wife, though they actually looked more like three sisters. We invited them to join us in one of their breaks and Romy Del Monte introduced us to his wife Lourdes, his son Luis and his two daughters Roselyn and Jane, young women in their early twenties.

They were all Christians and were living in Olongapo at the time we met them, though Romy and Lourdes, full-time professional entertainers who had already worked abroad in Japan and Vietnam, were hoping for more opportunities to travel. Roselyn's dream was to be a dentist. She was singing with her parents to earn the money she needed in order to complete her training.

During their three weeks at the White Rock, Mum and Dad became quite friendly with the Del Montes, and Mum invited them to lead a praise evening at our church. When they arrived we discovered that Romy and Lourdes had seven children, all of whom, right down to the three-year-old, took part in the singing. I was irresistibly reminded of the Von Trapp family in *The Sound of Music*.

We'd been working hard on one of the rooms at the rehab and by the time Dad left I was satisfied that Mum would be comfortable in it. It had a polished floor, some decent second-hand furniture and, unlike my house, it was screened against insects. I moved in with her and we shared the room for the rest of her stay, while Joy found a new room-mate in Leonalyn, a young girl we'd taken in at the request of her father who was a prisoner at Camp Maquinaya.

Over the next few weeks, Mum, Dondie and I saw a lot of Romy and Lourdes. They accepted an invitation to sing for the inmates at Iba Jail and took to the work so naturally it was hard to believe they'd never visited a prison before. The ease with which we all worked together, and their obvious delight in this new opportunity to serve the Lord, prompted us to ask them to consider whether God might be leading them to join the staff of the Philippine Outreach Centre.

While we waited for their decision, it struck me that if they accepted it would make life easier if they lived nearer to the rehab. Besides, their house in Olongapo was by the river and subject to flooding in the rainy season, while my own house, since I'd moved in with Mum, was lying empty. Mr Cruz, his goodwill apparently not yet exhausted, readily acceded to my request for the continued use of the house to accommodate Philippine Outreach staff.

Romy and Lourdes decided to join us. They would continue with their work at the White Rock, but since this was always in the evening they would be free during the day to use their talent to serve the Lord. Within a few short weeks, the whole family of nine moved into their new home.

Then it was Roselyn's turn. 'Sister Chrissy,' she said, simply, 'I want to help with the Philippine Outreach too. What do you need?'

'Well,' I replied, 'since you ask, we really need a teacher so that we can start a kindergarten here in the rehab.'

Mum and I had been concerned for some time about the small children in the rehab who were not attending school. Marie and Alex's children, for example, having recently moved from Manila, were not eligible to enrol until the beginning of the next school year, and there were others similarly placed. At the moment, they tended to spend their day roaming aimlessly around, whereas if we could start a school, or at least a kindergarten, they would be usefully occupied and could begin to develop their learning skills. It had remained just an idea, because we had no one who could teach them.

Roselyn went away to pray and returned a few days later to say that she felt she should make herself available to teach in the kindergarten. I had to tell her that while we would do our best to support her financially, it wouldn't be a large amount. 'Actually, Sister Chrissy, I'm not looking for a salary, but if I did have some support I could enrol at night school for an education course. That way I'd be properly qualified to teach.'

Just like that, she gave up her cherished ambition to be a dentist in order to serve the Lord.

Several women in the church volunteered to help Roselyn with the teaching and what she learned at night school she planned to pass on to her fellow teachers. Between them they began to devise a curriculum, to be taught in both English and Tagalog, though of course at the point of entry the children would not yet know any English. Lessons were to take place in the rehab, in the room we used for our church services. We also planned to provide a uniform for every child, made from a big roll of yellow material donated by my generous friends on the naval base, and Mum was kept busy at the sewing machine right up to the end of her stay.

The original intention of the kindergarten was to cater for our own children, but as we made our plans I began to feel that we couldn't ignore the needs of the children in our neighbourhood. There were many poor families who couldn't afford to send their children to school and others still more needy – the children of prostitutes and pimps who were being brought up in the bars where their parents worked. We all agreed that we should open up the kindergarten to them free of charge.

However, despite the fact that there was no free education in the Philippines at that time (though things are changing now under President Ramos), many people still harboured feelings of antagonism towards us and were reluctant to entrust their children to the dubious 'Born Agains'. As a result, at our first enrolment we had only twenty pupils altogether. We received little by way of thanks at first from those who did send their children, but in time we became aware that local opinion was softening somewhat, with even the first faint signs of approval here and there.

The Del Montes became an indispensable part of the team. Romy and Lourdes soon abandoned any idea of renewing their contract abroad and threw themselves full time into the prison ministry and the work of the church. Roselyn, of course, was the lynchpin of the kindergarten and Jane, when she discovered that the burden of clerical work was becoming an increasing worry, made herself available and enrolled at college on a secretarial course. Both girls offered themselves as interpreters for me in the children's outreaches when, shortly afterwards, Joy had to leave us.

They are all just as active in the work to this day and we continue to thank the Lord for that apparently chance encounter with The Family Band.

15

Wedding Plans

Mum wanted to have a serious talk with me before she went home. She liked Dondie, but to her mind he and I were nothing like as affectionate towards each other as an engaged couple ought to be and she was worried that something was seriously wrong between us. Hurriedly I began to formulate an explanation of the strict rules of conduct which governed relations between the sexes in the Philippines, but I couldn't carry it off and instead I burst into tears and confessed to Mum that I was worried too.

The cultural differences were very real. In provincial areas particularly, any open display of affection, especially between unmarried couples, was heavily frowned on. I'd even heard of men being forced into marriage by a girl's parents just because the couple had held hands in public. Dondie and I, as Christians with pastoral responsibilities, could easily create stumbling-blocks for others if we offended against the traditional code.

I understood this intellectually, but emotionally it was a different matter. I'd been brought up in a different culture and the need for so much discretion was hard to take. Until our engagement was official, Dondie wouldn't even introduce me to his mother because to her this

151

would in itself be tantamount to announcing our marriage; whereas in England, new boyfriends had taken me to meet their families at the earliest opportunity.

Being officially engaged didn't appear to make much difference. Surely it was natural, especially after we'd waited so long for things to come right for us, to expect Dondie to be eager to demonstrate his love for me and let the whole world see how proud he was of me? I so much wanted him to acknowledge our relationship by taking my hand, paying me compliments or singling me out with a look or a smile that was just for me. When instead he treated me just as if there were nothing special between us I felt rejected and insecure. I couldn't suppress the fear that cultural convention was only an excuse and that really he was ashamed to be seen holding hands with an English woman – or, even worse, that his feelings for me had changed.

When we were alone, which wasn't often, I taxed him with this and he would always deny it and do his best to reassure me of his love. But he wouldn't give ground over the need to abide by the restrictions imposed by the culture, while I, longing for tangible evidence of his love, continued to chafe under them.

I tried to convince Mum that Dondie and I could learn to adjust to these cultural differences, but I'm sure she realised I was trying to convince myself as much as her.

In fact, culture was not really the only factor in my unhappiness. I was also up against the fact that Dondie by nature was not given to extravagant expressions of his feelings or the sort of romantic gestures that I'd been used to from Stuart, and after Mum had left I began increasingly to compare the two of them. I remembered how good Stuart had been at creating an intimate world of romance in which 'our restaurant' and 'our song' had private significance, and a pebble picked up from the beach became a reminder of a special day. He'd plan surprises, and when he took me out to dinner or the theatre he always succeeded in making me feel like a fairy-tale princess. I didn't expect Dondie to shower me with expensive presents and outings, but I did long for little tokens such as a note or a secret smile.

I realised I was being unreasonable. Dondie was not Stuart, he was an individual in his own right with a person-ality of his own, and comparisons were not helpful. It was pointless to go on hankering for a fairy tale that had no basis in reality. And I couldn't doubt that God had spoken to me that night at Pinecrest.

Our wedding was set for 17th July, and in May I flew to England a month or so ahead of Dondie to finalise the arrangements. At the airport, my face was blotched with tears at the thought of leaving him for over a month, but he had his emotions well under control and while I wanted to delay the moment of parting as long as possible he seemed anxious to push me off to the departure area and get it over with. Fresh doubts assailed me and in this mood I set off to make plans for my wedding.

The dress I'd chosen a year ago was all ready apart from the final fitting, but there were plenty of other things to do. I tackled the preparations with a heavy heart, though remaining outwardly cheerful. David Chaudhary was to take the service, and David Greenow, founder of IGO, and his wife Emily agreed to stand in for Dondie's parents, as his widowed mother was much too frail to make the journey. Renee, my friend from Pinecrest, was coming over from the States to be my chief bridesmaid. Invitations were ordered, the reception was booked and everything was ready. Except me.

The nearer the wedding approached, the more my doubts increased. I loved Dondie, but if he wouldn't, or couldn't, show affection before we were married, how could I be sure it would be different afterwards? In addi-tion, the problem of living in an alien culture took on a new and frightening aspect. After five years in the Philippines I thought I'd adjusted pretty well, but I was now face to face with the fact that the adjustment was going to be permanent. The Philippines would be my home for the rest of my life. My children would be born and brought up there, thousands of miles from the rest of my family and in conditions far removed from the comforts and conveniences of the western lifestyle I'd known as a child. As a young woman I'd dreamed of sharing a beautiful house with my husband and children, of staying home and baking bread, inviting friends for dinner, going abroad for summer holidays. Now none of this was going to happen.

One day, when I'd been in England for about a week, I walked into town and bumped into Stuart. We stood talking about this and that and after a few minutes he said, 'How about a cup of coffee for old times' sake?'

'OK, why not? It will be our last opportunity!'

In the restaurant we chatted easily. Even after two broken engagements we still got on well and enjoyed each other's company, and as we lingered over the empty coffee cups I found myself fighting to repress a feeling of regret for what might have been.

'After all we've been through,' Stuart said, 'it seems a shame that we aren't going to end up together. It would have made a great novel, like *Love Story* or something.'

In my present state of emotional confusion, this wasn't a line of conversation I wanted to pursue, so I said firmly, 'I'm sorry. Letting go of you is a sacrifice for me, but the Lord is demanding it of me.' The memory of Pinecrest was as vivid as ever.

But the effect of my words on Stuart was the opposite of what I'd intended. I could almost see the thought forming in his mind and a glimmer of hope flickered over his face.

'Maybe it's like Abraham – when the Lord sees that you're willing to give me up, then he'll allow you to marry me, just as he allowed Abraham to keep Isaac.'

I didn't answer, but later, on my own, I started to wonder. Was he right? Was it like Abraham? Would the Lord let me marry Stuart after all? I'd thought everything would be plain sailing once the Lord told me who I was to marry, but I should have known Satan better than to imagine he would leave me alone. My fears and confusion, coupled with the unsatisfactory parting from Dondie, made me vulnerable to his schemes to lure me from God's purposes.

I passed from wondering whether Stuart was right to hoping that he was. I began daydreaming once more about having a home in England and just visiting the Philippines from time to time. I played over in my mind the memories of romantic walks and candlelit dinners with Stuart. 'Lord, is it so wrong to want this?' But God seemed far away and never answered.

It was no longer possible to keep my thoughts from my parents, and Dad's reaction was decisive: 'Chrissy, you can't marry Dondie if you feel like this about another man.'

'But what about the Lord speaking to me?'

'Well, if you're feeling the way you do, you must have misheard! There's no way I can allow you to get married when you're as uncertain as this. The wedding is off. Marriage isn't a sacrifice.'

I knew that. The sacrifice demanded of me consisted not in marrying Dondie but in letting go of Stuart, and all the dreams he represented. If God said, 'Dondie is the one,' I had to accept that he knew where my true happiness lay. And whatever Dad said, I knew I hadn't misheard. 'The sheep follow him, for they know his voice' (Jn 10:4). The question was whether, having heard, I was going to follow him or my feelings.

However, Dad was right about one thing: the wedding couldn't go ahead with me in my present state. I wrote to Dondie, explaining the situation and telling him the wedding was off. Since his flight was already booked and paid for, I left it to him to decide whether he wanted to make the trip anyway. I hardly knew myself what I wanted him to do. If he didn't come, it would surely be because he accepted that our engagement was over and I'd be free to marry Stuart. Another part of me, however, clung to the conviction that once I saw him again, everything would fall back into place and I'd regain the assurance that it was right to marry him.

While I waited for his reply, I continued to waver. Stuart and I even met to fast and pray, to see if the Lord would speak again.

'It's going to be OK. The Lord is for us,' said Stuart.

'It's not,' I wept. 'God hasn't changed his mind.'

It would have been easy to pretend that he had. So many of the people at church now thought Stuart and I were ideally suited and were strongly in favour of our getting married. Mum and Dad would have been glad to be able to keep me in England. I would have had everyone's approval except God's. Since he hadn't changed his mind, I asked the Lord to confirm the word he'd spoken at Pinecrest. He didn't reply, but his silence seemed to rebuke me: 'Chrissy, I've already told you. I won't repeat myself. You choose to trust me and obey, or not.'

It was a shock when I received Dondie's reply – 'Yes, I will arrive in England as scheduled' – but also a relief. Without him I felt I would probably give way to my feelings and marry Stuart. A day or two before Dondie arrived, I went to a crusade meeting in Warrington where, with uncanny accuracy, the speaker analysed my dilemma as if he knew every detail of my circumstances. His sermon about obeying the voice of the Lord spelled out in letters a mile high that my struggle was not to do with receiving direction from God, but with being willing to walk in it.

If he was asking me to give up my dreams, I knew my God well enough to know that what he had for me was even better. '"For I know the plans I have for you," declares the Lord, "plans to prosper you and not to harm you, plans to give you hope and a future"' (Jer 29:11, NIV). I'd known it all along; it was just the old ____ of translating knowledge into action and ending ____ional upheaval that was hurting not only me but

Stuart too, and all of my family. Life at home had been strained and difficult for weeks, and it was this atmosphere which greeted Dondie when he arrived, just a month before we'd been due to be married.

Imagine my dismay when it emerged that he hadn't understood the situation at all. Thinking that the wedding was merely postponed, though without any idea as to why, he had decided to make the trip as planned. Had he realised the truth, he would definitely have cancelled it. I expected him to be furious. To a Filipino, a broken engagement constitutes a huge scandal and he would have had every reason to feel that I'd humiliated him. But once the first shock was over, he amazed me by the quiet way in which he reacted. He, who of all of us had perhaps the most cause to be upset, was in fact the least perturbed.

In the following weeks, though he was actually staying with my brother, he spent most of his time with us at my parents' home, which wasn't easy for him or them. Mum especially was inclined to question him closely, because of the doubts she'd had about his love for me. But he made no attempt to ingratiate himself or plead his cause, nor did he in any way seek to put pressure on me. 'If it's God's will, it will happen,' was his only comment. Clearly he wasn't enjoying the uncertainty, but he never tried to turn the situation into a competition between himself and Stuart. When the two of them met, as they inevitably did at church, he gave no sign of being troubled at the thought of a rival, though he couldn't help but be aware that, materially at least, Stuart had so much more to offer me. Being only human I'm sure he struggled inwardly, but he never let me see it. I was baffled by his calmness; it was as if he had a secret source of tranquillity.

Though he hadn't set out to impress, his demeanour couldn't fail to have an effect on my family. It revealed more about his character than they would have learned in years under normal circumstances. A change came over me too. His refusal to try to win me by persuasion,

leaving me instead to seek the Lord for myself, confirmed
that he truly was the one for me, and suddenly I was able
to let go of Stuart. Immediately, my love for Dondie, so
long obscured, shone out again and all my doubts about
his love for me disappeared. When I was eventually able
to tell him that my fears and confusion had vanished, and
that the Lord's will was now also my own, there was of
course, Dondie being Dondie, no great explosion of
delight. His smile seemed to say that he had known all
along that I would reach this point.

Our only disappointment now was that the trial we'd
been through had robbed us of the wedding which was due
to have taken place in just a few days' time. Now that the
battle was over it was hard to face the prospect of delay, but
once we went back to the Philippines it would be a year or
more before we could return. Here we were, with a pile of
invitations and orders of service, the bride's and brides-
maids' dresses all ready and waiting – but no wedding.

After talking it over, Dondie and I decided to take
Mum and Dad out for a meal and ask whether they
would agree to our getting married before we went
back. The chances of persuading them were admittedly
slim because though they had been impressed by Dondie
they still thought highly of Stuart and knew how much
he wanted to marry me. Barring a miracle, they would
be sure to insist that we wait at least a year.

At the end of the meal, we put our proposal and prepared to be cross-questioned, but the expected interroga-
tion failed to materialise. Instead, they approved our plan
without argument – a bigger miracle than any we had
dared hope for. The date was fixed for 21st August, a
Sunday.

We chose to be married on Sunday as a way of dedicating the whole occasion to the Lord, but it turned out
to be a tremendous practical advantage in that booking a
reception, cars and a photographer would probably have
been impossible at such short notice for a Saturday. This

ime round I could thoroughly enjoy the whirl of preparation, but the moment which set the seal on my joy
came when Dondie finally told me his side of the story.

When he first became attracted to me he hesitated to
peak because of the many obstacles he foresaw to our
relationship. Having spent several years in America, where
wo of his sisters had settled, he was only too aware of the
high expectations of western women, and that I enjoyed a
very comfortable standard of living in England. He feared
oo the possibility of discrimination against us as a mixed-
race couple, not to mention the fundamental question of
whether two strong-willed personalities could ever make a
successful marriage.

While he was still debating with himself, the Lord
spoke to him: 'Chrissy will be your wife, not because of
our compatibility, nor because of your love for her, but
because I have a mighty work for you to do together.' My
etter from Pinecrest was simply a confirmation of what
he Lord had already said, and it was his complete cer-
ainty as to the Lord's will which had enabled him to
cope with my confusion so calmly. What thrilled me was
he fact that he had never till now disclosed the source of
his confidence; never sought to use it as a weapon to
pressurise me into accepting him.

David Chaudhary was still available to take the ceremony
and David and Emily to stand in for Dondie's parents.
Even my bridesmaid Renee phoned from America to say
he could make the revised date, despite the fact that her
sister was to be married only a couple of days later.

After a week of chilly rain, I woke on the morning of the
wedding to a sky of broken cloud and pale sunshine. We
were to be married in the beautiful old church which the
congregation, having long outgrown the original 'upper
room', had bought and lovingly restored. When I arrived
here with Dad, I half expected to find that many people
had stayed away; the postponement of the wedding had
generated a fair amount of controversy and I knew there

had been a widespread feeling that I should have married Stuart. But when I walked down the aisle on Dad's arm, following the rest of the bridal party as a Filipino bride does, I couldn't hold back my tears. I'd never seen the church so full. They were all there to lend their support and share my perfect day.

The only thing we really lost was our honeymoon. We had just four brief days in Mum and Dad's holiday home in Wales and then we were back on the road and back to work. Our first speaking engagement as Mr and Mrs Dondie Perillo was in Northallerton Prison and then, in September, we returned to the Philippines.

A few years later, Stuart found the woman God intended for him and is now happily married too.

16

'Let Us Not Grow Weary'

On our return, Dondie and I moved into a room in the rehab and within three weeks of our arrival we had our first child. The idea of adoption had always appealed to me: even if I couldn't solve the problems of all the unloved children in the world I could at least make a big difference for one child. I'd talked it over with Dondie before we were married, but his response was negative and he felt sure he wouldn't be able to love someone else's child as he would his own. That was until he heard from his mother about Carlo.

I didn't meet Dondie's mother before we were officially engaged, but when he showed me her photograph I immediately recognised her as a member of the Assemblies of God church in Olongapo which I'd attended with Dorothy and Linda when I first came to the Philippines. Some of Dondie's relatives still lived in their home province of Bicol in the south of Luzon, while others had moved north to Olongapo to find work. His mother had recently gone back to be with her family in the south and one day during our engagement he received a letter from her with news of Carlo, his sister Carmen's son.

For a variety of reasons Carmen had been forced to leave the four-year-old boy in the care of Dondie's mother, and though Carlo was very happy with her, Dondie was troubled. 'Mum is old now, and becoming quite frail,' he said to me. 'It's not fair for a boy so young.'

'Well, why don't you write and ask your sister if he can come and stay with us? After we're married she may even agree to us adopting him.'

Dondie duly wrote to his sister and to his mother and both agreed that once we were married Carlo could come to live with us, which was how I found myself with a four-year-old son within two months of my wedding. Carlo, however, was no trouble at all and quickly adjusted to life in the rehab, where he happily shared a room with one of the other kids. He loved riding in our jeepney and having lots of toys to play with and within a couple of weeks he was calling Dondie and me Dad and Mum.

We'd been keen to adopt Carlo straight away so that by the time we had children of our own his place in the family would be securely established and the others would always know and accept him as their brother. It was as well, then, that he was able to come to us so soon because a week or so later I discovered I was pregnant. Filipinos believe in big families, but this was fast work even for them: three months married, with one four-year-old and a baby on the way!

I suffered quite badly with morning sickness and while there were many times when I'd have been glad to spend the day at home I couldn't neglect the ministry in the jails. Romy and Lourdes were faithful helpers, as was Romy's brother Bill who'd joined us as our jeepney driver, but none of them was yet ready to teach and preach. Since there was no one to take my place I had to carry on, trusting the Lord to give me the spiritual strength to do his work, regardless of what I was feeling.

One of our visits to Camp Maquinaya at this time stands out as the catalyst which triggered a further fulfilment of my original vision for the Philippine Outreach Centre. It was an open-air service and as Lourdes led the singing we began to praise the Lord, with Romy playing his portable organ and me on the guitar. While the men were gathering round, my eyes were drawn to the unusually large number of children present. There had always been children, of course, living with their parents in the jail as the sole alternative to starvation on the streets, yet today there seemed to be so many more – though it may well have been that this perception was due less to any actual increase in their numbers than to the fact that the Lord was bringing them to my attention.

Though I continued to sing and play, I have to confess that my mind was not on praising and worshipping the Lord, but on the needs of these children. Many were old enough to be in kindergarten, if not in school, yet instead they were locked up within the confines of the jail, living alongside the inmates, some of whom at least were guilty of murder, rape, drug abuse and drug dealing.

As I looked at them I heard the Lord speak to me: 'Chrissy, now is the time to take these children out of this place.'

'But Lord, we're not ready for them yet. We haven't the money or the staff. We haven't even enough beds or any of the other things we'll need if we're to care for them.'

'Look around you. Haven't you more to offer them than this?'

I looked, and my excuses suddenly seemed lame, though I hadn't made them in order to evade responsibility for the children. I genuinely wanted to help them, but everything I'd said about our limited facilities was true and Dondie had often warned me that we were becoming over-stretched.

People are called to work in different ways. There are some (and I fully understand their thinking) who look to the Lord first of all to provide the facilities and equipment before embarking on a ministry project, and to be honest I'd much rather have things that way. It would be so much less demanding. (Ever since we opened the first rehab in 1985 we'd had to exercise our faith each month just to be able to feed everyone.) But in my case, the call to reach out to the needy came first and I therefore had to believe that the Lord would give us the necessary means to care for them.

I looked again at the tough, hardened men, covered in tattoos, heads shaved, puffing away at their cigarettes; I pictured the cells with no beds, bedding or bathrooms; and indeed I saw that nothing could in any case be worse than this.

'OK, Lord, but you will have to work on Dondie. Now that I'm married I can't do just as I please. If Dondie will agree, then I'm willing.'

This was no small 'if', because Dondie was constitutionally opposed to starting up new ventures for which we were not properly prepared and adequately equipped, and it seemed likely that my pregnancy and the additional responsibility of looking after Carlo would make him even more reluctant. I had no great hopes of obtaining his consent when, on my return to the rehab, I described to him, exactly as I'd experienced it, how the Lord had spoken to me. He confounded all my expectations by immediately agreeing that we should take the children in, on condition that the women in the rehab would do their part in caring for them.

It wasn't difficult to secure the co-operation of Alex's wife, Marie, Ronnie's wife, Norma, Helen Gerez and the rest of the women. They were all more than willing to help, and just as excited at the prospect as I was. Romy and Lourdes promised their support, and Roselyn professed herself happy to welcome any new additions to the kindergarten.

Everything now rested with the inmates themselves and their willingness to accept our plans, and the women in particular couldn't be expected to hand over their children, even temporarily, without a lot of heartsearching. Some of the mothers were prisoners' wives who had chosen to join their husbands in the jail because they couldn't support their families alone on the outside. Others were members of the very small population of female inmates who were accommodated just outside the prison compound in a separate cell designed to hold twenty women, though the actual number never rose above ten.

I had no idea beforehand how our proposal would be received, but in fact the initial reaction of many inmates was one of delight, and the prison officers were so much in favour of it that they offered to provide an armed escort so that parents could visit the rehab before making a decision. Several mothers took advantage of the offer and I was glad of the unexpected opportunity to reassure them that they would be able to find us without difficulty when they wanted to reclaim their children.

They made a subdued and silent party as they followed us round the rehab, subjecting everything to the minutest examination in their anxiety to be sure their children would be happy. It was not an easy decision, however bad conditions were in the jail, and these mothers were intent on satisfying themselves that we measured up to the standard they had set in their minds. When we reached the schoolrooms and then the bedrooms with their double bunks and real mattresses, I noted the first hint of approval in their eyes, but still not a word escaped them and they finished the tour as silently as they'd begun.

Afterwards, over refreshments, they finally delivered their verdict. It was unanimous, and at a stroke the children's dormitory gained eight new occupants who moved in just as soon as we were able to have beds made for them. Of the eight, only three-year-old Kristy refused to settle and had to be returned to the jail. The four-year-olds, Marilyn, Jennalyn and Angelica gave no trouble, sleeping soundly, eating well and enjoying their first encounter with education every bit as much as Jon, Joey, Sherley and Jefferson.

In later years we took in other prisoners' children, very few of whom actually left us when their parents moved away, and of all of them none brought me greater joy than Eddie Lazaro's son, Carlito.

After the tragedy of Eddie's death in 1983 I always kept in contact with his mother, Grace, and many times, when I saw how she was struggling to put her daughter through college, I offered to have Carlito live with us in the rehab. Grace was a widow and supplemented the small income from her cleaning job by earning commission on the vegetables and fish she sold on behalf of various friends. She consistently refused my offers of help because as a strict Roman Catholic herself she wanted Carlito to have a Catholic education, and while I was disappointed I couldn't help but admire her determination.

She managed to pay for him to attend a private Catholic school from kindergarten through to the final year of elementary school, but at this point her financial problems became overwhelming and she was at last compelled to seek my help.

'Sister Chrissy, Carlito is supposed to graduate this month, but the sisters at the school have warned me that if I don't pay my outstanding tuition fees, he won't be able to. Sister, Carlito says he would like to live with you at the rehabilitation home and if you are willing to sponsor him at school, we'll be really grateful.'

My heart leaped. By now Carlito was, I well knew, quite a mischievous teenager, but through the years I'd treasured the hope, for Eddie's sake, of being able to do something for his son. Paying off the outstanding fees would strain our budget to the limit, but I was confident that the Lord would meet this need and (it was still my practice not to hand over cash) arranged to go with Grace to the school to settle the debt.

That done, she invited me to her home, which was now in a district of Olongapo, and reaching it, she warned me, would involve quite a hike up the hillside. As we climbed the narrow dirt track worn by the constant passage of feet – there was no proper road – I wondered what it would be like to do this in the rainy season. It was treacherously slippery even when dry, but Grace, a grandmother in her fifties, scrambled nimbly to the top without a word of complaint.

The house was perched on the hillside with three others and though it was just a *kubo* (native Filipino house) with a dirt floor, Grace was very proud of it. Carlito was waiting there for our arrival, excited as he'd always been whenever I paid them a visit, and eager to talk to me. Conversation had to wait, however, until, at Grace's insistence, he'd changed out of his school uniform and hung it neatly on a hanger. 'Laundry soap is so expensive at the *tindahan* (corner shop),' she explained, 'but in Olongapo you can get a bargain. If you buy the whole bar you get one free, so I'm avoiding using soap until I can afford the full bar. Carlito knows how to keep his uniform clean so that it doesn't have to be washed every day.'

To look at Carlito you would never have guessed that his clothes were not washed daily; he looked as well turned out as any of the children at his private school. I caught a glimpse of the extent to which careful thrift had dominated Grace's life, enabling her to survive and support her family for so many years. How many people in Britain would think twice about buying a whole bar of soap? But in the Philippines such things are an inescapable fact of daily life for many. Laundry soap is sold in long bars which can be broken into four smaller pieces and as there are so many poor people who can't afford the whole bar, the smaller shops sell each piece separately. Similarly, you can buy a single stock cube instead of a full box and items such as shampoo and toothpaste are usually sold in small sachets because a full bottle or tube is beyond the means of the poor.

Grace had not been made bitter by the relentless need for economy, and her testimony was that God had met their every need. On one occasion, with her purse empty and no food in the house, she was walking home wondering how they were to eat that night when, glancing down, she saw a 500 peso note lying at her feet. For that she gave God the glory.

So Carlito came to live with us. He remained as mischievous as ever, but I continue to rejoice that we were able to lead him to accept Jesus as his Lord and Saviour.

When the children from Camp Maquinaya joined us we had been in the new rehab for almost two years and as the slow process of renovation neared completion we began to think about an official opening. In a few months' time I was expecting a number of visitors: Jonathan and Rodney, two of our trustees, were planning to visit the Philippines with a couple of missionary friends and would be calling in on us in January; and Nick, who'd given me my first lessons in evangelism, would be in the country at the same time. Best of all, Nanna Jean would be here too. I'd never imagined that she would be able to come, as she was now in her seventies, but so great was her desire to witness at first hand the work she'd prayed for and supported for so long, that she was prepared to risk the exhausting journey in order to be with us. It seemed the ideal time for the opening and we set the date for 7th January 1989.

We sent out invitations to missionary friends and local churches, and then set about the task of making the rehab ready for public viewing. We had a lot of decorating still to do, but the most expensive remaining job was finishing the windows, which at present had screening but no glass. Daily we brought our need to the Lord at the early morning prayer meeting, and with just a few days to go before the opening his answer came in the shape of an unusually large gift from our supporters back home.

The day arrived and while I escorted our guests from England on visits to the prisons and children's outreaches, the men were busy at the rehab finishing off the painting, putting up a platform for the opening service and erecting a tent covering over it to provide shade from the scorching sun. Meanwhile, the women were cleaning and preparing food for the banquet which was to follow the service. With so many visitors expected, there were five pigs to be slaughtered, three of which were spit-roasted over an open fire in traditional Filipino celebration style.

Like a bride on her wedding day, I was in a state of happy confusion as events flashed past me at bewildering speed, and though both the service and the banquet went according to plan I have only the haziest recollection of them. So many friends were there: members of various churches in Olongapo joined with us, and Romy's other brother, who was a pastor in Olongapo, brought his entire congregation; Pop Pederson, who had replaced Pop Houghton, came from the US Military Mission; and several fellow missionaries travelled from north and south to take part in our celebration.

But the greatest blessing was that so many of our unbelieving neighbours, having steadily opposed us ever since we moved into the district, were there that day to hear the testimonies of the ex-prisoners and the preaching of God's word. We had been praying for two years that the Lord would break down the barriers, and this was just a foretaste of what was to come. No doubt the prospect of sharing the banquet had played its part in persuading them to attend, but God's word is never sent out in vain and the planted seed would one day yield a harvest if we were patient. 'Let us not grow weary while doing good,' says St Paul, 'for in due season we shall reap if we do not lose heart' (Gal 6:9).

17

The Way to Success

Damp eyed, I gazed in wonder at my beautiful newborn daughter.

Dondie hadn't been able to leave the rehab to come with me when I flew to England to have the baby, so it was Mum and not he who was at my side when Monique was born on 6th June 1989. It was hard to be away from my husband for several months after being married for less than a year, and like most women I'd wanted him to be with me when I gave birth to our first child. It was only the sight of Monique, when the nurse laid her beside me, that eventually dried the tears I hadn't been able to hold back after Mum had gone.

I'd also been hoping to introduce Carlo to his new brother or sister straight away and but for delays in the processing of his adoption papers and visa documents he would have travelled with me. As it was, he'd had to stay behind in the Philippines with Dondie and now I wouldn't see either of them until September. While it was painful to be separated from my husband and son, I resolved to make the most of the opportunity to be with my loved ones in England, whom I might not see again for some considerable time. I was beginning to realise that trips to the UK would become rarer as our family grew because of the high cost of flying.

Within a very short time of Monique's birth I was back on the road for my usual round of speaking engagements, and the long journeys were now complicated by the routine of feeding and nappy changing which dominates life with a small baby. Before I spoke I would have to disappear for a while to give her a top-up feed, and then hand her over to her nanna. It certainly wasn't easy, but it had to be done if I were to fulfil my commitment to raise support for the Philippine Outreach Centre.

Thankfully, I had a companion to help me when I flew back in September. Vanessa was twenty years old and while attending a missions weekend at Hollybush had sensed God calling her to serve him for a time in the Philippines. She talked it over with Jonathan, one of the Hollybush staff and also one of my trustees, and he, knowing we desperately needed extra help, suggested that I should meet Vanessa and the missionary director of her church in Leeds. It was obvious to me that she just wanted the Lord to use her in whichever way he chose and the church elders testified to her faithfulness and zeal for evangelism, so it was soon agreed that she should join us for a year.

Vanessa settled in without difficulty. She quickly made friends with the young people in our church and having done a college course in pre-school education she was a great help in the kindergarten, where she and Roselyn were able to pool their resources and learn from each other's experiences. All her pupils loved her, and she them. She had a great gift for relating to people naturally and easily, and struck up a particular friendship with Albert, the brother of one of our young people. Albert had Down's syndrome and though he was nineteen he had never been to school because there was no provision for special educational needs in our area at that time. He was so fond of Vanessa that when he discovered she was a teacher in the kindergarten, nothing would satisfy him but to enrol as a pupil. He rarely missed a day until he graduated and went on to the local elementary school.

The kindergarten was doing extremely well. Our neighbours had set aside much of their earlier suspicion and started to trust us not to impose some alien religion on them, with the result that more of them were sending their children to us. It was equally gratifying to hear of the favourable opinions passed by staff at the elementary school on the quality of the graduates they received from our kindergarten.

At the rehab too everything seemed to be in excellent shape, with all the current residents making steady progress; none of them missed even the 6 o'clock morning prayer meeting, though we never made it compulsory. And Joseph's progress was little short of spectacular. Soon after that inauspicious beginning, when he turned up at our prayer meeting completely drunk, he had given his heart to the Lord and the change in his life was so dramatic that we readily acceded to his request for sponsorship at Bible school.

Basking in the warmth of these successes, we were totally unprepared for the violent upheaval which shook the rehab to its foundations. It was November, and I was hard at work in the office on our preparations for Christmas, when the quiet of the afternoon was ripped apart by shrill screams and the clamour of raised voices. I rushed out, and there at the centre of the commotion was Alex's stepdaughter, Maria Castillo. I'd never seen so much blood in my life; her school uniform was absolutely soaked in it. While Bill Del Monte hurried to get the jeepney started to take her to hospital, I tried to find out what had happened.

It appeared that Maria had suddenly started to bleed internally at school and her teacher had simply told her to go home. In that condition she'd walked all the way up the hill to the rehab, alone. Maria's mother, Marie, and her aunt, Norma, came with us in the jeepney and none of us spoke during the thirty-minute ride to the General

Hospital in San Marcelino, just to the north of Castillejos. I was thinking some very unwelcome thoughts.

Maria had known plenty of unhappiness in her short life. Before they came to the rehab her mother would often keep her away from school to help with the younger children, so that at fifteen she was still at elementary level. As a small child she had lost the sight of her left eye when her younger brother poked it with a stick, and the injury had destroyed the iris, giving her a freakish appearance which made other children afraid of her. We had sought the help of a mission on the US naval base and while nothing could be done to restore her sight she'd been fitted with a contact lens which worked well cosmetically and had given her the confidence of knowing she looked normal to her classmates.

And now fresh trouble of a much worse kind had come to her. Without my asking, the Lord had shown me the truth of what had happened to Maria and the knowledge dismayed me.

The hospital at San Marcelino, though quieter and cheaper than the General Hospital in Olongapo, was no better off as far as facilities were concerned and we waited a long time before the nurses came to attend to Maria. When they did come their treatment of her was anything but sensitive. They handled her roughly and one of them demanded, 'Who's the boy?' When Maria made no reply, she repeated impatiently, 'Come on, tell us! Who's the boy? Is it someone at school?'

'No, no!'

'Well, it must be somebody. Who was it?'

It was a painful scene; poor Maria was shaking her head in distress at the nurses' accusations, while to them the suspicion that she was miscarrying as a result of sex outside of marriage rendered her an object of contempt. Instead of offering comfort, Marie also turned on her daughter: 'Maria, tell us who it was!'

This made me angry as I was sure Marie must already know. I told them all to be quiet and leave the girl alone and demanded a private interview with the female doctor in charge. 'Please don't be so hard on her,' I said when we were alone. 'It's not her fault. I know her. She comes straight home from school every day and never goes out anywhere.'

'Then why doesn't she answer us?'

'I don't know for sure yet, but I think her stepfather is the one responsible.'

'Why doesn't she say so?'

'Probably she's afraid of him. He's an ex-prisoner with a violent history and she's very likely scared of what he might do.'

Having secured a promise that Maria would be treated more gently I went back to Maria herself, and without pressing her to talk assured her that I was there for her if she needed me. Leaving Norma and Marie to look after her, I went back to the rehab.

I decided to say nothing just yet to Alex. Anything I did would have repercussions both for Maria and the other five children under his authority and my first priority was to seek the Lord for wisdom in handling the situation. I realised now why Maria's elder sister Jackie had suddenly left the rehab a year or so ago. She'd gone out one day, ostensibly to do some shopping, and never returned. Afterwards, she wrote to Dondie and me, thanking us for all we'd done for her, but she didn't give her address or explain why she had left.

When talking to us about Alex's past, though they had spoken of his violence, neither Marie nor the children had ever hinted that he'd been guilty of sexual abuse. On the evidence available to us, therefore, we'd felt we had good reason to be encouraged by the progress he'd made since he joined us. His temper still flared up at times, but such occurrences were not common and, especially at the beginning, he'd seemed to be doing well in other ways. He began to develop a gift for preaching and had even asked us to pray that the door would be opened for him to return to his home town to spread the gospel there. It was undeniable, however, that when his brother Jim came to the rehab he had influenced Alex for the worse, and because Jim refused to leave the area after he was expelled, his influence remained.

When I confided to Dondie what I believed the Lord had shown me, we decided together that we should take no action until we had spoken to Maria and ascertained what she wanted to do. One morning shortly after this, when I arrived at San Marcelino to visit Maria, I found her aunt Norma sitting by the entrance to the hospital, distraught and red eyed. Struggling to get the words out, she managed to say, 'Oh, Sister Chrissy, you'll never believe it!' before breaking down again.

I put my arm round her. 'I know already. The Lord revealed to me that Alex is to blame. Has Maria told you?'

Still sobbing, she nodded in reply as we walked towards Maria's ward. Before we went in, Norma turned to me and said, 'Please don't tell Alex or Marie that you know. Maria hasn't told her mother yet. She's so frightened of what Alex will do if he discovers we all know.'

I spent a little while with Maria and she admitted to me herself that Alex was responsible. It had all happened while I was in England following the birth of Monique, and Maria had carried the burden of her dreadful secret all alone until now. Alex had planned his assault carefully. When the rehab's pigs were close to delivering their piglets, he would take his mosquito net and sleep outside by the pigsties in order to be on hand to help them. He had lured Maria out to him by insisting that she bring his coffee and it was there, where no one would see or hear anything, that he had raped her.

While Norma comforted Maria I went again to speak to the doctor. 'If the child wants to press charges against her stepfather, we'll support her. Can I rely on you to provide proof that she was raped, or at least that she had a miscarriage?' I asked.

'I've never said she had a miscarriage.' (This was true; it had been implied but never openly stated.) 'This kind of haemorrhage sometimes does occur in teenage virgins, though we don't know the cause.'

'How can you say that? When she was first admitted you were so certain there was a boy involved, you were condemning her for it. Now that she's confessed the truth, you're denying it.' I was utterly exasperated. There could be no rape case without medical testimony. Perhaps the doctor, knowing that Alex had a violent past, refused to get involved for fear of reprisals; it was certain that the medical records didn't disclose the true facts. When I checked them they said simply: 'Normal haemorrhage in adolescent female.'

In spite of the doctor's obduracy I assured Maria that I would still support her if she wanted to go ahead and file a rape charge. But she couldn't face the prospect of confronting Alex in court, nor did she want him to find out that we knew, and as no charge could be brought without her consent I accepted her decision. However, she agreed that for the sake of her nine-year-old sister Tina, and even the baby Mary Grace, she would expose Alex if he ever tried to harm her again.

Dondie and I were in a difficult position now. We couldn't charge Alex without Maria's consent, and in any case we'd given our word not to. If we confronted him ourselves he might well leave the rehab taking his family with him, and Maria's position would be worse than before. There seemed no alternative but to maintain a pretence of ignorance while we prayed for guidance.

Two weeks after Maria was discharged from hospital, as Vanessa and I were packing Christmas stockings for the children's outreaches, the rehab once more echoed to the sound of frantic screaming. It was Maria, thrown into a panic by Alex demanding that she bring him some coffee to the pigsties. Quickly, Dondie and I locked Maria in our room with Vanessa and Monique and rushed out to look for Alex, but there was no sign of him. He knew now that his sin had been exposed.

Several hours later we were all startled by a loud bang, then another – gunfire? Christmas fireworks? – followed by the sound of Alex's drunken shouting, which terrified everyone, especially his family who knew from past experience what he was capable of when drunk. The noise was coming from the kitchen and when Dondie and I hurried over there we heard Alex's voice: 'How about you, Brother Bill? You're a man. Are you willing to fight?'

We burst in to find that Alex had Bill firmly pinioned and was pressing a wicked foot-long *bolo* (knife) against his throat. Instinct took over and I ran towards them. 'Alex, in the name of Jesus, give me that knife.' He might as well have been made of stone. 'Alex,' I repeated more urgently, 'in the name of Jesus, give it to me.'

Slowly he released his hold on Bill, who darted away and ran for safety. Alex began to wave the knife at me and Dondie. 'How about you, then, Brother Dondie?'

Dondie and I were both convinced that he was planning to kill one of us and then take his own life, and each of us called on the Holy Spirit for wisdom to prevent him. All the others had cleared the area, keeping the women and children out of danger, so we were alone. We found the strength to ignore Alex's threats and speak to him calmly, discovering true wisdom in Solomon's words: 'A soft answer turns away wrath, but a harsh word stirs up anger' (Prov 15:1). Gradually his anger subsided and he began to show signs of remorse. 'There's no hope for me now. This time I've gone too far.'

If he would repent, we told him, the Lord would be faithful and just to forgive, provided his repentance was genuine. 'How can you forgive me for this?' he asked, handing the knife to Dondie.

'Alex, our heart's desire is to see you restored to the ot for you to be destroyed.'

ourse, for the children's sake we couldn't have

allowed him to stay at the rehab, but we didn't have to ask him to go. He left of his own accord immediately, quiet and broken, hanging his head. 'I've gone too far now,' he said softly.

Marie, afraid of what her husband might do, had already fled with Mary Grace and didn't come back till the next day, having spent the night in the market place. When she learned that Alex had left she decided to go after him, taking only Mary Grace and leaving the other children with us. They found a house in Pamatawan and Alex has since visited the church from time to time though as yet, like Esau, he has found no place for repentance.

Jackie and Maria are both married now with children of their own, and with the exception of one of the boys the rest of Alex's and Marie's children are still with us, including Mary Grace who returned to us a year or so after Alex left. The future looks bright for them all.

This incident was the worst we had yet encountered at the rehab. When it was over Bill Del Monte expressed his doubts to me: 'Don't you see now, Sister Chrissy, that you ought to give up with people like this? They'll never change. You're just wasting your time.'

I thought before I answered. 'Brother Bill, I'm not called to be successful and I'm not called to change these people. I know I could never change anyone. What I am called to be is obedient. We opened the rehab for people like Alex because the Lord told us to, not because we wanted to be successful and not for its sensation value. I can't stop just because of this failure.' I remembered my own failures which God had redeemed, and went on, 'I have to be obedient. If God tells us to stop, we will. What's important is our willingness to obey him.'

I can't deny that I feel disappointed when those whom I've tried so hard to instruct in the ways of God go astray. However, I always keep in the forefront of my mind a lesson which my mother taught me, gleaned from her own experience of similar disappointments with the young offenders who lived in our home. One of the boys had stolen her purse which was later found, empty, in a local pub. It had been hard enough for her to discover the theft, but to learn that he had spent the money on drink added insult to injury. She felt so let down after all she'd done for him. She told me, 'And then I cried out to the Lord. "What do I have to do for them? Do I have to die for them?"'

His reply shook her to the core: 'No, Mary. I did that.'

Without realising it, she had encroached on God's prerogative and lost sight of what was his responsibility and what was hers. Her ministry to the boys had filled her horizon to the exclusion of the need for God to act.

I learned from her mistake never to think that I have the power to change other people. I can lead them, guide them by example and treat them with love and compassion, but none of this will bring about a change in their lives. God alone can bring about that change in a man which will affect him for eternity. Man cannot even change himself by will power: '"Not by might nor by power, but by My Spirit," says the Lord of hosts' (Zech 4:6).

When there are changed lives and successes, I can't boast about them, 'for it is God who works in you both to will and to do for His good pleasure' (Phil 2:13). Equally, I can't complain about what appears to be failure; these situations too are in his hands.

What then constitutes success for a missionary, or a pastor, or any child of God? The secret of success, I believe, lies in these words:

> This Book of the Law shall not depart from your mouth, but you shall meditate in it day and night, that you may observe to do according to all that is written in it. For then you will make your way prosperous, and then you will have good success (Josh 1:8).

If by God's grace we are obedient to his word, then 'in due season we shall reap if we do not lose heart'.

18

Jimmy

Ever since I first met Mom and Pop Houghton in my early
days in the Philippines I'd kept up my links with the US
Military Mission's Servicemen's Home here in Subic. It was
an independent mission financed for the most part by
supporters in the States, with occasional additional funding
from the churches inside the Olongapo naval base, where
the Houghtons had numerous friends and contacts. It was
through Mom and Pop that I'd had invitations to speak on
the base and the Christians there had been extremely generous in their support of the Philippine Outreach Centre.

The Houghtons had been dear friends, helping and
encouraging me through some of my darkest times, and
I'd missed them when they returned to the States to continue their ministry with the Assemblies of God. However,
it wasn't long before I became acquainted with the Pedersons who came to replace them and with their daughter
and son-in-law, the Fishers. The Fishers were serving with
the US military and like Dondie and me were newlyweds,
with a son not much older than Monique.

When the Pedersons had to return unexpectedly to
America because of illness, they entrusted the care of the
Servicemen's Home to the Fishers, with whom Dondie and
I became good friends. For me especially, it was a treat to

spend time with people who came from a culture like my own and enjoy for a while the western comfort of the Home.

In their turn, the Fishers too needed to leave the Philippines quite suddenly and as they had no one to whom they could hand over the Servicemen's Home they turned to Dondie and me for help. Would we take over their role, just for a few months at most, until other arrangements could be made?

The suggestion was not as impossible as might first appear. For one thing, most of the work involved would be in the evenings; the purpose of the Home was to provide a drop-in centre for the men from the ships which were constantly coming and going at the base and we could expect visitors any time after 7pm. For another, the number of servicemen actually using the Home had been greatly reduced by the restrictions which sometimes placed Subic off limits to military personnel. (Ever since President Corazon Aquino defeated Ferdinand Marcos in the elections of 1986, the NPA [New People's Army], a group of Maoist insurgents whom Marcos had ruthlessly suppressed, had been threatening the US military, and a number of servicemen and some missionaries had been killed. Whenever trouble seemed imminent the military authorities would restrict the movements of their personnel and the men in our area would be confined to Olongapo.)

With this in mind, and since the job would be for only a short time, Dondie and I accepted, and in February 1990 we moved into the Home, which was just a five-minute drive from the rehab and closer to the centre of Subic. We soon fell into a routine, with Dondie spending most of the day up at the rehab while I continued as usual to visit Camp Maquinaya and Iba Jail with the Del Montes. The evenings, naturally, were spent at the Home waiting for any servicemen who might call, and if a crisis arose at the rehab during the night Bill, the jeepney driver, had instructions to come immediately to fetch us.

Some of our work for the Military Mission took us onto the base. On Friday evenings we joined a Bible study there, which gave us an opportunity to meet servicemen and invite them to the Home, and it also led to me being asked to teach once a week at a women's group. Every Wednesday we attended the chaplains' luncheon along with other military missionaries, local pastors and the military chaplaincy, and from time to time we received invitations to speak at the chapels on the base about the Servicemen's Home and the Philippine Outreach Centre.

Being responsible for two missions was hard work, but there were many compensations, of which access to certain facilities on the base was only one. Our visits to the servicemen's launderette each week after the Wednesday luncheon meant that Monique's baby clothes emerged beautifully soft from the tumble drier and we no longer used towels that felt like scrubbing brushes after being baked dry in the hot sun. And instead of taking Carlo and Monique to play on the beach, which was really none too clean, we were able to take them to McDonald's and the children's playground, treats they enjoyed enormously.

The Servicemen's Home itself, though it would have been judged ordinary by the standards of the better houses in Manila, was luxurious compared to those in Subic. It was two-storeyed and spacious, set in its own large garden, where Lora, the cook, had her own house. The lounge had a polished wooden floor and furniture (donated by a service family who'd been relocated) better than anything available in Olongapo. The small marble-tiled kitchen delighted me because in addition to a huge fridge it also contained the first oven I'd had since coming to the Philippines. An impressive wide stone stairway led to the first floor where the master bedroom boasted a king-size water bed, also the gift of a departing service couple, and, unbelievably, an en suite bathroom where the shower actually dispensed *hot* water, something unknown at the rehab. A door on the landing opened onto a large balcony directly over the lounge. Best of all, for the first time we had privacy and a place of our own as a family, so I wasn't too troubled when the months went by without any news of who was to replace us.

In the meantime, things were not standing still at the Philippine Outreach Centre while we were at the Home. John Morales, a converted ex-prisoner who had been detained at Muntinlupa and had heard of me from Mammie Olga, sought us out to ask if he could work with us in the prison ministry. He'd already gained experience by visiting the jail in his wife's home town of San Fernando and after taking him several times to Iba, where he quickly demonstrated a gift for communicating with the inmates, we gladly invited him to join us. He moved into the rehab with his wife and four children and in the year or so that they were with us, John was instrumental in expanding our work to include San Fernando Jail, about thirty miles north-east of Subic.

The church also was experiencing change. Dondie had been feeling for some time that the church's outreach would be more effective if our meeting place were nearer to the town centre than the rehab, and when he and I moved into the Servicemen's Home we noticed that a small restaurant on the same street was available for rent. It was small, but Dondie was satisfied that the location would benefit the work. He was right too, and church membership grew steadily from the time we began to meet there.

But it was meeting with Jimmy that sparked off the vision that was to live with me for the next three years. Not long after we moved to the Home I was asked by an anxious parent to visit a young man of twenty who was being detained at our local *barangay* station (a sort of small police station, but staffed by appointed civilians, where law breakers can be held until the police are informed and a formal arrest made). As the young man's offence was a minor one he would soon be released, and after speaking to him for a while I turned my attention to another detainee, wondering what on earth he could be guilty of. He looked about nine years old.

'What's your name?' I asked in Tagalog.

'Jimmy,' he replied shyly.

'And how old are you?'

'Twelve!'

'What has he done?' I asked the *barangay* captain.

'Oh, he was found roaming the streets at midnight, so he'll be kept here for three days.'

His mother, it appeared, worked in one of the nearby bars as a hostess, which was a euphemism for 'legal prostitute' (though street-walking was illegal, prostitution as a service provided in the bars was not). Jimmy's light skin and brown hair suggested that his father was a westerner, most probably an American serviceman.

I was overwhelmed with compassion for Jimmy, whose only crime was that he had no one to see that he was safely in bed at night. His mother hadn't been to see him since he was picked up, he told me, and he'd been too upset all that day to eat. Turning again to the captain, who knew of the Philippine Outreach Centre, I asked, 'Can I take him out for a while? I'll just show him round the rehabilitation home and give him something to eat, and I'll have him back within a couple of hours.'

'Sure, go ahead.'

'Jimmy, would you like to come with me?'

His little face lit up and his smile was all the answer I needed. He climbed happily into the old station wagon belonging to the Servicemen's Home and looked out of the window to see if any of his friends were around to notice him riding in a car with a white lady. To get to the rehab we had to pass the back of the bars and he pointed out to me the one where he lived with his mother and sister, at the same time waving and shouting to his friends, laughing at their wide-eyed astonishment.

At the rehab the children crowded round to be introduced to Jimmy. I took him on a tour of the building and he stared in silent delight at the kindergarten school rooms with their little red and green chairs and bright pictures, numbers and alphabets displayed on the walls. From the bedrooms, where I'm sure he could hardly believe there were such good strong bunks for all the children, we proceeded to the kitchen where he disposed of his rice and fish in record time, in spite of the attentions of the other kids who couldn't wait for him to finish so that they could show him their television.

When I asked him if he liked the rehab the answer was an emphatic 'Yes!'

'Would you like to stay here if your mum would let you?'

'Oh, yes!'

The two hours were soon up, and after I'd taken him back I decided to visit his mother. The atmosphere inside the bar was dark and close, and the dim illumination of the red light bulbs revealed hand-painted murals of half-naked women. Though the bars never actually closed, it was very quiet during the daytime. Jimmy's mother proved to be outside at the back and as I walked uneasily along an unlit corridor in search of her my feelings about her were mixed. This was no place for her to be bringing up a child; and yet I knew that many young teenagers from the provinces were sent by their families to earn money in the towns where, lacking education, they had little chance of finding a decent job and so ended up as this woman had.

When I found her she was washing clothes and instead of returning my smile she turned coldly away and went on with her work. She had already heard from her neighbours that Jimmy had been to the rehab and I could tell that she felt I was critical of her. Yet who was I to condemn her? But for the grace of God I might have found myself in the same position. I tried to convince her that what I felt was compassion, not criticism, and that I was only interested in helping her and her son. Jimmy would be welcome, I told her, to stay at the rehab if she became unable to support him; I knew that she must be earning less than usual since the restrictions kept servicemen away from the bars.

She eventually unbent a little, but she wouldn't allow Jimmy to come to us. Of course, I was disappointed. He was such a sweet little boy and I hated the thought of him living in the brothel, but even if I'd had the means I still couldn't help every child who tugged at my heartstrings. They had parents or guardians who loved them in their way and would never give them up, and now that I was a mother myself I understood this. I knew I would go to any length to prevent my children being taken away. I would scrub floors in order to feed them – anything rather than hand them over to someone else.

It was then that the Lord gave me a vision to start a school. We already had the kindergarten and it was doing very well, but at the age of seven the children had to move on to the local public elementary school, where those who had no other Christian influence in their lives would quickly forget what we had taught them about the ways of the Lord. If we had our own school they would have a Christian education from the age of three to sixteen and even if I couldn't care for all the Jimmys of Subic, some of them at least would have the chance of a better future. The rice and fish I'd given Jimmy would do him good for one day, whereas by educating a child in a good Christian school we could be instrumental in affecting both his eternal destiny and also the rest of his life on earth.

Jimmy himself moved away from the area the following year, but I would never forget him because it was through him that God gave me the vision for the Philippine Outreach Academy. I didn't know how long it would take to come to fruition and I'd learned by now that God can't be rushed. He has a perfect time for everything, and it's never early and never late.

In the meantime, however, I had to address more immediate concerns. My vision of a Christian school made me realise just how far the public school system was failing the rehab children. For one thing, because the school had no uniform they would set off each day in their flip-flops and ill-assorted clothes looking thoroughly dejected and untidy, and I was sure their lack of smartness was eroding their self-respect. They also appeared to have little enthusiasm or motivation in their work, which was hardly surprising as the teaching was erratic and they would often be sent home if the teacher was busy attending a meeting. Their academic achievement, in fact, was negligible.

Since, therefore, our own school was still in the future, I began to make enquiries about enrolling them in a private Christian school I knew of in Olongapo. White Stone Academy was run by Sister Onie, owner of the White Rock Hotel in Subic, and used an American system known as ACE (Accelerated Christian Education). I discovered, however, that to enrol our twenty children would cost far more than we could afford at present, so we all began to pray, especially the children who were very excited at the idea of going to a private school.

I was familiar with the ACE programme as my parents had once considered starting a school at the Upper Room, and I thought it would be useful for the children to follow an American curriculum because most professional jobs in the Philippines demand a good command of English. It would also be an advantage for them to have lessons conducted in English rather than Tagalog from elementary level as English was the language in which they would all be taught at high school. The ACE curriculum is divided into modules called 'paces' and there is a strong emphasis on self-directed study designed to prepare students for the sort of responsibility that will be required of them when they eventually go to college. Though a supervisor is always on hand, the children work individually, setting their own goals, checking and marking their own completed tasks and testing themselves on the contents of each pace prior to a mini-exam in which they must achieve at least ninety per cent before they can proceed to the next module. Motivation is stimulated by awarding prizes and privileges for good behaviour and academic achievement, and here in the Philippines the individual learning is supplemented by more interactive lessons in music, art and PE.

The standards reached in ACE schools were very high, even compared to other private schools, and I was satisfied that our children would benefit from the programme. The only problem (as usual!) was the cost. Even with the very generous discount which Sister Onie offered, the fees were still beyond what we could manage. On my last trip to England, Rodney, one of my trustees, had suggested starting a sponsorship programme to help with our finances, pointing out that our supporters might prefer to give to a particular person or project rather than to the Philippine Outreach in general. Though I hadn't yet followed up his suggestion, it struck me that many people might respond to a request to sponsor a child through school – if only we had time to ask them. But the time for enrolment was fast approaching and a decision had to be taken now.

After much prayer, I received the assurance that sponsors would come forward and that we should trust the Lord by enrolling the children immediately. Then the work began. Each student needed two uniforms, one for everyday and one for special occasions, which meant forty uniforms to be ordered. I got every child to trace the outline of his or her foot on a piece of paper so that I could go to Manila to buy twenty pairs of shoes, along with literally hundreds of notebooks, dozens of pencils and pencil sharpeners – the list was endless and the bills alarming. Through unexpected gifts and the support of my home church in England, God graciously provided for all these expenses and by June 1990 the children were ready for their first day at White Stone.

What a difference it was to see them setting off, excited and happy in their neat new clothes – white blouses and navy pleated skirts for the girls and short-sleeved white shirts and navy trousers for the boys. Proper shoes, too, and clean white socks. The uniforms were inspected daily at school and from taking pride in their appearance they grew in confidence and self-esteem, which spilled over into their work so that though some of them had initially been placed in a grade below the one they'd been in at the public school, they made rapid progress and soon caught up.

It had been a big step of faith when we enrolled them, but I never had cause to regret it. In addition to confirming my confidence in the ACE programme, the obvious benefit to the children gave me an added incentive to hold on to the vision God had given me and to look to the day when we could put the programme into practice in our own school. As the year went on, small groups, couples and individuals began to come forward to sponsor the children at White Stone and I believed even more strongly that the Lord would surely provide the means to make the Philippine Outreach Academy a reality.

When 1991 arrived, Dondie and I were still at the Servicemen's Home, 'a few months' having stretched to twelve, and even now there was no firm news of our successors. We began, however, to move ahead with plans to open our new school in the summer of that year. Everyone who will be responsible for running an ACE school – the principal, the pastor, the administrator and the teaching supervisor – has to undergo a short course of instruction in the implementation of the programme and in June, by which time I was three months pregnant with our second baby, we were all looking forward to our training when Pinatubo erupted and our plans, along with much else, were reduced to rubble.

19

Pinatubo

Dondie and I walked into a scene of unwonted confusion on the naval base when we arrived for the chaplains' luncheon on Wednesday 12th June. The owners of hundreds of cars, which were parked everywhere in the most unlikely places, were variously occupied in unloading their picnic baskets, walking their dogs or joining one of the long queues of people waiting to be allocated temporary accommodation.

It had been rumoured for several days that Clark Air Base in Angeles City was to be evacuated to the naval base as a safety precaution following news of the impending eruption of Mount Pinatubo, one of the more than thirty active volcanoes in the Philippines. Government warnings in the media instructed all those living within a twelve-mile radius of Pinatubo to evacuate for their own safety and there were regular broadcasts on the US military television network. American scientists were monitoring the volcano's activity and we were assured that Subic, thirty miles to the west of Pinatubo, was a safe area.

The following afternoon I was driving back from Olongapo with Dondie and as we neared Subic we saw that the market place was full of people all gazing upwards and pointing. There was a huge puff of grey smoke coming

191

from the direction of Pinatubo. Like the rest, we were awed rather than frightened by this spectacular but distant phenomenon. Tourists, Dondie had told me, came in large numbers to see the volcano in his home province of Bicol, especially when it was erupting, and it had never caused any danger in his lifetime.

On Friday morning we woke to find the garden of the Servicemen's Home lying under a thin covering of powdery light grey ash, like freshly fallen snow. Carlo and Monique were delighted; the Philippines never see snow, so it was an exciting novelty for them. Later on I had lunch on the base, a farewell party for a friend whose husband was being transferred elsewhere, and in the early evening, before going back to the base for the Friday Bible study, Dondie and I were planning to go house-hunting in Olongapo.

The restrictions on the movements of servicemen were hampering the work of the Home to such an extent that relocation to Olongapo, which unlike Subic was not off limits, seemed the only option. We didn't expect to be living in the new Home for long ourselves, because we'd had news at last that the Pedersons were hoping to return quite soon, but as Lora, the cook, would continue to work there after we'd left we invited her to join us in inspecting the property we had in mind.

We set off in the car in good time, but before we'd gone more than half a mile the sky went suddenly dark, not a rare occurrence in the rainy season. The rain, however, when it began to fall, turned out not to be rain at all, but mud, which spattered heavily onto the windscreen. The windscreen wipers achieved nothing other than to smear the thickly falling mud more effectively all over the surface of the glass, and with visibility down to virtually nil Dondie carefully turned the car in the direction of home. There was a fair amount of traffic and if other drivers hadn't exercised similar caution there could have been serious accidents.

With the help of a container of water begged from a

nearby house, and by stopping every minute or two to wash the mud from the windscreen, we made the half-mile journey home in just less than an hour, to find on arriving that the electricity had been cut off. We had no batteries for the radio so we went to bed that night no wiser as to what was happening and with no information about what it might signify.

Mud was no longer falling when we woke on Saturday, which was my birthday, and instead everything was covered by an inch of dark grey ash. I wasn't immune to the novelty myself this time and getting out my camera I happily finished the film taking shots of the strangely transformed landscape. There was still no electricity, so the radio remained dumb.

We had a busy day ahead. Joseph was to graduate from his Bible school in Angeles City and we planned to take a party of rehab residents and church members to attend the ceremony. Before that, straight after breakfast, I walked with Lora to the local store to buy some noodles, and flour for a cake, as it was something of a tradition for her to bake a cake when anyone had a birthday. It was only 8.30 when we got there, but the store was already packed with frantic shoppers hastily snatching at everything in sight, and the stock of tinned goods especially was disappearing rapidly. These people had obviously heard something we hadn't. Alarmed, we spent what little money we had with us on groceries and candles and I figured I'd have to come back with more money for a second foray.

But while we were still in the store, without warning the sky went dark as if a black curtain had suddenly fallen, instantaneously cutting off the light. Seconds later, ash, mud and stones began to rain down and there was a stampede for the checkout as panic-stricken people rushed to get home and out of danger. Lora and I joined the exodus and were soon liberally plastered with falling mud as we picked our way as quickly as we dared through the murk.

Back at the Home, lit by candles and the gas lamps kept for emergencies, we all sat and waited for the daylight which we felt sure must soon return. But over an hour later we were still marooned in our tiny island of light, with the thick darkness outside pressing blackly against the windows. Mid-morning brought the first of a series of minor earth tremors and at each one I felt a thrill of fear, remembering the devastation caused by a killer quake less than a year ago in Baguio City and Nueva Ecija. In an effort to keep a grip on normality, Lora prepared lunch (the cooker thankfully worked on Calor gas) and even went on to bake my birthday cake. It was a brave attempt, but impossible to sustain as the hours wore on.

It began to thunder, ear-shattering detonations that shook the ground and engulfed us in a solid wave of sound which terrified Carlo and Monique. In the intervals between the thunder cracks we heard the steady bombard-ment of stones bouncing off the corrugated iron roof, and the softer thudding of ash and mud. The ash fall had to be deep by now, but exactly how deep we couldn't tell because the only relief from the blackness outside came from flashes of lightning which shot across the sky like vivid streaks of red fire.

I'd often found comfort in difficult times by setting down my thoughts in a letter, and as the long afternoon drew to a close I sat in the candlelight and wrote to my parents.

Dear Mum and Dad,

How I wish I were back home with you now. Of all my experiences here so far (and I've been through and seen a lot) this is by far the worst – and on my birthday too! The volcano has been blowing all day and the whole area is covered by a black cloud of volcanic ash. It's now 5 o'clock and we haven't had an hour's daylight since early morning. We've been without elec-tricity since yesterday, and earlier today the water supply was cut off too. All day it's been raining volcanic clay, like wet cement, which must be deeper than six inches in the garden.

The thunder and lightning are bad enough to frighten even Dondie, and Monique is so scared we've been singing songs about Jesus to soothe her. Even as I'm writing we keep having minor earthquakes which make us want to get out of the house in case it collapses – except that the ash is so deep and stones are still raining down with the ash and clay.

Almost all the trees in the garden have just crashed down under the weight of the clay. Dondie is worried that the roof will be the next thing to give way, but doing anything about it means going outside, and the lightning is so scary. There's still no sign of light, so who knows how much longer the ash will go on falling?

There goes another earthquake. If it's frightening for us, how much worse must it be for those who don't trust the Lord in situations like this? It makes a big difference being a mother – I know I wouldn't be nearly as anxious if I didn't have the children to think about. I'm terrified to let them out of my sight in case a bigger earthquake comes, but I have to pretend I'm not worried because when Monique is afraid she looks to me for security. Oh Lord, I just wish this whole thing were over. Even if we needed to evacuate the house we couldn't go anywhere; the car is buried in clay, and the ash is too deep to drive through.

Dust is getting into the house now, covering absolutely everything. The only room that's free of it is the main bedroom, but the earthquakes feel so much stronger up there and if a big one came we'd be in trouble if we were upstairs. I don't think I can take much more of this. . . .

It's almost 8 o'clock, and we're still in total darkness. Monique and Carlo are giggling away now without a care in the world. Dondie and I just keep praying. This is the most frightening experience I've ever had. Still no water, and it will be at least another twenty-four hours before the electricity is reconnected, even if the volcano has died down by morning so that the engineers can begin work. . . .

Lora has just come back from her house with her son Christopher. He's thirteen. It's a little after 1am and we've been listening to the radio, using the batteries from Christopher's torch. It seems the earthquakes are a quite separate phenomenon, nothing to do with the volcano. We didn't listen for long because Dondie needed the torch. He's up on the roof now, shovelling off the ash while Christopher holds the torch for him. At least it's only ash falling now, not mud. While it's dry, the ash is much lighter than the mud, but we have to clear it in case there's rain during the night. It must be eighteen inches deep on the ground, even three feet in some places . . .

Monique and Carlo are both asleep. I'm tired too, but I daren't sleep for fear there might be a stronger earthquake. It's 3am and Dondie has just come down off the roof; he hasn't finished yet, but he's completely exhausted. A lot of houses nearby have already fallen under the weight of the mud and we're worried about the balcony over the lounge because it's pretty deep on there too. Poor Lora is trying to clear it . . .

Dondie's back on the roof, worn out but still working. Every time he hears another house cave in it makes him more determined to go on. And we haven't even started on Lora's house yet. We're still having earthquakes, but not so strong, and it's raining now, normal rain that is, so we might see some daylight tomorrow.

Well, my birthday is over and I can honestly say it's been the most memorable I've ever had. I've never been so scared in all my life. I don't know what I'd have done if I hadn't been able to pray.

Can't wait to be home.

Love, Chrissy

After a few hours' sleep we woke on Sunday to daylight at last. As far as the eye could see everything was dark grey, but the uniform blanket of ash couldn't hide the destruction the volcano had hurled down. It had been no respecter of persons and the houses of rich and poor, American and Filipino, had suffered equally. Fallen trees lay everywhere and the streets were strewn with electrical cables and telephone wires. From the balcony, as we continued to work at moving the ash, Dondie and I could see countless streams of bewildered refugees laden with sacks of rice, Calor gas bottles, beds, children and bags. One man was carrying a dead body. The ash was too deep for vehicles, and the evacuees had no choice but to walk.

Before the balcony was cleared, we heard news that

our new church building further down the street was seriously damaged and, fearing that the equipment would be pilfered, Dondie rushed off immediately to investigate, calling over his shoulder, 'I'll finish this when I get back.' I stayed on the balcony, and long before Dondie returned a passing friend called out, 'Chrissy, have you heard the latest news? The volcano is going to blow again and it will be worse than yesterday.'

I panicked. Apart from Tess, an eighteen-year-old who often helped us with baby-sitting, I was alone with the children. It had also started to rain heavily and the water on the balcony was being held by the remaining ash and starting to flood back into the house. Heavy lifting might harm my unborn baby, I might even miscarry, but if I did nothing the house could be damaged, endangering all of us, including Carlo and Monique. 'It's no good, I'll have to do it myself,' I thought, picking up the bucket, and for almost an hour I stuck to the back-breaking work of heaving the ash and water over the balcony wall, praying for the strength to go on and for protection for my baby.

Soon after Dondie returned with news that despite extensive damage to the building almost all our equipment had been spared, we spotted twenty or more of our church members from the *barangay* of Pamatawan.

'Where are you off to?' we asked.

'Manila! There's nothing left of Pamatawan, not a house left standing, and we've heard that the volcano is going to erupt again.'

The impracticability of the plan was a measure of the panic people were feeling: with the children and older people in the party it would take them weeks to walk to Manila, quite apart from the fact that they'd be in grave danger if the volcano were to blow again. They were easily persuaded to change their minds and stay with us for a while, which benefited us as well as them because with the help of the men Dondie was able to finish clearing the roof and balcony.

Suddenly Monique let out a loud scream. She'd fallen and banged her head hard on the corner of the stone steps. For me it was the last straw and I cried with her as I tried to comfort her. When she was calm, I slipped into the bedroom to be alone with the Lord. 'Lord, I can't take any more. Please do something so that we don't have to go through it all again.' I opened my Bible. The cataclysm which had overtaken Subic reminded me of the fate of Sodom and Gomorrah, and turning to Genesis I reread the account of their destruction. Abraham had pleaded with God not to sweep away the righteous with the wicked and God had promised to spare the cities if only ten righteous people were found there. 'Lord,' I prayed, 'there are more than ten righteous people here in Subic. For the sake of your own, please don't destroy it.' I felt my anxieties drain away and knew again his peace which passes understanding.

The arrival of Roy, one of the rehab kids, and then the Del Montes, brought welcome reassurance that everyone there was unhurt, and though the building was badly damaged it was not beyond repair. They were short of food, however, and completely out of rice.

The dreaded second eruption never came – at least, not in Subic. The volcano did indeed blow again, but the wind changed direction and carried the ash further north. We were desperately sorry for the people who lived there, knowing only too well what they must be suffering, but it was impossible not to feel relief that Subic had been spared a repeat of yesterday's disaster, which would surely have razed the whole town to the ground. Once again I slipped into my room, this time to thank the Lord for saving us from total destruction.

Dealing with the aftermath of catastrophe was made easier by reason of simple gratitude at being alive, and the difficulties, though many, were a small price to pay for our deliverance.

Even after the volcano had stopped erupting there was

still danger from sulphur in the ash, and for a time we had
to mask our mouths and noses during the daytime to
protect our lungs. But the most pressing problem was
food, both for ourselves and our Pamatawan evacuees
and for the rehab, as our present stock of rice would last
only a few days. After spending the whole of Monday
morning standing in line at the local store where, in order
to prevent disorder and panic buying, the customers at the
head of the queue had to wait outside while shop assistants
fetched the items they wanted, Dondie and I came away
with just a few groceries. The price of rice in Subic had
risen by a third which, at the rate we consumed it (a 100lb
bag every four days at the rehab alone), was more than we
could afford.

We decided to clean up the car and hope it would take us
as far as Olongapo. After a bit of a push it spluttered into
life and we set off along the main road which the Philippine
military had been busy clearing for the past twenty-four
hours. All the bars in Subic had collapsed and as we drove
past what was left of the funeral parlour we saw piles of
corpses lying haphazardly among the rubble. It was clear
from the number of fallen electricity poles that we could
expect to be without power for some time to come.

We stopped en route to offer a lift to a woman who was
hoping to reach Manila with her handicapped daughter,
and her evaluation of the disaster highlighted a crucial
difference between the western worldview and that of the
Philippines.

'God is really angry with us,' she said. 'It's obvious he's
telling us to put our lives right.' This woman had no
personal relationship with the Lord, but she recognised
the existence of a spiritual dimension in the situation.

Had the tragedy taken place in the west, most people
would have sought to understand it solely in terms of
physical cause and effect, paying heed to the explanations
of vulcanologists and seismologists and never thinking
about their relationship with God. The western nations

have largely lost their fear of God, but the Filipino people have a definite God-awareness which I believe he will use to bring the nation back to himself, working good through even such a calamity as we had suffered.

An hour's drive brought us eventually to Olongapo, which had been almost as badly hit as Subic. Churches, schools, hospitals and shops, if not completely flattened, were fearfully damaged and, more seriously for our immediate purpose, all the banks were closed. Until we could draw money from our account we couldn't replenish our dwindling store of food, but there was no sign as yet of any attempt to resume normal business. The only thing we could do was to bring our need to the Lord who says, 'Be still, and know that I am God' (Ps 46:10).

He answered our prayers just a couple of days later, when missionary friends from San Fernando managed to reach us with food and medical supplies. There was enough and more to see us through the immediate crisis, so we were even in a position to help others, church members and neighbours, who were in need.

Water too was in short supply for a while. The Servicemen's Home was connected to the town's water mains, but the water company had problems with its generator, which it could only operate for a few hours each day, and during the brief period when water was actually flowing the demand was so heavy that not a drop reached our taps. However, Dondie discovered that from around 2am there was a slow but steady flow trickling from the pipe in the garden and he and I would sit by it for a couple of hours collecting the water in bowls.

Having collected it, we used some to have a bath which we had to take right there in the garden; there were so many people sleeping in the house, and to carry the water indoors would disturb them. It didn't bother Dondie a bit, but I found it horribly embarrassing to be standing there in the open in the middle of the night having my bath fully clothed. Still, it wasn't the first time I'd had to do it. At east it was dark, and it was certainly better than no bath at all. We didn't throw the water away when we'd finished. We hoarded every drop that was used for bathing or washing clothes – it was far too precious to waste if we were to maintain the most basic standard of hygiene. Imagine (if you can bear to) the problem we faced with thirty people in one house and no water to flush the toilet.

After a week our household shrank back to its normal size when the evacuees returned to Pamatawan to salvage what they could from the debris and start to rebuild their homes and their lives. But there were some things which had gone for ever. As soon as there was light after the eruption, several ships had evacuated all the military personnel from the base to the island of Cebu, and we never saw any of our American friends again. The US decided to pull out of Subic and in fact military bases all over the Philippines were closed the following year. Without the base, the ministry of the Servicemen's Home naturally ended and from then on the Military Mission concentrated on its Home in Japan.

Our own outreach ministries in the schools and prisons came to a sudden halt. Camp Maquinaya had completely collapsed and the inmates were transferred to other prisons, while the roads and bridges to the jails at Iba and San Fernando were impassable and looked like remaining so for some time to come. San Agustin School was totally destroyed, and all the other schools in the area, including our own kindergarten, had discontinued classes. With so little for me to do, Dondie and I agreed that I should go to England earlier than planned to get the children to safety. He would follow later, in time for the baby's birth, leaving Joseph to oversee the church and the Del Montes to run the rehab in his absence.

Though the school and prison ministries were temporarily suspended, God was powerfully at work in the church, many people having been awakened by the disaster to an awareness of their spiritual need. Our numbers were also

swelled by members of two other congregations in th
area whose pastors had evacuated, leaving their flocks i
Dondie's care. We ourselves had no church building, s
our meetings were held in the Servicemen's Home.

It was over a month before I was able to leave, and in th
end a misunderstanding with the British Consul meant tha
Carlo couldn't travel with me and Monique, but woul
have to join us later with Dondie. When eventually th
plane took off (our first flight was cancelled after anothe
minor eruption) I breathed a long sigh of relief as th
nightmare unreality of the past six weeks fell away behin
me, and I began to look ahead to being reunited with m
family and the many opportunities which awaited me t
speak about our work.

I accepted engagements right up to the eighth month c
my pregnancy and when, on 17th December, I gave birt
to Nathanael, Dondie was with me, overjoyed to have hi
heart's desire, a healthy boy.

20

Philippine Outreach Academy

By the time I arrived back in Subic with the three children in the summer of 1992 (Dondie having returned ahead of us in March) the ravages inflicted by the volcano on the rehab and the church had been repaired, and everything there was back to normal. But Pinatubo hadn't finished yet. Lahar, hot volcanic mud, continued to flow from the mountain, and in the rainy season it was washed down into the valleys and low lying areas, causing huge devastation and killing many people. As near as Castillejos, the next town north of Subic where we had our first rehab, four construction workers died when the lahar hit suddenly in the night. Roads were blocked or destroyed and we were cut off for some time from both the San Fernando and Iba jails.

When Pinatubo erupted in June 1991 we had been on the point of beginning our training in preparation for opening our own ACE elementary school, but I delayed setting a fresh date. I'd lost none of the clarity of my original vision, and Roselyn, on whom as headteacher under my direction as principal so much would depend, was as committed to the idea of the school as I was. I hesitated solely because the director of ACE Philippines was not altogether happy either with the fact that our pupils, the graduates of our kindergarten, would include children of non-Christian parents or that we would not be charging fees. While I weighed the respective merits of going ahead with ACE or of adopting an alternative American curriculum I'd heard of, time was running out and it was only after several long nights of prayer that I received the assurance that it was God's will that we should choose ACE. There was little time for further delay if the school were to open in 1993, but at this crucial point we were once more rocked by a calamity as violent and destructive in personal terms as Pinatubo had been materially.

Romy was a devoted father, if inclined to be somewhat overprotective, especially of his daughters, and it was no secret that he strongly disapproved of Roselyn's fiancé Mike, a trainee civil engineer and member of our church. Though Roselyn, at twenty-seven, was three years beyond the age at which Filipino couples could marry without parental consent, Romy forbade her even to be seen walking alone with Mike. Most of the church members understood Romy's attitude and accepted that this was just the way he was, but there was also a lot of sympathy for Mike who, though he'd not been in the fellowship long, was well liked by the young people and endeared himself to everyone by the love and affection with which he always treated Roselyn.

In the New Year of 1993, however, I noticed a change in Roselyn. She said nothing to me, but she and I were very close and something in her manner led me to conjecture that her feelings for Mike had altered. Then Lourdes told me in confidence that Roselyn was planning to break off the engagement. It appeared that there was a side to Mike that no one outside the family, not even Dondie and I, had suspected. He so resented Romy's disapproval that, instead of showing him the respect required of a Filipino towards an older man and the father of his fiancée, he often treated Romy with contempt and there had been some heated exchanges between them. Roselyn, while conceding that her father might have been a little harsh in his dealings with Mike, could no longer contemplate marriage with a man who had reacted as Mike had done.

One evening a few days after this we held a breaking of bread service in the new house at the bottom of the hill below the rehab which Dondie and I had taken at the urging of our trustees, who felt that we needed separate living quarters for our family. Both Roselyn and Mike were there. The fact that they were sitting apart meant nothing, as they were never allowed to sit together in public, but then I saw that there was no engagement ring on Roselyn's finger. Romy would be glad, I thought, but how was Mike taking it?

Two days later, on Thursday afternoon, I was due to go with a team on one of our regular visits to San Agustin School and as usual I went to pick up the rest of the group in the car. Jane Del Monte was already waiting for me with Edilyn, one of the kindergarten teachers, and Joseph's sister Rose, but Roselyn, who was to teach that day, had just gone off somewhere with Mike and hadn't yet returned. Presumably they had things to discuss about the ending of their relationship, I thought, hoping it wouldn't take too long. But the minutes ticked by and in the end we waited so long for Roselyn that we had to call off the trip to San Agustin.

It was so unlike her that I was deeply uneasy, the more so when, some time later, Romy and Lourdes returned from searching for the couple without success. Most of the young people who heard about Roselyn's mysterious disappearance were unperturbed, taking it for granted that she and Mike had eloped, an expedient which was still quite commonly resorted to in the Philippines by couples unable to obtain parental consent to their marriage; the majority of parents would immediately withdraw their objections once the couple had spent a night together. Roselyn, of course, was old enough to marry without her parents' consent, but to the young people it probably appeared that Romy's disapproval was at the root of her disappearance.

It was an explanation which entirely failed to satisfy me. I knew Roselyn and I knew that her love for the Lord and her commitment to her ministry, as well as her self-respect, would never allow her to act so irresponsibly. My fears for her were intensified when Lourdes discovered that none of Roselyn's clothes were missing: it was obvious that she hadn't planned to go away.

Several days passed and still there was no word from Roselyn. Romy and Lourdes, then Dondie and I, all went to Mike's home in Barretto, near Camp Maquinaya, where his parents confirmed that he too hadn't been seen since Thursday afternoon. They promised to let us know if they learned where he was. Dondie, being more used to the Filipino way of thinking and knowing how much Mike wanted to marry Roselyn, was inclined to accept the elopement theory. He felt my anxiety was excessive and discouraged any further discussion between us, so I had to take my trouble to the Lord.

The following Wednesday we had our weekly overnight prayer meeting in the prayer garden which Dondie had constructed at the side of the disused hospital building. It was really just a roof of native materials for shelter, with some benches and a table, and each Wednesday Dondie and I would gather for prayer with a few other rehab residents from 7pm to 3am. While we prayed, I silently asked the Lord to show me where Mike and Roselyn were, and as I asked I saw a vision of a beach house on stilts. The only place I'd ever seen such a house before was at Baloy Beach in Barretto, between Subic and Olongapo, where I'd visited the Fishers before they took over the Servicemen's Home. It was a long beach with close to 100 houses, but I was sure I'd know the right one if I saw it.

I recognised it without difficulty when I drove to the beach later in the day. It was close to the entrance, which surprised me because I'd expected it to be somewhere

more secluded. It took only a few minutes to ascertain that
the house was empty, and when my enquiries at nearby
cottages failed to elicit any news of the missing pair, I drove
right to the end of the beach searching for another
house that matched the one in my vision. I found nothing, and returned home puzzled but still convinced that
Baloy Beach was connected in some way with Roselyn's
disappearance.

However, it was that same day which brought us our first
definite news and it came from Lourdes' cousin Jenny, who
lived in Manila. Jenny phoned through to Lourdes' sister-
in-law (neither we nor the Del Montes had a phone) and
left a message saying that Roselyn had visited her in Manila
and was now with Mike. Lourdes was given a phone number where she could contact Roselyn in a couple of days'
time. The message, which seemed deliberately vague and
evasive, did nothing to allay my fears and I was full of
questions when I went with Lourdes to return the call.
The phone was answered not by Roselyn but by Jenny,
who told Lourdes that Mike and Roselyn were to be married in Manila in a fortnight's time, on 3rd February. Jenny
didn't divulge the couple's present whereabouts, saying
only that Lourdes could see her daughter on the day of
the wedding at her cousin's house.

The news came as no surprise to Mike's parents, who
had broken their promise to tell us if they heard from him.
When Dondie and I went to see them we learned that his
mother had even been to see him and Roselyn, and she did
her best to assure us that Roselyn had run away so that
she'd be free to marry Mike. I frankly didn't believe her; I
was convinced that Roselyn was caught up in a web of
deception and concealment that was certainly not of her
own making.

It so happened that a group of us, including Romy and
Lourdes, were due to go to Manila on 3rd February for a
three-day seminar on leadership training, and Lourdes,
who was beginning to come to terms with the inevitability

of her daughter's marriage, arranged to leave the seminar to see Roselyn at Jenny's house and attend the wedding. Romy, however, refused to have any part in it. When Lourdes returned I asked how the ceremony had gone.

'The wedding was already over by the time I arrived. They'd been married by a judge in a courtroom, with dozens of other couples in a mass wedding. Mike's mother was their witness. Anyway, they'll be coming home on Saturday because Mike starts a job on Monday.'

'But how was Roselyn? Was she happy?'

'We were never alone so we had no chance to talk, but I must admit she didn't look very happy.'

'Then why did you leave her?' I asked, my voice rising in exasperation.

'Listen, it's done now,' snapped Lourdes. 'They're married. For Roselyn's sake, accept it.'

Lourdes and I never spoke to each other like this; it was a sign of the strain we were all under.

Early on Saturday morning Roselyn and Mike turned up on our doorstep. Mike was too frightened to face Romy alone and wanted Dondie to go with him. Leaving the two men together, I took Roselyn into another room on the pretext of asking her, as her employer, to explain her absence from the kindergarten. As soon as we were alone she needed no persuasion to talk, her words tumbling over each other in her eagerness to unburden herself.

'Sister Chrissy, I'm so sorry, but it was really not my fault.'

Mike had called for her when she finished work at the kindergarten on that Thursday, two days after she'd broken off the engagement, and asked her to take him to her house so that he could retrieve some things of his which he'd left there. As they walked down the hill from the rehab Roselyn noticed a tricycle (motorcycle taxi with passenger sidecar) waiting at the bottom. Turning to ask Mike about it, she realised that he'd dropped back, and just had time to see him throw a bottle into the long grass before he covered her face with a handkerchief soaked in chloroform. Half-conscious, she was forced into the tricycle, and through the haze of chloroform she dimly heard the driver saying, 'I thought you said the two of you planned this together?'

'Sister Chrissy, believe me, with all the strength I had left I begged the tricycle driver to help me, but he wouldn't.'

The tricycle took them to Baloy Beach and stopped at a house near the entrance where one of Mike's friends, the owner of the house, was waiting for them. When both the friend and the tricycle driver ignored her frantic pleas, Roselyn began to scream. Mike bundled her roughly into the house and beat her in the stomach, warning her to keep quiet.

Mike sent his friend to fetch a drink for Roselyn, whose mouth was very dry from the chloroform, and while he was gone she began screaming again. With the speed of a reflex, Mike lunged at her and pounded her brutally in the stomach until she promised to make no more noise.

I shuddered at the thought of Roselyn, so small and lightly built, at the mercy of a man as big and powerful as Mike.

She was terribly thirsty by the time the friend returned with a glass of fruit juice and gulped it down quickly, realising only when she'd almost finished it that it tasted of some kind of drug.

In her helpless and half-conscious state, Mike raped her.

Under the influence of the drug, she fell asleep. Hours later, in the middle of the night, Mike shook her awake and, weak and disoriented from the shock of abduction and the trauma of the rape, fearful too of being beaten again, she offered no resistance when he told her they were going to Manila. He took her to the house of his aunt and uncle who believed his story that he and Roselyn were eloping and welcomed them into their home.

For the next few days Roselyn was virtually a prisoner. She hadn't a peso in her purse and thus no means of getting back to her family, and Mike threatened to kill

her and himself if she tried to escape. She discounted the
idea of trying to reach a police station because even if she
reported the rape the police wouldn't pay her fare home
and she'd be stranded in Manila where Mike might easily
track her down. She pinned her hopes on gaining the
sympathy of Mike's relatives, but this would depend on
speaking to them alone and Mike never left the house.

Before they could be married, however, there were legal
formalities to complete and documents to obtain, and
eventually Mike had to go out. As soon as he'd left, Roselyn told the full story to his aunt who, not being his blood
relation, was initially sympathetic. But when she realised
that he could face a life sentence if Roselyn's family
pressed charges of rape, she changed tack and joined
the rest of the family in trying to persuade Roselyn to
consent to the marriage.

Finally, Mike slipped up by agreeing to give Roselyn the
money to buy some shampoo. It wasn't much, but it would
get her to her mother's cousin Jenny and the next time
Mike went out she slipped away and took a jeepney to
Jenny's house. Here, at last, was someone who would
help her to get away. But her hopes were short-lived.
Though she lived in Manila, Jenny's mental attitudes
were governed by the deeply engrained taboos of the provinces where, for a woman, sexual experience before marriage was an irretrievable scandal. Whatever the
circumstances, if her chastity were in question she had
forfeited any chance of finding a husband. For Jenny
the avoiding of such a scandal took precedence over
Roselyn's happiness and well being, and she ranged herself with Mike's relatives in urging her to go ahead with
the wedding.

It wasn't so very rare for these cultural attitudes to be
exploited by unscrupulous men if their offers of marriage
were refused. They knew that if they succeeded in seducing
a woman she would almost certainly agree to marriage in
order to preserve her reputation and escape the shame of

being labelled unchaste. Mike was unusual only in the degree of brutality and compulsion he employed. Even Roselyn, who knew in her heart that she herself had done nothing wrong, was made to feel guilty and ashamed by Jenny's arguments.

Her last hope vanished early next morning when Mike appeared at Jenny's house to reclaim her. Having guessed where she'd gone, he had easily traced the address in the telephone directory. By his crying and pleading he convinced Jenny that he genuinely loved Roselyn. Worn down by Jenny's repeated urgings, fearing too that Mike would fulfil his threat to kill her if she refused, and with her self-esteem undermined by irrational guilt, Roselyn allowed herself to be taken back. She had no more strength left to fight.

'There was no way I could get home without his help,' she explained. 'I thought my only hope was to marry him and once we were back in Subic I'd be able to run away and maybe find work with my cousin in Hong Kong.'

'But Roselyn, that wouldn't solve anything. There's no divorce in the Philippines and you'd never be free to marry someone else.'

'I know, but I'm prepared to stay single for the rest of my life.'

'He doesn't have the right to ruin your life like that. He kidnapped you, beat you, raped you and forced you into marriage against your will. Now he'll be expecting you to wash and iron his clothes and cook for him for the rest of his life. That can't be what you want. There has to be another way.'

I didn't know a great deal about Philippine law, but I was certain that it must be possible to end this travesty of a marriage.

'Roselyn, I'm sure you could have your marriage annulled.'

'No, Sister Chrissy,' she said in a defeated voice. 'I'll just stay with him for the time being.'

My heart ached for her. She was not only beautiful but gentle, caring and unselfish, the very last person to deserve the harrowing experience she'd been through, and I couldn't bear the thought of allowing her to suffer the consequences of it for the rest of her life. I couldn't understand why she seemed unwilling to let me help her.

'Roselyn, pray about it and think it over before you make up your mind, but remember, the longer you leave it the harder it will be to get an annulment. Don't say anything to Mike – he'll be working away for a week from Monday and you'll be free of him for a while. Tell me then what you've decided. I'll respect whatever decision you make and if you want to annul your marriage I'll do all I can to help you.'

With a faint gleam of hope in her voice she asked, 'Do you really think there's a possibility?'

'I'm sure of it. You were married under duress.'

'But what about the money? It will be very expensive.' This was the reason for her hesitation; she knew the process would involve a large amount which we couldn't afford.

'That's not a factor, the Lord will provide. What matters is what you want to do. And don't even consider Mike's suicide threats. If he could do what he did to you and call that love, it just shows that the person he loves most is himself. He'll never kill himself. Anyway, what do you want to do next week? Do you want to come back to work?' I thought that the nearer she was to us, the safer she'd be.

'Would you mind if I did? I'd love to, but there's bound to be gossip about me. The parents might object and it could damage our reputation.'

I assured Roselyn that I was in no way ashamed of her and that if others misjudged her, God would vindicate her. With that, we rejoined Mike and Dondie before Mike had time to become suspicious, and the four of us set off to see Romy and Lourdes.

They, of course, knew nothing of what had happened, but I managed to convey to them privately the essence of my conversation with Roselyn, stressing that for the moment we had to remain calm and keep up a pretence of ignorance until she had decided . what to do. Deeply shocked, they agreed and played their part magnificently during the brief visit. Lourdes also succeeded in extracting from an unwilling Mike, who could find no excuse for refusing so reasonable a request, his permission for Roselyn to spend one last week with her parents when he went away on Monday. When Roselyn went to collect her things from her old bedroom they secured a few precious moments alone with her, which allowed them to assure her of their love and support. Romy, who she'd feared might be of Jenny's opinion, hugged her and promised to move mountains if necessary to free her from the man who called himself her husband.

I shared their anguish as we watched Roselyn walk through the door with Mike. It would be a long weekend.

It took courage for Roselyn to return to work on Monday, knowing that the children's parents suspected that she had eloped. Setting aside her embarrassment she broached the subject herself and told them all frankly that she would never have considered eloping and had left under duress. One mother revealed that she had actually seen Roselyn being taken away in the tricycle and had assumed from her appearance that she was ill and on the way to hospital with Mike. There was no need to disclose any details of her ordeal; all the parents knew and respected her, and contrary to her fears they readily believed that she was not to blame. After her openness with the parents it was no great surprise when, once we were alone, she told me that she wanted to go ahead with the annulment.

'You're quite sure?' I asked.

'Sister Chrissy, I'm so scared of him and what he might do to me that I even have a knife here in my handbag. If I didn't annul the marriage, I'd have to run away.'

That same day I went with the Del Montes to Olongapo

to set in motion the legal process which would set Roselyn free. Ten years' experience of helping so many inmates through their own cases had given me a fairly wide circle of acquaintances among the lawyers and judges, one of whom put me in touch with a sympathetic man who was prepared to represent Roselyn for 15,000 pesos rather than the usual minimum fee of 25,000. I was assured that we had a strong case, especially if Mike could be persuaded not to contest it.

Back in Subic, Colonel Custodio, the chief of police and a kindly man, immediately arranged for Roselyn to make a statement at the police station and have a medical examination. He even went on to speak to several people in our *barangay*, asking them to look out for her safety. At the end of the day I was amazed by how much we'd accomplished and marvelled again at the answer to that prophetic prayer of David Chaudhary's all those years ago. God had indeed given us favour with the authorities.

As a further precautionary measure I arranged for Roselyn to stay with a missionary couple, the Vroomans. I hadn't known them well before Roselyn was abducted, but when I went to them for help they gave it unstintingly, opening their home to her for as long as she needed it. They gave her much more than a place to stay, spending hours talking through with her the irrational feelings of guilt and unworthiness which rape victims so often suffer, until she felt thoroughly assured that she was entirely innocent and had no need to be ashamed.

Before the week ended, news filtered through to Mike who immediately hurried back to Subic to see Dondie and me. He admitted the truth of everything Roselyn had said, but insisted that he loved her and had only wanted to hasten their marriage. He had already repented of his actions, he claimed, but made no demur when Dondie told him firmly that he must find another church. He had not, however, given up hope that Roselyn would return to him and was convinced that the annulment was all Romy's doing.

'Wake up, Mike,' I said. 'Even if she loved you once, how can she love you now after what you've done? She's simply afraid of you. Just be thankful that you're not facing a rape charge. It's over, Mike. Accept it.'

The case came up at the end of March and Roselyn and I were the only ones to give evidence. Mike had taken our advice and did nothing to contest it. I didn't know the judge who presided, but he seemed to be a compassionate man, and as far as I could tell the case appeared to be going well. It was a comfort too to know that in England friends and supporters, who were already hard at work raising the money to cover our legal costs, would be praying for us constantly.

Mercifully, the judge's decision was not long in coming and a few weeks after the conclusion of the case Roselyn received the documents which confirmed that her marriage was annulled and she was free. The mental scars would take longer to heal, but with God's help she could begin to put the past behind her. Our priority now was to do everything to ensure her complete recovery and though it was disappointing to have to postpone the opening of the school yet again, I accepted that it would have to wait until next year. I said nothing of this to Roselyn as she had more than enough to deal with, but it was she herself who raised the subject.

'Sister Chrissy, are we going ahead with the ACE training? We'll be too late if we don't apply soon.'

'But are you sure you're ready for that?'

'Actually, the more I have to do the better I am. It helps to keep my mind occupied and stops me dwelling on what happened to me. I'd much rather be busy.'

Roselyn's courage meant that there remained only one obstacle to the realisation of our long-treasured hopes – the ever present problem of finance. In addition to the teachers' salaries, which would be the biggest item in the budget, we would have to pay ACE eighteen pesos per student each month, plus the cost of the learning materials. There would also have to be a 'learning centre' which would take up most of the remaining space in the rehab, where each student could have an individual 'office' as specified by ACE. These consist of long tables divided by boards into separate cubicles, three offices to a table, the whole structure being easy to disassemble if more space is needed in the learning centre for joint activities.

One day, I was sure, there would be enough sponsors to finance the children through school, but at the moment our resources fell well short. Yet again we brought our problem to the Lord and one night in the prayer garden he spoke to me and assured me that he would meet our need. So it was with confidence that I told Roselyn to make the arrangements for our training. We had no difficulty in finding teachers. In Roselyn we already had the one fully qualified teacher required by the ACE programme and in the appointment of others we had the joy of gathering in the fruit of our past ministry.

Marivic and Lorna had expressed a desire to work for the Lord after graduating from San Agustin School, where I had taught them Scripture in their elementary and high school years, while Edilyn, now nineteen, was one of the firstfruits of our children's outreaches in Pamatawan almost ten years ago and was already teaching in the kindergarten. All three would teach in the mornings and use the money they earned to pay for their training in education at night school, as Roselyn had done. Tina was not a Christian when she enrolled her daughter in our kindergarten. She was converted at one of the meetings we held for parents, was subsequently baptised in the Holy Spirit and became a member of our church. A college graduate, she already had considerable experience of teaching in a private school, though not a Christian one.

Then there was Tess, the eldest child of a poor family,

whom we'd financed through high school in return for help in caring for Monique while I was working in the prisons and children's outreaches. She too intended to use her salary to study education at college. And it was a particular joy to have Dondie's niece Letty join us to help care for the rehab children and teach in the kindergarten. I had a great admiration for Letty who, without help from anyone, had pioneered a small house fellowship in a remote part of her home province of Bicol, where the activities of the NPA made the preaching of the gospel a hazardous undertaking. All of our teachers felt called of God to work at the Philippine Outreach Academy and were willing to do so for whatever salary we were able to pay them.

After we'd taken a step of faith in setting the date for our training, the Lord opened his hand liberally and help of all kinds began to flow in. First of all, the mail brought us a large and totally unexpected money order. Then an ACE school at a church in Lancashire, whose pastor was a friend of Dad's, agreed to send us their used paces, the modules of learning material, like brightly coloured comics, on which the curriculum is based. In the west, pupils write their answers directly onto the pace, but schools in third-world countries such as the Philippines are allowed to blank out the answers in used paces and the children write in notebooks instead.

We also discovered hidden treasure in our new driver, Tony, who joined us when Bill Del Monte returned to his home town in the province of Laguna. Tony, in addition to his skill as a car mechanic, turned out to have a gift for carpentry and he worked long into the night constructing fifteen 'offices' for our first intake of elementary pupils. Fifteen was the number of children graduating from kindergarten that year and it was only to these that the elementary school would be open; our older children who were already following the ACE programme at White Stone Academy would stay there for the sake of continuity. All was in readiness by the beginning of June and as enrolment week approached I surveyed the empty school-rooms which would soon be full of eager, happy children. With the addition of the elementary school, the Philippine Outreach Academy was an accomplished reality and by the grace of God would offer to the children of Subic the hope of a better future, both now and in eternity. Neither the fury of Pinatubo nor the personal tragedy which had over-taken Roselyn had been able to prevent the fulfilment of the vision.

It was a time for looking forward, but the future which lay ahead of me was founded on the experiences of the past. In the ten years since God called me to the Philippines he had gone before me, providing for my every need, redeeming my failures and lifting me over obstacles I could never have surmounted myself. Trust him, offer him your nothing, and he can do everything. To him be all the glory.

Afterword

Since the events described in this book, the Lord has given us many fresh challenges and opportunities. The Philippine Outreach Christian Fellowship currently has over ninety adult members (though numbers fall slightly in the rainy season) and has moved to larger premises. When we took it over in December 1994, the building, which had formerly been used as an arena for cockfighting, consisted of just a very rusty roof supported by wooden posts, with seating for a few hundred people; there were no walls and no cement floor. Since then, as we did with the rehab, we have been renovating it as and when we can.

Dondie and I both feel that the Lord is now leading us to extend the work beyond Subic and to plant four or five churches in other provinces of the Philippines. We have also been praying for revival, asking the Lord for 5,000 souls by the year 2000. Our vision for the future is shared by Joseph who, having pioneered a church in another *barangay* of Subic after graduating from Bible school, has returned to us as assistant pastor.

Two of the Christian inmates in San Fernando Jail are praying that on their release they might be involved with us in planting a church in the town of San Fernando. While still in the jail, they are leading Bible studies in their cells

220 LIVING UNDER THE VOLCANO

and one of them has been acting as my interpreter while Romy and Lourdes take a training course with YWAM. At Iba Jail, where we have been able to start the Iba Christian Inmates' Fellowship, the inmates have their own meeting room which, by means of their tithes and offerings and gifts from visitors, they have furnished and decorated themselves. Our ministry at Camp Maquinaya came to an end when Pinatubo erupted and so far we have been unable to resume it, but recently the way ahead has become clear and we shall be looking to the Lord to show us the right time to begin visiting there again.

The Philippine Outreach Academy has grown too, with the addition of a high school section to the pre-school, kindergarten and elementary levels, and all of our graduates have passed the national college entrance exam. Two of them have received scholarships to pay for their college courses and another, a talented musician who wants to use his gift to serve the Lord, has gained a place at music college in Manila; we are praying that funds will become available to finance him on the course. Three other graduates will be working part time at the Philippine Outreach Academy to support themselves through college.

Since we first started the Academy, government schools have greatly improved, though class sizes are still large (often more than sixty pupils) and ACE students continue to perform better than those from government schools. The general standard of living in the Philippines is rising too, but the very poor tend to get left behind and it is still our aim to offer them the lifeline of education as a way of escape from their poverty.

Our son Carlo is thirteen, and a Philippine Outreach high school student; as well as playing the drums in church services, he plays the guitar and is having piano lessons. His sister Monique, now eight, has reached grade three in our elementary school and is also learning to play the piano, while Nathanael, at five, has just started grade one. He wants to play the drums like his *kuya* (older brother). We have two more sons now: three-year-old Rannel, who has recently enrolled in our nursery, and Aaron, who will soon be two.

Since the school takes up ninety per cent of the rehab building we have no spare accommodation and cannot take in more ex-prisoners at present. But this is, I believe, only a temporary state of affairs. The old hospital next to the rehab still lies empty, waiting for us to enter into the promise of the Lord. 'For the vision is yet for an appointed time. . . . Though it tarries, wait for it; Because it will surely come. . .' (Hab 2:3).

Classics from KINGSWAY

The Kingsway Classics series presents favourite best-selling titles by well-known authors in special omnibus editions, for the same price as a single-volume paperback.

Classics from Jamie Buckingham
Risky Living, *Where Eagles Soar* and *A Way Through the Wilderness*.

Classics from Arthur Wallis
Living God's Way, *Going On God's Way* and *Into Battle*.

Classics from Watchman Nee Vol 1
The Normal Christian Life, *Sit Walk Stand* and *Changed Into His Likeness*.

Classics from Watchman Nee Vol 2
A Table in the Wilderness, *Love Not the World* and *What Shall This Man Do?*

Classics on Prayer
Learning the Joy of Prayer by Larry Lea, *Pray in the Spirit* by Arthur Wallis and *Praying Together* by Mike and Katey Morris.

Classics on Worship
Worship by Graham Kendrick, *The Believer's Guide to Worship* by Chris Bowater and *To the Praise of His Glory* by Dave Fellingham.

Classic Real-Life Stories
Vanya by Myrna Grant, *Blood Brothers* by Elias Chacour and *Streetwise* by John Goodfellow.

Kingsway Publications